# 30 DAYS TO

## THE

# TOEIC® TEST

Bo Arbogast • Elizabeth Ashmore • Trina Duke • Kate Newman Jerris

Melissa Locke • Sheridan MacInnes • Rhonda Shearin

A Chauncey
Group International
and
Peterson's
Partnership

A subsidiary of

 Educational
Testing Service

**THOMSON**
<hr>
**PETERSON'S**

Australia • Canada • Mexico • Singapore • Spain • United Kingdom • United States

## THOMSON
## PETERSON'S

**About The Chauncey Group International**

Founded in 1996, The Chauncey Group International is a subsidiary of Educational Testing Service (ETS®). The Chauncey Group and ETS share more than 25 years of experience in designing, developing, and administering occupational certificates and professional assessment programs. We have helped our customers define the competencies required for a variety of types of work and measure those competencies effectively and fairly. We are recognized as an industry leader in designing state-of-the-art assessment systems that meet professional testing standards. The Chauncey Group is headquartered in Princeton, New Jersey, with offices in Washington D.C., and and Paris.

**About Thomson Peterson's**

Thomson Peterson's (www.petersons.com) is a leading provider of education information and advice, with books and online resources focusing on education search, test preparation, and financial aid. Its Web site offers searchable databases and interactive tools for contacting educational institutions, online practice tests and instruction, and planning tools for securing financial aid. Peterson's serves 110 million education consumers annually.

**About the Chauncey • Peterson's Partnership**

The Chauncey Group International/Peterson's alliance is a model agreement for producing quality products and services to help people achieve their goals. With Peterson's print production capabilities, focus on the Internet, and distribution channels, The Chauncey Group can bring greater awareness of the TOEIC test to the international business community and provide viable tools to support English language instruction worldwide. By jointly publishing a guide with the same company that administers the test, Peterson's can give its customers a superior product that is the only "official" TOEIC preparation resource.

Visit www.TOEIC.com for more information about TOEIC and TOEIC-related products.

Visit Peterson's Education Center on the Internet (World Wide Web) at www.petersons.com

ISBN 0-7689-1097-8

Printed in Canada

10  9  8          07  06  05

# Acknowledgments

The following individuals provided invaluable assistance in the development of this book: Susan Ashmore, De'Travius Bethea, Rex Corlett, Sean Hainer, Barbara Korns, Krista Mathews, and Gina Wright.

# THE 30-DAY PROGRAM

*The Master Script for the audio that accompanies this book begins on page 281.*

# Day 1

## Get to Know the TOEIC Test

Before you start practicing for the TOEIC test, it is important to get to know the test. Let's look at the purpose of the TOEIC test as well as its content and format.

### WHAT IS THE TOEIC TEST?

The Test of English for International Communication (TOEIC®) is an English language proficiency test for people whose native language is not English. TOEIC test scores indicate how well people can communicate in English with others in the global workplace. The test does not require specialized knowledge or vocabulary; it measures only the kind of English used in everyday activities.

## What is the content of the TOEIC test?

The TOEIC test was designed to meet the needs of the working world. The test questions are developed from samples of spoken and written language collected from various countries around the world where English is used in the workplace. Test questions include many different settings and situations, such as:

*General business*—contracts, negotiations, marketing, sales, business planning, and conferences

*Manufacturing*—plant management, assembly lines, quality control

*Finance and budgeting*—banking, investments, taxes, accounting, billing

*Corporate development*—research, product development

*Offices*—board meetings, committees, letters, memoranda, telephone, fax and e-mail messages, office equipment and furniture, office procedures

*Personnel*—recruiting, hiring, retiring, salaries, promotions, job applications and advertisements

*Purchasing*—shopping, ordering supplies, shipping, invoices

*Technical areas*—electronics, technology, computers, laboratories and related equipment, technical specifications

*Housing/corporate property*—construction, specifications, buying and renting, electric and gas services

*Travel*—trains, airplanes, taxis, buses, ships, ferries, tickets, schedules, station and airport announcements, car rentals, hotels, reservations, delays and cancellations

*Dining out*—business and informal lunches, banquets, receptions, restaurant reservations

*Entertainment*—cinema, theater, music, art, media

*Health*—medical insurance, visiting doctors, dentists, clinics, hospitals

Becoming familiar with the language used in these settings will help you in the test, but please note:

- You do not need to know **specialized** business and technical vocabulary for the test.
- Your **skills and knowledge** in specialized areas will not be tested.

## What is the format of the test?

- The TOEIC test itself takes 2 hours to complete. Some extra time is needed to complete the biographical questions on the answer sheet and to respond to a short questionnaire about your educational and work history.
- It is a paper-and-pencil test.
- It is a multiple-choice test. For each question, you choose the answer that you think is correct and mark it with a pencil on your answer sheet.
- There are 200 questions in the test.
- The questions are divided into two main sections: Listening Comprehension and Reading. Each of these sections is timed separately. The Listening Comprehension section takes approximately 45 minutes. The Reading section takes 75 minutes.

Now you have a general idea about the test, its content, and its format. In the next part of the lesson, you will get to know the test in more detail by answering questions from the different parts of the test. The answers are printed at the end of the section.

## GET TO KNOW THE DIFFERENT TYPES OF QUESTIONS IN THE TEST

## Section 1: Listening Comprehension

In this section, there are 100 questions. During the test, you will listen to a recording of a variety of statements, questions, short conversations, and short talks and then answer questions based on the listening segments. There are four parts to this section.

### Part I: Photographs

There are 20 questions in this part. For each question, you will see a picture in your test book, and you will hear four short statements on the recording. You have to choose the statement that best describes what you see in the picture.

Here are some for you to try. Listen to the recording, look at the picture, and choose the correct answer.

Begin the recordings with Track 1 on CD 1; the audio is then consecutive with the exercises in this book.

1.  Ⓐ  Ⓑ  Ⓒ  Ⓓ

2.  Ⓐ  Ⓑ  Ⓒ  Ⓓ

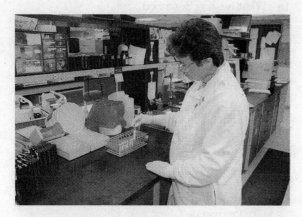

3.  Ⓐ  Ⓑ  Ⓒ  Ⓓ

4.  Ⓐ  Ⓑ  Ⓒ  Ⓓ

■ Now, STOP the recording.

## Part II: Question-Response

There are 30 questions in this part. You will hear a question asked by one speaker, followed by three responses from another speaker. You have to choose the most appropriate response to the question.

Here are some for you to try. Listen to the recording and choose the correct answer.

5.  Ⓐ  Ⓑ  Ⓒ
6.  Ⓐ  Ⓑ  Ⓒ
7.  Ⓐ  Ⓑ  Ⓒ
8.  Ⓐ  Ⓑ  Ⓒ
9.  Ⓐ  Ⓑ  Ⓒ

■ Now, STOP the recording.

## Part III: Short Conversations

There are 30 questions in this part. For each question, you will hear a short conversation between two people. In the test book, you will see a question about the conversation and four choices. You have to choose the correct answer to the question.

Here are some for you to try. Listen to the recording, read the question, and choose the correct answer.

10.  Where do the speakers work?
   (A)  In a clothing store.
   (B)  At a newspaper office.
   (C)  At a law office.
   (D)  In a bookstore.

   Ⓐ  Ⓑ  Ⓒ  Ⓓ

11.  How do the speakers think the problem should be addressed?
   (A)  By admitting fewer patients.
   (B)  By hiring more doctors.
   (C)  By enlarging the waiting room.
   (D)  By changing the hours of operation.

   Ⓐ  Ⓑ  Ⓒ  Ⓓ

12. When will the package arrive in London?

    (A) Tuesday morning.

    (B) Tuesday afternoon.

    (C) Wednesday morning.

    (D) Wednesday afternoon.

    Ⓐ Ⓑ Ⓒ Ⓓ

13. What is the man asking about?

    (A) The cause of increased sales.

    (B) Some overdue accounts.

    (C) Reductions in sales staff.

    (D) The results of a marketing survey.

    Ⓐ Ⓑ Ⓒ Ⓓ

14. Why will the speakers eat in the cafeteria today?

    (A) They can meet colleagues there.

    (B) The food is cheap there.

    (C) The seafood is fresh there.

    (D) They can eat quickly there.

    Ⓐ Ⓑ Ⓒ Ⓓ

■ Now, STOP the recording.

## Part IV: Short Talks

There are 20 questions in this part. You will hear several short talks. In your test book, you will read two or more questions about each short talk. Each question is followed by four choices, printed in the test book. You have to choose the best answer to each question.

Here are some for you to try. Listen to the recording and choose the correct answer.

15. Where is this talk most likely taking place?

    (A) At a post office.

    (B) At a factory.

    (C) On an airplane.

    (D) In a hospital.

    Ⓐ Ⓑ Ⓒ Ⓓ

16. What is being described?

    (A) Flight schedules.

    (B) Building repairs.

    (C) Exit procedures.

    (D) Work assignments.

    Ⓐ Ⓑ Ⓒ Ⓓ

17. In what area is Ms. Lee employed?

    (A) Human resources.

    (B) Telephone sales.

    (C) Customer service.

    (D) Product development.

    Ⓐ Ⓑ Ⓒ Ⓓ

18. What does Mr. Grieg want Ms. Lee to do?

    (A) Update a map.

    (B) Forward a list of names.

    (C) Attend a board meeting.

    (D) Accept a position.

    Ⓐ Ⓑ Ⓒ Ⓓ

■ Now, STOP the recording.

This is the end of the Listening Comprehension section.

## Section 2: Reading

In this section, there are 100 questions, printed in the test book. You will read a variety of materials and answer questions based on the reading materials. There are three parts to this section.

### Part V: Incomplete Sentences

There are 40 questions in this part. Each question consists of a sentence with a word or phrase deleted from it. Four words or phrases, marked (A), (B), (C), and (D), are given beneath each sentence. You have to decide which choice best completes the sentence.

The following are some for you to try:

19. Lyon Brothers, Inc., had a very small budget for advertising, so they decided to produce brochures - - - - - - - .

(A) itself

(B) oneself

(C) ourselves

(D) themselves

Ⓐ Ⓑ Ⓒ Ⓓ

20. Bianca Brunelli hopes to be - - - - - - - to government office in the spring.

(A) chosen

(B) elected

(C) preferred

(D) considered

Ⓐ Ⓑ Ⓒ Ⓓ

21. City College is now offering programs designed for students - - - - - - - to pursue a two-year certificate in information technology.

(A) Intending

(B) intended

(C) is intending

(D) has intended

Ⓐ Ⓑ Ⓒ Ⓓ

22. All department supervisors are required to attend the - - - - - - - on the new employee time-keeping policy.

(A) delegation

(B) summary

(C) commission

(D) seminar

Ⓐ Ⓑ Ⓒ Ⓓ

23. - - - - - - - the latest census, the population of the province has increased by eighteen percent in the last decade.

(A) In compliance with

(B) Depending on

(C) According to

(D) Along with

Ⓐ Ⓑ Ⓒ Ⓓ

## Part VI: Error Recognition

There are 20 questions in this part. For each question, you will read a sentence that has four words or phrases underlined. The four underlined parts of the sentence are marked (A), (B), (C), and (D). You have to identify the one underlined word or phrase that is incorrect.

Here are some for you to try:

24. There are several hotels in this area that
    A            B

provides discounts on tours of historical sites.
   C            D

Ⓐ Ⓑ Ⓒ Ⓓ

25. Information collection from shoppers through
            A            B

surveys is stored in secure files and is used to
                    C

tailor direct mailings.
      D

Ⓐ Ⓑ Ⓒ Ⓓ

26. Even though Ms. Herbert has been director
    A            B

for six months, she has not already visited the
  C               D

branch offices.

Ⓐ Ⓑ Ⓒ Ⓓ

27. <u>For</u> personal reasons, Mr. Chun has decided
 A

 <u>not to</u> apply for a <u>transference</u> at <u>this time</u>.
  B      C    D

 Ⓐ Ⓑ © Ⓓ

28. <u>All household</u> chemicals <u>they should</u>
   A       B

 be stored <u>well</u> out of the reach <u>of children</u>.
     C       D

 Ⓐ Ⓑ © Ⓓ

## Part VII: Reading Comprehension

There are 40 questions in this section. These questions are based on a selection of reading materials, such as notices, letters, forms, newspaper and magazine articles, and advertisements. Each text is followed by two or more questions.

Here are some for you to try:

**Questions 29–30** refer to the following letter.

## Kendar Office Supplies

*Kemapriatarum Road*
*Bangkok 10110*
*Thailand*

Ms. Pranee Udomsak
Director
Beni & Beni, Inc.
426 Silom Road
Bangkok 10110
Thailand

Dear Ms. Udomsak:

In checking our records, I noticed that you are no longer listed as a current customer of Kendar Office Supplies. When I called and spoke to your office manager, Peri Davis, I was informed that your company is now using one of our competitors for your office needs. Ms. Davis referred me to you as the individual who makes all purchasing decisions at Beni & Beni.

Ms. Davis kindly described some of the problems that led you to select another supplier. I'm pleased to tell you that Kendar has made many improvements to its product line and services, and we are certain Beni & Beni will find these attractive. We have introduced a whole new line of office and computer supplies, many of which are not available from any other supplier. In addition, Kendar now has the largest warehouse facility in the region.

If you need any additional information, please feel free to contact me. We welcome the opportunity to serve your company once again.

Sincerely,

Manee Chamchoy

29. For whom is this letter intended?
 (A) The director of Beni & Beni
 (B) The manager of Kendar Office Supplies
 (C) Peri Davis
 (D) Manee Chamchoy

30. What is the purpose of the letter?
 (A) To verify customer data
 (B) To register a formal complaint
 (C) To inquire about warehouse space
 (D) To restore a business relationship

**Questions 31–32** refer to the following information.

### Electrical Safety Requirements and Procedures

*An Up-to-Date, Intensive Two-Day Seminar*

### First Day

1. Introduction to Safety Standards
2. Conducting Electrical Inspections
3. Electrical Hazards
4. Training Requirements
5. Working on Energized Circuits or Parts
6. Installation of Electrical Equipment

### Second Day

1. Personal Protection
2. Servicing of Electrical Equipment
3. Clearance Distance Guidelines
4. Electrical Hazards in Confined Spaces
5. Portable Electrical Equipment
6. Test Equipment
7. Protective Equipment

This course presents electrical safety information based on national industry regulations and is designed to meet and exceed national safety training for the field. We have no affiliation with any supplier or manufacturer. We are therefore able to present a completely neutral view of the industry, without the sales bias inherent in many supplier-sponsored programs. To generate free and open exchange of information, tape recording of course sessions will not be permitted.

For registration and fees call:  (416) 555-1424 or visit our Web site at www.att.com

*The Association for Technological Training
3917 Stone St.*

TORONTO ON  M5A 1N1

31. Which topic will be covered on the second day?
    (A) Machinery installation guidelines
    (B) Equipment maintenance and repair
    (C) Hazardous waste disposal
    (D) Personnel management techniques

32. What is a stated advantage of the seminar?
    (A) The training is offered free of charge.
    (B) Recordings of the sessions can be ordered.
    (C) The course has no commercial sponsorship.
    (D) Participants will receive training certificates.

## YOUR FIRST IMPRESSIONS OF THE DIFFERENT TYPES OF QUESTIONS

Before you check your answers, think about the different types of questions in the TOEIC test. Which did you find the easiest? Which did you find the most difficult? Rank the seven different question types from 1 (easiest for you) to 7 (hardest for you). You could also make a note about why you think some types of question were harder for you than others.

| Question Type | Level of Difficulty (1 to 7) |
|---|---|
| Photographs | |
| Question-Response | |
| Short Conversations | |
| Short Talks | |
| Incomplete Sentences | |
| Error Recognition | |
| Reading Comprehension | |

Now, check your answers to the questions:

## Part I: Photographs

1. C
2. D
3. A
4. B

## Part II: Question-Response

5. B
6. A
7. B
8. C
9. A

## Part III: Short Conversations

10. B
11. C
12. C
13. A
14. D

## Part IV: Short Talks

15. B
16. C
17. A
18. D

## Part V: Incomplete Sentences

19. D
20. B
21. A
22. D
23. C

## Part VI: Error Recognition

24. C
25. A
26. D
27. C
28. B

## Part VII: Reading Comprehension

29. A
30. D
31. B
32. C

Now that you have checked your answers, would you change the way you ranked the types of questions in the test?

## HOW TO USE THIS BOOK

At the beginning of the book, you will find a table of contents that acts as an outline of the lessons in *30 Days to the TOEIC Test*. The 30 lessons follow the sequence of the different question types as they appear in the TOEIC test. Days 2 to 14 give tips, strategies, practice activities, and practice questions for the Listening Comprehension section of the test. Days 15 to 24 deal with the Reading section. Days 25 to 29 give you the opportunity to practice questions from both sections. Day 30 gives some general tips that relate to the whole test.

You can work through all the units in the order they appear, which mirrors the order of the actual test.

Alternatively, you can think about which types of questions you found most difficult when you tried the sample questions, and start by working on those first. For example, some people find listening comprehension harder than answering questions based on written material. If that is the case, you may want to spend more time working on Days 2 to 14. If you found one particular type of question in the Listening Comprehension section very difficult, the Question-Response type, for example, you might turn to Day 5 first, and work through Days 5, 6, and 7.

You may want to go straight to the set of practice questions for a particular type of question, see how you do on those, and then decide whether to work through the tips, strategies, and practice activities for that type of question. For example, if you want to work on Error Recognition questions, you will find a set of practice Error Recognition questions on Day 20. You can then go back to Days 18 and 19 to do more work on Error Recognition questions if you feel you need to.

## CHECK YOUR KNOWLEDGE OF THE TOEIC TEST

This lesson has given you an introduction to the TOEIC test and an opportunity to try some sample questions. Without looking back at the information given, find out how much you know about the test.

*Directions: Read the statements below. If you think the statement is a true statement about the TOEIC test, put a T next to it. If you think it is false, put an F next to it. When you have finished, check your answers below.*

*To the teacher:* Students should work together in pairs for this exercise. Ask them to discuss each statement and decide whether it is true or false. If they think it is false, they should correct the statement.

### True or False?

1. There are 200 questions in the TOEIC test.

2. "TOEIC" stands for "Test of English for International Commerce."

3. TOEIC questions test the type of English used in academic research papers.

4. The Listening Comprehension section comes before the Reading section.

5. The TOEIC test has multiple-choice questions: candidates choose the answer they think is correct for each question.

6. The TOEIC test is a computer-adaptive test.

7. All of the questions in the TOEIC test have four choices.

8. The TOEIC test is designed to test candidates' knowledge of the specialized vocabulary used in business and commerce.

9. In the Listening Comprehension section, the recording for each question is played once.

10. There is a separate writing assignment as part of the TOEIC test.

**Answers:**

1. T

2. F  "TOEIC" stands for "Test of English for International Communication."

3. F  TOEIC questions test the type of English used in everyday activities.

4. T

5. T

6. F  The TOEIC test is a pencil-and-paper test.

7. F  The Question-Response questions in Part II have only three choices.

8. F  You do not need to know specialized vocabulary for the TOEIC test.

9. T

10. F  There is no separate paper or writing assignment required as part of the test.

# Day 2

## An Introduction to the Listening Comprehension Section and Tips and Exercises for Part I: Photographs

The lessons for Days 2 to 14 deal with the four different question types in Section 1 of the test, the Listening Comprehension section.

## LISTENING COMPREHENSION SECTION OVERVIEW

The Listening Comprehension section consists of questions 1–100 of the TOEIC test. It is divided into four parts:

Part I: Photographs

Part II: Question-Response

Part III: Short Conversations

Part IV: Short Talks

In the Listening Comprehension section, you will hear an audio recording for each of the parts of the section. You will listen to a variety of statements, questions, short conversations, and short talks recorded in English, then you will answer the questions. For Parts I and II, you will hear only a recording. For Parts III and IV, you will also see questions and options written in your test book. In order to answer the questions in this section, you will use your ability to listen in English: for particular sounds, for details, and for the overall meaning of a statement or ques-

tion. You will have about 45 minutes to complete the Listening Comprehension section of the test.

Today's lesson starts with a tip to help you improve your listening skills in general and to help you select the correct answer in the Listening Comprehension section of the test.

## TIP  Pay attention to words that are stressed.

In spoken English, certain words in a sentence are stressed. That is, some words in a spoken sentence are pronounced more loudly, or with more emphasis, than other words. These are the words that the speaker thinks are important. Paying attention to the stressed words in speech can help you identify the main ideas. The stressed words are usually the words that give clues to meaning, such as nouns, verbs, and adjectives. Other words in a sentence are pronounced with little or no distinction. Very often, these are words that contain less information but contribute to the grammar of the sentence, such as the articles *a* and *the*, pronouns, prepositions, conjunctions, and auxiliary verbs.

Listen to this sentence:

**Example 1**

The doctor and a nurse are talking with a patient.

■ Now, STOP the recording.

In spoken English, the sentence above would most likely be stressed in four places: on the nouns *doctor, nurse,* and *patient,* and on the verb *talking.* The underlines indicate the syllables that are stressed when the sentence is spoken.

The <u>doc</u>tor and a <u>nurse</u> are <u>talk</u>ing with a <u>pa</u>tient.

The words that have little or no stress are the articles *the* and *a,* the conjunction *and,* the auxiliary verb *are,* and the preposition *with.* If you hear only the stressed words in this sentence, you can probably still understand what the sentence is about. The stressed words give you the main ideas.

**Example 2**

In this short passage, the words that convey grammatical information have been left out. These are the words that would not be stressed if the passage were spoken. The remaining words are those that convey content information. Read the passage through once. You should find that you can understand the main ideas of the passage even though the grammatical words have been left out.

If _____ have _____ PC _____ Internet access, _____ no better way _____ make _____ most _____ _____ than _____ use _____ _____ bank _____ us. Open _____ Lamberts Current Account _____ you _____ manage _____ money just how _____ want. _____ Current Account let _____ manage _____ money _____ _____ Internet any time _____ _____ day _____ night, _____ wherever _____ are _____ _____ world.

See the answer key at the end of this section for the completed version of this text.

## EXERCISE A: IDENTIFYING STRESS

On the recording, you will hear twelve sentences. The sentences are printed below. Read each sentence as you are listening to it, and underline the stressed words, or most important information. Each sentence will be read only once, as in the TOEIC test. They are typical of sentences you might hear on the recording for the Listening Comprehension section of the test. You will find the answers at the end of Day 2. If you find the exercise difficult, play the recording again while you are looking at the answers.

*To the teacher:* Start by giving some examples of simple statements in which the stress patterns can be easily identified. Write the sentences down and ask the students to identify the stressed words. Practice saying the sentences together, clapping your hands on each stressed syllable. Then play the recording, without stopping it, and ask the students to underline the stressed words. At the end of the recording, arrange the students in pairs and ask them to practice saying each sentence aloud together with the stress pattern heard on the tape.

1. The woman is carrying a tray of food.

2. When will you be leaving Jakarta?

3. I'd like to make an appointment with Dr. Simpson.

4. He said he would meet us at Delano's restaurant.

5. They're waiting to buy tickets from the box office.

6. Ms. Tanaka is coming to the budget meeting, isn't she?

7. I seem to have lost my umbrella somewhere.

8. The two men are shaking hands.

9. Have you met our new supervisor yet?

10. Welcome to Flight 346 to Los Angeles.

11. There's a table over there by the window.

12. It's expected to rain this afternoon.

■ Now, STOP the recording.

## TIPS AND EXERCISES FOR PART I: PHOTOGRAPHS

In the lesson for Day 1, you tried some sample questions from Part I of the test. This is the part of the test in which you see photographs of actions, objects, places, and people in your test book. On the recording, you will hear a speaker make four statements about each photograph. All four of the choices may sound like correct descriptions of the photograph, but only one describes accurately what you can see in the photograph. The following are important points to remember about this part:

There are 20 questions in the Photographs section.

The four choices are not printed in the test book. You will see only the photograph.

You hear the recording only once. This is the case throughout the Listening Comprehension section of the test.

In the Photographs section, there is a pause of 5 seconds between questions on the recording.

## TIP Take a quick look at the photograph before you hear the four statements.

Listening to spoken English is much easier when you have some idea about what you are going to hear. While you are waiting to hear the choices, look at the photograph and think about it. Ask yourself these questions about each picture:

Where was it taken?

What is the main subject?

What is happening?

Who are the people?

## EXERCISE B: THINKING ABOUT THE PHOTOGRAPH

There are four photographs below. Look at each one for 5 seconds and ask yourself these questions:

Where was it taken?

What is the main subject?

What is happening?

Who are the people?

*To the teacher:* Ask the students to do this exercise individually at first. You can ensure that they keep to the 5-second time limit. When they have finished, arrange the students in pairs to discuss and write down the answers to the questions.

1.

2.

3.

4.

## EXERCISE C: PRACTICE WRITING YOUR OWN DESCRIPTIONS OF PHOTOGRAPHS

Write down as many words and sentences as you can about the two photographs on the following page.

Follow the examples provided. Some possible answers are printed in the answer key at the end of the lesson.

*To the teacher:* Encourage the students to work together in pairs or small groups to "brainstorm" on this practice exercise. The exercise can easily be extended with other pictures cut from magazines, brochures, or newspapers. This could be developed into a "picture dictation" activity: students work together in groups of three or four and together discuss and draw the picture they are going to "dictate" to the rest of the class. One group is selected to begin the activity. Each member of the group says <u>one sentence</u> describing their group's picture. The other students have to draw the picture, without asking any questions. The results can be quite fun.

1.

**What is in the picture?**

_____

_____

_____

_____

**Sentences about the picture:**

_____

_____

_____

_____

2.

**What is in the picture?**

_____

_____

_____

_____

**Sentences about the picture:**

_____

_____

_____

_____

## EXERCISE D: LISTENING PRACTICE

Exercise C illustrated the fact that there may be many different ways to describe a photograph. In this exercise, you will look at some photographs and hear a number of different statements about each one. Some of these statements are correct descriptions of the photograph; some are not. Circle the letters of all the correct statements for each photograph. The answers are printed at the bottom of the page.

1.

A. They're putting the violins away.

B. The performance has begun.

C. They're standing on a stage.

D. The concert is taking place outdoors.

E. The curtain is beginning to rise.

F. They're drawing bows across the strings.

G. They're giving a concert.

2.

A. There are buildings near a lake.

B. The land in this area is very flat.

C. Buildings are reflected in the water.

D. There are houses on the hillside.

E. The water is very calm.

F. Factory chimneys rise above the village.

G. People are boating on the river.

3.

A. The men are wiring an appliance.

B. The men are all wearing hats.

C. Wiring is being placed underground.

D. A man is opening a window.

E. The men are setting a table.

F. The men are laying wheels on the ground.

G. A man is pulling a cable.

■ Now, STOP the recording.

# TIP Prepare yourself for authentic speech.

In the Listening Comprehension section of the TOEIC test, you will hear authentic English speech. The statements about the photographs in Part I will be spoken as a native speaker would say them. Thus, the speakers will use contractions as native speakers do.

### Contractions

| Informal English | Formal English |
|---|---|
| he's | he is or he has |
| they're | they are |
| it's | it is or it has |
| there's | there is |

## EXERCISE E: LISTENING TO STATEMENTS CONTAINING CONTRACTIONS

You will hear eight sentences on the tape, spoken in natural English with contractions. The second part of the sentence has been written down for you. Listen to the recording and complete the sentence, first in an informal style, as you hear on the tape, and then in a formal style.

1.  A.  Informal:  _____ the fish on the scales.

    B.  Formal:  _____ the fish on the scales.

2.  A.  Informal:  Next to the bench, _____ a bicycle.

    B.  Formal:  Next to the bench, _____ a bicycle.

3.  A.  Informal:  _____ just finished.

    B.  Formal:  _____ just finished.

4.  A.  Informal:  _____ cut the tree down.

    B.  Formal:  _____ cut the tree down.

5.  A.  Informal:  _____ the envelope.

    B.  Formal:  _____ the envelope.

6.  A.  Informal:  _____ land shortly.

    B.  Formal:  _____ land shortly.

7.  A.  Informal:  _____ very crowded.

    B.  Formal:  _____ very crowded.

8.  A.  Informal:  It looks as if _____.

    B.  Formal:  It looks as if _____.

■ Now, STOP the recording.

---
### ANSWER KEY FOR DAY 2
---

## Example 2

If you have a PC with Internet access, there's no better way to make the most of it than to use it to bank with us. Open a Lamberts Current Account and you can manage your money just how you want. Our Current Account lets you manage your money over the Internet any time of the day or night, from wherever you are in the world.

## Exercise A

1.  The <u>wom</u>an is <u>carry</u>ing a <u>tray</u> of <u>food</u>.

2.  <u>When</u> will you be <u>leav</u>ing Ja<u>kar</u>ta?

3.  I'd <u>like</u> to <u>make</u> an ap<u>point</u>ment with <u>Doctor</u> <u>Simp</u>son.

4.  He <u>said</u> he would <u>meet</u> us at Delano's <u>res</u>taurant.

5.  They're <u>wait</u>ing to <u>buy</u> tickets from the <u>box</u> of fice.

6.  Ms. <u>Tan</u>aka is <u>com</u>ing to the <u>budget meeting</u>, <u>isn't</u> she?

7.  I <u>seem</u> to have <u>lost</u> my um<u>brel</u>la <u>some</u>where.

8.  The <u>two men</u> are <u>shaking hands</u>.

9.  <u>Have</u> you <u>met</u> our new <u>super</u>visor <u>yet</u>?

10. <u>Wel</u>come to <u>Flight</u> <u>three</u> <u>four</u> <u>six</u> to Los An<u>geles</u>.

11. There's a <u>table</u> over <u>there</u> by the <u>window</u>.

12. It's ex<u>pec</u>ted to <u>rain</u> this after<u>noon</u>.

## Exercise C

### First photograph

**What is in the picture?**

Men

Glasses of water

Women

Papers and folders

Business people

People wearing suits

A large table

Some people sitting/standing

Lights hanging from the ceiling

People talking together

**Sentences about the picture:**

The people are having a meeting.

People are gathered around a large table.

Men and women are working together.

This is a formal business place.

There are lights in the center of the room.

People are on both sides of a long table.

### Second photograph

**What is in the picture?**

A tractor

Tools

A workshop

A large wheel

A mechanic

A window

A man

**Sentences about the picture:**

He's trying to fix the tractor.

The man's busy in the workshop.

He's repairing a tractor part.

It's quite dark in the workshop.

## Exercise D

1. B, F, and G

2. A, C, D, and E

3. B, C, and G

## Exercise E

This is what you heard on the tape:

1. He's putting the fish on the scales.

2. Next to the bench, there's a bicycle.

3. The concert's just finished.

4. They're about to cut the tree down.

5. She's sealing the envelope.

6. The plane's going to land shortly.

7. The restaurant isn't very crowded.

8. It looks as if it's going to rain.

These are the formal versions of the sentences you heard:

1. He is putting the fish on the scales.

2. Next to the bench, there is a bicycle.

3. The concert has just finished.

4. They are about to cut the tree down.

5. She is sealing the envelope.

6. The plane is going to land shortly.

7. The restaurant is not very crowded.

8. It looks as if it is going to rain.

# Day 3

## Further Exercises for Part I: Photographs

In this lesson, you will learn further strategies to help you make the correct choice in Part I of the test.

### TIP Prepare yourself for the language of descriptions.

Think about the type of English used by a native speaker when describing a picture. Look at these four photographs and some sentences that could describe them:

*To the teacher:* This section is intended as a brief grammar review for the students. In Exercise B, an opportunity will be given for them to practice using these structures. You may want to supplement this with extra explanations and exercises as you think necessary.

### Photograph 1

1. Some people are listening to the musicians.

2. A crowd of people has gathered to listen to the musicians.

3. The concert is taking place outdoors.

4. Some of the performers are seated.

5. A man is playing the violin.

## Photograph 2

1. A towel has been hung on the rack
2. There's a telephone on the bathroom wall.
3. He's looking at his reflection.
4. There's a large mirror in front of the man.
5. The man is wearing a patterned tie.

## Photograph 3

1. The path winds through the trees.
2. Nobody is walking along the path.
3. The trees are growing beside the path.
4. It is dark in the woods.
5. The area seems deserted.

## Photograph 4

1. The lid of the copying machine is open.
2. He's going to make a copy of a document.
3. He's about to close the lid.
4. The man is wearing a shirt and tie.
5. There are several people in the office.

## EXERCISE A: IDENTIFYING GRAMMATICAL FORMS

In the sentences above, can you identify the following verb tenses that are often used in descriptions?

- **Present continuous**—to describe what is happening in a picture
- **Present simple**—to mention the existence of someone or something in a picture (used with the impersonal subject "there"), to describe a state that exists in the picture, to describe the location of something in the picture
- **Present perfect**—to describe something that has happened or has been done. In the picture, you can see the result of that action.
- **Future**—to indicate what is likely to happen soon. When describing pictures, "going to" and the infinitive of the verb are often used when there is evidence in the picture of a future action. "About to" and the infinitive may also be used.

Now, identify the verb tense used in the descriptions of each photograph:

## Photograph 1:

1.  Some people are listening to the musicians.

    Verb tense: present continuous ("are listening")

2.  A crowd of people has gathered to listen to the musicians.

    Verb tense:

3.  The concert is taking place outdoors.

    Verb tense:

4.  Some of the performers are seated.

    Verb tense:

5.  A man is playing the violin.

    Verb tense:

## Photograph 2:

1.  A towel has been hung on the rack

    Verb tense:

2.  There's a telephone on the bathroom wall.

    Verb tense:

3.  He's looking at his reflection.

    Verb tense:

4.  There's a large mirror in front of the man.

    Verb tense:

5.  The man is wearing a patterned tie.

    Verb tense:

## Photograph 3:

1.  The path winds through the trees.

    Verb tense:

2.  Nobody is walking along the path.

    Verb tense:

3.  The trees are growing beside the path.

    Verb tense:

4.  It is dark in the woods.

    Verb tense:

5.  The area seems deserted.

    Verb tense:

## Photograph 4:

1.  The lid of the copying machine is open.

    Verb tense:

2.  He's going to make a copy of a document.

    Verb tense:

3.  He's about to close the lid.

    Verb tense:

4.  The man is wearing a shirt and tie.

    Verb tense:

5.  There are several people in the office.

    Verb tense:

In descriptions, the following parts of speech are also often used:

*   **Adjectives** are used to describe nouns.
*   **Prepositions** are used before a noun to describe relationships in space (location, movement) and time as well as other relationships.

Now, look at the sentences again. For each group of sentences describing a photograph, identify the adjectives and prepositions:

## Photograph 1:

Adjectives:_____

Prepositions:_____

## Photograph 2:

Adjectives:_____

Prepositions:_____

## Photograph 3:

Adjectives:_____

Prepositions:_____

## Photograph 4:

Adjectives:_____

Prepositions:_____

These are just some of the tenses and parts of speech that might be used in descriptions. In the next exercise, you will have the opportunity to describe some pictures yourself. As you do so, think about the grammatical forms and parts of speech you are using.

---

## EXERCISE B: PRACTICE WRITING DESCRIPTIONS

---

For each of the three pictures on pages 24 and 25, write down words related to the image and some statements that describe what you see. Your statements might look very similar to the choices on the TOEIC test!

1.

2.

3.

What is in the picture?

1. _____

2. _____

3. _____

Sentences about the picture:

1. _____

2. _____

3. _____

## EXERCISE C: FURTHER PRACTICE IN WRITING DESCRIPTIONS

Now, look through the pictures in a book, magazine, or newspaper. Try to find a variety of settings and situations. Look back at Day 1: "What is the content of the test?" for a list of the types of settings used in the TOEIC test. For each picture, write down words related to the image and some statements that describe what you see, as you did for the pictures on pages 24 and 25. In your descriptions, you will probably use many of the grammatical forms you identified in Exercise A as well as others.

When you finish, you could trade photographs with a friend or colleague. Have your friend describe the photographs without seeing what you wrote. Then, compare your work and decide which statement describes the picture most accurately.

*To the teacher:* As a homework activity, the students could be given the task of cutting out photographs from newspapers and magazines. Exercise C can then be done in class, with the students working on their own for the first part and then in pairs for the second part. For another class activity, you could cut out sets of five photographs from a magazine. Number each photograph and write a sentence describing each one. Display the photographs so that all the students can see them and read the sentences aloud one by one. Then, have the students identify which picture each sentence describes. Several sets of pictures could be prepared and the activity made more and more difficult. If the pictures in the set are quite different, it will be easy, but if there is some similarity between all the pictures in the set, for example a similar setting or the same people in each picture (you could use family photos), it will be more difficult.

Statements about a photograph may contain parts that are true. Listen carefully to determine if the entire statement, or only part of it, is true.

## TIP  Listen carefully to each statement about the photograph.

**Example**

He's adjusting the dials on a television set.

■ Now, STOP the recording.

While it is true that the man is adjusting dials, there is no television set in the picture. Therefore, the sentence in the example is not an entirely accurate description of what you see in the picture.

## EXERCISE D: PRACTICE LISTENING CAREFULLY TO EACH STATEMENT

Following are five pictures.  On the recording, you will hear two statements for each picture. Part of the first statement is incorrect. Listen to the recording and write in your book the incorrect part of the statement. Then, listen to the second statement, which is entirely correct, and write that down.

## Photograph 1

Statement 1: _____

Statement 2: _____

## Photograph 2

Statement 1: _____

Statement 2: _____

## Photograph 3

Statement 1: _____

Statement 2: _____

## Photograph 4

Statement 1: _____

Statement 2: _____

## Photograph 5

Statement 1: _____

Statement 2: _____

■ Now, STOP the recording.

*To the teacher:* It is important to reinforce the fact that part of the first statement about each picture is incorrect, and so the statement does not accurately describe the picture. To extend this activity, you could find some pictures and write the beginning of a sentence about each. Display the pictures one at a time, and read out the beginning of the sentence. Then have the students complete the sentence to make an accurate description of the picture.

## TIP Listen to all of the choices.

In Part I of the test, you are asked to choose the statement that best describes what you see in the picture. Be sure to listen carefully to all four statements for each photograph. Choice (B) may sound like the correct answer, but it is important to continue to listen to choices (C) and (D), because one of them might give a better description of the picture.

## TIP Get used to the timing and speed of delivery.

The speakers on the recording speak at a normal rate of speech. Take as many opportunities as you can to listen to authentic English speech, spoken at a normal speed. Be ready for the next question. There is a 5-second gap between the questions in this part of the test. If you are not ready for the next question, you will soon fall behind. On Day 4, you will be able to try a real Part I of the TOEIC test and get used to the speed of the speech and the pause between questions.

## ANSWER KEY FOR DAY 3

### Exercise A (Verb Tenses)

**Photograph 1:**

1.  Present continuous: *are listening*
2.  Present perfect: *has gathered*
3.  Present continuous: *is taking place*
4.  Present simple: *are seated*
5.  Present continuous: *is playing*

**Photograph 2:**

1.  Present perfect: *has been hung*
2.  Present simple: *is*
3.  Present continuous: *is looking at*
4.  Present simple: *is*
5.  Present continuous: *is wearing*

**Photograph 3:**

1.  Present simple: *winds*
2.  Present continuous: *is walking*
3.  Present continuous: *are growing*
4.  Present simple: *is*
5.  Present simple: *seems*

**Photograph 4:**

1.  Present simple: *is*
2.  Future: *is going to make*
3.  Future: *is about to close*
4.  Present continuous: *is wearing*
5.  Present simple: *are*

## Exercise A (Parts of Speech)

**Photograph 1:**

Adjectives:   1. Some   3. outdoors   4. Some

Prepositions: 2. of   4. of

**Photograph 2:**

Adjectives:   2. bathroom  3. his  4. large  5. patterned

Prepositions: 1. on   2. on   3. at   4. in front of

**Photograph 3:**

Adjectives:   4. dark   5. deserted

Prepositions: 1. through   2. along   3. beside   4. in

**Photograph 4:**

Adjectives:   1. copying, open   5. several

Prepositions: 1. of   2. of   3. about   5. in

## Exercise D

**Photograph 1:**

Statement one:  a microphone.

Statement two:  She's using a pay phone.

**Photograph 2:**

Statement one:  She's writing in

Statement two:  She's reading a book.

**Photograph 3:**

Statement one:  are getting off a bus.

Statement two:  The passengers are boarding the bus.

**Photograph 4:**

Statement one:  folding up

Statement two:  The man is looking at a newspaper.

**Photograph 5:**

Statement one:  A woman is opening up

Statement two:  A woman is pointing to the flip chart.

# Day 4

## Photographs: Practice Questions and Follow-up Exercises

In this lesson, you will have the opportunity to practice Part I of the TOEIC test. Before you do this, remind yourself of the tips given on Days 2 and 3:

- Pay attention to words that are stressed.
- Take a quick look at the photograph before you hear the four statements.
- Prepare yourself for authentic speech.
- Prepare yourself for the language of descriptions.
- Listen carefully to each statement about the photograph.
- Listen to all of the choices.
- Get used to the timing and speed of delivery.

### PRACTICE QUESTIONS

Now, try this practice Part I, working as if you were taking a real TOEIC test. On the recording, you will first hear the directions and an example item, as you would in a real TOEIC test.

Before you start, write the numbers 1–20 on a piece of paper to record your answers. Work straight through the section. Do not stop the recording. If you are not sure which is the correct answer, choose the one you think is closest. Do not leave any questions blank.

### Part I

*Directions: For each question, you will see a picture in your test book and you will hear four short statements. The statements will be spoken just one time. They will not be printed in your test book, so you must listen carefully to understand what the speaker says.*

**Sample Answer**
Ⓐ ● Ⓒ Ⓓ

When you hear the four statements, look at the picture in your book and choose the statement that best describes what you see in the picture.

Now, listen to the four statements.

Statement (B), "They're having a meeting," best describes what you see in the picture. Therefore, you should select statement (B). The answers are printed at the end of this section.

1.

4.

2.

5.

3.

6.

7.

8.

9.

10.

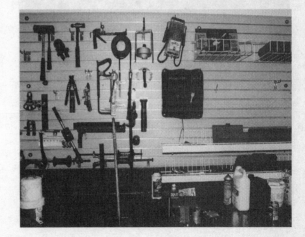

11.

12.

13.

14.

15.

16.

17.

18.

19.

20.

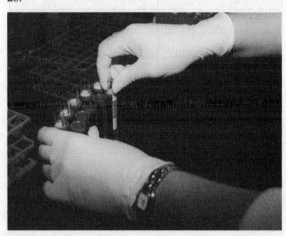

■ Now, STOP the recording.

You can check your answers with the answer key at the end of Day 4.

## FOLLOW-UP EXERCISES

### EXERCISE A: ANALYZING YOUR ERRORS

After you have checked your answers, go through the photographs and put an X and the letter of the answer you chose next to each photograph for which you chose the wrong answer. Then, listen to the recording again, and do two things:

1. Without looking at the answer key, try the question again.

2. Write a brief note, saying why your first choice was wrong. For example, look at the first photograph. Imagine you had chosen (B), "She's caring for a child," as the correct answer. You might make a note saying: "No child in photo."

When you have finished listening, check your answers again. Did you get more right the second time?

*To the teacher:* It is best to let the students try the questions at least twice without stopping the recording or referring to the recording script. After trying Exercise A individually, find out which questions caused the most difficulty. Arrange the students in pairs or small groups and let them work on those questions together. Play the recording for the difficult questions one at a time, giving them time to discuss the right answer and the wrong answers and make a short statement about why the distracters (wrong answers) did not accurately describe the picture.

## EXERCISE B: THINKING ABOUT THE CHOICES IN DEPTH

In this exercise, you will look at the script for the practice questions that is printed at the end of this section while you look at the photographs and listen to the recording. If possible, make a photocopy of the script to make this easier.

Play the recording for the first question, and make sure you understand why choice (A) was correct. Look at the script. Did you hear this choice correctly? Are there any words in this choice that you do not understand? If so, look them up in the dictionary. Look at the other three choices and think about why they were wrong. On the script, make a note of why you think the other three choices were wrong. For example, for choice (C) in Question 1, you might write: "not planting anything." Again, listen carefully to any words that you did not understand the first time, and look up any new words in the dictionary.

Follow this procedure for all 20 practice questions. This should give you a clear picture of the reasons for any wrong choices you made. Afterward, you might want just to listen to the recording again while looking at the photographs.

*To the teacher:* For this exercise, you could copy the script onto an overhead transparency and show the script to the students one question at a time as they listen to the recording. You could arrange the students in small groups and ask them to discuss the correct and incorrect choices together.

## EXERCISE C: THINKING ABOUT THE PHOTOGRAPHS

Look at the photographs again and think about the variety of locations in which they were taken.

Write the number of the photograph that you think was taken in each location.

| Location | Number of photograph |
|---|---|
| A.  laboratory | |
| B.  kitchen | |
| C.  elevator | |
| D.  warehouse | |
| E.  beach | |
| F.  reception area | |
| G.  meeting room | |
| H.  library | |
| I.  field | |
| J.  lakeside | |
| K.  restaurant | |
| L.  workshop | |
| M.  street | |
| N.  construction site | |
| O.  flower shop | |
| P.  balcony | |
| Q.  auditorium | |
| R.  filling station | |
| S.  seminar room | |
| T.  town center | |

Some answers are suggested in the answer key at the end of Day 4. Other answers may be possible. You could write your own list of locations.

*To the teacher:* This exercise is intended to encourage discussion of the locations in which the photographs were taken. Therefore, it is probably best done in groups. You might want to pre-teach phrases that could be used in the discussion, such as: "I think the photo was taken in _____" or "It could have been/ must have been taken at _____." You could also pre-teach phrases for agreeing and disagreeing. The different groups could be encouraged to come up with their own list of locations.

## EXERCISE D: WRITING DESCRIPTIONS OF THE PHOTOGRAPHS

1.  Look at photographs 3, 11, and 15.
    A.  Can you think of anything these photographs have in common?
    B.  Write three statements describing each photograph. Try to use all of these words:

    | | |
    |---|---|
    | fence | wings |
    | trees | horses |
    | grass | alone |
    | seaweed | fly (verb) |
    | hats | alone |
    | calm | flap (verb) |
    | sand | water | bridge |

2.  Look at photographs 1, 2, and 19.
    A.  Can you think of anything these photographs have in common?
    B.  Write three statements describing each photograph. Try to use all of these words:

    | | |
    |---|---|
    | board | glasses |
    | bend | sit |
    | hair | plant |
    | blinds | television |
    | explain | speak |
    | water | paper | clock |

3.  Look at photographs 16, 10, and 8.
    A.  Can you think of anything these photographs have in common?
    B.  Write three statements describing each photograph. Try to use all of these words:

    | | |
    |---|---|
    | floor | apron |
    | lights | desk |
    | tools | mend |
    | wear | wall |
    | study (verb) | books |
    | tiles | bend | clean (verb) |

See the answer key for some possible answers to the A questions in Exercise D. Other answers may be possible.

*To the teacher:* The exercise above is well suited to group work. Students can discuss together what the sets of photographs have in common, and together write the three statements. As an extension of this, divide the students into an even number of groups. Each group chooses three photographs from Practice Part I and writes a list of words to be used in descriptions of them. Name the groups A, B, etc. Group A challenges Group B to write three statements about Group A's photographs using all the words. Group B challenges Group A to do the same for the three photographs they chose. To draw the activity together, Group A reads out loud their statements in mixed order to Group B, who have to work out which picture each statement refers to. Group B then does the same.

## PRACTICE QUESTIONS SCRIPT

1.  (A) She's watering a plant.
    (B) She's caring for a child.
    (C) She's planting a tree.
    (D) She's drinking some water.

2.  (A) She's looking for her glasses.
    (B) She's picking up a pen.
    (C) She's holding a piece of paper.
    (D) She has a scarf around her neck.

3.  (A) They're riding horses.
    (B) They're jumping the fence.
    (C) They're feeding the animals.
    (D) They're farming the land.

4.  (A) She's stepping onto the escalator.
    (B) She's closing her handbag.
    (C) She's lifting the handle.
    (D) She's pushing the button.

5.  (A) The land around the building is flat.
    (B) The stadium is now full.
    (C) Planes have landed on the airfield.
    (D) The warehouse is many stories high.

6.  (A) A man is withdrawing money.
    (B) A man has hung a painting on a wall.
    (C) A man is writing in a notebook.
    (D) A man is on his hands and knees.

7.  (A) They're installing a sliding door.
    (B) They're climbing down a ladder.
    (C) They're working on the roof.
    (D) They're loading the truck.

8.  (A) The plates are being stacked.
    (B) The silver is being polished.
    (C) The shelves are being cleaned.
    (D) The floor is being mopped.

9.  (A) He's writing a receipt for the customer.
    (B) He's oiling the motorcycle engine.
    (C) He's pumping up the car's tires.
    (D) He's putting fuel in the automobile.

10. (A) The equipment is all being used.
    (B) The workspace is being cleaned.
    (C) The tools are hanging on the wall.
    (D) The workshop has not been organized.

11. (A) Dogs are lying on the riverbank.
    (B) Birds are flying over the water.
    (C) Birds are landing in the trees.
    (D) People are swimming in the lake.

12. (A) The highway is busy with traffic.
    (B) Some people are crossing the street at the light.
    (C) All the buildings along the street are identical.
    (D) There are cars parked on both sides of the road.

13. (A) The waiter is removing the tablecloth.
    (B) The waiter is presenting the bill.
    (C) The woman is drinking coffee.
    (D) The customers are waiting to be served.

14. (A) He's playing some music.
    (B) He's laying some pipe.
    (C) He's talking to a friend.
    (D) He's marching in a band.

15. (A) The area is crowded with people.
    (B) People are collecting seaweed.
    (C) A person is walking along the water's edge.
    (D) A person is selling drinks by the ocean.

16. (A) People are working at the tables.
    (B) The librarians are opening the windows.
    (C) The library is closed for the day.
    (D) Students are leaving the building.

17. (A) The people are seated on a bench.
    (B) The woman is leaning on a railing.
    (C) The man is taking a picture of the view.
    (D) The people are looking for a parking place.

18. (A) Flowers are arranged in buckets.
    (B) Vegetables are planted in a garden.
    (C) The trees are in full bloom.
    (D) Sacks of flour are on the ground.

19. (A) The speaker is facing the audience.
    (B) They are changing the channel on the television.
    (C) They are closing the blinds.
    (D) The man is pointing toward the board.

20. (A) She's wearing gloves.
    (B) She's studying for a test.
    (C) She's tasting the food.
    (D) She's shaking hands.

## ANSWER KEY FOR DAY 4

### Practice Questions

1. A
2. C
3. A
4. D
5. A
6. D
7. C
8. D
9. D
10. C
11. B
12. D
13. D
14. A
15. C
16. A
17. B
18. A
19. D
20. A

### Exercise C

Suggested answers:

A. 20
B. 8
C. 4
D. 5
E. 15
F. 1
G. 2
H. 16
I. 3
J. 11
K. 13
L. 10
M. 6
N. 7
O. 18
P. 17
Q. 14
R. 9
S. 19
T. 12

### Exercise D

Possible answers:

1. A. The photographs all show outdoor scenes.

2. A. The photographs all have an office setting.

3. A. The photographs all show the interiors of rooms.

# Day 5

## Tips and Exercises for Part II: Question-Response

In the lesson for Day 1, you tried some sample questions from Part II of the test. Today, you will start to work on Part II, the Question-Response section. This is the part of the test in which you hear a question asked by one speaker, followed by three responses from another speaker. All three of the responses are correct English, but only one is an appropriate response to the question. The following are important points to remember about this part of the exam:

- There are 30 questions in the Question-Response section.
- Neither the questions nor the responses are printed in the test book. You will see only the words "Mark your answer on your answer sheet" in the test book.
- You will hear three choices only.
- You will hear the recording only once, as in the rest of the Listening Comprehension section.
- On the recording, there is a pause of 5 seconds between questions.

Here are some suggestions for improving your ability to select the best response in this part of the test.

### TIP  Focus on the purpose of the question.

In order to choose the correct response to a question, you should understand what the purpose of the speaker's question is. Ask yourself: Why is the speaker asking that question?

Sometimes the purpose of the question is to ask for specific information, such as time, location, or reason.

For example, look at the following questions:

| Question | Information asked for |
|---|---|
| What time does the bus for Stuttgart leave? | Time |
| Where did you put the plans for the new office building? | Location |
| How will you be traveling to the conference? | Method of transportation |
| Do you have any idea why she's decided to quit her job? | Reason |
| Has Peter decided who will be arranging the deliveries while you're away? | Person |
| Which cup of coffee is yours? | Identification |

## EXERCISE A: ASKING FOR INFORMATION

Listed above are some types of information that a speaker might ask for.

1. Think of a question to ask for these other types of information. If there are any words in the right-hand column that you do not know, look them up in the dictionary.

| Question: | Information asked for: |
|---|---|
| _____ | ? Distance |
| _____ | ? Duration |
| _____ | ? Ownership |
| _____ | ? Cost |
| _____ | ? Opinion |
| _____ | ? Frequency |
| _____ | ? Instructions |
| _____ | ? Directions |

*To the teacher:* For this exercise, the students could work in groups of four. Ensure that learners' dictionaries of English are available, and ask them first to discuss the meaning of the words in the right-hand column and then to decide on the questions. Compare the questions from the different groups, then rearrange the students in pairs so that the members of each pair are from different groups. In their pairs, the students take turns to read out a question and elicit a suitable response from their partner, as in Exercise B. You could extend the practice of thinking about questions by asking the pairs to think of other types of information they might ask for and make up some examples of questions to elicit that information.

2. Think of a possible response to each of the questions you wrote in 1.

When you have finished, compare the questions you wrote for 1 with those suggested in the answers section at the end of Day 5. There are many possible questions and responses that could be written for this exercise.

We have looked at questions asked in order to gain information, but people do not only ask questions for information. A question may have a different purpose.

Here are some examples:

| Question: | Purpose of the question: |
|---|---|
| You're responsible for quality control, aren't you? | Asking for confirmation (person) |
| Could you take down the minutes, please? | Requesting (action) |
| Would you like to come over for dinner one evening? | Inviting |
| How about moving that bookshelf over there to make more space? | Making a suggestion |
| Why don't you write and complain about the delay? | Giving advice |
| Do you mind if I open the window? | Asking for permission |
| You're not going to stay late again, are you? | Expressing disbelief |

## EXERCISE B: IDENTIFYING THE PURPOSE OF A QUESTION

Listen to the following questions and then match them with the letter that best corresponds to the purpose of each question. This exercise will help you understand why the speaker is asking the question. The answers are printed at the bottom of the page.

*Sample Question:* Where is the nearest post office?
*Purpose:* Asking for information (location)

**Question:**

1. Who's coming to the reception?

2. When are you taking your vacation?

3. Is it okay if I change the air filter?

4. Do you know why they built the new museum so far from the old one?

5. The play starts at 7:30, doesn't it?

6. You're not really taking a new job, are you?

7. Shouldn't we hire a new designer?

8. Would you like to join us for lunch?

**Purpose of the question:**

A. Asking for information (person)

B. Making a suggestion or request

C. Asking for confirmation (time)

D. Asking for information (time)

E. Extending an invitation

F. Expressing disbelief

G. Asking for information (reason)

H. Asking for permission (action)

■ Now, STOP the recording.

> *To the teacher:* After trying Exercise B on their own, the students could then check their answers with a neighbor. Then each student should write another question for each purpose (without showing it to their partner). They should take turns to ask each other the question and elicit a response.

## EXERCISE C: FURTHER PRACTICE IN IDENTIFYING THE PURPOSE OF A QUESTION

As in Exercise B, listen to the following questions and then match them with the letter that best describes the purpose of each question. This time, the questions are not written out for you, so you will need to listen carefully. After you have done the exercise, check your answers below. You can then listen to the tape again, write down the questions and think of a suitable response for each.

**Question:**

1.

2.

3.

4.

5.

6.

7.

8.

**Purpose of the question:**

A. Asking for information (frequency)

B. Giving advice

C. Asking for permission

D. Inviting

E. Asking for information (ownership)

F. Requesting (action)

G. Asking for information (duration)

H. Asking for information (cost)

■ Now, STOP the recording.

## TIP Listen for question words.

A question word, such as *when*, *where*, *who*, or *how* may be used in a question. The question word helps the listener to identify the purpose of the question.

---

### EXERCISE D: LISTENING FOR THE QUESTION WORD

---

Listen to these questions and write down the question word used in each one. Be careful—the question word does not always come at the beginning of the question.

1.

2.

3.

4.

5.

6.

7.

8.

■ Now, STOP the recording.

There are two points to note from this exercise:

• A question that contains a question word is often asking for information, but not always.

• The question word does not always come at the beginning of the question. In Questions 3, 4, and 5 above, the question word is in the middle of the question. The speaker uses an introductory phrase before asking the actual question, or the question with the main purpose. (These questions are sometimes called *indirect questions*.) It is important to listen to the introductory phrase as well as the actual question, because doing so will help you identify the correct response. Questions 3, 4, and 5 were:

3. Does Tom remember which travel agent he booked the tickets through?

4. Would you mind showing me how to use the copier?

5. You don't know whose coat this is, do you?

The introductory phrases were:

3. Does Tom remember. . .

4. Would you mind showing me. . .

5. You don't know. . .

---

### EXERCISE E: IDENTIFYING PHRASES THAT INTRODUCE INDIRECT QUESTIONS

---

All of these questions come from the first part of the lesson for Day 5, in which you focused on the purpose of the question. All of these questions contain question words, and all of them are indirect questions. Read them and underline the phrase that introduces the question in each one.

1. Do you have any idea why she's decided to quit her job?

2. Has Peter decided who will be arranging the deliveries while you're away?

3. Could you tell me how far it is to the station, please?

4. Have you got any idea how often we have to replace the printer cartridge?

5. Do you know why they built the new museum so far from the old one?

6. Does anybody know whose umbrella this is?

Now, write some more indirect questions using different introductory phrases.

*To the teacher:* Elicit further introductory phrases for indirect questions and write them on the board. Think of various situations in which indirect questions might be asked, and write them on cards. Examples:

1. It's your first day at a new job, and there are a lot of things you don't know about the job and the office. Ask a colleague.

2. You're studying in the U.S.A. for three months, staying with an American family. It is the beginning of your stay, and you're not familiar with American home life. Think of some questions you might ask a member of the family.

   Arrange the students in groups of four. Hand out a card to each group and ask them to think of some indirect questions for that situation, using the phrase on the board. You could then rearrange the students into pairs, so that each pair is made of students from two different groups, and ask them to role-play the situations. The person asking the questions needs to explain the situation first.

## ANSWER KEY FOR DAY 5

## Exercise A

Here are some possible questions for Part 1:

| Question: | Information asked for: |
| --- | --- |
| Could you tell me how far it is to the station, please? | Distance |
| How long is the planning meeting expected to last? | Duration |
| Whose briefcase is this? | Ownership |
| How much is this tie? | Cost |
| What do you think about the collapse of the stock market? | Opinion |
| Have you any idea how often we have to replace the printer cartridge? | Frequency |
| Can you show me how to use this projector? | Instructions |
| How can I get to the airport from here? | Directions |

## Exercise B

1. A
2. D
3. H
4. G
5. C
6. F
7. B
8. E

## Exercise C

1. D
2. B
3. G
4. A
5. F
6. C
7. H
8. E

## Exercise D

1. How (+ wide)
2. When
3. Which
4. How
5. Whose
6. Why
7. What (+ about)
8. Why

## Exercise E

The phrases you should have underlined are

1. <u>Do you have any idea</u> why she's decided to quit her job?
2. <u>Has Peter decided</u> who will be arranging the deliveries while you're away?
3. <u>Could you tell me</u> how far it is to the station, please?
4. <u>Have you got any idea</u> how often we have to replace the printer cartridge?
5. <u>Do you know</u> why they built the new museum so far from the old one?
6. <u>Does anybody know</u> whose umbrella this is?

# Day 6

# Further Exercises for Part II: Question-Response

In today's lesson, you will learn further strategies to help you make the correct choice in Part II, as well as tips to improve your understanding of authentic spoken English, which you will be able to apply to all the tasks in the Listening Comprehension section.

## TIP Be prepared for questions without a question word.

Many questions do not contain a question word. One example is questions requiring a "yes" or "no" answer. In the question "Are we going to the party?" the word order, rather than a question word, indicates that this is a question. The answer to this might be "Yes, we are" or "No, we aren't" or even "I'm not sure." Another example is questions in which the speaker is asking for confirmation of information, such as "You're in charge of training new recruits, aren't you?" Here, the question tag "aren't you?" indicates that this is a question. The answer might be "Yes, that's right" or "No, that's Frank's responsibility."

## EXERCISE A: UNDERSTANDING QUESTIONS WITHOUT A QUESTION WORD

On the recording, you will hear a number of questions. Part of the question is written out for you. Listen to the recording and complete the question. Then, choose a suitable response to each question from the list below. The answers are given at the end of today's lesson.

🎧

1. _____ helping me with this suitcase?

2. _____ buy that car, is he?

3. _____ on Friday, doesn't she?

4. _____ first visit to the United Kingdom?

5. _____ a ride to the theater this evening?

6. _____ stay late today, or finish this in the morning?

7. _____ to confirm that appointment?

8. _____ coffee, or tea?

9. _____ last year's conference, didn't we?

10. _____ that proposal done on time?

■ Now, STOP the recording.

Now, choose one suitable response to each question from this list:

A. That's right.

B. No, I've never been there.

C. That would be a great help.

D. I just don't see how I can.

E. No, she didn't.

F. I certainly hope not.

G. No, I've been here a couple of times.

H. No, not at all.

I. Not as far as I know.

J. Coffee, please.

K. Yes, that's an excellent proposal.

L. I've never seen that suitcase before.

M. She actually goes on Saturday morning.

N. We might as well get it done today.

*To the teacher:* This exercise serves to provide a few examples of questions without a question word. Depending on the ability of your students, you might want to do some grammar practice in forming questions at this point. The exercise could be followed by a discussion of the purpose of each question, a discussion of why one response is correct and another not and then eliciting as many other possible responses as they can think of for each question.

## TIP   Prepare yourself for authentic English speech.

Throughout the Listening Comprehension section of the TOEIC test you will hear authentic English speech. The questions and responses in Part II will be spoken as a native speaker would say them. In the lesson for Day 2, we looked at the use of contractions in informal English when we described the photographs in Part I of the test. Contractions will also be heard in the questions and responses on the recording for Part II. For example, you will hear "he's" instead of the more formal "he is" or "he has" and "won't" instead of the more formal "will not."

In the Listening Comprehension section, you should also be prepared to hear elisions and phonetic linking:

### Elisions

In natural English speech, each word is not spoken as a separate, distinct entity. Some sounds, and in fact whole syllables, may not be pronounced. This omission of a sound is called *elision*. Thus, when saying "last night" a native speaker generally leaves out the "t" so that you hear "las night." In "going to" both the "g" at the end of "going" and the "t" at the beginning of "to" will generally be left out, so that "going to" sounds like "gonna."

| Informal Spoken English | Formal English |
| --- | --- |
| *wanna* | *want to* |
| *dunno* | *do not know* |
| *sanwich* | *sandwich* |
| *what sis* | *what is this* |
| *nex week* | *next week* |
| *gimme* | *give me* |

### Phonetic Linking

Natural English speech involves a phenomenon called "phonetic linking." It is very common in spoken English to break up syllables and words up so that they begin, if at all possible, with consonants [b, p, d, r, l, k, etc.] instead of with vowels [a, e, i, o, u].

If a syllable does not begin with a consonant in written English, then the speaker takes the last consonant from the preceding syllable and uses it as the first sound of the next syllable. Thus "selling" is pronounced "se-lling" and "broken" becomes "bro-ken." This happens across word boundaries as well as within words, so that "what is" becomes "wha-tis" and "just a minute" becomes "jus-ta-mi-nute."

| Spoken English | Written English |
| --- | --- |
| par-kings | parking is |
| wha-ta-bout | what about |
| doe-sit-work | does it work |

## EXERCISE B: PRACTICING USING NATURAL SPEECH

Practice saying the following sentences aloud. Use elisions and linking to make them sound as natural as possible. Some hints are given in the brackets, and you should also look back at the examples above. Being able to speak English naturally yourself will help you to understand natural spoken English.

1. What about having lunch together? (linking: *what + about*)

2. I don't know what his name is. (elision: *don't know*, elision: *what his*, linking: *name is*)

3. I'd like a ham sandwich, please. (linking: *like + a*, elision: *sandwich*)

4. How does it work? (linking: *does + it*)

5. I'll see you next week. (elision: *next week*)

6. I want to finish this as soon as possible. (elision: *want to*, linking: *this + as, soon + as*)

7. I'll be with you in a minute. (linking: *in + a*)

8. He left last night. (elision: *left last night*)

*To the teacher:* First practice the examples from the explanation above with the students. When they seem to have grasped the idea of elisions and linking, ask them to prepare for Exercise B by marking the linked words in the book, using a curved line underneath the end of one word to link it to the next, and indicating sounds that are omitted or changed through elision. They could work in pairs for this. Then ask them to practice saying each sentence aloud. Encourage babbling rather than speaking in chorus. Finally, choose individual students to say the sentences. Work on natural stress and rhythm, which should lead to natural pronunciation.

## Vocabulary

In the Listening Comprehension section of the test, you will also hear vocabulary that is used in informal speech. Here are some examples of these words, together with their equivalents in a more formal style of English.

| Informal English | Formal English |
| --- | --- |
| lots of | many |
| boss | director or supervisor |
| get in touch with | contact |

## EXERCISE C: UNDERSTANDING VOCABULARY USED IN INFORMAL ENGLISH

Informal vocabulary is used in these statements and questions. Underline the informal words, then rewrite the sentences in formal English.

1. When you're through with that journal, can I have it?

2. Could you give me a hand with this?

3. She said she'd be here at six o'clock sharp.

4. Yes, she quit her job last week.

5.    He was late so many times they finally fired him.

6.    The boss said he'd get in touch with me early next week.

7.    I don't have a clue where that file is.

8.    Your boss called while you were out.

## TIP Listen for a natural response to the question.

Listen to the following example:

### Example 1

Who's going to be in charge of processing paychecks now?

(A) Yes, I have a credit card.

**(B) The assistant accountant.**

(C) It's a complicated process.

■ Now, STOP the recording.

In authentic speech, the response to a question is not always grammatically linked to the question. Based on the grammar of the question here, you might expect the answer to contain the phrase "is going to be in charge." Although choice (B) does not contain this phrase, it is an acceptable and natural response to the question "Who?"

### Example 2

Where is the employee cafeteria?

(A) He's out sick today.

(B) Yes, I'm really hungry.

**(C) I'm not sure; I just started here.**

■ Now, STOP the recording.

Based on the grammar of the sentence, you might expect the answer to this question to contain the phrase "It is located..." Although choice (C) does not contain this phrase, choice (C) is a realistic response to a request for directions. People don't always know the answer to a question. Remember that TOEIC test questions are examples of authentic English speech. Think of different ways of responding to a question when you don't know the answer, or perhaps don't want to answer the question. For example, look at the following questions and responses:

| Question | Response |
|---|---|
| Would you like a sandwich, or some soup? .................... | I think I'll just have a drink. |
| When did they send out that order? ......................................... | They didn't say. |
| Can you recommend a restaurant around here? ........ | I don't usually eat out. |
| Is there a shuttle bus to the airport? .................. | Ask the receptionist, over there. |

## EXERCISE D: LISTENING FOR A NATURAL RESPONSE

Listen to these questions from Exercise B from Day 5. Then, match the question with the appropriate response from the list on the right, thinking about which would be a natural response to the question.

*Sample Question:* Where is the nearest post office?
*Answer:* There's one across from the city park.

### Question

1.    Who's coming to the reception?

2.    When are you taking your vacation?

3. Is it okay if I change the air filter?

4. Do you know why they built the new museum so far from the old one?

5. The play starts at 7:30, doesn't it?

6. You're not really taking a new job, are you?

7. Shouldn't we hire a new designer?

8. Would you like to join us for lunch?

## Response

A. Nothing closer was available.

B. Yes, I start in two weeks.

C. The entire department is invited.

D. Yes, we should.

E. I thought it was at eight.

F. I haven't decided yet.

G. Sorry, but I have a noon meeting.

H. Only if it's really dirty.

■ Now, STOP the recording.

*To the teacher:* This exercise is probably best done in pairs. Encourage discussion of which response is the most natural for each question. After the students have finished the exercise, ask them to practice the questions and responses, encouraging natural speech. Then, prepare them to practice making up their own responses to these questions. One person in each pair works with the book closed. The other person asks the first question and the partner responds with a brief, natural response. After the first four questions, they switch roles.

## ANSWER KEY FOR DAY 6

## Exercise A

Complete questions:

1. Would you mind helping me with this suitcase?

2. He's not going to buy that car, is he?

3. She leaves on Friday, doesn't she?

4. Is this your first visit to the United Kingdom?

5. Would you like a ride to the theater this evening?

6. Shall we stay late today, or finish this in the morning?

7. Did Mr. Richardson phone to confirm that appointment?

8. Would you prefer coffee, or tea?

9. We met at last year's conference, didn't we?

10. Do you think you will get that proposal done on time?

Suitable responses:

1. H

2. F

3. M

4. G

5. C

6. N

7. I

8. J

9. A

10. D

## Exercise C

Possible answers:

1. May I have that journal when you finish reading it?

2. Could you help me with this?

3. She said she would be here at exactly six o'clock.

4. Yes, she resigned from her job last week.

5. He was late to work so often that they finally dismissed him.

6. The manager said he would contact me early next week.

7. I do not know where that file is.

8. Your supervisor telephoned while you were out of the office.

## Exercise D

1. C

2. F

3. H

4. A

5. E

6. B

7. D

8. G

# Day 7

## Question-Response: Practice Questions and Follow-up Exercises

In this lesson, you will have the opportunity to practice Part II of the TOEIC test. Before you do this, remind yourself of the tips given on Days 5 and 6:

- Focus on the purpose of the question.
- Listen for question words.
- Be prepared for questions without a question word.
- Prepare yourself for authentic English speech.
- Listen for a natural response to the question.

As with Part I of the test, be sure to listen to all of the choices. There is a pause of 5 seconds between each Question-Response item. Use this practice Part II to get used to the timing and speed of delivery.

## PRACTICE QUESTIONS

Now try this practice Part II, working as if you were taking a real TOEIC test. On the recording, you will first hear the directions and an example item, as you would in a real TOEIC test. Before you start, write the numbers 21–50 on a piece of paper to record your answers. Work straight through the section. Do not stop the recording. If you are not sure which is the correct answer, choose the one you think is closest. As in all mutiple-choice tests, never leave a blank.

## Part II

*Directions: In this part of the test, you will hear a question or statement spoken in English, followed by three responses, also spoken in English. The question or statement and the responses will be spoken just one time. They will not be printed in your test book, so you must listen carefully to understand what the speakers say. You are to choose the best response to each question or statement.*

Now, listen to a sample question.

You will hear:

● Ⓑ Ⓒ

You will also hear:

The best response to the question "How are you?" is choice (A), "I am fine, thank you." Therefore, you should choose answer (A). The answers are printed at the end of this section.

21. Mark your answer on your answer sheet.

22. Mark your answer on your answer sheet.

23. Mark your answer on your answer sheet.

24. Mark your answer on your answer sheet.

25. Mark your answer on your answer sheet.

26. Mark your answer on your answer sheet.

27. Mark your answer on your answer sheet.

28. Mark your answer on your answer sheet.

29. Mark your answer on your answer sheet.

30. Mark your answer on your answer sheet.

31. Mark your answer on your answer sheet.

32. Mark your answer on your answer sheet.

33. Mark your answer on your answer sheet.

34. Mark your answer on your answer sheet.

35. Mark your answer on your answer sheet.

36. Mark your answer on your answer sheet.

37. Mark your answer on your answer sheet.

38. Mark your answer on your answer sheet.

39. Mark your answer on your answer sheet.

40. Mark your answer on your answer sheet.

41. Mark your answer on your answer sheet.

42. Mark your answer on your answer sheet.

43. Mark your answer on your answer sheet.

44. Mark your answer on your answer sheet.

45. Mark your answer on your answer sheet.

46. Mark your answer on your answer sheet.

47. Mark your answer on your answer sheet.

48. Mark your answer on your answer sheet.

49. Mark your answer on your answer sheet.

50. Mark your answer on your answer sheet.

■ Now, STOP the recording.

## FOLLOW-UP EXERCISES

## EXERCISE A: GENERAL PROBLEMS WITH PART II

Think about any problems you had. Here are some typical comments from students, with some suggestions that might help them. Read through the problems and suggestions. Did you have any of these difficulties? Are there any other general problems that you had? Would any of the suggestions given here help with your problems?

**Problem:** "There were quite a few words I didn't understand."
**Suggestion:** *Don't worry if you don't understand all the words. Try to get the main idea, and focus on the words you do know.*

**Problem:** "I was sure I had chosen the right answer, but it turned out to be wrong."
**Suggestion:** *Always listen to all of the choices. Choice (A) or (B) may seem to be right, but keep listening and you may feel that choice (C) is definitely the correct one.*

**Problem:** "The speakers spoke too quickly. I got completely left behind."
**Suggestion:** *Don't spend too long thinking about each one. After you have listened to the 3 choices, there are 5 seconds before you hear the next question. If you cannot decide on the answer, pick the one that seems closest. There's a chance that it's right!*

**Problem:** "I understood the question, but I didn't understand all the responses."
**Suggestion:** *Take a guess. Never leave a blank!*

**Problem:** "The first speaker asked about something called 'laundry.' I don't know what that is, so I couldn't answer that one."
**Suggestion:** *But you may have understood some other words in the question. Use them to help you make a choice.*

*To the teacher:* For this activity, it would be best to put the students into groups of four, seated in small circles. At this point, the discussion should be about general difficulties with this part of the test, not about particular items. You could type the problems on cards. Each group discusses the problems and decides on suggestions for each problem. Students add any other general problems they had and discuss suggestions for those problems. At the end, the groups could compare their results with each other or with the suggestions in the book.

Now try Part II again. Cover the answer key. Play the recording straight through once more, and try the questions you got wrong again. Afterward, check your answers. How did you do the second time?

## EXERCISE B: LOOKING AT THE CHOICES IN DEPTH

These are the answers that a student chose for the first ten questions:

21. A
22. A
23. B
24. B
25. C
26. B
27. C
28. A
29. B
30. B

Look at the practice questions script that begins on page 59 and listen to the recording for these questions. After each one, stop the recording and think about these points:

• Did the student choose the right answer?

• Why do you think the student chose this answer?

• Look at the question and the correct answer. Think about why it is correct.

For example, look at number 21. This is what you heard on the recording:

**(Woman)**   Have they delivered our lunch yet?

**(Man)**   (A)   I like chicken.

          (B)   On Monday.

          (C)   Yes, it's here.

Here's a possible explanation:

The student chose (A). The correct answer is (C). The student probably chose (A) because the question was about "lunch" and (A) mentions "chicken," something you might eat for lunch. The word order in the question shows that a "yes" or "no" answer is expected. "It" in (C) could be "lunch."

Check your explanations of the student's answers for numbers 22–30 against the explanations here. Did you have similar explanations?

22. The student chose (A). The correct answer is (B). The student probably chose (A) because the question asks "when" and (A) states a time. However, the question asks when something happened in the past, and (A) tells about the time when something happens in the present, every day. "Ago" in (B) shows that this choice is about something in the past, which fits with the question. "Three weeks ago" answers the "when" question.

23. The student chose (B), the correct answer. The woman cannot identify what the noise was, so "I don't know" is an appropriate answer.

24. The student chose (B). The correct answer is (A). The student probably chose (B) because it mentions "a shirt," which could be "laundry." (B) cannot be the answer because it does not answer the "when" question. (A) gives a suitable answer to a question about something happening in the future, because "in about two hours" means two hours from now.

25. The student chose (C), the correct answer. The question asks "who" and (C) gives the name of a person. Neither (A) nor (B) supplies that information.

26. The student chose (A), the correct answer. The word order of the question suggests a "yes" or "no" answer is expected. (A) answers "yes," using the past tense, which would be appropriate for answering a question in the present perfect tense. (C) also gives a "yes" answer, but it answers with a future time, which is not appropriate for the question.

27. The student chose (C). The correct answer is (A). The student might have chosen (C) because the question asks about a "staff meeting" and (C) mentions "staff." (C) could be a response to "Who will attend the staff meeting?" (A) answers the question "how long" by giving a period of time.

28. The student chose (A). The correct answer is (B). The student probably heard "time" and "play" in the question as well as in (A) and decided to choose that answer. The question asks "What time?" The woman does not have that information, so (B) is an appropriate answer.

29. The student chose (B). The correct answer is (A). The question is about a "briefcase," which is a kind of bag. (B) contains the word "case," but it would probably mean a legal case, not a bag. (A) provides an appropriate answer to the question about the briefcase, because "it" could refer to a briefcase.

30. The student chose (B), the correct answer. The question is about a train that is delayed, and asks "why" that is so. (B) gives a possible reason.

You can now look at your answers to the rest of the practice questions in the same way that we just looked at questions 22–30. Analyzing your answers in this way will help you to understand how to make the correct choice.

*To the teacher:* If possible, it would be helpful to do this exercise in groups of three or four, each group having the recorded version to listen to, so that the groups can work at their own pace. After working on the answers chosen by the sample student for the first ten questions, the students could work individually on their own answers for the questions. This could be set as a homework assignment.

## EXERCISE C: THINKING ABOUT THE INCORRECT CHOICES

This exercise will help you understand why the two incorrect choices would not be appropriate answers to the question the first speaker asks.

Look at the recording script for questions 31–40. Read through and circle the correct answer for each question. Make sure you understand why that is the correct answer by thinking about the purpose of the question and what type of response is expected.

Now look at the other two choices. They are both possible utterances in English. For each one, write a question that would produce that response.

For example, look at number 31:

**(Man)**       You want me to retype this document, don't you?

**(Woman)**     (A)   That type would be best.

              (B)   I would appreciate it.

              (C)   I can't document that.

There are many possible questions that could be written. For choice (A), you might write, "Is this the type of camera you want?" and for (C), you might write, "Do you have any proof that you bought the vacuum cleaner here?" Both of these questions are quite different from the one asked by the first speaker. This should help you to understand why (A) and (C) are incorrect.

*To the teacher:* The students may find it quite difficult to think of suitable questions, so it would be best for them to work in pairs or small groups. As they are working, listen to the discussion in the groups and note down ten correct questions that apply to different distracters (incorrect choices). When they have finished working in groups, discuss some of the questions as a class. Then ask them to close their books and try this oral exercise: one by one, ask the questions that you gathered as they were working, and elicit a quick response.

## EXERCISE D: IF YOU HAVE MORE TIME

This exercise shows that there are many possible responses to a question in English.

- Make a set of question cards. On one side of the card (or small piece of paper), write a question in English. Underneath the question, write the purpose of the question. See the examples below.

- Write down as many possible responses to the question as you can think of on the other side of the card. Take examples of real speech that you have heard in your place of work, on TV or the radio, or in films.

- Make several of these cards and practice with a friend or colleague. Read the questions out loud and ask your friend to give some appropriate answers. Compare your friend's answers with the answers you prepared on the back of the card.

Your cards may be like these examples:

---

Card 1: front

Question: Where is Mr. Davidson going?

Purpose: Asking for information (location)

---

Card 1: back
Possible responses:
- He's going to a café.
- He's going to go home.
- He's starting a new job at Bailey Incorporated.

---

Card 2: front

Question: Do you know what time the plant opens?

Purpose: Asking for information (time)

---

Card 2: back
Possible responses:
- It's open 24 hours.
- I'm not sure.
- Ask Ms. Chang.

---

*To the teacher:* This activity could lead into a game. Seat the students in a large circle and provide a ball or bean bag to throw. Give it to one student, who asks one of these questions and throws the object to someone in the circle, who has to respond. If a suitable response is given, this person asks the next question and throws the object to another person in the circle, who gives a response. If they cannot give an appropriate response, they are out of the game, and the object goes back to the first person, who asks another question. The game continues until everybody has asked a question, or until all players but one are out.

## PRACTICE QUESTIONS SCRIPT

21. **(Woman)** Have they delivered our lunch yet?

    **(Man)** (A) I like chicken.

    (B) On Monday.

    (C) Yes, it's here.

22. **(Man)** When did you begin your new job?

    **(Woman)** (A) At nine o'clock every morning.

    (B) Three weeks ago.

    (C) A sales associate.

23. **(Man)** What was that loud noise I just heard?

    **(Woman)** (A) Yes, I think it was.

    (B) I don't know.

    (C) No, cameras are not allowed.

24. **(Woman)** When will my laundry be ready?

    **(Man)** (A) In about two hours.

    (B) Two dollars a shirt.

    (C) I've already cut it.

25. **(Woman)** Who will go with you on the business trip?

    **(Man)** (A) By train.

    (B) The Excalibur Hotel.

    (C) Ms. Preston.

26. **(Woman)** Has the director already left?

    **(Man)** (A) Yes, he had an appointment.

    (B) It's on the right, actually.

    (C) Yes, in three months.

27. **(Woman 1)** How long do you think the staff meeting will last?

    **(Woman 2)** (A) An hour at the most.

    (B) In the conference room.

    (C) All the staff in our department.

28. **(Man)** What time does the play begin?

    **(Woman)** (A) This is the first time I've played.

    (B) I'll call the theater to find out.

    (C) I couldn't really hear the music.

29. **(Woman 1)** Don't you want to take your briefcase with you?

    **(Woman 2)** (A) No, it's too heavy.

    (B) Because we're starting a new case.

    (C) No, she's in a hurry.

30. **(Man 1)** Why is this train running late?

    **(Man 2)** (A) We met them two hours ago.

    (B) I think there are mechanical problems.

    (C) It's scheduled for Platform 7.

31. **(Man)** You want me to retype this document, don't you?

    **(Woman)** (A) That type would be best.

    (B) I would appreciate it.

    (C) I can't document that.

32. **(Woman)** Would you like to order a calendar for next year?

    **(Man)** (A) Yes, they can.

    (B) Thanks, but I already have one.

    (C) Except for December.

33. **(Man 1)** What do you think I should wear to the party?

    **(Man 2)** (A) A suit and tie.

    (B) A nice gift.

    (C) On Main Street.

34. **(Woman 1)** Shall we send you a reminder for your next dental appointment?

    **(Woman 2)** (A) No, I can't remember.

    (B) Yes, that would be helpful.

    (C) No, I'd like a complete set.

35. **(Woman)** Where should I put these lab materials when I've finished using them?

    **(Man)** (A) I've had them since last week.

    (B) You can get them from any supervisor.

    (C) Take them to Dr. Reynold's office.

36. **(Man)** Whose coffee cup is this on my desk?

    **(Woman)** (A) It's not his desk.

    (B) I was wondering where I left it!

    (C) Cream and sugar, please.

37. **(Woman)** Why didn't you let us know you'd be late?

    **(Man)** (A) I couldn't find a phone.

    (B) I'll try again tomorrow.

    (C) You do have permission.

38. **(Man 1)** Who's the new chef at Fontaine's bakery?

    **(Man 2)** (A) They now open at seven in the morning.

    (B) The bakery has been there for five years.

    (C) A man who worked at Central Pastry Shop.

39. **(Man)** Why don't we go out this evening?

    **(Woman)** (A) David and Caroline.

    (B) Sorry, I've already made plans.

    (C) I didn't enjoy that movie either.

40. **(Man)** What is the fine for overdue books?

    **(Woman)** (A) You can borrow videos, too.

    (B) Yes, it's an excellent book.

    (C) It's ten cents a day.

41. **(Man)** You don't really want to start a new project this late in the day, do you?

    **(Woman)** (A) In the beginning.

    (B) I still have time.

    (C) Yes, it really is.

42. **(Man)** Should I wait here at the counter or follow you back to the warehouse?

    **(Woman)** (A) I put the scale on the counter.

    (B) My house is not far from here.

    (C) Oh, come with me please.

43. **(Man 1)** Your managing director resigned yesterday, didn't he?

    **(Man 2)** (A) Yes, it was quite a surprise.

    (B) The letter is ready for you to sign.

    (C) Yes, I can give you directions.

44. **(Woman)** How will you get to work tomorrow?

    **(Man)** (A) I'll get my car back from the mechanic tonight.

    (B) I go home early on Fridays.

    (C) I applied for several jobs.

45. **(Man 1)** Is Ms. Liu from the payroll department here today, or is she still on vacation?

    **(Man 2)** (A) She works in payroll.

    (B) She'll be back on Monday.

    (C) I haven't been on vacation.

46. **(Woman 1)** Where should we meet so we can all go to the game together?

    **(Woman 2)** (A) The team is very good this year.

    (B) Let's meet at the stadium entrance.

    (C) It should be over by ten o'clock.

47. **(Man 1)** How can we be sure that the order will arrive on time?

    **(Man 2)** (A) Express service is very reliable.

    (B) At about five in the afternoon.

    (C) To buy some.

48. **(Woman)** Didn't anyone train the new employee to use the copier?

    **(Man)** (A) John takes the bus to work.

    (B) The copier's in the staff room.

    (C) Mike showed him how everything works.

49. **(Woman 1)** What do you think, plain or patterned carpet in the waiting room?

    **(Woman 2)** (A) Not much longer, I hope.

    (B) There's no room on the plane.

    (C) Either one is fine with me.

50. **(Man)** Wilma gets reimbursed for the cost of driving her car to the meeting, doesn't she?

    **(Woman)** (A) I'll have a look in my purse.

    (B) Yes, but she has to submit a claim form.

    (C) No, we've already met, several times.

## ANSWER KEY FOR DAY 7

| | | | |
|---|---|---|---|
| 21. C | | 36. B | |
| 22. B | | 37. A | |
| 23. B | | 38. C | |
| 24. A | | 39. B | |
| 25. C | | 40. C | |
| 26. A | | 41. B | |
| 27. A | | 42. C | |
| 28. B | | 43. A | |
| 29. A | | 44. A | |
| 30. B | | 45. B | |
| 31. B | | 46. B | |
| 32. B | | 47. A | |
| 33. A | | 48. C | |
| 34. B | | 49. C | |
| 35. C | | 50. B | |

# Day 8

## Tips and Exercises for Part III: Short Conversations

In the lesson for Day 1, you tried some sample questions from Part III of the test. Today, you will start to work on Part III, the Short Conversations section. This is the part of the test in which you hear a conversation between two people. In the test book, you will read a question about the conversation, and you will also see four choices. You should choose the best answer to the question from the four choices. The following are important points to remember about this part:

- There are 30 questions in the Short Conversations section.

- In the test book, you will see only the question and the four choices. You will not see the text of the conversation.

- As in the rest of the Listening Comprehension section, you will hear the recording only once.

- On the recording, there is a pause of 8 seconds between questions.

Today's lesson begins with a tip that will help you select the best answer when you hear the conversation.

### TIP  Read the question first.

Try to read each question before you listen to the conversation. If you have time, quickly read the four choices, too. Reading the question first can help you to focus your listening and may give you some idea of what the conversation is about.

Consider the following question:

How long will Mr. Olmos be away?

After reading the question, you can see that you need to find out *how long* something will happen. You can then listen to the conversation to find out the length of time that Mr. Olmos will be away.

**Example 1**

On the recording, you will hear:

| (Woman) | Have you heard? Mr. Olmos is going to Africa. |
| (Man) | Is that right? I guess he'll be gone for some time. |
| (Woman) | Not too long, really. Just for fourteen days. |

■ Now, STOP the recording.

In your test book, you will read:

How long will Mr. Olmos be away?

(A) Four days.

(B) One week.

(C) Two weeks.

(D) Over one month.

When you listen to the conversation, it is not necessary to note *where* Mr. Olmos is going. The answer to the question can be heard when the woman says, "…just fourteen days." Because fourteen days is the same as two weeks, (C) is the best answer.

Now, read the following question:

What does the woman want to do?

Now that you have read the question, when you hear the conversation, you can listen for *what* the woman wants. You know that you do not need to know where the people are, who they are, or what the woman is doing.

**Example 2**

On the recording, you will hear:

**(Woman)**:   Is that today's paper? I want to see if our advertisement is in it?

**(Man)**:   No, this is yesterday's. Today's hasn't come in yet.

**(Woman)**:   Oh, I'll call downstairs and see if they have a copy.

■ Now, STOP the recording.

In your test book, you will read:

What does the woman want to do?

(A) Put an advertisement in the paper.

(B) Order a newspaper subscription.

(C) Have some photocopies made.

(D) Check the paper for an advertisement.

In the first line, the woman says, "I want to see…." If you have already read the question, you will realize that you are about to hear the answer. The woman says that she wants to see if the advertisement is in the paper. *See* and *check* have a similar meaning in this situation. Choice (D) is therefore the best answer.

## EXERCISE A: LISTENING FOR REQUIRED INFORMATION

In Example 1, the key words, or the words that supply the answer, are "just fourteen days." In Example 2, the key words are "want to see…advertisement." In Exercise A, you'll practice listening for required information. Look at the question and read the choices before you listen. On the lines underneath, answer the question and write the key words that help you answer the question.

1.   Where are the photographs?

   (A)  In the woman's office.

   (B)  On the conference table.

   (C)  On the man's desk.

   (D)  In the break room.

   _____

   _____

2.   What does the woman say about the electrical equipment?

   (A)  It can be modified easily.

   (B)  It was made in Europe.

   (C)  It was bought at a trade show.

   (D)  It operates quickly.

   _____

   _____

3.   When is the man's economics class?

   (A)  On Tuesdays.

   (B)  On Wednesdays.

   (C)  On Thursdays.

   (D)  On Fridays.

   _____

   _____

■ Now, STOP the recording.

## TIP Try to imagine the setting of the conversation and who is speaking.

The sample questions in Exercise A all asked about specific details from the conversations. With other types of questions, you will have to imagine the setting of the conversation and to think about who is speaking in order to choose the correct answer. These questions will ask you to make an inference, or to come to a conclusion about what is happening. Questions such as "Who are the speakers?" and "Where does the conversation probably take place?" ask you to make an inference or to guess the most likely answer. The exact answer to the question may not be heard in the conversation.

As you listen to the conversations, ask yourself the following questions:

Who are the speakers?

Where are they?

What are they doing?

What is their relationship?

The question written in the test book can often help you to determine the setting of the conversation. For example, from the question

Who mailed the reports?

you might guess that the speakers work in an office.

Certain vocabulary words in the conversation can also help you figure out the setting. For example, if you hear the following words:

| | |
|---|---|
| assembly line | plant supervisor |
| shift | foreman |
| technicians | production line |

you might guess that the setting of the conversation is a factory or a production facility of some kind.

If you hear the words:

| | |
|---|---|
| patient | x-ray |
| doctor | exam |
| appointment | medicine |

you might guess that the conversation takes place in a hospital or medical clinic. When you imagine the setting, or picture the scene of the conversation, you can prepare yourself to answer questions about it.

Now, listen to Example 3. Think about who the speakers are, where they are, and what they are doing.

### Example 3

| | |
|---|---|
| **(Man)** | Thanks for your help with our trip to New Orleans. The hotel was beautiful and we had a great time. |
| **(Woman)** | My pleasure. I guess you're planning another trip? |
| **(Man)** | Yes, and I'll be needing plane tickets, a rental car, and of course, a hotel recommendation. |

■ Now, STOP the recording.

The man thanks the woman for her "help with our trip." He also tells her he will need "plane tickets, a rental car, and…a hotel recommendation." The woman asks the man if he is "planning another trip." These are services usually provided by a travel agent. Therefore, you can infer from the conversation that the woman is a travel agent and the man, a customer. The conversation may be taking place at a travel agency.

## EXERCISE B: IMAGINING THE SETTING AND WHO IS SPEAKING

As you listen to the recording, imagine the setting and who is speaking. You will have to make conclusions based on what you hear. It may not be possible to answer all the questions for each example, but try to write down key words that tell you *who* the speakers probably are, *where* they probably are, *what* they could be doing, and what their *relationship* might be.

1.  Who are the speakers?        _____

    Where are they?              _____

    What are they doing?         _____

    What is their relationship? _____

2.  Who are the speakers?        _____

    Where are they?              _____

    What are they doing?         _____

    What is their relationship? _____

3.  Who are the speakers?        _____

    Where are they?              _____

    What are they doing?         _____

    What is their relationship? _____

4.  Who are the speakers?        _____

    Where are they?              _____

    What are they doing?         _____

    What is their relationship? _____

5.  Who are the speakers?        _____

    Where are they?              _____

    What are they doing?         _____

    What is their relationship? _____

■ Now, STOP the recording.

## FOR ADDITIONAL PRACTICE

*To the teacher:* The following class activity can help students practice imagining the setting and who is speaking. Prepare slips of paper beforehand. On half of the sheets, write an occupation; on the other half, a setting. A student draws a slip of paper from one of the piles. If the student draws an occupation slip, the student says something that might be spoken by a member of that occupation. If the student draws a setting slip, the student says something that might be spoken in that setting. Have other students guess what is written on the slip. Use the recommendations here, or choose your own:

| Occupations | Settings |
|---|---|
| Doctor | A beach |
| Secretary | An office |
| Police officer | An airport |
| Taxi driver | A clothes shop |
| Teacher | A highway |
| Waiter | A market |
| Pilot | A bank |
| Mechanic | A post office |
| Shoe salesman | A library |

## SCRIPT FOR DAY 8

### Exercise A

1.  **(Woman)**  Where are the pictures from the Atlanta Conference?

    **(Man)**  I put them upstairs in your office. Didn't you want them there?

    **(Woman)**  Well, I left them here in the break room for people to look at.

2. **(Man)** Have you shipped the electrical equipment to the European trade show?

   **(Woman)** We have to make some modifications to it, but that won't be difficult. I'm sure we can do it.

   **(Man)** We've got to do it quickly. We don't have that much time.

3. **(Woman)** I thought you had an economics class on Tuesday nights.

   **(Man)** No, it was switched to Wednesdays, and the finance class was canceled, so now I'm free on Tuesdays and Thursdays.

   **(Woman)** Well, since you're free, why don't we meet at the library later?

## Exercise B

1. **(Woman)** I didn't expect to see so many people here this early. The show doesn't start for another hour, and half the seats are already full.

   **(Man)** Well, the lead actor is very popular these days. He's been in a number of successful plays.

   **(Woman)** Not only that, but the set design is supposed to be quite unique.

2. **(Woman)** Your story on last night's game was very good, but I've suggested some changes.

   **(Man)** I hope it won't take much time. I've got to get to the stadium for an interview this afternoon.

   **(Woman)** You just need to make it a bit shorter. We want to add another photo.

3. **(Man)** And this is the latest model. You'll save money because it doesn't use much hot water or electricity.

   **(Woman)** I don't know. The restaurant can get very busy. How fast is it?

   **(Man)** Faster than the machine you're using now. You'll find it cleans pots and pans better, too.

4. **(Woman)** I understand you had to shut down the third assembly line this morning. What happened?

   **(Man)** A power supply problem. The electrician had to replace a cable. It was off for about an hour.

   **(Woman)** Have him check the cables in lines one and two and let me know if there are any more problems. I'll be in my office.

5. **(Man)** We should have just ordered from the catalog. This will take all afternoon.

   **(Woman)** This store is cheaper, and they deliver. Besides, I don't want to see a picture; I want to see what we're getting.

   **(Man)** Well, we need filing cabinets, desks, and chairs. Let's look at the cabinets first.

---

## ANSWER KEY FOR DAY 8

### Exercise A

| | Answers: | Possible key words: |
|---|---|---|
| 1. | A | "I put them...in your office." |
| 2. | A | "make...modifications" and "that won't be difficult" |
| 3. | B | "switched to Wednesdays" |

### Exercise B

Possible answers:

1.  They are in a theater. They are waiting for a play to begin.

2.  They are in a newspaper office talking about a story. The man is a sportswriter, and the woman is an editor.

3.  The man is trying to sell a dishwasher, and the woman is a restaurant owner. They may be in an appliance store.

4.  They are in a factory. The woman may be a supervisor, and the man might be a foreman.

5.  They are shopping at an office supply store. They may be colleagues. They may have just started their own business.

# Day 9

## Further Exercises for Part III: Short Conversations

On Day 8, you learned that you should read the question while you are waiting to hear the recorded conversation. You also learned that you should try to imagine the setting of the conversation, and you practiced answering two types of questions: questions that ask about specific details and questions that ask you to come to a conclusion. In today's lesson, you will learn additional strategies for the Short Conversations portion of the TOEIC test.

### TIP Look at all four choices carefully before answering.

Words that are spoken in the conversation often appear in the four choices. You need to determine if these repeated words provide an answer to the question or not. Consider the following example:

**Example 1**

On the recording, you will hear:

| (Man) | Sally, can you give me a hand with this marketing project this afternoon? |
| --- | --- |
| (Woman) | Well, I need to finish this product proposal today, then I'm going to catch a train at 5:15. |
| (Man) | OK. Could we start on it first thing tomorrow morning, then? |

■ Now, STOP the recording.

In your test book, you will read:

What does the man want Sally to do?

(A) Postpone the proposal

(B) Hand him some papers.

(C) Tell him what time the train leaves.

(D) Help him with a project.

Choice (A) mentions the woman's proposal. It's true that she is working on a proposal. However, the man never tells her to *delay* working on it.

In Choice (B), the man asks for "a hand," which means to ask for help. However, he does not ask her *to hand*, or to give, him anything.

Choice (C) mentions what time the train leaves. The woman does mention the time of the train, but this is not what the man wants to know.

Choice (D) is correct because the man asks for help, or *a hand*, with the project.

## EXERCISE A: READING THE CHOICES CAREFULLY BEFORE ANSWERING

In the next three questions, words that are spoken in the conversation appear in the four choices. Read the question and listen to the recording. Then read the choices carefully before answering.

1. What does the woman suggest?
   (A) Trying different colors.
   (B) Changing the style.
   (C) Using other fabrics.
   (D) Opening a new account.

2. What is Mr. Brower's current position?
   (A) Driver.
   (B) Salesman.
   (C) Partner.
   (D) Manager.

3. What sport did the man see last night?
   (A) Basketball.
   (B) Rugby.
   (C) Soccer.
   (D) Baseball.

■ Now, STOP the recording.

When you listened to the conversations, you probably heard some of the words written in the four choices. Look at the scripts and the answer key at the end of this section to check your answers. If you selected any wrong answers, try to decide why.

Ask yourself the following questions:

• Did you read the question first?
• Did you try to imagine the setting of the conversation?
• Did you carefully read all four choices?
• Did you listen to the entire conversation?

## TIP  Be aware of different ways of answering the question.

When choosing your answer in Part III of the test, be aware that there will be only one correct choice. The phrasing of that choice, however, may be different from what you heard in the conversation.

### Example 2

Consider the following question:

When will the woman leave for Hawaii?

The correct answer may be a day, a date, a time, or a period of time.

Now listen to the conversation:

**(Man)**     I'm very tired. At least it's Friday and I can sleep late tomorrow.

**(Woman)**   I won't be sleeping late. I'll be up at five since the plane for Hawaii leaves at seven.

**(Man)**     That's right. Tomorrow, you're starting your vacation. Have a good time!

■ Now, STOP the recording.

There are different ways to answer the preceding question. Look at the following choices. Which ones are possible answers to the question?

When will the woman leave for Hawaii?
A.  Tomorrow
B.  Today
C.  At five
D.  At seven
E.  In the morning
F.  In the afternoon
G.  On Friday
H.  On Saturday

Choices A, D, E, and H all correctly answer the question. Any of these answers may appear as the correct choice on the test.

## EXERCISE B: LOOKING AT DIFFERENT WAYS OF ANSWERING THE QUESTION

Read through the following lines from Short Conversations (they are not complete conversations). The line from the conversation—*in italics*—is followed by a question. Try to come up with as many answers for each question as possible. When you have finished, go back and decide which answers are the most likely and which are the least likely.

*The file you need is upstairs in my office in the top drawer.*

Where is the file?

_____

_____

_____

*The prices are a bit high here, but the styles are up-to-date.*

Where is the conversation taking place?

_____

_____

_____

*There's going to be an hour delay. Let's see if we can find a coffee shop nearby.*

Where is the conversation taking place?

_____

_____

_____

*I expected his presentation to be interesting and informative, but it wasn't.*

What does the woman think about the presentation?

_____

_____

_____

*Our products are sold mostly to teenagers. I think we would be wasting money on late-night advertising.*

Who is probably speaking?

_____

_____

_____

## TIP Understand the purpose of the question.

In the lesson for Day 5, you practiced identifying the purpose of the question. This skill is useful throughout the test. In the following conversation, for example, there are different ways to ask a "when" question. Look at this conversation:

**Example 3**

**(Man)**   I'm calling to let you know that your credit card payment is several weeks overdue.

**(Woman)**   Hmm…I thought I paid that last month. Perhaps it was delivered to the wrong address.

**(Man)**   Well…please check your records to see if you've already paid.

Here are two possible questions "when" questions for the conversation:

1.   When was the payment due?

2.   When does the woman think she made the payment?

In Exercises C and D, you'll practice writing your own questions and answers.

## EXERCISE C: UNDERSTANDING THE PURPOSE OF THE QUESTION

Listen to the following conversation. Then write questions for the answers that are given. Some possible answers are listed at the end of this unit. Your answers may be slightly different.

| (Man) | I'm calling to let you know that your credit card payment is several weeks overdue. |
| (Woman) | Hmm…I thought I paid that last month. Perhaps it was delivered to the wrong address. |
| (Man) | Well…please check your records to see if you've already paid. |

■ Now, STOP the recording.

## Questions

1. _____
_____

2. _____
_____

3. _____
_____

4. _____
_____

5. _____
_____

6. _____
_____

7. _____
_____

8. _____
_____

## Answers

1. To check her records.
2. She thought she had already paid her bill.
3. Several weeks ago.
4. Last month.
5. She missed a credit card payment.
6. Because the woman missed a payment.
7. A credit card payment.
8. In a billing office.

## EXERCISE D: PRACTICE WITH DIFFERENT TYPES OF QUESTIONS AND ANSWERS

For this exercise, there are three conversations on the recording. Listen carefully to each conversation, then write either a question or an answer in the space provided. You might need to listen to each conversation more than once.

## Questions

1. A. Where does the man want to go?

B. _____
_____

C. What does the man ask the woman to do?

D. _____
_____

2. A. Where is the woman going?

B. _____
_____

C. When is the woman going to the new restaurant?

D. _____
_____

3.  A.  _____
        _____

    B.  What does the man say about the reception?

    C.  _____
        _____

    D.  Why is the woman disappointed?

## ANSWERS

1.  A.  _____
        _____

    B.  To a doctor's appointment.

    C.  _____
        _____

    D.  He will take a taxi.

2.  A.  _____
        _____

    B.  He has other plans.

    C.  _____
        _____

    D.  Going to the new restaurant again next week.

3.  A.  The visiting professors.

    B.  _____
        _____

    C.  At the beginning of next month.

    D.  _____
        _____

■ Now, STOP the recording.

## For Additional Practice

- Make a set of conversation cards. See the sample below. On one side of the card (or small piece of paper), write one of the Part III conversations from this chapter or from other sections of this book.

- On the other side of the card, write possible questions for the conversation. Read the conversation out loud then turn the card over and try to answer the questions without looking at the conversation again.

- Make several cards and practice with a friend or colleague. Read the short conversations out loud and ask your friend to answer the questions that you have prepared. Repeat the process with cards that your friend has made.

---

*Front of card*

**(Woman)**  We should think about finding another hotel for staff meetings.

**(Man)**   Why? The food and service are great here, and there's plenty of space!

**(Woman)**  Yes, but the prices keep going up.

---

---

*Back of card*

Why is the woman unhappy with the hotel?

What does the man think about the hotel?

Where is this conversation probably taking place?

Who are the speakers?

---

## Scripts for Day 9

### Exercise A

1.  **(Man)**   We've tried different colors and different fabrics, but we haven't been able to satisfy the client.

    **(Woman)** This client isn't interested in new colors and fabrics. You'll have to try changing the style. I don't want to lose this account.

    **(Man)**   I'll go back to production and get started again.

2.  **(Man)**   Did you hear that Mr. Brower is retiring next month?

    **(Woman)** I know. Is he an area manager or a partner?

    **(Man)**   He's a partner. He started forty years ago as a driver and worked as a salesman, too.

3.  **(Woman)** I hear you took some French clients to the baseball game last night. How was it?

    **(Man)**   They said that they still prefer soccer and rugby to baseball.

    **(Woman)** Maybe you should try basketball next time. It's more exciting.

## Exercise D

1. **(Man)**    Could you take me to the station after my meeting?

   **(Woman)**  Sorry, I'm not going downtown. I have a doctor's appointment near here.

   **(Man)**    That's OK. I'll get a taxi.

2. **(Woman)**  We're planning to go to the new Italian restaurant this afternoon. Would you like to join us?

   **(Man)**    I'd love to, but I've already made plans for lunch. Maybe we can go some time next week.

   **(Woman)**  OK. If it's good, I'm sure everyone will want to go back again.

3. **(Man)**    I heard this morning that Wednesday's reception for the visiting professors has been postponed.

   **(Woman)**  Really? I was looking forward to meeting Dr. Greene and the others.

   **(Man)**    They've rescheduled it for the beginning of next month.

---

## ANSWER KEY FOR DAY 9

---

### Exercise A

1. B

2. C

3. D

### Exercise B

Possible answers:

1. Upstairs. In the man's office. In the top drawer. In a desk.

2. A shoe store. A clothing store. A boutique. A department store.

3. An airport. A train station. An office.

4. It was boring. It was dull. It was not informative.

5. A marketing executive. A business owner. A company president.

### Exercise C

Possible questions:

1. What does the man ask the woman to do?

2. Why is the woman surprised?

3. When was the payment due?

4. When does the woman think she made the payment?

5. What mistake has the woman made?

6. Why did the man call?

7. What is overdue?

8. Where does the man probably work?

### Exercise D

Possible questions and answers:

| Questions | Answers |
|---|---|
| 1. A. | To the station. |
| B. Where is the woman going? | |
| C. | Take him to the station. |
| D. How will the man get to the station? | |
| 2. A. To an Italian restaurant. | |
| B. Why is the man not able to go to the Italian restaurant today? | |
| C. | This afternoon. |
| D. What does the man suggest? | |
| 3. A. Who is the reception for? | |
| B. | It has been postponed. |
| C. When will the reception been held? | |
| D. | She wants to meet the professors. |

## Day 10

# Short Conversations: Practice Questions and Follow-up Exercises

In this lesson, you will have the opportunity to practice Part III of the TOEIC test. On Days 8 and 9, you learned the following tips to help you in this part:

- Read the question before you listen to the conversation.
- Try to imagine the setting of the conversation and who is speaking.
- Look at all four choices carefully before answering.
- Understand the purpose of the question.

### PRACTICE QUESTIONS

Now try this practice Part III, working as if you were taking a real TOEIC test. On the recording, you will first hear the directions for Part III, as you would in a real TOEIC test. Be sure to listen to each conversation on the recording completely. The question and four choices are not on the recording; they are printed in the book. There is an 8-second pause between each conversation to give you time to mark your choice and prepare yourself for the next conversation.

Before you start, write the numbers 51–80 on a piece of paper so that you can mark your answers. Work straight through the section. Do not stop the recording. If you are not sure which is the correct answer, choose the one you think is closest. Do not leave any questions blank.

### Part III

*Directions: In this part of the test, you will hear 30 short conversations between two people. The conversations will not be printed in your book. You will hear the conversations only once, so you must listen carefully to understand what the speakers say.*

*In your book, you will read a question about each conversation. The question will be followed by four answers. You are to choose the best answer to each question. The answers are printed at the end of this section.*

51. What are the speakers probably doing?
    (A) Driving in a truck.
    (B) Having some lunch.
    (C) Working in a warehouse.
    (D) Shopping in a store.

52. Why is the woman returning the blouse?
    (A) It is the wrong size.
    (B) She does not like the color.
    (C) She already has one like it.
    (D) The style is out of fashion.

53. How does the woman feel about her job?
    (A) Her work is dull.
    (B) The location is too far away.
    (C) The job is better than her last one.
    (D) Her coworkers are friendly.

54. What was probably the problem with the printer?
    (A) It was not connected.
    (B) It did not have paper.
    (C) It needed more ink.
    (D) The cord was damaged.

55. Where are the speakers?
    (A) At a post office.
    (B) At a department store.
    (C) At an airport.
    (D) At a hotel.

56. What are the women discussing?
    (A) A newspaper article.
    (B) Library hours.
    (C) Book prices.
    (D) A fiction writer.

57. Who are the speakers?
    (A) Teachers.
    (B) Students.
    (C) Business executives.
    (D) Office assistants.

58. Why did the woman miss the training session?
    (A) She had the wrong information.
    (B) She was not feeling well.
    (C) She did not get to the station in time.
    (D) The room number had been changed.

59. What is the man reserving?
    (A) A conference site.
    (B) A table for breakfast.
    (C) A hotel room.
    (D) An early-morning taxi.

60. Where are the speakers?
    (A) At a supermarket.
    (B) In an office.
    (C) At a restaurant.
    (D) On a beach.

61. Why will they go into the shop?
    (A) To make a purchase.
    (B) To see a friend.
    (C) To get a haircut.
    (D) To ask for information.

62. Why is the man concerned?
    (A) A package has been lost.
    (B) Business is very slow.
    (C) A deadline is approaching.
    (D) An employee has been fired.

63. When will the tour begin?
    (A) 11:30 A.M.
    (B) 12:00 P.M.
    (C) 12:30 P.M.
    (D) 1:00 P.M.

64. When does this conversation take place?
    (A) Spring.
    (B) Summer.
    (C) Autumn.
    (D) Winter.

65. Who is seeking a new position?

    (A) Mr. Parker.

    (B) Ms. Lee.

    (C) Mr. Parker's manager.

    (D) Ms. Foley.

66. Where will the plants be placed?

    (A) Next to the window.

    (B) Just outside the building.

    (C) Near the water cooler.

    (D) On either side of the front door.

67. Where does this conversation take place?

    (A) In a library.

    (B) In a furniture store.

    (C) In a restaurant.

    (D) In a fitness center.

68. How many times a year does the woman travel to Argentina on business?

    (A) Once.

    (B) Twice.

    (C) Three times.

    (D) Five times.

69. Who will be buying a house?

    (A) Susan.

    (B) Roberto.

    (C) Douglas.

    (D) Beth.

70. What does the man like about the café?

    (A) The size.

    (B) The menu.

    (C) The prices.

    (D) The service.

71. How will they resolve the problem?

    (A) By replacing the contractor.

    (B) By testing the wiring.

    (C) By adding new workstations.

    (D) By contacting the installers.

72. What does Mr. Garcia have to do?

    (A) Inspect an apartment building.

    (B) Contact the moving company.

    (C) Ask the tenant to sign an agreement.

    (D) Help to move some boxes.

73. What are they discussing?

    (A) A business meeting.

    (B) A bank loan.

    (C) An employee's behavior.

    (D) A late payment.

74. What does Sam have to do?

    (A) Buy a magazine.

    (B) Finish a project.

    (C) Take a business trip.

    (D) Call a friend.

75. How many tablets is the woman going to buy?

    (A) 50.

    (B) 100.

    (C) 150.

    (D) 200.

76. What does the woman want the man to do?

    (A) Get her some medicine.

    (B) Keep the window closed.

    (C) Exchange seats with her.

    (D) Open the curtains.

77. Who will the man talk to next?

    (A) The hotel manager.

    (B) A designer.

    (C) An accountant.

    (D) The personnel manager.

78. When is the administration department going to meet?

    (A) This morning.

    (B) This afternoon.

    (C) Tomorrow morning.

    (D) Tomorrow afternoon.

79. How will Mr. Smith get the specifications?

    (A) By post.

    (B) By hand.

    (C) By fax.

    (D) By e-mail.

80. Why do the speakers need to talk to Brenda?

    (A) To ask her to hire workers.

    (B) To get some data from her.

    (C) To ask her to write a report.

    (D) To get her to help analyze data.

■ Now, STOP the recording.

## FOLLOW-UP EXERCISES

### EXERCISE A: LOOKING AT THE QUESTIONS AND CHOICES CAREFULLY

Check your answers for the Part III practice questions against the answer key at the back of this section. Put a circle around the number of each question for which you chose the wrong answer. Prepare yourself to try again by reading the question and choices carefully for each of these. Underline any words you don't understand and look them up in a dictionary.

*To the teacher:* Have the students work in pairs to discuss the questions and choices for any answers they got wrong. Listen to see if there are any questions that were difficult for a number of the students. Write the questions and choices for these on the board and discuss any problems. Also discuss what can be learned from the questions and choices about the conversation setting and the speakers. Don't discuss the dialogues at this point.

Now, try the section again. Play the recording straight through without stopping. Listen to the ones you got right as well as those you had difficulties with.

When you have finished, check your answers again. How did you do the second time?

### EXERCISE B: FOCUSING ON THE DIALOGUES

You have studied the questions and choices carefully. Now focus on the dialogues themselves.

At the end of this section, you will find the recording script for the Short Conversations practice questions. Play the recording again, looking at both the script and the questions and choices while you are listening. Listen to all of the conversations, but pay particular attention to those you got wrong. For these, stop the recording and replay it, making sure you understand the conversation. On the script, underline the words or phrases that help you choose the correct answer. Write down what you think the setting of the conversation is and who the speakers are.

*To the teacher:* If language laboratory facilities are available, the students can work individually on Exercise B. If not, find out which questions caused the most difficulty and work on those with the class. Use an overhead projector to project the script onto the board. Elicit suggestions as to setting, speakers, and words and phrases to underline. Circle any parts that students had difficulty understanding on the recording and practice the pronunciation of these. Finally, pair up the students so they can practice role-playing the dialogues.

### PRACTICE QUESTIONS SCRIPT

51. **(Man 1)**   Don't stack more than four boxes on top of one another, Bill.

    **(Man 2)**   Should I move them down to that area over there?

    **(Man 1)**   Yes, that's near where the truck will drop off the rest of the crates.

52. **(Woman)**   I'd like to return this blouse. I have the receipt here.

    **(Man)**   What's the reason for the return?

    **(Woman)**   It doesn't fit very well.

53. **(Man)** So, Jennifer, how are you enjoying your new job?

**(Woman)** Well, so far it's not very interesting, actually.

**(Man)** Hmm. Maybe things will get better after the first few months.

54. **(Woman)** This printer doesn't seem to be working.

**(Man)** Uh ...check the cord. It may have been unplugged.

**(Woman)** You're right. Maybe someone used it with a laptop computer.

55. **(Woman)** May I bring this bag with me onto the flight?

**(Man)** I'm afraid that's too large ma'am. You'll have to check it in.

**(Woman)** OK, as long as it's handled carefully.

56. **(Woman 1)** Have you read Joan Smith's new novel?

**(Woman 2)** No, but I didn't really like her last story about the journalist.

**(Woman 1)** I love her books. She writes so well.

57. **(Man)** What are you doing in your Business Writing class today?

**(Woman)** I'm giving a test. What about you?

**(Man)** We're still reviewing. My students are having trouble with business letters.

58. **(Man)** Why weren't you at the training session?

**(Woman)** I thought it was canceled.

**(Man)** No, yesterday's session was canceled, but not today's.

59. **(Man)** I'd like to make a reservation for the night of September fourth.

**(Woman)** Yes, of course. Would you like our business traveler rate, which includes breakfast in the room?

**(Man)** Yes. I'd also like to be on either the first or second floor.

60. **(Woman)** This soup is much too salty. I think I'll send it back.

**(Man)** I'm surprised. The food here is usually very good.

**(Woman)** I know. I've brought clients here many times.

61. **(Man 1)** That's funny. I'm sure there used to be a pharmacy on this corner.

**(Man 2)** Well, now it's a barbershop.

**(Man 1)** Let's go in. Maybe the barber will know where the pharmacy moved.

62. **(Man)** How late can we submit this bid?

**(Woman)** Well, the notice of tender gives a May tenth deadline.

**(Man)** Wow! We'd better get moving on this then!

63. **(Man)** Two tickets for the 12:30 tour, please.

**(Woman)** Here you go. We're running about thirty minutes behind schedule, so you'll be leaving at one.

**(Man)** That's fine. We have to go exchange some more money anyway.

64. **(Man 1)** We need to send a buyer to New York to look at the new lines of summer clothes.

**(Man 2)** Winter isn't even over yet! How can they plan so far in advance?

**(Man 1)** Designers are always at least two seasons ahead.

**65. (Man)** Ms. Lee, why are you interested in transferring to another department? You've worked in Customer Service for almost six years.

**(Woman)** Well, my current manager, Mr. Parker, suggested I apply.

**(Man)** I see. Well, I'll send your résumé to Ms. Foley.

**66. (Man)** Where would you like to put these plants, Ms. Kim? By the window?

**(Woman)** No, they don't need that much light. How about over here by the water cooler?

**(Man)** OK. I'll push them back so they're away from the door.

**67. (Man 1)** Can I help you, sir?

**(Man 2)** Yes, I'd like to know if this table is marked down.

**(Man 1)** Yes, that one has been reduced for our clearance sale.

**68. (Woman 1)** How often do you come to Argentina?

**(Woman 2)** Well, usually twice for business and at least once for leisure each year.

**(Woman 1)** Really. So you're here quite often?

**69. (Man)** Susan, I hear that you finally decided to buy that house you were looking at!

**(Woman)** Yes, I did, Roberto. I hope it's the right decision.

**(Man)** My friends Douglas and Beth bought a house in that same area last year. They're very pleased so far.

**70. (Woman)** What's that café across the street like?

**(Man)** They have a great menu, but it's kind of small and a bit overpriced.

**(Woman)** That's okay, as long as it has something different from all the other places around here.

**71. (Man)** If we replace the workstations, we'll need to re-cable the whole floor.

**(Woman)** How can we be sure of that? Let's check with the installers first.

**(Man)** OK. I'll find the phone number.

**72. (Man 1)** Mr. Garcia, did the new tenant sign his lease yet?

**(Man 2)** No, he's busy unpacking some boxes that just came off the moving van.

**(Man 1)** Please get his signature on it by the end of the day.

**73. (Woman)** I'm giving a presentation to the board of directors today.

**(Man)** Make sure to give a clear statement of our marketing strategy.

**(Woman)** I think they'll be more interested in how the money's being spent—at least initially.

**74. (Man 1)** It's been good talking with you, Sam. I guess I'd better let you get back to work.

**(Man 2)** Yes. I need to finish this design so I can submit it by Friday. The company wants to have it ready for next month's magazine.

**(Man 1)** Yes. Once that's done, you'll be able to relax a little bit!

**75. (Woman)** I'd like to buy some aspirin, please.

**(Man)** We have bottles with 50, 100, or 150 tablets. Which would you like?

**(Woman)** The smallest one, please.

**76. (Man)** Excuse me, the sun is shining right on my seat and it's a bit warm. Would you mind if I opened the window?

**(Woman)** Yes, actually. I have a cold and I'd rather keep it closed.

**(Man)** Oh, I'm sorry. Never mind.

77. **(Man)** I'm thinking of having the lobby re-decorated this year.

   **(Woman)** Are you going to hire an interior decorator this time?

   **(Man)** Not until I talk to someone in Accounting!

78. **(Woman 1)** Can we use the conference room for an Administration Department meeting tomorrow morning?

   **(Woman 2)** No, it's already been reserved. It is free in the afternoon, though.

   **(Woman 1)** Okay. We'll reschedule for tomorrow at 2 P.M. Can you make the reservation, please?

79. **(Woman)** I just received an e-mail from Mr. Smith at the factory. He needs product specifications immediately. Are you still planning to see him today?

   **(Man)** Yes, I'll be leaving in about a half hour.

   **(Woman)** Great. I'll get the information ready and you can give it to him when you see him.

80. **(Woman 1)** Do you think we should hire some temporary workers to finish this data entry?

   **(Woman 2)** Yes, then the two of us can concentrate on writing the reports.

   **(Woman 1)** All right, I'll call Brenda in Personnel and see what she can do.

## PRACTICE QUESTION EXPLANATIONS

The following are explanations of the correct answers for the Short Conversations practice questions. Refer to these if you are still uncertain about why a particular choice is correct.

51. (C) The men are moving boxes and talking about where a truck will drop off crates. These activities commonly occur in a *warehouse*, a place where goods are stored and transferred.

52. (A) The phrase *it doesn't fit well* indicates that the blouse is the wrong size, either too large or too small.

53. (A) The phrase *not very interesting* is an indirect way of saying that the job is *dull* or boring.

54. (A) The man suggests, and the woman confirms, that the printer was *unplugged*, which means that it was *not connected*.

55. (C) The speakers mention a *flight* and *checking in* a bag, along with limits on the size of a bag. All of these ideas are associated with an *airport*.

56. (D) The first woman mentions Joan Smith's new *novel* and comments that Smith *writes* well; from this we know that Ms. Smith is a *writer of fiction*.

57. (A) The speakers are discussing plans for *teaching* their classes: the man will *review* business letters with his students and the woman will *give a test*.

58. (A) The woman thought that today's training session had been *canceled*, but the man informs her that she was mistaken.

59. (C) The woman asks the man if he would like the rate that includes *breakfast in the room*, so the man is probably reserving a *hotel room*.

60. (C) The speakers mention *soup*, *food*, and the fact that they entertain their clients in this place, all of which indicate that it is a *restaurant*.

61. (D) The first man suggests that the *barber* might know something about the *pharmacy*; the men will therefore go into the barbershop *to get information*.

62. (C) After hearing the deadline for a bid, the man expresses surprise and says that they *had better get moving*, or must work quickly. Therefore, it can be assumed that the *deadline is approaching*, or coming up soon.

63. (D) The woman tells the man that the tour is running thirty minutes *behind schedule*; in other words, the tour will start late. Since the man is purchasing tickets for the 12:30 tour, this means that his tour will not actually begin until 1:00.

64. (D) After the first man mentions summer clothes, the second man says that *winter isn't even over*, which is another way of saying that it is still winter at the time of the conversation. The first man also states that lines of clothing come out *at least two seasons ahead*. Two seasons ahead of summer is *winter*.

65. (B) The man asks the woman, whom he addresses as Ms. Lee, why she is interested in *transferring to*, or working for another department.

66. (C) The woman suggests that the plants should go *over by the watercooler*, and the man agrees with her.

67. (B) The second man asks if a table has been *marked down*, or reduced in price, and the first man confirms that the table's price has been reduced for a sale. Because the men are discussing a sale on furniture, they are probably in a *furniture store*.

68. (B) The second woman states that she usually visits Argentina *twice for business* each year.

69. (A) The man addresses the woman as Susan and says that he has heard she will be *buying a house*. Susan confirms this.

70. (B) The man says that the café has *a great menu*.

71. (D) The man is concerned about having to re-cable the entire floor. The woman suggests *checking with*, or contacting, *the installers* to find out if re-cabling will be necessary.

72. (C) The first man tells Mr. Garcia to get the tenant's *signature* on *the lease*, or rental agreement, by the end of the day.

73. (A) The woman mentions a *presentation* to the *board of directors*, and the man speaks of a *marketing strategy*. This indicates that the woman will be attending a business meeting.

74. (B) Sam says that he needs to finish *a design* that he has been working on. This is a *project* he is involved with at work.

75. (A) The man says that tablets are sold in bottles of 50, 100, or 150. The woman indicates that she would like *the smallest one*, so she is going to buy a bottle with 50 tablets.

76. (B) The man asks the woman if he can open the window because he is warm. The woman states that *she would rather keep it closed*, which is a polite way of refusing his request.

77. (C) The man says that he wants to redecorate the lobby, but he wants to talk to *someone in Accounting* before he hires an interior decorator.

78. (D) The first woman wants to set up a meeting for *tomorrow morning*, but she changes her mind when she hears that the conference room is unavailable then. She says she will *reschedule for tomorrow at 2 P.M.*

79. (B) The woman says that she will get the *information*, or specifications, ready so that the man can give it to Mr. Smith when he sees him later in the day. To give someone something *by hand* means to deliver it in person.

80. (A) The women want to *hire some temporary workers* to finish entering some data. They need to *call Brenda in Personnel* to get her to hire the workers.

## Exercise C: Imagining the Setting

Look quickly through the recording script and see if you can find a conversation that is likely to take place in each of these settings. Does imagining the setting help you choose the correct answer?

A. On the street.

B. On a train.

C. In an office.

D. At an airport.

E. On the phone.

F. In a pharmacy.

G. In a furniture store.

H. At a warehouse.

*To the teacher:* Arrange the students in pairs for Exercise C. Encourage them to be able to say why they think the conversation takes place in a particular setting.

## Exercise D: Thinking about the Speakers

Look at the script and find conversations that you think could be spoken by these pairs of speakers:

A.  two colleagues

B.  a shop assistant and a customer

C.  a hotel guest and a receptionist

D.  a secretary and a boss

E.  two customers

F.  two friends

---

### FOR ADDITIONAL PRACTICE

Pick a pair of speakers from Exercise D and a setting from Exercise C and write a short conversation of your own that could be spoken by those two speakers in that setting. If possible, practice saying it with a friend. Try making up several conversations with different combinations of speakers and settings.

*To the teacher:* The students can write the conversations in pairs. When they are ready, ask them to act out their conversations—also in pairs and preferably without looking at their scripts. The other students in the class can then guess what the setting is and who the speakers are.

---

## ANSWER KEY FOR DAY 10

---

### Practice Questions

51. C
52. A
53. A
54. A
55. C
56. D
57. A
58. A
59. C
60. C
61. D
62. C
63. D
64. D
65. B
66. C
67. B
68. B
69. A
70. B
71. D
72. C
73. A
74. B
75. A
76. B
77. C
78. D
79. B
80. A

### Exercise C

Possible answers:

A. Conversation 61
B. Conversation 76
C. Conversation 54
D. Conversation55
E. Conversation 58
F. Conversation 75
G. Conversation 67
H. Conversation 1

### Exercise D

Possible answers:

A. Conversation 57
B. Conversation 75
C. Conversation 59
D. Conversation 78
E. Conversation 60
F. Conversation 56

# Day 11

## Tips and Exercises for Part IV: Short Talks

In the lesson for Day 1, you tried some sample questions from Part IV of the test. Today you will take a closer look at the Short Talks portion of the TOEIC test. This is the part of the test in which you will hear several short talks, each consisting of authentic examples of spoken English from workplace, travel, and leisure situations. These talks will vary in level of formality and will include such spoken language as announcements, short speeches, and advertisements. The following are important points to remember about this part:

- There are 20 questions in this part of the test.
- In the test book, you will see two or three written questions about each talk, with four choices for each question. You will not see the text of the talk.
- Each talk is read by one speaker only and will be read one time only.
- On the recording, there is a pause of 8 seconds between questions.

Here are some suggestions for improving your ability to make the best choice.

## TIP  Read the questions first.

Each talk will have two or three questions related to what you hear. Try to read the questions before you listen to the talk. Reading the questions can help you to focus your listening and may give you some idea of what the talk will be about. Reading the questions and choices can also let you know if you need to listen for general information or for details. Consider the following types of questions:

**General Information Questions:**

What is the purpose of this talk?
Where is this talk being given?
Who is the speaker?

All of these questions ask for general information about a short talk. To find the answers to general information questions, concentrate on listening for the main ideas.

Now consider these questions:

**Questions about Details:**

What is the final destination of the flight?
How long is the flight to Dubai?
Where will the plane stop first?

All of these questions ask about specific details of the short talk. To answer questions about details, you will need to pay attention to specific facts, times, and dates.

Now listen to a short talk. As you listen, try to answer the general information and detail questions listed previously. Notice that you can guess that the talk will be about an airline flight—even before you have heard the recording.

## Example 1

Good afternoon and welcome aboard Global Air Flight 875 from Copenhagen to Bangkok, with intermediate stops in Dubai and Calcutta. We are preparing to depart in a few minutes. At this time, your seat back should be returned to its full upright position and your seat belt should be fastened. Our anticipated flying time to Dubai is six hours and twenty-five minutes. We hope you enjoy the flight.

■ Now, STOP the recording.

## Inference Questions

The information that you need to answer a question may not always be stated directly. You may need to make inferences, or draw conclusions, from information given in the talk. These conclusions may be about general information or specific details.

In Example 1, the general information question "Who is the speaker?" requires an inference. We infer from the entire talk that the speaker is a flight attendant. A question about specific details may also require you to make an inference. For example, "Where will the plane stop first?" is not directly answered in the talk. However, we can infer that the first stop is Dubai, because the speaker states the flying time to that city.

The first question in Exercise A is also an inference question. You can infer from the talk who the speaker is, although that information is not directly stated.

---

### EXERCISE A: READING THE QUESTIONS FIRST

Read the following questions and choices and decide whether you are being asked to listen for general information or for details.

1.  Who is speaking?

    (A) A police officer.

    (B) A weather forecaster.

    (C) A radio announcer.

    (D) A bus driver.

2.  According to the report, what is causing the traffic delays?

    (A) Traffic accidents.

    (B) Fog.

    (C) Road construction.

    (D) Floods.

Now cover up the following short talk with a piece of paper, listen to the talk, and try to answer both questions.

**Questions 1 and 2** refer to the following report.

And for all of you getting ready for your drive home, I'm happy to report that there are no major traffic delays in the metropolitan area. There are, however, a few minor problems. On Route 9 near River Road, expect delays due to paving. Also, because of the rebuilding of the Lincoln Bridge, only one lane will be open. Stay tuned for an update in twenty minutes.

■ Now, STOP the recording.

Notice that the first question is asking about general information, while the second question is asking about a specific point. Did reading the questions before you heard the talk help you to choose the correct answer?

> **TIP Don't worry if you don't understand every word of the talk.**

On Day 2, you learned about listening for stressed words. Remember, these are usually the most important words for understanding the meaning of spoken English. If you listen for stressed words, then you don't have to worry if you do not understand every word of the talk. Practice listening for stressed words as you complete the following exercise:

## EXERCISE B: LISTENING FOR STRESSED SYLLABLES

Read the question and choices first:

1.  How are the apartments described?
    (A) They are up-to-date in design.
    (B) They have two bedrooms.
    (C) They are in the middle of the city.
    (D) They are very small.

Now listen to the talk. As you listen, follow the text and underline the syllables that are stressed. You may need to play the recording more than once. When you have finished, find the words that relate to describing an apartment and answer the question.

It's your life. Live each moment to the fullest! Imagine living in a spacious, modern apartment in a country-club setting where activities and facilities can keep you constantly busy. Close to the city, yet rural enough to grow a garden and have a pet. We offer luxurious one-bedroom apartments for $1,500 a month. Your rent includes membership in our private health and fitness club. Find out how beautiful life can be. Call or write for a free brochure or video, or make an appointment for a tour. Don't delay, call today. Only a limited number of one-bedroom apartments remain.

■ Now, STOP the recording.

Now answer another question about the details of the talk. Let the stressed syllables help you find the important information. Don't worry if you don't understand every word of the talk. If necessary, listen to the recording again.

2.  What is included in the rent?
    (A) Country-club fees.
    (B) Gardening services.
    (C) A health-club membership.
    (D) A video.

The correct answer for question 1 is (A). Since "up-to-date" means "modern," hearing the word "modern" in the text can help you choose the correct answer. For question 2, hearing the word "membership," followed by "health," "fitness," and "club" should help you choose the correct answer, (C). You might not have understood the phrase "live each moment to the fullest" or the words "rural" or "luxurious," but it is still possible to choose the correct answer even if you did not understand every word.

**Note:** The test book will not indicate which questions refer to each talk. This is indicated on the recording before you hear the talk itself. For example, before the first talk, you will hear the speaker say, "Questions 81 and 82 refer to the following message." From this, you know that when you are listening to the first talk, you should look only at questions 81 and 82. Question 83 will be about the next talk.

## TIP Listen to the whole talk before answering the questions.

Although it is a good idea to read the questions before you hear the talk, do not try to answer the questions until you have heard the entire talk. There may be important details at the end of the talk. You may also need to consider all the information to understand the main ideas or to make inferences.

**Example 2**

Consider the following question:

What time will the game start?
(A) At 3:00 P.M.
(B) At 4:00 P.M.
(C) At 7:00 P.M.
(D) At 8:00 P.M.

Now listen to the first part of the talk:

The baseball game scheduled for 7:00 tonight has been postponed due to rain.

■ Now, STOP the recording.

If you listen no further, you may think that (C), 7:00 P.M., is the answer. Now listen to the whole talk:

The baseball game scheduled for 7:00 tonight has been postponed due to rain. The game will be played on Saturday at 4:00 P.M. instead.

■ Now, STOP the recording.

You can see that two times are mentioned, but the information you need to answer the question is in the last sentence of the talk.

## EXERCISE C: LISTENING TO THE WHOLE TALK BEFORE ANSWERING THE QUESTIONS

Listen to the following excerpts from short talks. Then answer the question that follows each talk. Notice that you must listen to all of the excerpt in order to get the information you need to answer the question. The scripts for the talks are printed at the end of this section.

1. What does the speaker say about making candles?

Answer: _____

2. What is the new completion date of the project?

Answer: _____

3. When was Compton founded?

Answer: _____

■ Now, STOP the recording.

*To the teacher:* You may want to play only the first part of each excerpt aloud, and then have students answer the question. Then play the rest of the excerpt and ask the question again, so students can see that they may get a different answer after hearing everything. You can also have students underline the word in each talk that signals a contrast between the information presented in the first part of the talk and the second.

## EXERCISE D: PRACTICING ALL OF TODAY'S TIPS

Listen to the following short talk to practice using the tips on the previous pages. Read the questions first, look for main ideas and details, make inferences, listen for stressed words, and consider all the information before answering. Check your answers against the answer key at the end of this section.

**Questions 1 and 2** refer to the following report.

The Eastern Gas Company has been given permission to increase the charges for natural gas service. The revised rate for natural gas service will not be effective until March first of next year. The overall increase will amount to 20 cents per cubic meter. Details of this change are available at the gas company billing office.

■ Now, STOP the recording.

1. What will increase, according to the report?
   (A) The area serviced by the company.
   (B) The number of company offices.
   (C) The length of the billing cycles.
   (D) The price of natural gas service.

2. When will the increase go into effect?

(A) March 1.

(B) March 8.

(C) March 20.

(D) March 30.

## SCRIPT FOR DAY 11

### Exercise B

1. Many people believe that making your own candles is difficult. We're here today to show you that it's not so hard. Just watch this quick and simple technique.

2. The Crosstown Bridge project was originally scheduled for completion by the end of this August. However, work has been slowed down by the recent storms, delaying the proposed completion date until early October.

3. History books have long reported that the town of Compton was founded 300 years ago. But surprising new evidence shows that it was probably really founded closer to 500 years ago.

## ANSWER KEY FOR DAY 11

### Exercise A

1. C

2. C

### Exercise C

Possible answers:

1. It is easy to do.

2. In early October.

3. 500 years ago.

### Exercise D

Answers and explanations:

1. The answer is choice (D). Lines 1 and 2 of the talk contain the phrase "increase the charges for natural gas service." If you miss hearing this detail, you might hear "the revised rate" and "overall increase…to 20 cents." All of these details will help you understand that the main idea is about an increase in the price of natural gas service.

2. The answer is choice (A). The third line of the talk contains the phrase "March first of next year." Do not be confused by other numbers you may hear in the report.

## FOR ADDITIONAL PRACTICE

Listen to a radio or TV program in English in which speakers give brief talks, such as a news report, weather report, advertisement, or interview. If you can, record them. After the short piece is finished, consider the following questions:

Who is the speaker?

Where does the talk take place?

What is the main idea of the talk?

Who is the intended audience?

Take notes while you are listening to the talk and write your own questions about the main ideas and details of the talk.

Exchange your taped talks and questions with a friend or colleague. Practice listening and answering each other's questions.

# Day 12

## Further Exercises for Part IV: Short Talks

Today you will continue to become familiar with the Short Talks section of the test.

Before each short talk begins, you will hear the speaker say something like:

*Questions 81 and 82 refer to the following announcement…(or talk, advertisement, speech, etc.)*

Paying special attention to the introduction can be helpful. If you know that the short talk is a speech, that fact narrows down the contexts where it could have taken place. A speech might be heard at a retirement banquet or political gathering, for example. Likewise, if the talk is a news report, it might have been given on the radio or television.

After you hear the introduction about the type of talk you will be hearing, listen very carefully to the first one or two sentences of the talk. These sentences can often help you understand who the speaker is and where the talk takes place. Understanding the setting can help you prepare for and understand the rest of the talk.

For instance, you might hear the following:

**Example**

*Questions 1 and 2 refer to the following announcement.*

I'd like to take this opportunity to welcome you all to our seventh annual electronics sales convention. This year we are proud to announce…

■ Now, STOP the recording.

After hearing only this information, you will be able to answer questions such as the following:

| **Questions** | **Answers** |
|---|---|
| Where is this talk probably being given? | (a sales convention) |
| What is the speaker's job? | (an electronics salesperson or conference organizer) |
| How often are the conventions held? | (annually, or once a year) |
| What type of products might be presented at this convention? | (cameras, VCRs, electronic parts, etc.) |

## EXERCISE A: PAYING ATTENTION TO THE BEGINNINGS OF TALKS

Here are some examples of introductions and beginnings of talks. Listen carefully and see how much information you can get just by listening to this part of the talk. The scripts for these talks are printed at the end of this section.

**Talk 1:**

1.  Where would this talk probably be heard?

    Answer: _____

2.  How can Super Wax be used?

    Answer: _____

3.  What is one advantage of Super Wax?

    Answer: _____

**Talk 2:**

4.  What can visitors take a tour of?

    Answer: _____

5.  What time do the tours begin?

    Answer: _____

6.  How often are tours given?

    Answer: _____

7.  Where can visitors go to buy tickets?

    Answer: _____

**Talk 3:**

8.  What is the main subject of this news report?

    Answer: _____

9.  Where is the park located?

    Answer: _____

10. Who attended the ceremony?

    Answer: _____

11. What can be found in the park?

    Answer: _____

■ Now, STOP the recording.

*To the teacher:* You can expand this exercise by assigning various categories of talks (news report, advertisement, announcement, etc.) to students and asking them to make up a few lines of a talk. Other students can then try to guess what kind of talk they are hearing, where it takes place, who is speaking, and other information.

## EXERCISE B

Cover up the following talk with a piece of paper. While you listen to the recording, try to match the questions printed in the book with the appropriate answers.

Welcome to Hoffberg Fine Instrument Company. I'm Paul York and I'll be conducting the tour today. Our facility here, one of the five operated by Hoffberg, is where the company's famous violins are manufactured. To start, we'll tour the production area, where we'll observe skilled craftsmen completing the assembly process. Then we'll visit the audiovisual room, where we'll see a short film on the history of Hoffberg Fine Instruments. Before we begin, are there any questions?

■ Now, STOP the recording.

1.  Who is probably speaking?

2.  What will the visitors do first?

3.  How is the history of the company presented?

4.  What does Hoffberg Company produce?

A. Medical instruments

B. A tourist

C. With a videotaped film

D. Take a tour of production

E. With a slide presentation

F. A company employee

G. Violins

H. Go to the audiovisual room

## EXERCISE C

Cover up the short talk below with a piece of paper. Then, listen to the recording and try to decide which vacation package would be most appropriate for the following people:

1. A family with two young children

   Pick one:    Vacation Package 1

                Vacation Package 2

                Vacation Package 3

   Why is this the best vacation package for these people? _____

2. A couple who enjoy sporting adventures

   Pick one:    Vacation Package 1

                Vacation Package 2

                Vacation Package 3

   Why is this the best vacation package for these people? _____

3. A university student with limited finances

   Pick one:    Vacation Package 1

                Vacation Package 2

                Vacation Package 3

   Why is this the best vacation package for this person? _____

Happy Travel is pleased to announce three new vacation packages. The first is a grape-picking holiday in Southern Italy. We offer reasonably priced room and board and a discounted round-trip airline ticket. Make friends and enjoy the beautiful scenery. Our second package is a fun-for-all beach-resort vacation. Shopping, snorkeling, and bike rentals are all available, and there are supervised activities for the young. Thrill seekers will want to try our luxury scuba diving package off the coast of Greece. Our top-class diving instructors will make sure you have an underwater experience that's out of this world! Call now for details on all three packages.

■ Now, STOP the recording.

## EXERCISE D

Listen to the following talk and complete the questions. There is more than one way to fill in each blank.

Where _____?

Who _____?

What _____?

Why _____?

When _____?

*Questions 1 through 4 refer to the following short talk.*

Our next topic today is the schedule change for the new office building on Center Street. We're starting construction in November of this year—not in March of next year, as we had originally planned. As a result of this change, we'll need all preliminary drawings, site plans, and renderings ready for the client in two weeks. I realize this new schedule may present a challenge to many of you, so we will adjust your workload to accommodate the extra work.

■ Now, STOP the recording.

*To the teacher:* Have students work together to compare and check their completed questions. You can then write several completed questions from different students on the board and have students check the talk to see whether or not they are plausible.

## SCRIPT FOR DAY 12

### Exercise A

#### Talk 1

*Questions 1 through 3 refer to the following radio advertisement.*

Are you tired of spending hours waxing your car? Now you can get the shine without the work! Introducing new Super Wax. Cheaper than most waxes…

#### Talk 2

*Questions 4 through 7 refer to the following tour information.*

Welcome to Franklin Dairy. Tours of the cheese factory are given every hour beginning at two o'clock. If you'd like to join a tour, please go to the ticket window…

#### Talk 3

*Questions 8 through 11 refer to the following news report.*

In local news, the new park was dedicated this morning in a ceremony attended by the mayor. The park, called Gordon Park because it is located on Gordon Avenue, has a playground, tennis courts…

## ANSWER KEY FOR DAY 12

### Exercise A

1.  On the radio
2.  To wax cars
3.  It is cheaper than other waxes
4.  A cheese factory
5.  At 2:00
6.  Every hour
7.  At the ticket window
8.  A park dedication
9.  On Gordon Avenue
10. The mayor
11. A playground and tennis courts

### Exercise B

1.  F
2.  D
3.  C
4.  G

### Exercise C

Suggested answers:

1.  Package 2: the beach-resort vacation…because there are activities for children
2.  Package 3: the scuba-diving vacation…because it's an adventurous sport, it's expensive, and it cannot be done with children
3.  Package 1: the grape-picking holiday…because it's inexpensive

### Exercise D

Possible questions:

Where is this talk probably taking place?

Who is probably speaking?

What is going to change?

Why must work begin as soon as possible?

# Day 13

## Short Talks: Practice Questions and Follow-up Exercises

In this lesson, you will have the opportunity to practice Part IV of the TOEIC test. Before you do this, remind yourself of the tips given on Days 11 and 12:

- Read the questions first.
- Don't worry if you don't understand every word of the talk.
- Listen to the whole talk before trying to answer the questions.
- Pay special attention to the introduction and the first part of the talk.

---

### PRACTICE QUESTIONS

Now try this practice Part IV, working as if you were taking a real TOEIC test. On the recording, you will first hear the directions for Part IV. Be sure to listen to each talk all the way through. The questions and four choices are not on the recording; they are printed in the book. There is a pause of 8 seconds between each talk to give you time to mark your choices and prepare yourself for the next question.

Before you start, write the numbers 81–100 on a piece of paper so that you can mark your answers. Work straight through the section. Do not stop the recording. If you are not sure which is the correct answer, choose the one you think is closest. Do not leave any questions blank.

### Part IV

*Directions: In this part of the test, you will hear several short talks. Each will be spoken just one time. They will not be printed in your test book, so you must listen carefully to understand and remember what is said.*

*In your book, you will read two or more questions about each short talk. The questions will be followed by four answers. You are to choose the best answer to each question. The answers are printed at the end of this section.*

81. For whom is this message most likely intended?

    (A) A nursing assistant.

    (B) A receptionist.

    (C) A patient.

    (D) A teacher.

82. By when should Ms. Giovanni arrive?
    (A) By 10:00.
    (B) By 10:30.
    (C) By 11:00.
    (D) By 11:30.

83. Where is this announcement being made?
    (A) In a factory.
    (B) In a computer store.
    (C) In a shopping center.
    (D) In a school.

84. Why is the building closing early?
    (A) The staff are having a meeting.
    (B) Workers have become ill.
    (C) There are problems with the computers.
    (D) The equipment is being replaced.

85. What is the topic of this talk?
    (A) A new employee.
    (B) A recent election.
    (C) A work schedule.
    (D) A branch office.

86. Who most likely is Patricia Wright?
    (A) An interviewer.
    (B) A publisher.
    (C) A politician.
    (D) An editor.

87. For about how long was Patricia Wright overseas?
    (A) A few weeks.
    (B) A few months.
    (C) A year.
    (D) Two years.

88. Why was Flight 109 delayed?
    (A) The flight crew was stuck in traffic.
    (B) The plane had mechanical trouble.
    (C) The weather was bad.
    (D) The connecting flight was canceled.

89. What is the new departure time?
    (A) 7:30.
    (B) 8:00.
    (C) 8:30.
    (D) 9:00.

90. What problem is the speaker addressing?
    (A) Conference meeting schedules have changed.
    (B) The demand for programs is greater than the supply.
    (C) Some items have been removed from the information desk.
    (D) The guest speaker for the conference has not arrived.

91. What will happen in the afternoon?
    (A) Guests will be able to register.
    (B) New meeting times will be announced.
    (C) The opening session will begin.
    (D) More programs will be available.

92. Where does this talk probably take place?
    (A) In a restaurant kitchen.
    (B) At an appliance repair company.
    (C) On a factory floor.
    (D) At a dry cleaner's.

93. What should the user do if the items do not come out clean?
    (A) Stack them on the cart.
    (B) Wash them by hand.
    (C) Put them through the machine again.
    (D) Contact customer service.

94. Who is making this announcement?
    (A) A sports team physician.
    (B) A travel agent.
    (C) A company administrator.
    (D) A radio announcer.

95. What will begin on Thursday?

    (A) Physical examinations.

    (B) Training sessions.

    (C) Film screenings.

    (D) Sales presentations.

96. Who is the speaker most likely addressing?

    (A) A potential buyer.

    (B) A construction crew.

    (C) A house cleaner.

    (D) A group of tourists.

97. Which part of the house has been renovated recently?

    (A) The kitchen.

    (B) The bedroom.

    (C) The garage.

    (D) The stairways.

98. What is mentioned as a possible disadvantage of the house?

    (A) The distance from the house to town.

    (B) The size of the building.

    (C) The price of making improvements.

    (D) The condition of the structure.

99. Who most likely is the speaker?

    (A) A bank manager.

    (B) A store supervisor.

    (C) A machine operator.

    (D) A security consultant.

100. What is the topic of the talk?

    (A) Salary increases.

    (B) Staff absences.

    (C) A rise in profits.

    (D) Stolen merchandise.

■ Now, STOP the recording.

## EXERCISE A: MAKING SURE YOU UNDERSTAND THE QUESTIONS

It is important that you fully understand the questions. Have another look at the written questions for the practice questions. At this point, do not study the choices. Find the following words in the questions and write down their meanings:

**Words**               **Meanings**

1.  overseas _____

2.  topic _____

3.  renovated _____

4.  intended _____

5.  addressing _____

6.  likely _____

7.  items _____

8.  delayed _____

9.  departure _____

Underline any other words in the questions that you do not know and look them up in a dictionary.

Now read both the questions and the choices. You may find that you don't understand every word in the choices. If you like, look up the words you don't know in the dictionary. When you are taking the test, try not to worry if you don't understand all of the words in the choices: you may not need to understand every word in all of the choices in order to answer the questions correctly.

Now try the practice questions again, playing the recording straight through without stopping. When you have finished, check your answers again. How did you do the second time?

## EXERCISE B: UNDERSTANDING THE MAIN IDEAS OF THE TALK

As mentioned in Day 11, some of the questions about the short talks are general information questions. To answer them, you need to understand the main ideas of the talk. To do this, you often need to gather information from different parts of the talk. You may then need to draw a conclusion based on those various pieces of information.

Below are the scripts for the first two talks from the practice section together with the questions that are asking about the main ideas. Read the question, then start the Day 13 recording again so you can listen to the talks. On the script, underline the words and phrases that help you to choose the correct answer.

**Questions 81 and 82** refer to the following message.

Ms. Giovanni, this is Janet from Dr. Rossi's office calling to remind you of your annual physical exam tomorrow at 10:30. Please be on time. The appointment should take about an hour.

81. For whom is this message most likely intended?

   (A) A nursing assistant.

   (B) A receptionist.

   (C) A patient.

   (D) A teacher.

**Questions 83 and 84** refer to the following announcement.

Attention all employees. The power outage in plant number two has been resolved. However, our main computers are still down. We will be closing the production line early today so that technical services can correct the problem. Plan to leave by 2:30 P.M. unless told otherwise by your supervisor. Please make sure all manufacturing equipment is turned off before you leave. Thank you.

83. Where is this announcement being made?

   (A) In a factory.

   (B) In a computer store.

   (C) In a shopping center.

   (D) In a school.

■ Now, STOP the recording.

In the first short talk, you might have underlined "message," "This is Janet from Dr. Rossi's office," "your annual physical exam," and "appointment." From these, you can conclude that the person leaving the message for Ms. Giovanni is a doctor's receptionist and that Ms. Giovanni, for whom the message is intended, is a patient.

In the second short talk, you might have underlined "employees," "supervisor," "plant number two," "production line," and "manufacturing equipment." All of these help you to understand that the announcement is being made at a factory.

## EXERCISE C: LISTENING FOR SPECIFIC DETAILS

Some of the questions about the short talks ask about specific details. This exercise will help you focus on the details in the talks. Below, you will see the script for the next two talks in the section and the questions that are asking about specific details. The words or phrases that you need to understand in order to make the correct choice have been omitted. Look at the question and choices first, then listen to the recording for each talk and fill in the missing words. Stop and start the recording as often as you wish.

**1. Questions 85 through 87** refer to the following short talk.

Good morning everyone. As you know, we have been holding interviews for a new editor to join our team. Ms. Patricia Wright has been chosen for the position. She will begin her orientation program this week and will be on staff by the end of the month. Ms. Wright has a good deal of experience in our field, both here and abroad. She worked for a major publication in _____ for _____ before returning to this country.

■ Now, STOP the recording.

87. For about how long was Patricia Wright overseas?

   (A) A few weeks.

   (B) A few months.

   (C) A year.

   (D) Two years.

   **2. Questions 88 and 89** refer to the following announcement.

This is to announce the new departure time for Flight 109 to Jakarta. Severe thunderstorms delayed the connecting flight from Tokyo. The plane is on the ground and is being serviced. _____ is now scheduled for _____. Meal vouchers will be available for passengers scheduled on this flight. Passengers are asked to please be back to the gate by 8:00 for boarding.

88. What is the new departure time?

   (A) 7:30.

   (B) 8:00.

   (C) 8:30.

   (D) 9:00.

## EXERCISE D: LISTENING WITH THE SCRIPT

Go through all the practice questions again, talk by talk. Look at the script while you are listening to the recording. Make sure you understand why the correct answer is correct for each question. Consider whether each question is asking about a main idea or a detail. Then cover the script and listen to the talk again. Think about these questions:

- Do you have trouble understanding some words because of phonetic linking or elisions? If so, you may want to look back at Day 6.

- Are you paying attention to the stressed words, which usually contain the main ideas? Look back at Day 2 to remind yourself about stress. Remember, you don't always need to understand every word. Even when you are listening to somebody speaking in your own language you may not hear every single word, but you can still understand the meaning of what they are saying.

- Do you feel the people on the recording are speaking quickly? If so, practice listening to authentic spoken English as much as possible so that you can get used to the speed at which people speak. Watch English television, listen to English radio or books on tape and talk to native English speakers as much as possible.

## PRACTICE QUESTIONS SCRIPT

**Questions 81 and 82** refer to the following message.

Ms. Giovanni, this is Janet from Dr. Rossi's office calling to remind you of your annual physical exam tomorrow at 10:30. Please be on time. The appointment should take about an hour.

**Questions 83 and 84** refer to the following announcement.

Attention all employees. The power outage in plant number two has been resolved. However, our main computers are still down. We will be closing the production line early today so that technical services can correct the problem. Plan to leave by 2:30 P.M. unless told otherwise by your supervisor. Please make sure all manufacturing equipment is turned off before you leave. Thank you.

**Questions 85 through 87** refer to the following short talk.

Good morning everyone. As you know, we have been holding interviews for a new editor to join our team. Ms. Patricia Wright has been chosen for the position. She will begin her orientation program this week and will be on staff by the end of the month. Ms. Wright has a good deal of experience in our field, both here and abroad. She worked for a major publication in Hong Kong for over two years before returning to this country.

**Questions 88 and 89** refer to the following announcement.

This is to announce the new departure time for Flight 109 to Jakarta. Severe thunderstorms delayed the connecting flight from Tokyo. The plane is on the ground and is being serviced. Departure time is now scheduled for 8:30. Meal vouchers will be available for passengers scheduled on this flight. Passengers are asked to please be back to the gate by 8:00 for boarding.

**Questions 90 and 91** refer to the following conference announcement.

Ladies and gentlemen, some of you have been asking for additional conference programs. Unfortunately, we can't give anyone an extra program until we're sure that we have enough for the conference guests who haven't arrived yet. If you've lost yours and need to check your meeting schedules, you can use the copies that we have at the information desk. Those of you who still need an extra program can check with us this afternoon. By then, we will have additional copies.

**Questions 92 and 93** refer to the following short talk.

This dishwasher might look intimidating, but it's really quite easy to use. Start by taking an empty dish rack and load the dishes so that none of them are touching each other. Place the rack at the opening of the machine and hit the power switch so that the rack automatically feeds through the machine. Check the dishes when they come out on the other side and if they aren't completely clean,

run the rack through the machine again. When they're done, take the dishes out and stack them on the dish cart.

**Questions 94 and 95** refer to the following announcement.

Though we have no official dress code for traveling while on business, employees should remember that their physical appearance affects customers' impressions of our company. Beginning this Thursday, I will offer the first in a series of three workshops on business dress and conduct for travel in foreign countries. I hope the sessions will be informative and thought provoking.

**Questions 96 through 98** refer to the following talk.

As you can see, the house is in excellent condition. It's worth far more than the asking price. The present owners carried out some renovation work recently and put in a whole new bathroom and kitchen. They were careful to retain the charming character of the house, as I'm sure you'll appreciate. When you go upstairs, you'll see how cozy the bedroom is. The house is a bit small, but you could easily build an extension over the old garage. The property is in a very desirable location—just minutes away from the train station, a supermarket, and some restaurants.

**Questions 99 and 100** refer to the following talk.

I've called this meeting because, since the beginning of the year, our store has been losing over 1500 Euros a month due to theft. Last month, this figure rose to nearly 2000 Euros. We believe that a group of shoplifters has been operating in the building for the last few weeks and that this may account for the losses that occurred in September. We've been in touch with our security consultants, who will be investigating the matter and drawing up a report on their findings.

---

## ANSWER KEY FOR DAY 13

### Practice Questions

81. C

82. B

83. A

84. C

85. A

86. D

87. D

88. C

89. C

90. B

91. D

92. A

93. C

94. C

95. B

96. A

97. A

98. B

99. B

100. D

### Exercise C

1. Hong Kong; over two years

2. Departure time; 8:30

## Day 14

# Listening Comprehension Section: Sample Questions from Parts I to IV, with Explanations of the Answers

In today's lesson, you will answer sample questions from all four parts of the Listening Comprehension section of the TOEIC test and read detailed explanations for correct and incorrect answers.

Play the recording for Day 14. Cover the explanation. Then, as you listen to the recording, fill in the circles for the correct answers on your answer sheet. Use the TOEIC Sample Questions Answer Sheet on page 115 as you answer the questions. You may choose either to play all the listening samples at once or to stop the recording after each question. Uncover the script and explanation for each sample question to check your answers. Read the explanations carefully to find out why your answers are either correct or incorrect.

### Example Question 1

(A) They're leaving the office.

(B) They're working with the projector.

(C) They're moving the files.

(D) They're looking through a microscope.

### Question 1 Explanation

(A) One woman is seated over her work. The other is standing behind a table and working with her hands. Thus, neither is leaving the room.

**(B) A projector is a piece of equipment that is used to show pictures.**

(C) While offices frequently contain files, no files are visible in this photo.

(D) The equipment is used for viewing but is not a microscope. The standing woman is looking at, but not through, the projector.

## AUTHENTIC TOEIC LISTENING COMPREHENSION QUESTIONS WITH EXPLANATIONS

### Part I Photographs

**Sample Question 1**

On the recording, you will hear:

(A)  *The people are waiting outside a hotel.*

(B)  *All the people have left the room.*

(C)  *Several people are gathered near a table.*

(D)  *Two women are drinking coffee.*

**Question 1 Explanation**

(A)  People seem to be *waiting*, but they are *inside* a hotel.

(B)  People are still *in the room*.

**(C)  Four men are standing in front of the *table*. They seem to be waiting in line for their turn.**

(D)  A coffee cup is on the table, but the women are not *drinking* coffee.

**Sample Question 2**

On the recording, you will hear:

(A)  *She's talking on the telephone.*

(B)  *She's reading a newspaper.*

(C)  *She's copying a document.*

(D)  *She's standing in a telephone booth.*

**Question 2 Explanation**

**(A)  The woman is holding the *telephone* to her ear and appears to be having a conversation.**

(B)  The woman is looking at a *paper*, but it is not a *newspaper*.

(C)  The woman is holding a *document* (something written), but she is not *copying* it.

(D)  The woman is at a work area in an office and is seated, not *standing*.

## Sample Question 3

On the recording, you will hear:

(A) *The drivers are leaning against the trucks.*

(B) *The trucks are lined up along the road.*

(C) *The engines are being repaired.*

(D) *The workers are unloading the trucks.*

### Question 3 Explanation

(A) There are trucks in the photo, but no *people* are visible.

**(B) Four trucks are parked in a *line* alongside the road.**

(C) There is nothing to show that the trucks are being *repaired*.

(D) As in (A), there are no people in the picture.

## Sample Question 4

On the recording, you will hear:

(A) *He's filling in a form.*

(B) *He's using a keyboard.*

(C) *He's signing a contract.*

(D) *He's writing on a board.*

### Question 4 Explanation

(A) The man is writing but he is not filling out a *form*, which would be *a printed paper*.

(B) The man is writing on a *board* on the wall. He is not typing on a computer *keyboard*.

(C) A *contract* would be printed on paper. The man is writing, but he is not *signing* his name to a legal document.

**(D) The man is *writing* words on a large *board* so others can read them.**

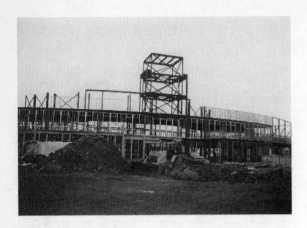

## Sample Question 5

On the recording, you will hear:

(A)  *A crane is moving material to the top of a building.*

(B)  *The frame of a building is exposed.*

(C)  *The construction of a building is completed.*

(D)  *People are attending a groundbreaking ceremony.*

### Question 5 Explanation

(A)  The photo shows a construction site, but no *crane*. A crane is a big piece of equipment used for raising and lowering large objects.

**(B)  The building is being constructed. So far only the supporting structure, or *frame*, is in place.**

(C)  The building is not finished, since the walls and roof have not been added yet.

(D)  A groundbreaking ceremony takes place at the *start* of a construction project; this project is already underway. A bulldozer is moving earth, but no people can be seen at a ceremony.

## Part II Question–Response

### Sample Question 6

On the recording, you will hear:

(Man)      *Would you mind changing seats with me?*

(Woman)  (A)  No, I don't mind at all.

(B)  Sorry, I don't have change.

(C)  There are no more seats available.

### Question 6 Explanation

**(A)  The woman does *not mind* changing seats; in other words, she will do so *willingly*.**

(B)  The question uses *change* as a verb meaning to make a switch, not as a noun meaning *coins* or *money*.

(C)  Both the man and the woman already have seats. The man does not ask if there are other seats, but rather if he can have the woman's seat.

### Sample Question 7

On the recording, you will hear:

(Woman 1)  *Why don't you let me leave the tip?*

(Woman 2)  (A) Because I need you here.

(B)  It's not too far.

(C)  I've already taken care of it.

### Question 7 Explanation

(A)  The first woman wants to *leave the tip*, or *gratuity*. She does not say *leave on a trip*.

(B)  Again, *leave the tip* means *to give money*. The conversation is not about how far or near something is.

**(C)  The second woman has already *taken care of* the tip, meaning she has already *left it*.**

## Sample Question 8

On the recording, you will hear:

(Man 1)   *Haven't you worked here longer than Mrs. Kim?*

(Man 2)   (A) No, it's very close to the office.

          (B) No, we were hired at the same time.

          (C) No, she won't have to wait much longer.

### Question 8 Explanation

(A) The word *longer* here refers to time, not distance.

**(B) The second man has worked here for the same length of time as Mrs. Kim, since they were *hired at the same time*.**

(C) The conversation is about how long Mrs. Kim has worked, not how long she must *wait*.

## Sample Question 9

On the recording, you will hear:

(Woman)   *The leadership training with Mr. Garcia begins at ten o'clock, doesn't it?*

(Man)   (A) No, it leaves at eleven.

       (B) It's not raining now.

       (C) I thought it was at nine.

### Question 9 Explanation

(A) The woman says *training*. This response would refer to a *train*.

(B) This response would refer to the weather (*raining*).

**(C) The woman asks when the training will start. She gives a time, 10:00, followed by a tag question, which is a way to check if she is right. The man gives her the correct starting time, which is 9:00.**

## Sample Question 10

On the recording, you will hear:

(Man 1)   *Should I turn off these lights?*

(Man 2)   (A) Just keep driving straight along this road.

          (B) No, only the ones in your office.

          (C) Yes, it's too heavy for me.

### Question 10 Explanation

(A) The first man is not asking for directions on *where to turn*.

**(B) He asks about turning out the electric lights. The answer is to turn out just those in his own office.**

(C) The word *lights* is used as a noun, not as an adjective.

## Sample Question 11

On the recording, you will hear:

(Woman 1)   *Do you like this hot weather, or do you prefer the cold?*

(Woman 2)   (A) I have trouble with the heat.

            (B) It's just an allergy.

            (C) Yes, I'm feeling much better, thanks.

### Question 11 Explanation

**(A) *Cold* refers to the temperature of the *weather*.**

(B) *Cold* here does not mean a *sickness*. They are not discussing whether the woman has a cold or an allergy.

(C) They are not discussing the woman's health.

# Part III Short Conversations

## Sample Question 12

In the test book, you will read:

12. What is the man's problem?

  (A) His folder is missing.

  (B) The woman gave him the wrong paper.

  (C) He forgot to hand in the folder.

  (D) He is late for a meeting.

On the recording, you will hear:

(Woman)   *Here's the schedule. Do you have everything you need?*

(Man)   *I can't find my folder with the guidelines in it.*

(Woman)   *You just had it in your hand a minute ago!*

## Question 12 Explanation

**(A) The man says he can't find his folder; therefore, the folder is *missing*.**

(B) The woman is not giving him the wrong paper; she is giving him the *schedule.*

(C) The man cannot find his folder, but he did not forget to *hand it in,* or *submit,* it.

(D) There is no mention of a *meeting.*

## Sample Question 13

In the test book, you will read:

13. When should the patient return to the doctor's office?

  (A) Today.

  (B) Tomorrow.

  (C) After one week.

  (D) After two weeks.

On the recording, you will hear:

(Man)   *Before I leave, is there anything else I need to know, doctor?*

(Woman)   *Well, you should start your medication this evening, and take it for two weeks. I'll need to see you here again after that.*

(Man)   *OK. I'll make an appointment on my way out.*

## Question 13 Explanation

(A) The man should start his *medication* later today.

(B) The man says *to know,* not *tomorrow.* The doctor wants to see the man again, but not so soon.

(C) There is no mention of *one week.*

**(D) The medicine should be taken for two weeks. The doctor wants to see the man again when it is finished.**

## Sample Question 14

In the test book, you will read:

14. Where does this conversation probably take place?

  (A) At the man's house.

  (B) At the man's office.

  (C) At a jewelry store.

  (D) At a clothing store.

On the recording, you will hear:

(Man)   *Excuse me, I think I dropped my watch in the fitting room when I was trying on a suit here this morning. Has anyone found it?*

(Woman)   *I don't see it here, but if you leave your name and phone number, I'll call you if it turns up.*

(Man)   *Thanks. I'll give you my office number and my home number.*

## Question 14 Explanation

(A) The man says he will leave his *home* telephone number. A fitting room is not found in one's home, or *house.*

(B) He will also give his *office number,* but he is not at his office.

(C) A watch is *jewelry,* but the man says that he *dropped* his *watch.* He is not shopping for one.

**(D) The man mentions a *fitting room* and *trying on a suit.* He must be in a *clothing store.***

## Sample Question 15

In the test book, you will read:

15. What will happen three months from now?

    (A) Road repairs will begin.

    (B) The trip downtown will take over an hour.

    (C) The trip downtown will become shorter.

    (D) Main Street will be closed.

On the recording, you will hear:

(Woman)  *They've started the road repairs on Main Street.*

(Man)  *I know. For the next three months, it'll take over an hour to get downtown.*

(Woman)  *Yes, but after that we'll be able to get there much faster.*

## Question 15 Explanation

(A) The road repairs *have started* already.

(B) The trip will take an hour only while repairs are going on.

(C) **After three months, the road repairs will be finished and the trip will be faster, or *shorter*.**

(D) The man says, "For the next three months ...," implying that the road repairs will take that long. Three months from now, Main Street should be back to normal.

## Sample Question 16

In the test book, you will read:

16. Who is the woman talking to?

    (A) A hotel clerk.

    (B) A flight attendant.

    (C) A taxi driver.

    (D) A long-distance operator.

On the recording, you will hear:

(Man)  *Good evening, front desk. May I help you?*

(Woman)  *Yes, I have a 7:45 flight tomorrow morning, so I'll need a wake-up call. How long does it take to get to the airport?*

(Man)  *If you get a cab from here by 6:30, it should only take 15 minutes. Should I call you at 5:45?*

## Question 16 Explanation

(A) **She has reached the *front desk* to ask for a *wake-up call*, so she must be talking to a hotel clerk.**

(B) She will be going to the *airport* in the morning, but she is not talking to a flight attendant.

(C) She will take a *cab* in the morning, but is not now talking to the driver.

(D) She is requesting a wake-up call, not a *long-distance* call.

**Sample Question 17**

In the test book, you will read:

17. Why doesn't the man move to an apartment near the university?

    (A) The rent is too high.

    (B) He doesn't want to live there.

    (C) The apartments are all currently occupied.

    (D) There are no nice apartments in that area.

On the recording, you will hear:

(Man)     *It's so hard to find an apartment in this city. They're either too small or too expensive.*

(Woman)     *Have you looked over by the university?*

               *Rents are low around there, and some of the apartments are really nice.*

(Man)     *I tried that area, but there's nothing available until summer.*

**Question 17 Explanation**

(A) Although rents in the city are expensive, they are *lower* near the university.

(B) He already tried to find an apartment there, but none were *available.*

**(C) The apartments near the university are all rented until the *summer.***

(D) The woman says that the apartments in that area *are* nice.

## Part IV Short Talks

**Sample Questions 18 and 19**

On the recording, you will hear:

**Questions 18 and 19 refer to the following announcement:**

> *Attention health-club members. Back by popular demand, our expert instructor, Elena Pappas, will again offer her International Folk Dancing sessions beginning January 15. Enjoy the fun of moving to music, gain the benefits of physical conditioning, and meet new people while you learn the basics of folk dances from around the world. Enrollment is limited to sixteen. See Maria Sandor at the front desk for details.*

In the test book, you will read:

18. Who is Elena Pappas?

    (A) A front desk clerk.

    (B) A physician.

    (C) A tour guide.

    (D) A dance teacher.

**Question 18 Explanation**

(A) Maria Sandor is the front desk clerk.

(B) *Physical conditioning* is mentioned, not *physician.*

(C) *International* and *around the world* refer to the *folk dances,* not to tourism.

**(D) Elena Pappas is an *instructor* who will *offer dancing sessions.***

19. Where is the announcement being made?

    (A) At a trade fair.

    (B) At a health club.

    (C) At a language school.

    (D) At a folk festival.

## Question 19 Explanation

(A) There is no mention of a *trade fair*.

**(B) The talk addresses *health-club members*.**

(C) Although the word *international* is mentioned, there is no mention of a *language school*.

(D) The announcement is about folk *dancing*, not a folk *festival*.

On the recording, you will hear:

## Sample Questions 20 through 22

On the recording, you will hear:

## Questions 20 through 22 refer to the following announcement:

*The anniversary committee is finalizing plans for the celebration of our twenty-fifth anniversary on Saturday, June second. In the event of rain, the celebration will be held on June ninth. The official ceremonies are scheduled to begin at five o'clock in Oak Park and will include speeches by visiting dignitaries and the dedication of two cherry trees as a salute to past presidents of the association. Special events for children are also being planned. Anyone who would like to assist the anniversary committee should contact Tom Suzuki before April twenty-ninth.*

In the test book, you will read:

20. What is the celebration for?
    (A) To officially open Oak Park.
    (B) To welcome a new president.
    (C) To mark an anniversary.
    (D) To salute future association leaders.

## Question 20 Explanation

(A) Oak Park, where the celebration will be held, is mentioned only as the location for the celebration, not the reason for it. There is no mention of opening Oak Park.

(B) Past presidents of the association will be *saluted*, or *honored*. No mention is made of a new president.

**(C) *Anniversary* is a key word. The celebration is in honor of the twenty-fifth anniversary of the association.**

(D) Mention is made of *past* leaders, but not of *future* leaders.

21. If it rains, when will the celebration take place?
    (A) April 25.
    (B) April 29.
    (C) June 2.
    (D) June 9.

## Question 21 Explanation

(A) April 25 is not referred to in this text. The association is 25 years old.

(B) April 29 is the last date for people to contact Tom Suzuki if they want to help the committee.

(C) Saturday, June 2, is the planned date for the celebration to take place if the weather is good.

**(D) If it rains on June 2, the celebration will be held on June 9 instead.**

22. Which activity will be included in the celebration?
    (A) Reports on the year's achievements.
    (B) Speeches by new association officers.
    (C) Planning for future children's activities.
    (D) Dedication of commemorative trees.

## Question 22 Explanation

(A) No mention is made of the achievements of the association.

(B) Speeches will be made by *visiting dignitaries,* visitors who are persons of high standing, not by members of the association.

(C) Children's activities are being planned for *this* celebration, not *future* celebrations.

**(D) Two cherry trees will be dedicated to *salute,* or *honor,* the past presidents of the association.**

On the recording, you will hear:

## Sample Questions 23 and 24

On the recording, you will hear:

## Questions 23 and 24 refer to the following report:

*Union workers at Gemini Industries are in their fifth day of a strike in protest of the growing use of temporary workers. More and more workers are seeing their full-time jobs replaced by non-salaried, short-term positions without benefits or job security. Gemini President Raymond Singh insists that the company reduce payroll costs to remain competitive.*

In the test book, you will read:

23. What are the workers concerned about?
    (A) Payroll costs.
    (B) Job security.
    (C) Salary cuts.
    (D) Factory security.

## Question 23 Explanation

(A) Only *Mr. Singh,* the company's president, is concerned about the payroll.

**(B) The workers are worried because full-time jobs are being replaced by short-term, temporary jobs without benefits or *job security.***

(C) *Salary cuts* means *reductions in pay.* The word *non-salaried* is used, but it refers to jobs, not to reductions in pay.

(D) Gemini Industries sounds like the name of a factory. However, the workers are worried about their *jobs,* not the security of the factory.

24. What is Mr. Singh's attitude toward the workers' complaints?
    (A) He insists on hiring only full-time workers.
    (B) He supports the workers' strike.
    (C) He rejects the company policy.
    (D) He maintains that expenses must be cut.

## Question 24 Explanation

(A) The company is hiring more temporary workers *instead* of full-time workers.

(B) The workers are striking against the company. Mr. Singh, the president of the company, agrees with the *company,* not the workers.

(C) Mr. Singh *defends* the company policy.

**(D) He insists that the company must reduce expenses by cutting payroll costs (the amount spent on workers' pay).**

■ Now, STOP the recording.

## TOEIC SAMPLE QUESTIONS ANSWER SHEET

1.  Ⓐ  Ⓑ  Ⓒ  Ⓓ
2.  Ⓐ  Ⓑ  Ⓒ  Ⓓ
3.  Ⓐ  Ⓑ  Ⓒ  Ⓓ
4.  Ⓐ  Ⓑ  Ⓒ  Ⓓ
5.  Ⓐ  Ⓑ  Ⓒ  Ⓓ
6.  Ⓐ  Ⓑ  Ⓒ  Ⓓ
7.  Ⓐ  Ⓑ  Ⓒ  Ⓓ
8.  Ⓐ  Ⓑ  Ⓒ  Ⓓ
9.  Ⓐ  Ⓑ  Ⓒ  Ⓓ
10.  Ⓐ  Ⓑ  Ⓒ  Ⓓ
11.  Ⓐ  Ⓑ  Ⓒ  Ⓓ
12.  Ⓐ  Ⓑ  Ⓒ  Ⓓ
13.  Ⓐ  Ⓑ  Ⓒ  Ⓓ
14.  Ⓐ  Ⓑ  Ⓒ  Ⓓ
15.  Ⓐ  Ⓑ  Ⓒ  Ⓓ
16.  Ⓐ  Ⓑ  Ⓒ  Ⓓ
17.  Ⓐ  Ⓑ  Ⓒ  Ⓓ
18.  Ⓐ  Ⓑ  Ⓒ  Ⓓ
19.  Ⓐ  Ⓑ  Ⓒ  Ⓓ
20.  Ⓐ  Ⓑ  Ⓒ  Ⓓ
21.  Ⓐ  Ⓑ  Ⓒ  Ⓓ
22.  Ⓐ  Ⓑ  Ⓒ  Ⓓ
23.  Ⓐ  Ⓑ  Ⓒ  Ⓓ
24.  Ⓐ  Ⓑ  Ⓒ  Ⓓ

# Day 15

# An Introduction to the Reading Section and Tips and Exercises for Part V: Incomplete Sentences

The lessons for Days 15 to 24 deal with the three different question types in Section 2 of the test, the Reading section.

## READING SECTION OVERVIEW

The Reading section consists of questions 101–200 of the TOEIC test. It is divided into three parts:

Part V: Incomplete Sentences

Part VI: Error Recognition

Part VII: Reading Comprehension

In the Reading section, you will read both individual sentences and longer texts. In order to answer the questions, you will use your knowledge of English grammar, usage, and vocabulary, as well as your overall reading skills.

You will have 75 minutes to complete the entire Reading section. You can work at your own pace to complete all three parts.

Today's lesson starts with a tip that applies to the whole of the Reading section.

## TIP Prepare yourself for formal written English.

The language used in the Reading section represents formal written English and does not usually contain the contractions or informal language found in the Listening Comprehension section.

Look at these examples of different levels of formality:

### Informal English

I'm sorry I can't come.
Please call back.
Can you give me a hand with this?

### Formal English

I regret that I will be unable to attend.
I look forward to your reply.
I would appreciate your assistance in this matter.

Now, look at the different language used in the following two announcements, one spoken and one written:

### A spoken excerpt from a staff meeting

There aren't enough parking spaces for everyone going to the party at the hotel on Wednesday night, so they're arranging a shuttle bus to pick us up and drop us off there. Please use the bus so that the hotel has enough room for their own guests.

## A written communication from a hotel

Because the hotel does not have sufficient parking spaces for everyone attending the reception on Wednesday evening, we have arranged a shuttle bus to bring guests to the hotel entrance. We ask that you take advantage of this service so that we may accommodate our overnight guests.

In the written communication above, the sentence structure is more complex and the vocabulary used is more formal. For example, *enough* becomes *sufficient*, and *please use* is replaced with *we ask that you take advantage of*.

## EXERCISE A: USING INFORMAL AND FORMAL ENGLISH

In the list below, fill in the formal words and phrases used in the written communication from the hotel. The first two have been done for you.

| Informal English | Formal English |
|---|---|
| 1. enough | sufficient |
| 2. please use | we ask that you take advantage of |
| 3. going to | |
| 4. the party | |
| 5. has enough room for | |

*To the teacher:* To practice changing informal English to formal English, put students in small groups of three to four students to role-play informal meetings. Suggested meeting situations:

1. Students at a language school meet with the social secretary or event coordinator to suggest social events for the next term.

2. To increase productivity, a company has proposed cutting everyone's lunch break from 1 hour to 45 minutes. Some colleagues who object to this proposal get together to discuss it.

3. A supervisor, who has worked at a company for many years, is retiring. A committee gets together to discuss plans for a party and a retirement gift.

After the role-played meetings, ask the students to write a formal report or a document such as a formal petition, proposal, or memorandum based on their meeting. Ask the students to change the informal language they used in their meeting to more formal language for their report.

## TIPS AND EXERCISES FOR PART V: INCOMPLETE SENTENCES

Questions 101–140 of the TOEIC test consist of 40 sentences that are each missing a word or phrase. Under the sentence, you will see four words or phrases, marked (A), (B), (C), and (D). You must select the word or phrase that best completes the sentence.

Here are some important points to remember about the Incomplete Sentences part of the test:

- There are 40 questions in this part.
- You have 75 minutes for the entire Reading section. Questions in Part V are not timed, so don't spend too long on each question. Instead, come back to a question if you still have time at the end of the test.
- Mark an answer for every question.

In the lessons for Day 15 and 16, there are tips and exercises to help you improve your ability to find the best word or phrase to complete the sentence.

**TIP Decide if the question requires knowledge of vocabulary or grammar.**

Read all of the choices carefully. In some cases, you must select the correct vocabulary item. In other questions, you must select the correct grammatical form of a particular word.

Consider the following examples:

## Example 1

Everyone should have periodic eye examinations to make sure any problems are quickly - - - - - - - .

(A) produced

(B) responded

**(C)** discovered

(D) prepared

## Example 2

Everyone should have periodic eye examinations to make sure any problems are quickly - - - - - - - .

(A) discovering

(B) discover

**(C)** discovered

(D) to discover

In Example 1, all of the choices are past participles of different verbs. You must choose the word that is appropriate in the context of the sentence. A medical problem must be *discovered* quickly so that it can be treated.

In Example 2, the choices come from the same root word, *discover*. Here, you must select the correct grammatical form of the word. The verb should be passive. The past participle *discovered* completes the passive construction—*problems are quickly discovered.*

*To the teacher:* At this point, it may be a good idea to review the different parts of speech to make sure the students know them. You could ask them to identify the nouns, verbs, adjectives, adverbs, prepositions, and conjunctions in a short, formal text. The students could then work in pairs to discuss their answers.

Here are some more examples. Read each sentence, study the four choices, and select an answer. Did you need to select a vocabulary item or pick a grammatical form to complete the sentence?

## Example 3

The publishers suggested that the envelopes be sent to - - - - - - - by courier so that the film can be developed as soon as possible.

(A) they

(B) their

(C) theirs

(D) them

## Example 4

Conservatives predict that government finances will remain - - - - - - - during the period of the investigation.

(A) authoritative

(B) summarized

(C) examined

(D) stable

## Example 5

Updating your skills is the only way to remain - - - - - - - in today's job market, according to economist Chun Ho Suk.

(A) competitor

(B) competition

(C) competitive

(D) competed

## Example 6

Not only did the suppliers send the wrong - - - - - - - for the machine, but they also sent them to the wrong department.

(A) particles

(B) components

(C) technicians

(D) principles

Look at the following explanations for Examples 3–6. Do they agree with your answers?

*Example 3:* You have to choose the correct form of the pronoun *they* to use after the preposition *to* for the indirect object of the verb *sent*. The correct choice is (D), *them*.

*Example 4:* From the four choices, you have to select the vocabulary item with the correct meaning in this context. You need to find the adjective that could be used to describe *government finances*. The correct choice is (D), *stable*.

*Example 5:* The four choices are different grammatical forms of the word *compete*. Think about the sentence carefully. What would the word in the space describe? The phrase *for a person* could be inserted after *the only way*. This makes it clear that the correct choice has to be an adjective that could be used to describe a person. The correct choice is (C), *competitive*.

*Example 6:* From the four nouns, you have to select the one with the correct meaning in this sentence. The correct word would be one describing something that the suppliers might send and that is connected with a machine. The answer is (B), *components*.

## TIP Consider the overall meaning of a sentence to determine a missing vocabulary item.

Understanding the general idea of a sentence can help you determine the missing vocabulary item. In fact, it is a good idea to ignore, or even cover up, the choices at first so that you can focus on the meaning of the whole sentence.

Consider the following example:

**Example 7**

The firm - - - - - - - Mr. Morrison as its accountant after it was learned that he had not been mishandling funds.

(A) reinstated

(B) distracted

(C) determined

(D) reprimanded

The last part of this sentence indicates that Mr. Morrison had not done anything wrong. Ask yourself, "What would a firm be likely to do in this situation?" Only choice (A), *reinstated*, provides a meaningful answer. Mr. Morrison was reinstated, or returned, to his position.

## EXERCISE B: THINKING ABOUT THE OVERALL MEANING OF THE SENTENCE

Answer the following Incomplete Sentence questions for which you are required to select the appropriate vocabulary item. Cover up the choices with a piece of paper at first, and think about the overall meaning of the sentence. Ask yourself, "What is the sentence about?" Then uncover the choices and pick the one that would be meaningful in the sentence. Write notes about what helped you to choose the answer.

1.  Our studies show that increases in worker productivity have not been adequately rewarded by significant increases in - - - - - .

    (A) compensation

    (B) commodity

    (C) compilation

    (D) complacency

2.  Two assistants will be required to - - - - - - - reporters' names when they arrive at the press conference.

    (A) remark

    (B) check

    (C) notify

    (D) ensure

3.  The Trade Ministry's report asserts that the growing - - - - - - - of skilled labor is limiting business expansion.

    (A) opportunity

    (B) scarcity

    (C) danger

    (D) enlargement

4.  Even when two parties seem radically opposed to one another, an - - - - - - - negotiator can help find common ground.

    (A) incompetent

    (B) authentic

    (C) effective

    (D) appreciative

*To the teacher:* To encourage the students to think about the overall meaning of the sentence, try this activity. On separate papers, type the sentences in Exercise B without the four choices. (You can also type up incomplete sentences from other chapters in the book.) Have the students work in pairs to answer the questions "Where might you read this sentence?" and "What is the sentence about?" for each sentence. When the answers to these questions have been agreed upon by the whole class, have the students open their books and answer the questions (this time, choosing one choice from the four choices) in pairs. Allow them to use dictionaries for the second part of this activity.

## TIP Apply your knowledge of prefixes, word stems, and suffixes to select the best vocabulary item.

**prefix:** a letter or group of letters at the beginning of a word

**stem:** the main part of a word

**suffix:** a letter or group of letters at the end of a word

Use your knowledge of the different parts of words to choose the correct answer. For example, if you know that the prefix *pre-* means *before,* and that *re-* means *again,* you can determine the meaning of words like *pre*arrange, *pre*season, and *pre*flight, as well as *re*appear, *re*attach, and *re*install.

If you know that the stem *view* means *see,* then you can understand that *preview* means *see before* and *review* means *view again.*

Here are examples of common prefixes, stems, and suffixes and their meanings or uses.

### Prefixes

| | |
|---|---|
| **anti-** | against |
| **auto-** | self |
| **bi-** | two |
| **ex-** | out, former |
| **mono-** | one |
| **multi-** | many |
| **pre-** | before |
| **syn-** | with |
| **tri-** | three |
| **re-** | again |
| **un-** | not |
| **fore-** | before |
| **under-** | below |
| **co-** | together |

### Stems

| | |
|---|---|
| **bio** | life |
| **biblio** | book |
| **cycle** | circle, round |
| **demo** | people |
| **dict** | say |
| **dorm** | sleep |
| **duct** | lead |
| **flect** | bend |
| **graph** | writing |
| **labor** | work |
| **lingua** | language |
| **temp** | time |
| **vis** | see |

### Suffixes

| | |
|---|---|
| **-er** | a person who does something |
| **-ful** | full of |
| **-less** | without |
| **-ly** | forms an adverb from an adjective |
| **-ness** | forms a noun from an adjective |
| **-ion** | forms a noun from a verb |

**Examples**

biographer—a person who writes a story of a life

reflection —light bent back

monolingual—speaking one language

dormitory—a place to sleep

laboratory—a place to work

laborer—a person who works

**Note:** Breaking apart a word into prefix and stem can help you guess the meaning of many words. Some words, however, may seem to have prefixes but really do not. For example, in the words *precious*, *premier*, and *pressure*, *pre-* is not a prefix meaning *before* but is part of the stem of the word. Look for word parts, but be aware that a word might not always contain a prefix or suffix.

*To the teacher:* Use the list to elicit examples of words with these prefixes, stems, and suffixes. Seat the students in groups of three or four and ask them to choose five prefixes, three stems, and three suffixes. Ask each group to think of words for each of their choices. You could provide dictionaries for this activity so that students can look up the meanings of their words. Walk around the groups and check that they understand the meaning of each word they come up with. As groups finish, ask them to write three of their words on the board, to make a list of about twelve words. Ask the groups to either write the meanings of their words on the board or explain the meanings orally. You can also ask students in one group to give the meanings of the words written down by a different group.

---

## EXERCISE C: PRACTICE WITH PREFIXES

Match the prefix on the left with a suitable word ending on the right. Use each prefix and word ending only once. Be sure you understand the meaning of each word. Then choose the most appropriate word to use in each of the sentences.

| Prefixes | Word endings |
|---|---|
| re- | -portation |
| pre- | -estimated |
| fore- | -colored |
| under- | -necessary |
| bi- | -operation |
| co- | -lingual |
| multi- | -see |
| trans- | -cycle |
| un- | -dictable |

**Sentences:**

1. Fluctuations in the stock market are not always - - - - - - - .

2. We failed to - - - - - - - the effect of the new shopping center on traffic patterns.

3. Public - - - - - - - can be used to get to the conference center.

4. Ms. Curtis was dissatisfied because she felt her abilities were - - - - - - - by her supervisor.

5. An advertisement has been placed for a - - - - - - - secretary.

6. The management apologizes for any inconvenience and asks for your - - - - - - - while the construction is in progress.

7. Taking notes during the slide presentation is - - - - - - - because handouts will be distributed at the end.

8. A - - - - - - - sign would attract attention to the new restaurant better than a black-and-white sign.

9. Employees are asked to - - - - - - - all used paper and envelopes.

*To the teacher:* Seat the students in pairs to work on Exercise C. When the pairs have completed the exercise and you have checked their answers, move them into groups of four and ask them to complete each sentence with different words than they have been given in the exercise. Have them think of as many words as they can to complete each sentence. Then have each group choose a new answer for each sentence and write all their answers clearly on a piece of paper. (Make sure that they write the answers in a different order than the sentences and that they do not number them.) The groups then exchange papers and try to fit the words to the sentences.

---

## ANSWER KEY FOR DAY 15

### Exercise A

3.  attending

4.  the reception

5.  may accommodate

### Exercise B

1.  A

2.  B

3.  B

4.  C

**Examples of notes:**

1.  The sentence is about some research that has been carried out. The research was about worker productivity and its relationship with increases in something else. You'd expect increases in productivity to be rewarded by increases in pay. Choice (A), *compensation*, is another word for *pay*.

2.  The sentence is about arrangements for a press conference. Reporters will be attending to interview somebody, probably an important public figure. What will assistants need to do to reporters' names? The answer is (B), *check* them, probably against a list of people that have been invited.

3.  The sentence is about the results of a report from the Trade Ministry. According to the report, something is *limiting business expansion* or preventing businesses from growing. The limiting factor has something to do with *skilled labor*. This means workers who are qualified to do a particular job. It is the *lack* of such workers that would limit business expansion. Choice (B), *scarcity*, means *lack*.

4.  *Parties* would be groups of people. The sentence is about helping two groups of people who are *radically opposed to one another*, or have very different ideas to *find common ground*, which means *come to an agreement*. What type of negotiator would be able to achieve this? The answer is (C), an *effective* negotiator.

### Exercise C

1.  predictable

2.  foresee

3.  transportation

4.  underestimated

5.  bilingual

6.  cooperation

7.  unnecessary

8.  multicolored

9.  recycle

# Day 16

## Further Exercises for Part V: Incomplete Sentences

In today's lesson, you will learn additional strategies and practice using your knowledge of vocabulary and grammar to help you make the correct choices in Part V of the TOEIC test.

**TIP  Note that some words are often used together in set expressions.**

Certain combinations of words typically occur in English. For example, the verb *make* can be used with *an appointment, a date,* or *a mistake,* while the verb *do* is frequently used with *a job, homework,* or *an errand.* For example, *I made a mistake when I was doing my homework.*

Keep in mind that an Incomplete Sentence question may be assessing your knowledge of English language usage.

Consider the following examples:

**Example 1**

Mr. Dupré has asked me to send his - - - - - - - regards to you and your staff.

(A) **warm**

(B) firm

(C) close

(D) good

The word *regards* is usually used with the words *warm* or *best.* While *close* and *good* might seem to make sense, they are not used to modify *regards.*

**Example 2**

He has - - - - - - - a great deal of time on this project.

(A) passed

(B) **spent**

(C) cost

(D) paid

The word *time* can be used with *passed* or *spent,* but the meanings of the two expressions are different. *To pass time* means to let the time go by while you are relaxing or waiting. This would not make sense in the above sentence. *To spend a lot of time* on something means that you use the time for a special purpose.

## EXERCISE A: CHOOSING THE MISSING WORD FROM A SET EXPRESSION

Below are six Incomplete Sentences. In each one, the missing word forms part of a set expression.

First, read each sentence and underline the word or words that the missing word combines with to form a set expression. For example, looking at *Example 1* above, *warm regards* is the set expression, so you would underline *regards*. In *Example 2*, you would underline *time* because it forms a set expression with the missing word *spent*. When you have thought about all the sentences in this way, try to choose the correct answer.

1.  I am writing in - - - - - - - to the position of events manager advertised in August's Entertainment Monthly.

    (A) comment

    (B) account

    (C) notice

    (D) reference

2.  Please call the dentist's office at your - - - - - - - convenience to make an appointment for your six month check up.

    (A) soonest

    (B) quickest

    (C) earliest

    (D) easiest

3.  It is essential that we operate - - - - - - - the parameters of time and a limited budget.

    (A) among

    (B) about

    (C) within

    (D) onto

4.  Reservations for the fish restaurant recently opened by John Larchmont need to be - - - - - - - several weeks in advance.

    (A) conducted

    (B) left

    (C) enlisted

    (D) made

5.  The success - - - - - - - the new manufacturing process has doubled the number of requests for the product.

    (A) to

    (B) of

    (C) for

    (D) by

6.  We apologize for informing you of the change in location of the conference at such - - - - - - - notice.

    (A) brief

    (B) tight

    (C) short

    (D) small

Now check your answers against the answer key at the end of Day 16.

*To the teacher:* To practice other set expressions, try making some fill-in-the-blank exercises. Look for short articles in newspapers or magazines that contain some set expressions. Type the article out again, omitting one word from each set expression. Have the students supply the missing words. Perhaps you could find a text with several set expressions containing a verb. You could then supply a set of verbs for the students to choose from when filling the blanks.

## TIP  Identify the missing part of speech to determine the correct grammatical form.

Identifying the missing part of speech (noun, verb, adjective, adverb, preposition, conjunction, etc.) can help you eliminate some of the choices. If the missing word is a verb, for example, you can rule out the choices that are not verbs. Consider the following example:

**Example 3**

Please - - - - - - - your face with a mask when using welding materials.

(A) protection

**(B) protect**

(C) protecting

(D) protective

In this example, the sentence is grammatically correct when completed with a verb form that expresses a command—the imperative form of the verb.

Choices (A) and (D) are not verbs, so you can eliminate these choices immediately. Choices (B) and (C) are both verb forms. Choice (C), *protecting*, is not an imperative, so choice (B), *protect*, is the correct answer.

**Note:** Understanding suffixes can help you determine the part of speech of a word. It is important to recognize, for example, that many *adjectives* end in -*ent*, as in *silent* and *persistent*, while *nouns* with the same stem end in -*ence*, as in *silence* and *persistence*.

*To the teacher:* Before the students work on Exercise B, make sure that they know the terms for the different parts of speech and elicit some examples of each. The answers to Exercise B should be discussed before moving on to Exercise C. It is probably best for students to work on these individually and then compare their answers with a neighbor.

---

## EXERCISE B: IDENTIFYING MISSING PARTS OF SPEECH

Read the following sentences and decide what part of speech is missing in each case. Choose one of the parts of speech listed below and write it in the blank at the end of the sentence. The first one is done for you.

| | | |
|---|---|---|
| noun | preposition | verb |
| adverb | conjunction | adjective |

1. In order for the conference to run smoothly, we will need hundreds - - - - - - - volunteers. (<u>preposition</u>)

2. The need for skilled workers in the manufacturing trade will - - - - - - - dramatically over the next decade. (_____ )

3. West Street has the city's - - - - - - - concentration of art galleries, museums, and restaurants. (_____ )

4. The RBI Corporation has - - - - - - - maintained that its greatest growth potential lies overseas. (_____ )

5. The airline industry announced yesterday that it had canceled a $3.5 billion - - - - - - - for jet airplanes. (_____ )

6. The audience is reminded that neither cameras - - - - - - - recording equipment will be permitted in the auditorium. (_____ )

---

## EXERCISE C: COMPLETING SENTENCES

Now complete the same sentences from Exercise B using words of your own.

1. In order for the conference to run smoothly, we will need hundreds - - - - - - - volunteers.

2. The need for skilled workers in the manufacturing trade will - - - - - - - dramatically over the next decade.

3. West Street has the city's - - - - - - - concentration of art galleries, museums, and restaurants.

4. The RBI Corporation has - - - - - - - maintained that its greatest growth potential lies overseas.

5. The airline industry announced yesterday that it had canceled a $3.5 billion - - - - - - - for jet airplanes.

6. The audience is reminded that neither cameras - - - - - - - recording equipment will be permitted in the auditorium.

## TIP Look for grammatical relationships between parts of the sentence.

When you are choosing the correct grammatical form to complete the sentence, look at how the parts of the sentence fit together. Information from one phrase often affects other parts of the sentence.

Consider the following examples:

**Example 4**

The notebook computer is the - - - - - - - profitable of all the products that are presently on sale.

(A) as

(B) so

(C) more

**(D) most**

The phrase *of all the products* tells you that the notebook is being compared with more than one other product. A superlative adjective is required. Choice (D) forms the superlative of the adjective, so you should choose it as your answer.

**Example 5**

Mrs. Hayashi - - - - - - - from her trip to Jakarta late yesterday evening.

(A) return

**(B) returned**

(C) returns

(D) be returned

Here, the clue is the phrase *late yesterday evening.* This phrase indicates that the action took place in the past. Choice (B) is the simple past tense and is the correct answer.

## EXERCISE D: RECOGNIZING THE GRAMMATICAL RELATIONSHIPS IN THE SENTENCE

Before you try to choose the correct answers to these questions, cover up the choices. Decide what type of word you would use to fill in the blank. What types of words do you expect to see in the choices? Underline the word or phrase in the sentence that helps you to decide what should go in the space. Then uncover the choices and answer the questions.

1. Mr. Kobayashi spoke quite - - - - - - - while he was making his sales presentation.

(A) exciting

(B) excitable

(C) excitedly

(D) excitement

2. Over the next two years, production at the Landsbury plant - - - - - - - to double in order to meet increased demand.

(A) needed

(B) will need

(C) has needed

(D) was needing

3. The new computers we are installing are far more powerful - - - - - - - those we are currently using.

(A) as

(B) than

(C) and

(D) so

4. Regrettably, Mr. Jenkinson was found to be - - - - - - - good at his work nor easy to get along with.

(A) either

(B) nor

(C) both

(D) neither

5.  While you are in the building, please wear your identification badge at all times so that you are - - - - - - - as a company employee.

(A) recognize

(B) recognizing

(C) recognizable

(D) recognizably

*To the teacher:* Students should be encouraged to look for clues when they are attempting Incomplete Sentences in which they have to choose the correct grammatical form. Sometimes these clues are in a different part of the sentence from the missing word, as in the examples above, and sometimes they are adjacent to the space. Underlining the clue will help students to focus on what grammatical form is needed. Have students practice underlining clues in and completing gap-filling exercises, which you can easily make from short reading texts from newspapers, magazines, and other sources.

**TIP  Try to develop your knowledge of vocabulary.**

## FOR ADDITIONAL PRACTICE

### Keep a Reading Vocabulary Notebook

One of the best ways to increase your reading proficiency is to find reading materials that you enjoy and to read for pleasure as often as you can. In order to increase your understanding of English grammar and vocabulary, you may also want to do the following:

- Find material that you can read easily without having to stop frequently to look up words in a dictionary.

- As you read, underline unknown words and guess at their meaning from the context in which they appear. Do not stop and check these words in your dictionary at this point.

- When you have finished reading, choose five to ten words that you think you have understood from the context.

- Now, write those five words in a vocabulary notebook (see sample below) and check in your dictionary for the part of speech and the meaning of the word as it appears in the passage.

- Next, use the words in sentences of your own. If you can, have a teacher or native English speaker check your sentences to see if you have used the words correctly.

Entries in your reading vocabulary notebook might look like these:

| New Vocabulary | Part of Speech | Meaning | Example Sentence |
|---|---|---|---|
| *Recipient* | Noun | a person who receives | The recipient of the award gave a speech of thanks. |
| *Draft* | Verb | draw or write the first version of | Mr. Ito has drafted the proposal, but it has not yet been reviewed. |

## ANSWER KEY FOR DAY 16

### Exercise A

1.  D    Set expression:    "with reference to"

2.  C    Set expression:    "at your earliest convenience"

3.  C    Set expression:    "within the parameters"

4.  D    Set expression:    "reservations need to be made"

5.  B    Set expression:    "success of"

6.  C    Set expression:    "at short notice"

### Exercise B

1.  preposition

2.  verb

3.  adjective

4.  adverb

5.  noun

6.  conjunction

### Exercise C

Possible answers:

1.  of (only possible answer)

2.  increase, decrease, rise, fall

3.  highest, largest, finest

4.  always, recently, predictably

5.  contract, proposal, plan, agreement

6.  nor (only possible answer)

### Exercise D

1.  **(C)** is the correct answer. A word is needed to describe the way in which Mr. Kobayashi *spoke*. *Spoke* is a verb, so an adverb is needed.

2.  **(B)** is the correct answer. The words *over the next two years* indicate that the verb will be in the future tense.

3.  **(B)** is the correct answer. The comparative adjective *more powerful* shows you that two things are being compared. In a comparison, *than* is used with the comparative adjective.

4.  **(B)** is the correct answer. The words *nor easy* indicate that the conjunction *neither* is required before the adjective *good*.

5.  **(C)** is the correct answer. An adjective is required here to describe the pronoun *you*. The adjective should mean *can be recognized*.

# Day 17

## Incomplete Sentences: Practice Questions and Follow-up Exercises

In this lesson, you will have the opportunity to practice Part V of the TOEIC test. Before you begin this lesson, remind yourself of the tips given on Days 15 and 16:
- Prepare yourself for formal written English.
- Decide if the question requires knowledge of vocabulary or grammar.
- Consider the overall meaning of a sentence to determine a missing vocabulary item.
- Apply your knowledge of prefixes, word stems, and suffixes to select the best vocabulary item.
- Note that some words are often used together in set expressions.
- Identify the missing part of speech to determine the correct grammatical form.
- Look for grammatical relationships between parts of the sentence.
- Try to develop your knowledge of vocabulary.

## PRACTICE QUESTIONS

Now, try this practice Part V, working as if you were taking a real TOEIC test. Before you start, write the numbers 101–140 on a piece of paper to record your answers. First, read the directions and the example item, then work straight through the section. Write down the time you start and the time that you finish the section. It should take you about 15 to 20 minutes. If you are not sure of the correct answer, choose the one you think is closest. Do not leave any questions blank.

## PART V

*Directions: Questions 101–140 are incomplete sentences. Four words or phrases, marked (A), (B), (C), (D), are given beneath each sentence. You are to choose the one word or phrase that best completes the sentence.*

**Example:**

Because the equipment is very delicate, it must be handled with - - - - - - - .

(A) caring
(B) careful
(C) care
(D) carefully

*Sample Answer*

Ⓐ Ⓑ ● Ⓓ

The sentence should read, "Because the equipment is very delicate, it must be handled with care." Therefore, you should choose answer (C).

Now, begin work on the questions. The answers are printed at the end of this section.

101. Battery-operated reading lamps - - - - - - - very well right now.

    (A) sale

    (B) sold

    (C) are selling

    (D) were sold

102. In order to place a call outside the office, you have to - - - - - - - nine first.

    (A) tip

    (B) make

    (C) dial

    (D) number

103. We are pleased to inform - - - - - - - that the missing order has been found.

    (A) you

    (B) your

    (C) yours

    (D) yourself

104. Unfortunately, neither Mr. Sachs - - - - - - - Ms. Flynn will be able to attend the awards banquet this evening.

    (A) but

    (B) and

    (C) nor

    (D) either

105. According to the manufacturer, the new generator is capable of - - - - - - - the amount of power consumed by our facility by nearly ten percent.

    (A) reduced

    (B) reducing

    (C) reduce

    (D) reduces

106. After the main course, choose from our wide - - - - - - - of homemade deserts.

    (A) varied

    (B) various

    (C) vary

    (D) variety

107. One of the most frequent complaints among airline passengers is that there is not - - - - - - - legroom.

    (A) enough

    (B) many

    (C) very

    (D) plenty

108. Faculty members are planning to - - - - - - - a party in honor of Dr. Walker, who will retire at the end of the semester.

    (A) carry

    (B) do

    (C) hold

    (D) take

109. Many employees seem more - - - - - - - now about how to use the new telephone system than they did before they attended the workshop.

    (A) confusion

    (B) confuse

    (C) confused

    (D) confusing

110. - - - - - - - our production figures improve in the near future, we foresee having to hire more people between now and July.

    (A) During

    (B) Only

    (C) Unless

    (D) Because

111. The prime minister is expected to arrive at the convention hall at - - - - - - - 7:00 p.m.

    (A) approximated

    (B) approximates

    (C) approximate

    (D) approximately

112. Responses to the proposed work schedule changes are - - - - - - - outstanding from several departments.

    (A) until

    (B) yet

    (C) still

    (D) since

113. As the filming location has not yet been - - - - - - -, the release date has been postponed.

    (A) detained

    (B) determined

    (C) delayed

    (D) deleted

114. Extreme - - - - - - - should be used when the fork-lift truck is being operated.

    (A) caution

    (B) cautioned

    (C) cautiously

    (D) cautious

115. The county hospital is currently - - - - - - - volunteers to staff the reception desk.

    (A) look to

    (B) looking for

    (C) looking around

    (D) looking into

116. We are a major international company with a growing number of - - - - - - - in North America.

    (A) inferences

    (B) instances

    (C) instincts

    (D) interests

117. The report indicates that the Tilbrook Fund is acting properly by delivering policy advice - - - - - - - rather than announcing it to the public.

    (A) privacy

    (B) privately

    (C) private

    (D) privatize

118. This presentation will demonstrate how Metron computers are superior - - - - - - - those of our competitors in terms of both features and speed.

    (A) from

    (B) than

    (C) to

    (D) as

119. The Executive Council of the Fashion Buyer's Congress is - - - - - - - of fifteen members from various branches of the fashion industry.

    (A) compose

    (B) composing

    (C) composed

    (D) to compose

120. Though their performance was relatively unpolished, the actors held the audience's - - - - - - - for the duration of the play.

    (A) attentive

    (B) attentively

    (C) attention

    (D) attentiveness

121. Dr. Abernathy's donation to Owston College broke the record for the largest private gift - - - - - - - given to the campus.

    (A) always

    (B) rarely

    (C) once

    (D) ever

122. Savat National Park is - - - - - - - by train, bus, charter plane, and rental car.

(A) accessible

(B) accessing

(C) accessibility

(D) accesses

123. In Piazzo's latest architectural project, he hopes to - - - - - - - his flair for blending contemporary and traditional ideals.

(A) demonstrate

(B) appear

(C) inspect

(D) position

124. Replacing the office equipment that the company purchased only three years ago seems quite - - - - - - - .

(A) waste

(B) wasteful

(C) wasting

(D) wasted

125. On - - - - - - -, employees reach their peak performance level when they have been on the job for at least two years.

(A) common

(B) standard

(C) average

(D) general

126. We were - - - - - - - unaware of the problems with the air-conditioning units in the hotel rooms until this week.

(A) complete

(B) completely

(C) completed

(D) completing

127. If you send in an order - - - - - - - mail, we recommend that you phone our sales division directly to confirm the order.

(A) near

(B) by

(C) for

(D) on

128. A recent global survey suggests - - - - - - - demand for aluminum and tin will remain at its current level for the next five to ten years.

(A) which

(B) it

(C) that

(D) both

129. Rates for the use of recreational facilities do not include tax and are subject to change without - - - - - - - .

(A) signal

(B) cash

(C) report

(D) notice

130. We conduct our audits in accordance - - - - - - - generally accepted auditing standards.

(A) of

(B) with

(C) in

(D) across

131. The Director of Educational Programs works collaboratively with the Ministry of Education to - - - - - - - that the programs are meeting the needs of the institution.

(A) ensure

(B) define

(C) accept

(D) imply

132. The Armstrong Group has the - - - - - - - management team of the three companies under consideration.

    (A) impressive

    (B) more impressive

    (C) impressively

    (D) most impressive

133. There are over thirty keyboard commands that can prompt word-processing procedures, but common usage - - - - - - - only a few.

    (A) involves

    (B) receives

    (C) subscribes

    (D) corresponds

134. The recent storms have led to the - - - - - - - closure of our overseas office.

    (A) temporal

    (B) temporary

    (C) temporarily

    (D) temporaries

135. "Accounts receivable" is money owed to a company, - - - - - - - "accounts payable" is money owed by the company to creditors.

    (A) whereas

    (B) otherwise

    (C) such as

    (D) in order that

136. Cooks must remember that some raw foods are very - - - - - - - and should be refrigerated or chilled until ready to be eaten or cooked.

    (A) peripheral

    (B) perishable

    (C) periodic

    (D) permanent

137. If savings could have been made elsewhere, we - - - - - - - to give financial support to local community service organizations last year.

    (A) continue

    (B) continued

    (C) had continued

    (D) would have continued

138. The telecommunications department is completing a detailed - - - - - - - of each factory site to determine the types of equipment and features needed in each area.

    (A) elaboration

    (B) evolution

    (C) evaluation

    (D) expansion

139. Proposed changes that are not - - - - - - - with existing safety regulations will not be considered.

    (A) dependent

    (B) compliant

    (C) relating

    (D) supportive

140. The lectures will cover the relevant methods of - - - - - - - the impact of currency fluctuations on international transactions.

    (A) determination

    (B) determined

    (C) determining

    (D) determine

## FOLLOW-UP EXERCISES

### EXERCISE A: EXPLAINING THE ANSWERS

These are the answers that one student chose for the first fifteen questions:

101. B

102. C

103. D

104. C

105. D

106. C

107. A

108. C

109. A

110. D

111. D

112. B

113. C

114. D

115. B

First, check with the answer key to see which ones are right and which are wrong. Study each one the student got wrong, and think about the following:

- Why would this be the wrong choice to complete the sentence?
- Which is the correct choice?
- Why is it the correct choice? Could you explain to the student why it is correct?

Write notes to answer these questions. Then check your notes with the sample notes given at the end of Day 17.

*To the teacher:* Students could work on Exercise A in pairs, role-playing student and teacher, and changing roles halfway through the exercise. Stress that the "teacher" has to provide a clear explanation for the "student."

### EXERCISE B: LOOKING CAREFULLY AT YOUR OWN ANSWERS

Look at questions 116–140 and put a mark by each one that you answered incorrectly. Look at the sentence and the four choices again and think about these points:

- Why is the answer you chose incorrect?
- Which is the correct choice? Try the question again without looking at the answer key.
- Why is this the correct choice? Could you explain to another student why it is correct?

Write notes for each question, as you did for numbers 100–115. When you have finished, check your notes with the explanations given at the end of Day 17. They explain the correct choice and the three incorrect choices.

*To the teacher:* Have students work on Exercise B individually. You could walk around the class, helping with any questions the students find particularly difficult. This will also help you to see what kind of difficulties the students are having so that you can determine areas for further work.

### EXERCISE C: VOCABULARY REVIEW

#### Part 1: Identifying the Part of Speech

These words have been taken from the sentences and choices in the practice section. The number of the question in which each appears is given in parentheses. Complete the table by putting each word into the correct column according to its part of speech, as used in the question. There should be one word in each space in the table.

caution (114)

accessible (122)

approximately (111)

confirm (127)

foresee (110)

donation (121)

indicates (117)

demonstrate (123)

currently (115)

variety (106)

privately (117)

well (101)

complaints (107)

missing (103)

collaboratively (131)

determined (113)

duration (120)

capable (105)

current (128)

peak (125)

| Verbs | Nouns | Adjectives | Adverbs |
|-------|-------|------------|---------|
|       |       |            |         |
|       |       |            |         |
|       |       |            |         |
|       |       |            |         |
|       |       |            |         |

*To the teacher:* Have students work on Part 1 of Exercise C in pairs. Encourage them to look carefully at each word as it is used in the question to decide what part of speech it is. Afterwards, discuss the fact that some of these words can be used as a different part of speech. Elicit examples of how these words could be used as other parts of speech.

## Part 2: Thinking about Meaning

Now, complete these sentences with the appropriate words from the list above. Think about what part of speech the word in the space should be, as well as its meaning. You will not use all of the words from the table.

1. The - - - - - - - of this journey will be - - - - - - - 3 hours and 45 minutes.

2. Several - - - - - - - have been received about the service in the hotel restaurant.

3. Plans are in progress to ensure that the theater is easily - - - - - - - to wheelchair users.

4. The computer training center - - - - - - - has four hundred trainees on its books, following many different courses.

5. This letter is to - - - - - - - the travel arrangements for your trip to Tokyo on April 14.

6. The refurbishment of the senior citizens' leisure center can now be carried out, thanks to a - - - - - of $10,000 from a local company.

7. These new machines are - - - - - - - of doubling the factory's output.

8. We will dispatch the - - - - - - - components from your order by courier within twenty-four hours.

9. Representatives of the local community are working - - - - - - - with Stavely City Council on the plans for Greenhills Park.

10. Bearing in mind the present economic situation, we do not - - - - - - - that we will be able to offer any permanent contracts to new employees in the near future.

11. The - - - - - - - sales record for new cars is thirty-five in a quarter and is held by Peter Briggs, sales executive at our Portland branch.

12. The steps outside the canteen can be slippery in wet weather, so please proceed with - - - - - - - .

---

## ANSWER KEY FOR DAY 17

---

## Practice Questions

101. C

102. C

103. A

104. C

105. B

106. D

107. A

108. C

109. C

110. C

111. D

112. C

113. B

114. A

115. B

116. D

117. B

118. C

119. C

120. C

121. D

122. A

123. A

124. B

125. C

126. B

127. B

128. C

129. D

130. B

131. A

132. D

133. A

134. B

135. A

136. B

137. D

138. C

139. B

140. C

## Exercise A

### Answers and Explanations

101. (B) is wrong because of the words *right now*, which indicate that the present continuous tense of the verb is needed. (C), *are selling*, is the present continuous form of the verb *to sell*.

102. (C) is correct. When you are making a phone call, you *dial* the number.

103. (D) is incorrect. *Yourself* is a reflexive pronoun, used when the subject and object of the verb are the same person—for example, *You* wash *yourself* every morning. Here, the subject of the verb *inform* is *we*, not *you*. (A) is correct because *you* is used for the indirect object of *inform*.

104. (C) is correct. *Nor* is the negative conjunction used with *neither*.

105. (D) is incorrect. *Reduces* is the third-person singular form of the simple present tense of the verb *to reduce*. It cannot be used after *is capable of*. The gerund form of the verb is needed after the preposition *of*. This is (B), *reducing*.

106. (C) is incorrect. *Vary* is a verb. There is already a verb, *choose,* in the sentence. A noun is needed after the adjective *wide.* (D) is correct because *variety* is a noun.

107. (A) is the correct choice. *Enough* could be used with *not* to describe *legroom,* which is an uncountable noun.

108. (C) is the correct choice. The verb *hold* is part of a set expression. It is the verb commonly used with *party.*

109. (A) is incorrect. *Confusion* is a noun. *Confusion* over how to use the telephone system may exist, but a noun would not be used to describe the noun *employees.* (C), *confused* is correct. It is the past participle of the verb *to confuse,* used to describe the way the employees feel.

110. (D) is incorrect. *Because* would not be used with *improve,* which is the present simple tense of the verb. (C) is the correct choice. The use of the present simple *improve* indicates that this is a conditional sentence. *Unless* is a conjunction used to introduce a condition.

111. (D) is the correct choice because the adverb *approximately* is used with a specific time to mean *roughly.*

112. (B) is incorrect. *Yet* would not be used with the adjective *outstanding,* which here means "have not been submitted." Also, *not* would need to be used with *yet.* The time adverb *still,* which is choice (C), is needed to qualify *outstanding.*

113. (C) is incorrect. A *location,* or place, cannot be *delayed. Delayed* refers to time. (B) is the correct choice. The release date of the film has had to be *postponed,* or made later, because the location has not yet been decided upon. *Determined* means *decided upon.*

114. (D) is incorrect because a noun is needed after *extreme. Cautious* is an adjective. The correct choice is (A) because *caution* is a noun. The adjective *extreme,* which means *great,* describes the noun *caution.*

115. (B) is the correct choice. The phrasal verb *looking for* means *trying to find.*

## Exercise B

### Answers and Explanations

116. (D) In this sentence, *interests* refers to a company's economic or financial involvements in a given area, in this case the geographical area North America. (A) An *inference* is a conclusion based on known facts. (B) An *instance* is a particular example or occurrence of something. (C) An *instinct* is a natural tendency. Neither (A), (B), nor (C) makes sense in this context.

117. (B) This sentence calls for an adverb that can describe the manner in which the advice was given. (A) *Privacy* is a noun. (C) *Private* is an adjective. (D) *Privatize* is a verb.

118. (C) The preposition *to* should follow the phrase *are superior* to make a comparison. (A) *From,* (B) *than,* and (D) *as* cannot combine with *are superior* in this way.

119. (C) The expression *is composed of* is a set phrase that means "to be made up of or to consist of." (A) *Compose* and (D) *to compose* cannot follow *is* to make a complete verb. While (B) *composing* can combine with *is,* it cannot be followed by the preposition *of.*

120. (C) A noun is needed to act as the object of the verb *held*: the actors *held* the audience's *attention.* (A) *Attentive* is an adjective. (B) *Attentively* is an adverb. (D) *Attentiveness* is a noun, but it cannot serve as the object of the verb *hold.*

121. (D) Here, only the adverb *ever* can express the idea that this was the largest gift given *at any time* in the history of the college. (A) *Always* would indicate that the gift was given repeatedly. (B) *Rarely* would indicate that the gift was given not often, but more than once. When used as an adverb, (C) *once* would express the idea that this gift had been given on one previous occasion, which does not make sense in this context.

122. (A) An adjective is needed to modify the proper noun *Savat National Park*, and *accessible* is the only adjective among the choices. (B) *Accessing* can be either a gerund or part of a verb form. (C) *Accessibility* is a noun. (D) *Accesses* is a verb.

123. (A) This sentence requires a verb that can take as its object the word *flair*, which means a creative ability to do something well: Piazzo hopes to *demonstrate his flair*, or show his ability, to blend styles. (B) *Appear* is an intransitive verb and so cannot take an object. Flair is not a physical object, so it does not make sense to (C) *inspect* or (D) *position* it.

124. (B) An adjective is needed to modify the gerund *replacing*, which is the subject of this sentence. (A) *Waste* can be a verb or a noun and (C) *wasting* can be a gerund or part of a verb phrase, but neither word can be an adjective. (D) *Wasted* is most often a verb. (In American English, *wasted* can also be used as a slang adjective meaning "strongly under the effects of drugs or alcohol," but that meaning would not make sense in this context.)

125. (C) Of the choices given, *average* is the only one that can combine with the preposition *on*. The phrase *on average* usually introduces an idea that is a generalization. (A) *Common* and (D) *general* most often combine with *in*, as in the phrases, "a lot in common" and "in general." (B) *Standard* most commonly combines with prepositions in the phrases "up to standard" and "below standard."

126. (B) Only an adverb can be used to modify the adjective *unaware*. Both (A) *complete* and (C) *completed* can either be adjectives or verbs and (D) *completing* can be either a gerund or part of a verb phrase, but none of these three words can be an adverb.

127. (B) It is the preposition *by* that combines with *mail* to create a prepositional phrase meaning "through the use of the postal service." Though they can all serve as prepositions, (A) *near*, (C) *for*, and (D) *on* cannot combine with *mail* to create this meaning.

128. (C) The relative pronoun *that* is required here to introduce the relative clause that acts as the object of *suggests*. (This clause has *demand* as its subject and *will remain* as its verb). While (A) *which* is also a relative pronoun, it would be used to give more information about something already mentioned in the sentence, which is not the case here. Neither (B), *it*, or (D), *both*, is a relative pronoun.

129. (D) The expression *be subject to change without notice* (or *without further notice*) functions as a set phrase. The nouns (A) *signal* and (C) *report* are grammatically countable and thus would require an article or other determiner if being used as the object of a preposition. Although (B) *cash* is an uncountable noun, and so could fit grammatically in the sentence, its meaning does not make sense in this context.

130. (B) The noun *accordance* regularly combines with the prepositions *in* and *with* to create the phrase *in accordance with*. The prepositions (A) *of* and (D) *across* do not combine with *accordance* in this way. While the preposition (C) *in* can precede the noun *accordance*, it cannot follow it.

131. (A) The key phrase here is *works...to ensure that*. The context makes clear that the sentence should express the idea of making certain that something happens. (B) *Define*, (C) *accept*, and (D) *imply* cannot express this idea.

132. (D) Because this sentence makes a comparison among three companies, the superlative form *most impressive* is needed. The adjective (A) *impressive* and the adverb (C) *impressively* cannot be used to make comparisons. The comparative form (B) *more impressive* would be correct if the sentence were comparing only two things.

133. (A) The word *usage* means the ways in which people use something, here a computer word-processing program. Of the choices given, only *involves* expresses an idea that can combine with *usage*. Because *usage* is abstract and non-concrete, it does not make sense to use it with the verbs (B) *receives* or (C) *subscribes*. (D) *Corresponds* could be used with *usage*, but it would have to be followed by the preposition *to*.

134. (B) An adjective is needed to modify the noun *closure*. *Temporary* means "lasting for a limited period of time." The adjective (A) *temporal* has a more general meaning, "of or relating to time," which does not make sense in this context. (C) *Temporarily* is an adverb, and (D) *temporaries* is a plural noun.

135. (A) A coordinating conjunction is needed to express the relationship between these two clauses, either of which could stand on its own as a complete sentence. *Whereas* expresses the idea that both of these sentences are true, though there is a degree of contrast to their meanings. (B) *Otherwise* would create a conditional meaning, (C) *such as* would be used to give an example, and (D) *in order that* would be used to express a purpose. None of these three meanings fits the context of the sentence.

136. (B) Raw foods can be described as *perishable*, meaning that they can spoil in a short period of time. It does not make sense to describe foods as (A) *peripheral*, meaning of secondary importance, as (C) *periodic*, meaning happening repeatedly at a fixed interval, or as (D) *permanent*, meaning continuing unchanged for a long period of time.

137. (D) The word *if* and the verb form *could have been made* in the initial clause indicate that this is a conditional sentence occurring in the past. Thus, the correct verb form following *we* is *would have continued*. Neither the simple present (A) *continue*, nor the simple past (B) *continued*, nor the past perfect (C) *had continued* can be used to express this conditional meaning in the past.

138. (C) Neither (A) an *elaboration* nor (B) *evolution* is something that can be completed. While both (C) *evaluation* and (D) *expansion* can serve as the object of *is completing*, only an *evaluation* would "determine the types of equipment and features needed."

139. (B) Of the four adjectives given as choices, only *compliant* can combine with the preposition *with*. (A) *Dependent* usually combines with *on*, (C) *relating* usually combines with *to*, and (D) *supportive* usually combines with *of*.

140. (C) This sentence requires a word that can be the object of the preposition *of* and can also take the noun *impact* as its object. Only the gerund *determining* can do both of these things. The noun (A) *determination* can be the object of a preposition, but cannot take *impact* as an object. The verbs (B) *determined* and (D) *determine* can take *impact* as an object, but cannot serve as the object of a preposition.

## Exercise C

### Part 1

| Verbs | Nouns | Adjectives | Adverbs |
| --- | --- | --- | --- |
| foresee | caution | accessible | approximately |
| demonstrate | duration | missing | currently |
| confirm | donation | capable | privately |
| indicates | variety | current | collaboratively |
| determined | complaints | peak | well |

### Part 2

1. duration, approximately
2. complaints
3. accessible
4. currently
5. confirm
6. donation
7. capable
8. missing
9. collaboratively
10. foresee
11. current
12. caution

# Day 18

## Tips and Exercises for Part VI: Error Recognition

On Day 15, you began to work on the Reading section of the TOEIC test. Today, you will start to work on the Error Recognition part of this section. This part of the test consists of 20 written sentences. Each sentence contains an error in vocabulary, grammar, or usage. Four words or groups of words are underlined in each sentence. You must choose which of the four underlined words or phrases contains the error.

Here are some important points to remember about the Error Recognition part of the test:

- There are 20 questions in this part.
- You must choose the option that is *incorrect*.
- You have 75 minutes for the entire Reading section. Part VI is not timed, so avoid spending too much time on each question. Instead, come back to a question if you still have time at the end of the test.
- Mark an answer for every question.

## TIP Remember that the words NOT underlined are correct.

On Day 15, you learned that in the Incomplete Sentences, the parts of the sentence that are correct can provide clues about the parts that are being tested. The same is true for sentences in the Error Recognition part of the test. For example, if a verb is underlined, check to see if it agrees with its subject. If a pronoun is underlined, check to see if it agrees with the noun to which it refers.

Consider the following sentences:

**Example 1**

Three colleagues from China, who will be <u>conducting research</u> in this country,
　　　　　　　　　A

<u>needs</u> housing <u>in the downtown area</u>
　**B**　　　　　　　**C**

from June 7 <u>to July 31</u>.
　　　　　　D

The subject of this sentence, *three colleagues*, is plural, so the plural form of the verb is required. Therefore, choice (B) contains the error.

**Example 2**

Because there were only <u>a few applicants</u>
                              A

for the position, it <u>is expected</u> that
                          B

Mr. DaSilva will be able <u>to</u> do all the
                              C

interviewing by <u>itself.</u>
                   **D**

In the parts of this sentence that are not underlined, there is no noun that the pronoun *itself* may refer to. Therefore, choice (D) contains the error.

> *To the teacher:* Before the students try Exercise A, check that they can identify subject and verb or pronoun and its referent in sentences without errors. Follow up the exercise with further work on agreement. Lack of agreement is a common mistake in the writing of non-native speakers. Ask the students to write a paragraph on a particular topic. Ask them to check for agreement errors in their own paragraph, then exchange papers with their neighbor and look for agreement errors in that paragraph. Introduce a symbol to indicate an agreement error in your students' writing. Do not correct their agreement errors—use the symbol and ask them to try to correct the error themselves.

## EXERCISE A: IDENTIFYING AGREEMENT RELATIONSHIPS

Examples 1 and 2 illustrate how different parts of a sentence can be linked together in terms of number and gender. In this exercise, you will practice identifying the parts of a sentence that should agree with one another. In each of the following sentences, an incorrect verb form or pronoun has been underlined. Circle the corresponding subject or referent in each sentence. Then, above the underlined word, write the correct form of the verb or pronoun.

1. The vehicle should be driven at highway speeds for at least 20 minutes to warm <u>him</u> up.

2. Managers know that a small loss sometimes leads to bigger losses and <u>become</u> a problem.

3. The project manager has brought together a team of engineers, and each one <u>have signed</u> a contract, pending approval from the home office.

4. In order for this organization to survive, it must immediately focus <u>their</u> resources on projects with high potential for success.

5. Any company with ten or more employees <u>are</u> required to file a statement of assets before the first of the year.

6. The new director <u>promise</u> to be a very dynamic leader because of his energetic personality.

7. During <u>her</u> many trips to England, Mr. Mueller became interested in the design of formal gardens.

8. Some retailers require a sales receipt for returns, and many <u>charges</u> restocking fees for some merchandise.

## TIP  Check each underlined item to see if it contains an error.

In Exercise 1, each error involved disagreement between different parts of a sentence. Sometimes, though, the error may be contained within one part of the sentence only. You should therefore check to see if the error is within the underlined word or phrase.

Consider the following sentences:

**Example 3**

Because <u>some of our</u> existing clients
              A

<u>will not requiring</u> our services <u>this season,</u>
       **B**                          C

we <u>must increase</u> our marketing efforts.
         D

In this sentence, the auxiliary verb *will* must be followed by the verb form *require, be required, be requiring,* or *have required* to form a grammatical sentence. Therefore, choice (B) contains the error.

**Example 4**

The executive department's plans to move

the offices <u>from downtown</u> to a suburban
                    A

area <u>met with</u> little resistance; <u>indeed</u>, most
        B                              C

employees **<u>look forward to move</u>**.
                    D

In this sentence, the error is in choice (D). *Look forward to* is an expression that is usually followed by a gerund (or noun made from the verb form by adding *–ing*)—*look forward to moving.*

---

## EXERCISE B: UNDERSTANDING VERB FORMS

---

In this exercise, you will practice changing the tense of some verbs. This will help you to understand verb forms. It will also help you to check that different parts of the sentence fit together; for example, if you change a past-tense verb form to the future tense, you will have to check that all parts of the sentence still make sense.

Read each sentence, paying special attention to the verb forms that are underlined. Then rewrite the sentence, changing the underlined verbs according to the instructions at the end of the sentence. Remember, you may also need to change other time references in the sentence.

*To the teacher:* Before the students try the exercise, write a couple of example sentences on the board, one to be changed from past to future, and one from future to past. Point out the time expression and ask them to change that first, and then change the verb tenses accordingly. Then ask them to work on the exercise individually, comparing answers with their neighbor afterwards. If they found the exercise difficult, provide some more sentences to work on, supplying the new time expression to be used. Focussing on the link between the time expression and the verb tense will encourage the students to look for clues in the Error Recognition sentence to check each underlined part for correctness.

1. We <u>had already shipped</u> your order when we <u>received</u> your cancellation letter last week. (change to the FUTURE)

2. After leaving Los Angeles, the flight <u>will make</u> a stop in Honolulu before arriving in Seoul this afternoon. (change to the PAST)

3. By last March, the company <u>had been trying</u> for five years to improve the financial performance of one of its subsidiaries with a complex restructuring plan. (change to the FUTURE)

4. The budget report <u>will be sent</u> to the printer tomorrow in order to be ready for Friday's distribution. (change to the PAST)

5. Nationwide Airlines <u>has teamed up</u> with several four and five star hotels to create unforgettable vacation packages. (change to the FUTURE)

6. When he <u>retires</u> next month, Marco <u>will have worked</u> for the bank for more than 40 years. (change to the PAST)

7. Thank you for providing us with the opportunity to review the project schedule before the implementation plan <u>begins</u> in a month's time. (change to the PAST)

These changes will involve just a few of the verb forms that occur in written English. When you have finished with these, you could try changing the tenses of verbs in sentences from an English language magazine or newspaper. (Don't forget that a change in verb tense might affect other words in the sentence.) The more familiar you are with the different forms of English verbs, the more easily you will be able to recognize errors in those forms.

> ## TIP  Become familiar with phrasal verbs and collocations.

**Example 5**

We <u>recognize</u> that <u>many of you</u> have had to
  A                      B

<u>put up occasional</u> disruptions in the workplace
       C

<u>during</u> our recent renovations.
  D

In this sentence, there is a missing preposition in choice (C). *To put up with* something means to tolerate it. This is an example of a phrasal verb, which is a verb that is combined with one or more prepositions and/or adverbs to form a meaning distinct from its parts. Learning phrasal verbs and using them correctly can improve your English proficiency as well as help you prepare for the Error Recognition section of the test.

Here are some examples of commonly used phrasal verbs and their meanings:

### Phrasal Verbs

get through with ......finish
get into ................enter
get on with ...............continue
get over ...................recover from
look into ...................investigate
look forward to ........anticipate gladly
look over...................examine
put in for ..................request formally
put off......................postpone
put up with................tolerate

Phrasal verbs are most often used in informal communication but can sometimes be used in written communication. Exercises C and D will help you learn to recognize phrasal verbs and use them appropriately.

## EXERCISE C: COMBINING VERBS AND PARTICLES TO MAKE PHRASAL VERBS

In this exercise, you will practice putting verbs together with prepositions and adverbs to create phrasal verbs. You may need to refer to a dictionary to check whether the combination is a possible one. In the two boxes below are verbs and particles (prepositions or adverbs). Choose a verb from the first box and then choose the word or words from the second box that combine with the verb to give it a new meaning. On the lines below, write the phrasal verb, the meaning of the phrasal verb, and then a sentence using the phrasal verb. You may need to use some of the particles more than once.

> *To the teacher:* The students could first work on the exercise individually. Encourage them only to write down verb + particle combinations that they are sure they have come across before, rather than trying to guess at possible combinations. They may not be able to fill all the lines. When they have written down the combinations they know, arrange them in groups of three or four to compare answers. They may then be able to fill more of the lines. Finally, write the verbs up on the board and find out how many phrasal verbs the class found made with each verb. Explain the meanings and provide correct examples.

**Verbs:**

| fall | give | come | get | go |
|------|------|------|-----|-----|
| meet | set | put | pull | break |

**Particles:**

| up | off | with | together | along |
|-----|------|------|----------|-------|
| after | down | apart | into | out |

1. Phrasal Verb: _____

   Meaning: _____

   Example sentence: _____

   _____

2. Phrasal Verb: _____

   Meaning: _____

   Example sentence: _____

   _____

3. Phrasal Verb: _____

   Meaning: _____

   Example sentence: _____

   _____

4. Phrasal Verb: _____

   Meaning: _____

   Example sentence: _____

   _____

5. Phrasal Verb: _____

   Meaning: _____

   Example sentence: _____

   _____

6. Phrasal Verb: _____

   Meaning: _____

   Example sentence: _____

   _____

7. Phrasal Verb: _____

   Meaning: _____

   Example sentence: _____

   _____

8. Phrasal Verb: _____

   Meaning: _____

   Example sentence: _____

   _____

9. Phrasal Verb: _____

   Meaning: _____

   Example sentence: _____

   _____

10. Phrasal Verb: _____

    Meaning: _____

    Example sentence: _____

    _____

## EXERCISE D: UNDERSTANDING DIFFERENCES BETWEEN SIMILAR-LOOKING PHRASAL VERBS

Some verbs can be combined with many different adverbs and prepositions to make phrasal verbs. Verbs like *get*, *look*, and *put* in the chart above are examples of verbs that combine to make several phrasal verbs. Sometimes the difference in meaning between two phrasal verbs that share a common verb is very small. In this exercise, you will complete sentences by selecting the best phrasal verb from several that look very similar. Read each sentence. Then choose the phrasal verb that best completes the sentence.

1.  Mr. Stevens hopes to - - - - - - - the training seminar with a greater understanding of his strengths and weaknesses.

    (A) come away from

    (B) come across

    (C) come out with

2.  The administration has decided to - - - - - - - the teachers' suggestion for a spring fundraiser.

    (A) go through

    (B) go along with

    (C) go under

3.  If Mr. Schmidt can - - - - - - - attending the scheduled four o'clock meeting, he will be free to meet with you on Friday afternoon.

    (A) get along

    (B) get back

    (C) get out of

4.  Obviously, we'll find it easier to stay competitive if we - - - - - - - developments in the market.

    (A) keep out of

    (B) keep up with

    (C) keep away from

5.  Young Sook - - - - - - - his father; he is tall and athletic.

    (A) takes after

    (B) takes over

    (C) takes up

6.  Due to a scheduling conflict, the conference has been - - - - - - - until the end of July.

    (A) put off

    (B) put on

    (C) put back

*To the teacher:* Exercises C and D should raise the students' awareness of phrasal verbs. Encourage them to note down any new phrasal verbs they come across together with their meaning and an example sentence. As a homework exercise, they could cut out a short newspaper article (no more than three paragraphs), underline the phrasal verbs and use a monolingual learners' dictionary to check the meaning and find another example sentence.

---
**ANSWER KEY**
---

## Exercise A

1.  The ⟨vehicle⟩ should be driven at highway speeds for at least 20 minutes to

        it
    warm <u>him</u> up.

2.  Managers know that a small ⟨loss⟩ sometimes leads to bigger losses and

    becomes
    <u>become</u> a problem.

3.  The project manager has brought together a team of engineers, and each ⟨one⟩

    has signed
    <u>have signed</u> a contract, pending approval from the home office.

4.  In order for this ⟨organization⟩ to survive,

            its
    ⟨it⟩ must immediately focus <u>their</u> resources on projects with high potential for success.

5.                         is
    Any ⟨company⟩ with ten or more employees <u>are</u> required to file a statement of assets before the first of the year.

6.              promises
    The new ⟨director⟩ <u>promise</u> to be a very dynamic leader because of his energetic personality.

7.        his
    During <u>her</u> many trips to England, ⟨Mr. Mueller⟩ became interested in the design of formal gardens.

8.  Some ⟨retailers⟩ require a sales receipt for returns,

            charge
    and many <u>charges</u> restocking fees for some merchandise.

## Exercise B

1.  We <u>*will already have shipped*</u> your order when we <u>*receive*</u> your cancellation letter *next* week.

2.  After leaving Los Angeles, the flight *made* a stop in Honolulu before arriving in Seoul *that* afternoon.

3.  By *next* March, the company *will have been trying* for five years to improve the financial performance of one of its subsidiaries with a complex restructuring plan.

4.  The budget report *was sent* to the printer yesterday in order to be ready for Friday's distribution.

5.  Nationwide Airlines *will team up* with several four- and five-star hotels to create unforgettable vacation packages.

6.  When he *retired last* month, Marco *had worked* for the bank for more than 40 years.

7.  Thank you for providing us with the opportunity to review the project schedule before the implementation plan *began a month later*.

## Exercise C

1.  *Phrasal Verb:* fall off

    *Meaning:* decline

    *Example sentence:* Exports have fallen off over the last quarter.

2.  *Phrasal Verb:* give up

    *Meaning:* stop

    *Example sentence:* Mr. Ahmed has recently given up smoking.

3.  *Phrasal Verb:* come along

    *Meaning:* accompany someone

    *Example sentence:* We're going to the movies. Would you like to come along?

4. *Phrasal Verb:* get together

   *Meaning:* meet

   *Example sentence:* Let's get together at four o'clock to discuss this matter further.

5. *Phrasal Verb:* go after

   *Meaning:* try to get

   *Example sentence:* We are going after three big construction contracts this month.

6. *Phrasal Verb:* meet with

   *Meaning:* encounter

   *Example sentence:* The proposal to hold extra classes in the evening met with opposition from parents.

7. *Phrasal Verb:* set out

   *Meaning:* display

   *Example sentence:* The shoes that are on sale are set out on tables outside the store.

8. *Phrasal Verb:* put in

   *Meaning:* to make an application

   *Example sentence:* I have put in for two weeks' vacation in July.

9. *Phrasal Verb:* pull out

   *Meaning:* withdraw

   *Example sentence:* Plans for the merger had to be shelved when one company suddenly pulled out.

10. *Phrasal Verb:* break down

    *Meaning:* fail

    *Example sentence:* Following disagreements over prices, negotiations between the two parties broke down completely.

## Exercise D

1. A
2. B
3. C
4. B
5. A
6. A

# Day 19

## Further Exercises for Part VI: Error Recognition

In today's lesson, you will learn additional strategies to help you select the correct answers in the Error Recognition part of the test. You will also find tips and exercises to increase your knowledge and control of English grammar, which will aid your performance on all parts of the TOEIC test.

## TIP Consider the structure of complex sentences.

Before we look at complex sentences, let's review independent clauses, dependent clauses, and common sentence types.

- An independent clause contains a subject and a verb and can stand alone as a sentence (if it has the right punctuation).

- A dependent clause also contains a subject and a verb, but it cannot stand alone as a sentence. A dependent clause contains a word or phrase like *if, when, because, which,* or *whether* that makes the idea expressed in the clause subordinate—or dependent—on another idea. This subordinate idea <u>depends</u> on the idea expressed in an independent clause.

There are three basic types of sentences:

- A simple sentence is a sentence that contains one independent clause and no dependent clauses.

- A compound sentence contains two or more independent clauses.

- A complex sentence contains one independent clause and one or more dependent clauses

(There is also a compound-complex sentence type, which contains at least two independent clauses and one dependent clause.)

When you are answering questions in the Error Recognition part of the TOEIC test, pay special attention to the structure of complex sentences.

Here are examples of complex sentences:

- *Although* replacement work on gas lines will begin on Monday, employees will not be affected.

- Replacement work on gas lines, *which* will begin on Monday, will not affect employees.

In the first sentence, the independent clause is *Employees will not be affected*. The dependent clause is *Although replacement work on gas lines will begin on Monday*. In the second sentence, the independent clause is *Replacement work on gas lines will not affect employees*. The dependent clause is *Which will begin on Monday*. Notice that the independent clauses are sentences by themselves—they can stand alone—but the dependent clauses are NOT sentences by themselves—they need independent clauses and ideas to make them complete sentences.

Consider the words *although* and *which*, which are used to establish the relationships between the independent and dependent clauses.

Consider the following examples:

**Example 1**

<u>However</u> we normally close the theater doors
   A

<u>after the show</u> begins, latecomers will
     B

<u>be seated</u> during <u>the intermission</u>.
  C          D

In this sentence, the word *however* can connect the two clauses when it is placed at the beginning of the *second* clause after a semi-colon:

We normally close the theater doors after the show begins; *however,* latecomers will be seated during the intermission.

*Although* is a more appropriate word choice to begin this sentence:

*Although* we normally close the theater doors after the show begins, latecomers will be seated during the intermission.

**Example 2**

ABC Textiles <u>realized</u> a profit <u>of approximately</u>
         A          B

DM 95 million last year, <u>**so**</u> makes them
               C

<u>one of</u> the industry leaders in Germany.
  D

In this sentence, the second clause is a dependent clause and should be introduced with the pronoun *which:*

ABC Textiles realized a profit of approximately DM 95 million last year, *which* makes them one of the industry leaders in Germany.

*To the teacher:* Before the students try Exercise A and B, give them further practice in identifying simple and complex sentences using a text they are familiar with. Draw attention to the words used to link the clauses in the complex sentences and ask them to write other complex sentences using these linking words. Each of the exercises should be worked on individually, followed by whole class discussion of the best way of dividing and combining the sentences.

## EXERCISE A: DIVIDING COMPLEX SENTENCES

The following paragraph includes complex sentences. Divide the complex sentences into simple sentences where it is possible to do so.

As you explore the Yangtze on this affordable cruise, enjoy some of China's most beautiful landscapes and ancient towns. Four nights aboard one of our ships, which are equipped with first-class accommodation and leisure facilities, are offered in combination with three nights in comfortable, centrally located hotels in Beijing and Shanghai. If you are part of a group of 20 or more passengers you will be provided with a special escort who will act as both interpreter and guide.

## EXERCISE B: COMBINING SIMPLE SENTENCES

In this exercise, you'll practice building compound and complex sentences from simple ones. The following paragraph includes simple sentences. Combine the simple sentences to form compound and complex sentences where possible.

Prague is a cultural capital of Europe. Prague offers a glimpse of the past. Prague provides a sense of the future. Our tour takes you to popular places. Popular places include the Hradcany Castle area. The Hradcany Castel area is a favorite among tourists. Popular places include Golden Lane. Golden Lane is a collection of tiny fourteenth- and fifteenth-century houses. Kafka lived in Golden Lane. The price of this trip is per person. The price of this trip does not include taxes. The price of this trip includes breakfast daily. The price of this trip includes a round-trip airfare from London. London is a short, 3-hour flight from Prague.

## TIP  Study the sentence for indications of time and space.

Words and phrases in the sentence may indicate the correct verb tenses to be used. Consider the following time expressions:

| | | |
|---|---|---|
| last month | today | tomorrow |
| yesterday | now | in two weeks |
| since Tuesday | always | next July |

These expressions indicate a past, present, or future time frame. When they are used in a sentence, check to see that the appropriate verb tenses are used.

Consider the following sentence:

**Example 3**

The new brochures <u>describing</u> <u>all our</u> services
                                    A            B

were delivered to us <u>late yesterday</u> and
                              C

**<u>were shipped out</u>** early tomorrow morning.
   D

Time expressions in this sentence are the phrases *late yesterday* (past) and *early tomorrow morning* (future). The first part of this sentence refers to the time that the brochures were delivered. In the second part of the sentence, the phrase *tomorrow morning* indicates that the shipping will take place in the *future*.

The brochures *will be shipped out* early tomorrow morning. Therefore, choice (D) contains the error.

Make certain that words that indicate space or location are also used correctly. Consider the following prepositions and adverbs of place:

above
across
away
down
near
opposite
outside
through
toward
underneath

Now, consider the following sentence:

**Example 4**

The <u>fastest way</u> to <u>get to</u> England from France by
      A                B

car is **<u>over the tunnel</u>** linking <u>the two countries</u>.
           C                                  D

In this sentence, the word *tunnel* is a clue to the error. While it is possible to drive *over* a bridge, you would have to drive *through* a tunnel. Therefore, choice (C) contains the error.

*To the teacher:* In Day 18 attention was drawn to time expressions and their link with verb tenses. For further practice, find a text containing a number of time expressions. Type it out again, leaving a space for each verb linked to a time expression. Type the infinitive of the verb in parentheses after each space and ask the students to put the verbs into the correct tenses. Find another text containing prepositions and adverbs of place. Ask the students to identify them. Then ask them to write a paragraph describing their home town using some of the words indicating space or location that you have discussed. To practice prepositions and adverbs used when there is movement, ask them to write a paragraph describing a journey they have made.

## EXERCISE C: SKILL BUILDING

Circle the letter of the *incorrect* sentence in each of the following pairs. The answers appear at the bottom of the page.

1.  A. The airline has slowly <u>built up</u> service to ten European and Asian destinations.

    B. The airline has slowly <u>build up</u> service to ten European and Asian destinations.

2.  A. The new factory <u>will locate</u> south of the town and will employ workers from the entire province.

    B. The new factory <u>will be located</u> south of the town and will employ workers from the entire province.

3.  A. Investors in the fund <u>stand to be made</u> substantial profits.

    B. Investors in the fund <u>stand to make</u> substantial profits.

4.  A. To request vacation time, employees should seek <u>prior</u> approval from their supervisors.

    B. To request vacation time, employees should seek <u>prior to</u> approval from their supervisors.

5.  A. Experience shows that <u>preparation the key</u> to the negotiation of any settlement.

    B. Experience shows that <u>preparation is the key</u> to the negotiation of any settlement.

6.  A. There are <u>much more</u> reasons to analyze this economic theory than have been stated.

    B. There are <u>many more</u> reasons to analyze this economic theory than have been stated.

7.  A. <u>All and every company</u> car must be returned to the central parking lot after use.

    B. <u>Each and every company</u> car must be returned to the central parking lot after use.

8.  A. Wages have never been <u>as high</u> as they are now.

    B. Wages have never been <u>as higher</u> as they are now.

9.  A. Despite a late start, Mrs. Cho was eventually able to <u>achieve competent</u> in the French language.

    B. Despite a late start, Mrs. Cho was eventually able to <u>achieve competence</u> in the French language.

10. A. Advertising agencies sometimes ask customers to <u>pay their bills</u> in advance.

    B. Advertising agencies sometimes ask customers to <u>pay its bills</u> in advance.

*To the teacher:* Exercise C includes a variety of different errors. After the students have worked on it individually, either discuss the errors with the whole class, or, if your class is strong in grammar, ask them to take turns with their neighbor in explaining the errors.

## EXERCISE D: STRUCTURE PRACTICE

The following exercise in controlled writing can help you practice focusing on important structural aspects of written English.

Select an article from a book, magazine, or newspaper. Make sure that it is an article that you can read and understand easily. Rewrite one or two paragraphs (about 100–200 words) of the article according to one of the following instructions. You may have to make other revisions to the passage so that it still makes sense (see Example 5). After you have completed the exercise once, choose another instruction and revise the passage according to that instruction.

1. Divide all complex sentences into smaller, simpler sentences where possible.

2. Combine simple sentences into complex sentences where possible.

3. Find synonyms for adjectives in the text. Make sure the passage still makes sense.

4. Change single subjects to plural subjects where possible. Change other parts of each sentence, such as verb forms and pronouns, to fit the new subject.

5. Change plural subjects to single subjects where possible. Change other parts of each sentence, such as verb forms and pronouns, to fit the new subject.

6. Change any female subjects to male subjects, and change the pronouns as necessary.

7. Change any male subjects to female subjects, and change the pronouns as necessary.

8. Identify prepositions and prepositional phrases of time and location.

The following is a sample passage using Instructions 1 and 5:

### Example 5

Original Text:

**Currently, all work sites within the company have safety rules that every worker is expected to follow. Many of the rules concern special clothes or other safety items that must be worn, the safe way to perform work tasks, and the use of equipment while working.**

1. Divide any complex sentences into smaller, simpler sentences where possible.

Currently, all work sites within the company have safety rules. Every worker is expected to follow these rules. Many of the rules concern special clothes or other safety items. These items must be worn, etc.

5. Where possible, change plural subjects to single subjects.

Currently, one work site in the company has a safety rule that a worker is expected to follow. The rule concerns a special piece of clothing or a safety item that must be worn, etc.

## Answer Key for Day 19

### Exercise A

Possible rewrite:

You will explore the Yangtze on this affordable cruise. Enjoy some of China's most beautiful landscapes and ancient towns. Four nights aboard one of our ships are offered in combination with three nights in comfortable, centrally located hotels in Beijing and Shanghai. The ships are equipped with first-class accommodation and leisure facilities. You are part of a group of 20 or more passengers. You will be provided with a special escort. The escort will act as both interpreter and guide.

### Exercise B

Possible rewrite:

Prague is a cultural capital of Europe that offers a glimpse of the past and a sense of the future. Our tour takes you to popular places including the Hradcany Castle area, a favorite among tourists, and Golden Lane, a collection of tiny fourteenth- and fifteenth-century houses, which is also notable for being the neighborhood where Kafka lived. The price of this trip is per person and does not include taxes. It does include breakfast daily and a round-trip airfare from London, which is a short, 3-hour flight from Prague.

### Exercise C

1. B
2. A
3. A
4. B
5. A
6. A
7. A
8. B
9. A
10. B

# Day 20

## Error Recognition: Practice Questions and Follow-up Exercises

In this lesson, you will have the opportunity to practice Part VI of the test. Before you do this, remind yourself of the tips you learned on Days 18 and 19:

- Remember that the words NOT underlined are correct.
- Check each underlined item to see if it contains an error.
- Become familiar with phrasal verbs.
- Consider the structure of complex sentences.

## PRACTICE QUESTIONS

Now try this practice Part VI, working as if you were taking a real TOEIC test. Before you start, write the numbers 141–160 on a piece of paper to record your answers. First, read the directions and example item, then work straight through the section. Write down when you start and finish the section. It should take you about 10 to 15 minutes. If you are not sure of the correct answer, choose the one you think is closest. Do not leave any questions blank.

## Part VI

*Directions: In Questions 141–160, each sentence has four words or phrases underlined. The four underlined parts of the sentence are marked (A), (B), (C), (D). You are to identify the one underlined word or phrase that should be corrected or rewritten.*

### Example

All <u>employee</u> are required <u>to wear</u> their
    A                            B

<u>identification</u> badges <u>while</u> at work.
  C                     D

*Sample Answer*

● Ⓑ Ⓒ Ⓓ

The underlined word "employee" is not correct in this sentence. This sentence should read, "All employees are required to wear their identification badges while at work." Therefore, you should select choice (A). Now begin work on the questions.

141. <u>Being</u> sure <u>to complete</u> the evaluation form
       A            B

     <u>before</u> you <u>leave</u> the seminar.
       C      D

142. The years I <u>spent</u> working with the children's
             A

     home <u>was</u> the most <u>rewarding</u> of <u>my life</u>.
         B         C      D

143. <u>After</u> checking <u>the features</u> of the X120 computer,
       A          B

     we <u>finally</u> decided to buy <u>the another</u> model.
          C           D

144. <u>Although</u> the reorganization of the storage
       A

     system caused <u>some</u> disruption, <u>at first</u> there
               B         C

     were <u>much</u> benefits.
          D

145. <u>If</u> clients <u>do not</u> know <u>how respond</u> to a
      A      B      C

     questionnaire item, ask them to <u>circle</u> "I
                                 D

     don't know."

146. <u>More and more</u> companies <u>has developed</u> new
        A                 B

     employee <u>compensation</u> packages that offer lower
             C

     fixed <u>salaries</u> and more money in the form of
          D

     commissions and bonuses.

147. When you send a fax <u>from</u> this machine,
                  A

     <u>remember</u> to enter the area code <u>for number</u>
       B                    C

     that you <u>are dialing</u>.
          D

148. Before <u>submitting</u> the draft document to the vice
          A

     president, <u>see that</u> it <u>has been</u> reviewed <u>thorough</u>.
             B     C           D

149. <u>Even</u> we <u>had been</u> behind schedule <u>at</u> one point,
      A     B              C

     the proposal was submitted <u>on time</u>.
                   D

150. The new <u>lounge</u> furniture has arrived <u>and</u> will
          A                B

     be in place by the <u>end next week</u>.
       C         D

151. <u>Effective</u> immediately, Craig Wu <u>will be</u> the new
       A                  B

     branch <u>management of</u> the Mottsboro <u>division</u>.
           C              D

152. Monica <u>moved</u> to the city <u>last</u> year because she
          A         B

     was tired <u>for</u> driving so far to work <u>every morning</u>.
           C             D

153. <u>Perhaps</u> Mr. Rhenquist is not <u>quite</u> as well
       A                B

     qualified for the position <u>as</u> Mr. Robbins <u>does</u>.
                C       D

154. <u>Designing</u> and implementing <u>successful</u>
       A              B

     incentive pay plans <u>are</u> a complex undertaking
               C

     for <u>any</u> business.
        D

155. <u>Shipment</u> of windows ordered on or near the
       A

     fifteenth <u>of the month</u> will be <u>delay</u> due to
            B         C

     staffing <u>shortages</u>.
         D

156. From <u>next year</u>, the London office <u>will be</u>
            A                         B

    responsible <u>of</u> all the European news <u>coverage</u>.
              C                        D

157. Revitalization of the transportation system <u>would</u>
                                                A

    be a major <u>victor</u> for Glenville, which is showing
              B

    signs of recovering <u>following</u> years of <u>economic</u>
                         C                  D

    decline.

158. Ms. Jacobs in Personnel can be relied <u>upon</u> to
                                      A

    provide <u>an excellent</u> advice <u>on how</u> to conduct
              B              C

    interviews with job <u>applicants</u>.
                        D

159. The provincial government is <u>offering</u> Bristol
                              A

    Corporation a $10-million <u>incentive</u> package to
                          B

    build <u>a new</u> office buildings <u>in the center</u> of Selisburg.
              C                  D

160. Clients <u>using</u> travel agency vouchers <u>should stay</u>
            A                               B

    in hotels <u>that accept</u> vouchers and should present
              C

    <u>it</u> on arrival.
    D

The correct answers can be found at the end of Day 20. When you have finished, check your answers. Then try again to answer any questions that you answered incorrectly the first time. How did you do the second time?

## FOLLOW-UP EXERCISES

### EXERCISE A: LOOKING CAREFULLY AT THE QUESTIONS

Below, you will find explanations of the correct choices for the Error Recognition questions. Since the task in Part VI is to identify the underlined word or phrase that is incorrect in the sentence, the explanation describes only why that word or phrase is incorrect. The other three underlined parts are correct. Study the explanations. Then, using what you have learned from them, write out a correct version of each sentence you had difficulty with. You are not required to correct the error when you are taking the actual test, but it is better to have a correct sentence in your mind rather than an incorrect one.

*To the teacher:* Establish which questions your class found most difficult and work on those with the whole class. Write each one on the board and elicit possible explanations of why the incorrect word or phrase is incorrect. Point out any clues in other parts of the sentence. Finally, elicit a correct version of the sentence and write it up. Use the students' performance in the practice questions as an indicator of the areas of grammar on which they need extra work. For homework, ask them to study the explanations for the questions not discussed in class.

## PRACTICE QUESTION EXPLANATIONS

141. (A)  This sentence is in the form of a command, and therefore, the main verb should be in the imperative form: *be* sure to complete.

142. (B)  The main verb of the sentence must be the plural form *were* in order to agree with its plural subject, *years*. The relative clause in this sentence, which has *I* as its subject and *spent* as its verb, does not affect this relationship.

143. (D) The determiner *another* is a combination of the article *an* and the adjective *other*. Because it contains an article, *another* can never be used with another article such as *the*.

144. (D) The adverb *much* can only be used to modify words that are grammatically non-countable, while *many* is used in similar situations to modify plural words. (For example, we say *much money* but *many dollars*.) Because the word *benefits* is plural, it must be modified by *many*, not *much*.

145. (C) In this sentence, the words *know how to* work together as a single unit, and so the word *to* must be inserted between *how* and *respond*.

146. (B) The plural subject of this sentence, *companies*, requires a plural verb: companies *have* developed new compensation packages.

147. (C) The singular noun *number* should be preceded by an article. Here, because there is a specific number to be dialed, the definite article *the* should be inserted: *for the number*.

148. (D) The adverb *thoroughly* is called for here to modify the verb *reviewed*. *Thorough* is an adjective.

149. (A) The conjunction *even though* should be used to introduce a subordinate clause that contrasts with the idea in the main clause. Here, the proposal was submitted on time in spite of some earlier difficulties.

150. (D) The preposition *of* is needed to complete the phrase *the end of next week*.

151. (C) A noun is needed to name Craig Wu's new position. The non-count noun *management* refers to a group of people. The singular noun *manager*, which refers to one person, should be used here.

152. (C) The adjective *tired* does not combine with the preposition *for*. Two possible substitutions would be *tired of*, meaning that she no longer enjoyed the drive, or *tired from*, meaning that the drive made her physically tired.

153. (D) To maintain the parallel structure, the same linking verb, *is*, must be used in the first and the second parts of the sentence: Mr. Rehnquist *is* not as qualified as Mr. Robbins *is* (qualified).

154. (C) The conjunction *and* joins the verbs *designing* and *implementing* to create a single compound subject, which the sentence describes as *a complex undertaking*. This singular subject requires a singular verb form, *is*.

155. (C) This sentence requires the past participle of the verb *delay* to complete the passive verb form: Shipment *will be delayed*.

156. (C) Someone or something can be responsible *for* a particular task, meaning that it is that person's job to complete the task. The preposition *of* cannot combine with the adjective *responsible*.

157. (B) The adjective *major* modifies a noun. The word *victor*, meaning a person who is successful, is a noun, but it is not appropriate here, where the success of an event is being described. The noun *victory* should be used here.

158. (B) *Advice* is a non-count noun, so it cannot be preceded by an indefinite article: Ms. Jacobs provides excellent advice.

159. (C) The plural noun *buildings* should not be preceded by the singular indefinite article *a*. The plural indefinite determiner *some* could be used here: *some new office buildings*.

160. (D) The object pronoun *it* refers to the noun phrase *travel agency vouchers* and should agree with it in number. The plural object pronoun *them* would be correct here.

## Exercise B: Thinking about Complex Sentences

On Day 19, you learned about complex sentences. You practiced making a complex sentence into two or more simple sentences and combining simple sentences to make a complex sentence. You also learned about words such as *however* and *although* (connectors), which are used to show the relationships between the clauses in a complex sentence.

A number of the sentences in the practice Error Recognition questions that you tried today are complex sentences. Below are the first parts of some of these sentences. Without looking back at the practice questions, write two different endings for each sentence. Don't try to reproduce the original sentence. Then circle the connector in each one.

> *To the teacher:* Working on the exercise in pairs will help the students to think of two different endings for each sentence. When they have finished, write the original sentences on the board so that you can discuss the grammar of the original ending with the class. At the end of the lesson, ask the students to hand in their sentences so that you can check them for grammatical accuracy.

1.
A. When you send a fax from this machine, _____.

B. When you send a fax from this machine, _____.

2.
A. Although the reorganization of the storage system caused some disruption, _____.

B. Although the reorganization of the storage system caused some disruption, _____.

3.
A. Ms. Jacobs in Personnel can be relied upon to provide excellent advice on how _____.

B. Ms. Jacobs in Personnel can be relied upon to provide excellent advice on how _____.

4.
A. Monica moved to the city last year because _____.

B. Monica moved to the city last year because _____.

5.
A. Although we had been behind schedule at one time, _____.

B. Although we had been behind schedule at one time, _____.

6.
A. Before submitting the draft document to the vice president, _____.

B. Before submitting the draft document to the vice president, _____.

7.
A. If clients do not know how to respond to a questionnaire item, _____.

B. If clients do not know how to respond to a questionnaire item, _____.

When you have finished, compare your sentences with the original sentence. Are they similar in grammatical structure?

## EXERCISE C

On Day 18, you practiced identifying agreement relationships in sentences. In this exercise, you will practice identifying the subject of the verb and checking whether the verb is in agreement with the subject.

The following sentences are taken from the practice Error Recognition questions in this chapter. In each sentence, a verb has been highlighted. First circle the subject of the highlighted verb, then check "Yes" if the verb agrees with the subject, and "No" if it does not. Note that errors used in this exercise are not necessarily the same as the errors in the practice questions.

1. The years I spent working with the children's home <u>was </u>the most rewarding of my life.

&#10063; Yes   &#10063; No

2. If clients <u>do not know</u> how to respond to a questionnaire item, ask them to circle "I don't know."

&#10063; Yes   &#10063; No

3. More and more companies <u>has developed </u>new employee compensation packages that offer lower fixed salaries and more money in the form of commissions and bonuses.

&#10063; Yes   &#10063; No

4. The new lounge furniture <u>have arrived </u>and will be in place by the end of next week.

&#10063; Yes   &#10063; No

5. Revitalization of the transportation system would be a major victory for Glenville, which <u>is showing</u> signs of recovering following years of economic decline.

&#10063; Yes   &#10063; No

6. Clients using travel agency vouchers should stay in hotels that <u>accept</u> vouchers and should present them on arrival.

&#10063; Yes   &#10063; No

## EXERCISE D

On Day 18, you learned that you should check each underlined item in a sentence in the Error Recognition part of the test to see if it contains an error. In the letter that follows, a word or phrase has been underlined in each sentence. Check each underlined part, decide whether it contains an error, and, if so, how you would correct that error.

> *To the teacher:* As well as deciding which underlined parts contain an error, the students should be prepared to support their decisions. Further exercises of this type can be made using other formal business documents.

# Kendar Office Supplies  *Kemapriatarum Road, Bangkok 10110, Thailand*

Ms. Pranee Udomsak
Director
Beni & Beni, Inc.
426 Silom Road
Bangkok 10110
Thailand

Dear Ms. Udomsak:

In checking our records, I noticed that you are no longer listed as <u>a current customer</u> ₁ of Kendar Office Supplies. When I called and spoke to your office manager, Peri Davis, I was informed that your company is now using one of our competitors for <u>their</u> ₂ office needs. Ms. Davis referred me to you <u>as individual</u> ₃ who makes all purchasing decisions at Beni & Beni.

Ms. Davis <u>kindly described</u> ₄ some of the problems that led you to select another supplier. I'm pleased to tell you that Kendar has made many improvements to its product line and services, and we are certain Beni & Beni will find <u>these attractive</u> ₅. We have introduced a whole new line of office and computer supplies, many of which <u>they are not</u> ₆ available from any other supplier. In addition, Kendar now has <u>the largest</u> ₇ warehouse facility in the region.

<u>For you need</u> ₈ any additional information please feel free to contact me. We <u>are welcome</u> ₉ the opportunity to serve your company once again.

Sincerely,

*Manee Chamchoy*

Manee Chamchoy

---

## ANSWER KEY FOR DAY 20

### Practice Questions

141. A

142. B

143. D

144. D

145. C

146. B

147. C

148. D

149. A

150. D

151. C

152. C

153. D

154. C

155. C

156. C

157. B

158. B

159. C

160. D

### Exercise B

The connectors in each sentence are

1. when

2. although

3. how

4. because

5. although

6. before

7. if

### Exercise C

| Subject | Subject-Verb Agreement? |
|---------|------------------------|
| 1. years | No |
| 2. clients | Yes |
| 3. companies | No |
| 4. furniture | No |
| 5. Glenville | Yes |
| 6. hotels | Yes |

### Exercise D

1. no error

2. incorrect pronoun: *your* should be used

3. definite article is missing: the underlined part should read *as the individual*

4. no error

5. no error

6. the pronoun *they* is not needed

7. no error

8. the connector *if* should be used in place of *for*

9. the verb *are* is not needed

# Day 21

## Tips and Exercises for Part VII: Reading Comprehension

In today's lesson, you will begin to work with the Reading Comprehension part of the TOEIC test.

The Reading Comprehension part consists of a number of reading passages, each followed by a set of between two and five questions. There are 40 questions in all. The passages vary in format and represent the kinds of materials that are found in travel, leisure, and workplace situations.

Questions in this part of the test will ask you to do the following:

- identify the main idea of a text or the purpose for which it was written

- look for details, sometimes in different words from those in the text itself

- make inferences about the text

Here are some suggestions and exercises to improve your ability to select the best answer in this part of the test.

### TIP Allow enough time to read and reread the passages.

This part of the test will take longer than the two previous reading parts. You may need to spend more than half of the 75 minutes on the reading passages. On Day 23 and Day 29, you will have the opportunity to try a practice test for Part VII (Reading Comprehension). This will give you an idea of how much time you need to allow for this part.

### TIP Become familiar with the layout of texts used in the workplace.

When you become familiar with text layout, or the way a text appears on the page, you will often be able to make predictions about the content of the text. Familiarity with the layout may help you locate some of the most important information in the text.

For example, you may be asked to identify the recipient of a letter (that is, the person who will receive a letter) or the name or title of the writer. Usually, the name of the sender or writer is at the bottom of the page in a business letter, while the recipient's name and title are found at the top. In an office memorandum, however, the names of both sender and receiver are at the top of the page, under the date. Knowing this can help you locate the required information quickly.

## Example 1

Questions 161–162 refer to the following memorandum.

---

**Date:** July 31

**To:** Marketing Division

**From:** Stephen Schneider, Director—Planning & Research

**Re:** *The Market Monthly* Newsletter

Attached is a copy of *The Market Monthly,* a newsletter published by the Marketing Division, designed to keep you updated on competitors, trends, and events that impact the markets of interest to this company. If there are individuals in your area who do not receive the newsletter and should be added to the distribution list, please contact the *Monthly's* managing editor, Maria Lopez, at ext. 240.

I would appreciate receiving any comments or suggestions you have regarding *The Market Monthly.* Please feel free to contact me at ext. 167.

---

161. Whom should readers contact with suggestions?

(A) The company director

(B) The marketing manager

(C) **Mr. Schneider**

(D) Ms. Lopez

At the bottom of the memo, the writer invites suggestions. If you are familiar with office memos, you will know that the writer's name is usually at the top of the memo, following the word *From.* Readers should contact Mr. Schneider, choice (C).

Here are some common types of written business communication:

- advertisements
- business letters
- charts
- coupons
- e-mails
- evaluations
- faxes or facsimiles
- graphs
- informal notes
- invitations
- itineraries
- memos or memoranda
- notices
- schedules
- tables
- telephone messages
- tickets
- vouchers

Familiarize yourself with the kinds of reading texts found in many areas of daily life, including leisure, travel, and the workplace. Reading passages in the TOEIC test are based on authentic examples of written English from a variety of settings.

*To the teacher:* Use the list above to help you gather examples of written business communication. Familiarize the students with the names of the various types. As a homework assignment, ask them to work in groups of three to gather one example of each type of written communication. Give them time in class to mount their examples on paper and label them according to the type of communication each one represents. If possible, hang them on the wall and give the students time to look at and discuss each others' collections.

## EXERCISE A: THINKING ABOUT THE LAYOUT OF THE TEXT

Below you will see two texts: a job advertisement and a telephone message. Read the two texts to get a general idea of what they are about. Then study the layout of the texts and answer the questions about their layout. Finally, use the information about the layout to help you answer the comprehension questions.

### Text 1

Questions 1–3 refer to the following job advertisement.

---

**CHIEF INFORMATION OFFICER**

We are one of the fastest-growing major health-care facilities in the country, with an immediate need for a Chief Information Officer. Our CIO is responsible for all information-systems activities, including systems analysis, management reporting, and computer functions. This person sets information-systems policies, procedures, and technical standards and acts as a liaison between Information Services and other management departments. The ideal candidate has an advanced degree and 7 years' experience in health-care information systems, including at least 4 years of supervisory experience. Programming experience is not necessary, but experience with systems conversions is beneficial. We offer a competitive salary and excellent benefits, along with the opportunity to work in a dynamic, growing organization. Please send résumé with cover letter and salary history to:

University Medical Center
P.O. Box 1234
Dubai, UAE
ATTN: Human Resources

Phone, fax, and e-mail applications will not be processed.

---

### Questions about layout

1. Where is the title of the position usually indicated in a job advertisement?

2. Where in the advertisement would you expect to find details about how to apply for the job?

3. Where would you expect to find general information about the company or organization that is advertising the post?

### Comprehension questions

1. Who placed the advertisement?
   (A) A secretarial school
   (B) The Dubai chief information officer
   (C) A computer company
   (D) A hospital

2. What must an applicant submit?
   (A) An employment history
   (B) An application fee
   (C) Personal references
   (D) Medical records

3. How should an application be submitted?
   (A) In person
   (B) By fax
   (C) By mail
   (D) By e-mail

## Text 2

Questions 4–5 refer to the following message.

| | |
|---|---|
| **Message for:** | *Mr. Ibrahim* |
| **From:** | *Michel LeBlanc* |
| **Taken by:** | *Henri* |
| **Time:** | *2:15 p.m., Thurs.* |

**Message:**

*Michel LeBlanc at Batir Construction called. Has finished updating the contract but can't meet you on Friday at 3. Wanted to know when he can reach you to reschedule. Will be at home this evening, but will try to contact you before then. If he doesn't get in touch with you, call him after 8 p.m. at home at 24-55-5123.*

### Questions about layout

1.  What details are usually given in the top part of a telephone message?

2.  Where would you expect to find information about why the caller telephoned?

### Comprehension questions

4.  Why did Mr. LeBlanc call Mr. Ibrahim?
    (A) To reschedule a meeting
    (B) To ask for some building work to be done
    (C) To find out when a meeting will end
    (D) To request a work order

5.  What is Mr. LeBlanc going to do?
    (A) Meet Mr. Ibrahim on Friday
    (B) Revise the contract
    (C) Go out for the evening
    (D) Telephone again this afternoon

*To the teacher:* Example 1 and Exercise A have introduced three types of written business communication: memoranda, job advertisements, and telephone messages. From the materials you have collected, select some other types and devise some simple questions about the layout of the texts to help the students locate information. If possible, copy the texts onto overhead transparencies for ease of presentation.

## TIP Read the sentence that introduces the text.

The introduction to the text will often tell you important information about the kind of text you are about to read.

### Example 2

Questions 163–164 refer to the following instructions.

Our FAX machine is easy to use.

First, place the document on the feeder tray, face down.

Next, enter the recipient's fax number.

Finally, press the start button.

Looking at the introduction to the text will often help you find the information you are looking for. In the introduction to Example 2, the word *instructions* tells you that you will read a series of steps or directions. If you want to identify a particular step in the instructions, for example, you can assume that those steps will be written in the order in which they will be carried out.

## EXERCISE B

Below are the first parts of some reading comprehension texts and several sentences introducing texts. Write the number of each text before the appropriate sentence below.

_____ refers to the following coupon.

_____ refers to the following letter.

_____ refers to the following advertisement.

_____ refers to the following e-mail message.

_____ refers to the following order form.

_____ refers to the following article.

### Text 1

> # Mach Motors Company, Inc.
>
> Fredriksdalsgatan 100 412 GS Göteborg, Sweden
>
> Dear Customer:
>
> The satisfaction and safety of all our customers are of prime concern to us. We are therefore contacting all owners of this year's Meteor to alert them to improvements in the design of one of the car's features. You may have noticed that the rear . . .

### Text 2

| | |
|---|---|
| To: | Robert O'Neill, <oneill@shannon.com.ie> |
| From: | Georges Bemanajara, <beman@les.dts.mg> |
| Subject: | Europe Trip |
| Date: | Tues, 07 Sept 11:53:05 |

> Just want to leave my phone number in the Netherlands with you: 23-319501. I'll be in Amsterdam until the 15<sup>th</sup> but want to keep in touch. I plan to be in London the…

### Text 3

Name: _____

Address: _____

_____Zip code:_____

Please send me _____ copies of PREDICTING ECONOMIC CHANGE at $20.99

each plus $2.50 per book postage and packing. I enclose a check for $ _____ made payable to Cooper and Wallace Publishing.

### Text 4

**WHITE TENT CIRCUS**

**HAMMERTON**

**Sunnyvale Park**

**Mon 11<sup>th</sup> to Sun 24<sup>th</sup> May**

Weekdays: 4.30pm and 7.30pm
Saturdays: 3.00 pm and 6.00pm
Sundays: 2.00pm and 5.00pm
**HALF
PRICE
COUPON
ANY SEAT, ANY DAY
(VALID AT TIME OF TICKET PURCHASE ONLY)**

Adults:  £10 rear circle   £12 side circle
         £15 front circle   £20 ringside

**Children: …**

**Text 5**

### Now Clothing to close stores

High street clothing store Now Clothing is expected to close hundreds of outlets after almost two years of falling sales. The US retailer, which trades in Britain, Italy and Spain, is likely to reveal a sharp fall in its third-quarter profits today. The results are expected to be accompanied by an announcement that it is closing…

**Text 6**

### HOLBERRY COUNTRY HOUSE HOTEL

- 20 elegant bedrooms, some with four-poster beds

- Extensive breakfast and dinner menu

- 5 minutes to shops, restaurants, and lake

- Free use of nearby luxury leisure facilities

- Special weekend rates

*To the teacher:* The students should be familiar by now with the names of the various types of business communication. This exercise could be used with the students working in small groups. Copy the six texts and the introductory sentences so that each group can have a set of texts and sentences. Cut them up so that each text and each sentence is on a separate piece of paper. Then ask the students to work on the matching exercise in their groups. A further matching exercise could be made using the materials you collected earlier.

## TIP  Relate what you read to what you already know.

When you read the passage, use what you already know to help you make sense of the material. As you read, form ideas about the text. Find evidence in the text to support your ideas as they develop, or use the evidence to change your first thoughts.

**Example 3**

| Billing Date: January 2 | Policy: Automobile | Policy #: A34 9256681 |
|---|---|---|
| Due Date: January 25 | Minimum Due: $58.28 | In full: $524.52 |

Original premium: $582.80
Last payment: $58.28 CR

This bill offers you a choice of convenient payment plans to meet your individual needs. You may pay "in full" and avoid incurring a finance charge. Or you may pay the "minimum due" now and the balance in future monthly payments. A periodic rate of 4% per month will be applied to the outstanding balance.

Consider this example of how a reader might think about the above text:

"This must be a bill, because it says *billing dat*e. A *policy* often refers to insurance of some kind. This must be an insurance bill. Automobile? Yes, that's a kind of insurance in many countries. And *premium* is used with insurance bills; this must be a bill for car insurance."

"I wonder what *CR* stands for. It says *last payment*, so it must be money already paid. Maybe it stands for 'credit.' Why do they offer a payment plan if payment has already been made? I guess the last payment must have been for the previous year."

*To the teacher:* Encourage your students to make use of all the information in the text to help them fully understand it. Find other texts where meaning of words or phrases might be deduced from the context. Type them onto overhead transparencies, underline the words and phrases you think might be new, and demonstrate how the meaning could be deduced. Ask the students to think about whether they have come across similar documents before and to make comparisons with other documents.

# ANSWER KEY FOR DAY 21

## Exercise A

### Text 1

#### Questions about layout

1. The heading of an advertisement usually gives the title of the job.

2. Details about how to apply for the job are usually given at the end of an advertisement.

3. Information about the company or organization that is advertising the post is likely to be given in the first paragraph, or at the beginning, of an advertisement.

#### Comprehension questions

1. D

2. A

3. C

### Text 2

#### Questions about layout

1. In the top part of a telephone message, the following details are usually given: who the message is for, who telephoned, who wrote down the message, and when the message was taken.

2. Information about why the caller telephoned is likely to be found under the message heading.

#### Comprehension questions

4. A

5. D

## Exercise B

Text 1: refers to the letter.

Text 2: refers to the e-mail message.

Text 3: refers to the order form.

Text 4: refers to the coupon.

Text 5: refers to the article.

Text 6: refers to the advertisement.

# Day 22

## Further Exercises for Part VII: Reading Comprehension

In today's lesson, you will learn further strategies to help you make the correct choice in Part VII of the test.

**TIP  Skim the entire passage quickly once to get an idea of what the passage is about.**

Skimming, or quickly reading the text, can give you an idea of what the passage is about. Pick out key words and phrases that you are familiar with, and do not focus on unknown words. This strategy can help prepare you to answer questions about a main idea.

Consider the following example. Read the passage on this page. Selected words have been shaded to demonstrate that you need to read only certain parts of the passage to get the main idea. Then, cover the passage at the top of the next page and read question 165 and try to answer it.

### Example 1

Questions 165–167 refer to the following article.

Economic Slump Blamed on Bad Weather

downturn       economy
attributed       last year's typhoon.
destruction

much smaller production figures

affected overall
consumer sales.
next year

rebuild facilities.

**Economic Slump Blamed on Bad Weather**

The recent downturn in the economy has been attributed to last year's typhoon. The destruction of several key electronics manufacturing plants on the eastern side of the nation has led to much smaller production figures in that key industry. The resulting demand has driven prices up and affected overall consumer sales. Industry experts predict a sharp rebound next year as many industries take advantage of the opportunity to update and rebuild facilities. Damage to residential areas was also significant, and housing reconstruction has been strong throughout the last year.

165. What is the main idea of the article?

(A) A major storm is approaching the area.

(B) New manufacturing plants have been constructed.

(C) A large company is going out of business.

(D) A major storm has affected businesses.

The correct answer is (D). If you read only the words or phrases *economic slump, blamed, downturn, typhoon, destruction,* and *affected overall consumer sales,* you can see that a storm, or a typhoon, has affected businesses.

*To the teacher:* Make sure the students try to answer the question using only the ideas acquired from the key words and phrases. Demonstrate how these indicate the main idea of the article. Then give them an opportunity to read the whole article, but avoid focussing on unknown words. Draw attention to the title, which can give information about the main idea.

## EXERCISE A: SKIMMING THE PASSAGE FOR KEY WORDS AND PHRASES

In this exercise, there are two passages in which some of the less important words have been shaded and the key words have been left unshaded. Read each passage once and then decide whether the statements beneath it are true. The complete passages and answers are given at the end of Day 22.

*To the teacher:* The statements should only be studied after reading the whole passage through once to get the main ideas. Make sure that the students also consider the layout of Text 1 and the title of Text 2 before attempting the true/false statements.

### Text 1

Ms. Rose Kemper
Kemper Garments Ltd.
Edgeware
Middlesex HA8 9XG
ENGLAND

Paul Timmerman
Het Overloon 1
Postbut 6500
NL-6401 JH Heerlen
The Netherlands

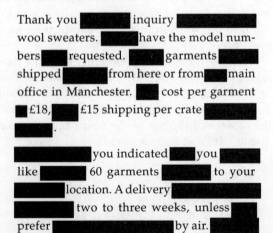

Dear Mr. Timmerman:

Thank you ▓▓▓ inquiry ▓▓▓▓▓ wool sweaters. ▓▓▓ have the model numbers ▓▓ requested. ▓▓▓ garments ▓▓▓ shipped ▓▓▓ from here or from ▓▓ main office in Manchester. ▓▓ cost per garment ▓ £18, ▓▓ £15 shipping per crate ▓▓▓ ▓▓ .

▓▓▓▓▓ you indicated ▓▓ you ▓▓▓ like ▓▓▓ 60 garments ▓▓▓ to your ▓▓▓▓ location. A delivery ▓▓▓▓▓ ▓▓▓▓ two to three weeks, unless ▓ prefer ▓▓▓▓▓ by air.

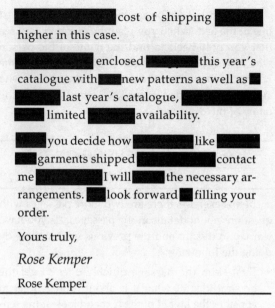

███████████ cost of shipping ██████ higher in this case.

████████████ enclosed ████████ this year's catalogue with ███ new patterns as well as ██ ██████ last year's catalogue, ███████ ██████ limited ███████ availability.

██████ you decide how ██████████ like ████ garments shipped ████████████ contact me ███████████ I will ███████ the necessary arrangements. ███ look forward ███ filling your order.

Yours truly,

*Rose Kemper*

Rose Kemper

1. Rose Kemper works in the garment industry. Yes No

2. Rose Kemper is requesting a shipment. Yes No

3. Paul Timmerman lives in England. Yes No

4. The requested garments are available. Yes No

5. Kemper Ltd. has two locations. Yes No

6. Paul Timmerman has indicated how the goods should be shipped. Yes No

7. Two catalogues are enclosed with the letter. Yes No

**Text 2**

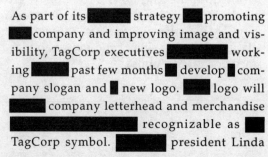

**Slogan Effort Underway at TagCorp**

As part of its ██████ strategy ███ promoting ████ company and improving image and visibility, TagCorp executives ██████████ working ██████ past few months ██ develop ██ company slogan and ██ new logo. ██████ logo will ██████ company letterhead and merchandise ████████████████ recognizable as ██ TagCorp symbol. ████████ president Linda

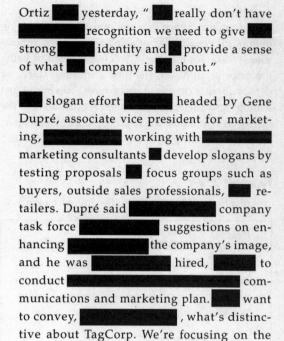

Ortiz ████ yesterday, " ███ really don't have ████████████ recognition we need to give ██ strong ████ identity and █ provide a sense of what ███ company is ██ about."

████ slogan effort ███████ headed by Gene Dupré, associate vice president for marketing, ████████████ working with ████████████ marketing consultants ██ develop slogans by testing proposals ██ focus groups such as buyers, outside sales professionals, ███ retailers. Dupré said ████████████ company task force ████████ suggestions on enhancing ██████████ the company's image, and he was ██████████ hired, ███████ to conduct ████████████████ communications and marketing plan. ███ want to convey, ████████████ , what's distinctive about TagCorp. We're focusing on the excellent value we offer ████████ breadth of products ███ develop here."

1. The company has worked on this project for several years. Yes No

2. The company is trying to increase product recognition. Yes No

3. Linda Ortiz was hired to lead the project. Yes No

4. Proposals have been tested on outside professionals. Yes No

5. TagCorp produces many different products. Yes No

**TIP  Read the questions before you read the text again.**

It is a good idea to read the questions before you reread the text. When you read a real advertisement, memo, or agenda, for example, you usually have some reason for reading it. You might want to know the price of an object, the time a meeting starts, or details about a change in procedures. You might just want to find a telephone number. A quick look at the questions that follow the reading passage in this part of the test can help you determine what you should be reading for.

**Example 2**

Questions 168–169 refer to the following card.

---

Welcome, **Ms. Martelli**                                      ,

to the Star Plaza Hotel. We hope you have a pleasant stay. Please present this card when enjoying our restaurant, coffee shop, and sporting facilities and when signing charges to your room account.

Check Out Date: **10th December**

Room No.  **635**                        **P. Angelo**
                                          *Desk Clerk*

---

168. When did the guest receive the card?

   **(A) When checking into the hotel**

   (B) When ordering a meal at the restaurant

   (C) When paying the bill

   (D) When making a room reservation

169. Who issued this card to the guest?

   (A) Ms. Martelli

   **(B) P. Angelo**

   (C) The restaurant cashier

   (D) The accounts manager

Question 168 can be answered by reading the first line of the text. The word *welcome* indicates that the guest has just arrived. The next line, *We hope you have a pleasant stay,* confirms this. It is not necessary to keep reading to know that choice (A) is the answer.

Question 169 can be answered by reading the last line of the text. When you read the question, you see that you only need to find the name of the person who *issued this card.* You can then go straight to the bottom of the text, to the name of the *desk clerk* who signed, or issued, the card. Choice (B) gives the name of the desk clerk.

---

## EXERCISE B: FOCUSING ON THE QUESTIONS

---

In this exercise, there are two more passages with questions about details in the passages. As you have learned in this tip and the previous tip, try these by doing the following:

- First skim the passage quickly once to get the general idea of what it is about (don't forget to consider the layout of the text and look at the sentence that introduces the text).

- Next read the questions and make sure you understand them.

- Then read the passage again, looking for the information that you need to make the correct choice.

- Read the choices carefully and decide which one provides the best answer to the question, based on what you have read in the passage.

*To the teacher:* Observe your students as they are working on the two texts to make sure they are following the procedure outlined above. Stress that they should be sure to read all the options carefully. After the students have worked on the questions individually, give them time to discuss the answers with a neighbor. Then go through the questions with the class, discussing where the information for each one can be found.

**Text 1**

Questions 161–162 refer to the following notice.

On June 7, the company will hold its first world-wide videoconference. All twenty facilities will be linked by a satellite broadcasting system so that employees can see and speak with each other. Officials of the Zurich head office will begin the conference by telling us about their goals for the next ten years. Next, each facility manager will speak about current challenges. The last hour will be devoted to questions from the floor at all locations. Due to time differences, employees in Asia and South America will have to come to their broadcast facilities outside of regular business hours. Additional pay will be provided for them for this inconvenience. If this format proves productive, we hope to schedule worldwide and regional videoconferences periodically.

161. What will be the first agenda item at the conference?

(A) Plans for a decade
(B) Twenty-year goals
(C) Present challenges
(D) Questions from employees

162. Why will some employees receive extra pay?

(A) They must speak at the conference.
(B) The conference will take place before or after work.
(C) They must travel to other offices to attend.
(D) Their departments have met certain goals.

Questions 163–164 refer to the following newspaper article.

WASHINGTON—A government study released yesterday said that businesses should implement widespread commercial use of encryption, mathematical formulas to scramble electronic data, to curb the theft of computer data, wireless communications, and other electronic information. A committee of the government research council, which gives science and technology advice, said a broad use of encryption would help industries in many ways, including by making banking and telecommunications networks more secure and by giving people greater privacy. The committee also recommended that export controls on encryption technologies be progressively relaxed but not eliminated.

163. What does the study suggest businesses do?

(A) Curb electronic information sharing
(B) Use special technology to scramble electronic data
(C) Progressively relax government export controls
(D) Invest in government research

164. According to the article, how will the committee's recommendations benefit businesses?

(A) Science and technology advice will be available.
(B) Computer data will be processed more quickly.
(C) Government resources will be shared.
(D) Telecommunications networks will be more secure.

**TIP When you want to identify the main idea, read the title and the first sentence of each paragraph.**

Key points are often contained in specific areas of a text. Reading the first sentence of each paragraph can help you to get the general idea of a passage that has several paragraphs. In shortened texts, such as advertisements or announcements, reading the first words or phrases in each part of the text can help you answer questions about the text.

## Example 3

Questions 170–173 refer to the following advertisement.

---

**SEARCHING FOR AN APARTMENT?**

*Apartments Fast, Inc.,* makes it quick and simple!

We offer up-to-date availability on the type of rental you are searching for:

- Apartments, Studios, Duplexes, Corporate Suites
- All Price Ranges
- Short- and Long-Term Leases
- Furnished or Unfurnished

**Specializing in Corporate Apartments**

We specialize in completely furnished apartments with all the necessities and comforts of home. Whether you wish to entertain clients in a corporate apartment or secure temporary housing, we will make all the necessary arrangements.

Our service is tailored to your needs while working within your budget. You'll find that our prices are much less than what you would pay at a regular or extended-stay hotel. And we have a wide variety of apartments conveniently located throughout the city for you to choose from.

**CALL NOW: 123-4321**

For your free apartment search

---

170. What service does Apartments Fast, Inc., offer?

(A) Cleaning people's homes and apartments

**(B) Helping people to find places to rent**

(C) Buying and selling apartments and homes

(D) Moving furniture and appliances for people

To answer question 170, you need to understand the purpose of the advertisement. If you read the first sentences in each block of writing, you will read

*We offer up-to-date availability on the type of rental you are searching for…,*

*We specialize in completely furnished apartments with all the necessities and comforts of home…,* and

*Our service is tailored to meet your needs while working within your budget.*

These key phrases indicate that choice (B) is correct.

The title of the passage and the first sentence of each paragraph often tell the reader what the topic of the passage or the paragraph is. Details about the topic will then follow. In Exercise C, you will practice identifying the topic.

*To the teacher:* Ask the students to highlight the title, the heading, and the first sentence in each block of writing in the advertisement to help them see where the key ideas are located. Cut out other short texts from newspapers and magazines for further practice and follow the same procedure.

---

## EXERCISE C: IDENTIFYING THE TOPIC

Find the word in each of the following lists that gives the category, or description, of the other words in the same list. The first one is done for you.

*To the teacher:* Students should work on the exercise in pairs to encourage discussion of the topics. Ask them also to supply one or two more words to add to each list. Then place them in groups of four to compare their additional words. Give each group two more topic words to make lists for. Papers can then be exchanged between the groups so that each group can try to pick out the topic or category word in each list.

1.  cat      lion      rabbit      monkey
    (animal)      dog      cow

2.  receptionist   employee   manager
    executive     assistant     director

3.  desk      cabinet      bookcase
    table      furniture      chair      stool

4.  rain      snow      weather
    wind      fog      ice

5.  cement      steel      wood
    glass      material      brick

6.  kitchen      room      basement
    closet      parlor      bathroom

7.  circle      square      triangle
    shape      rectangle

8.  emotion      anger      love
    boredom      fear      pleasure

9.  painting      sports      music
    hobby      cooking      gardening

10. hammer      wrench      sander
    drill      tool      saw

## ANSWER KEY FOR DAY 22

### Exercise A
**Text 1**

Dear Mr. Timmerman:

Thank you for your inquiry regarding our wool sweaters. We do have the model numbers you requested. These garments can be shipped directly from here or from our main office in Manchester. The cost per garment is £18, plus £15 shipping per crate of 40 garments.

In your letter, you indicated that you would like to have 60 garments shipped to your business location. A delivery of this size usually takes two to three weeks, unless you prefer the shipment to arrive by air. I should mention that the cost of shipping will be higher in this case.

Finally, I have enclosed a copy of this year's catalogue with our new patterns as well as a copy of last year's catalogue, for which we have limited product availability.

Once you decide how you would like to have the garments shipped to you, please contact me directly and I will make the necessary arrangements. We look forward to filling your order.

Yours truly,

*Rose Kemper*

Rose Kemper

**Answers:**

1.  Yes
2.  No
3.  No
4.  Yes
5.  Yes
6.  No
7.  Yes

## Text 2

Slogan Effort Underway at TagCorp

As part of its overall strategy for promoting the company and improving image and visibility, TagCorp executives have been working for the past few months to develop a company slogan and a new logo. This logo will adorn company letterhead and merchandise and be immediately recognizable as the TagCorp symbol. TagCorp president Linda Ortiz said yesterday, "We really don't have the kind of recognition we need to give us a strong visual identity and to provide a sense of what the company is all about."

The slogan effort is being headed by Gene Dupré, associate vice president for marketing, who has been working with a number of marketing consultants to develop slogans by testing proposals on focus groups such as buyers, outside sales professionals, and retailers. Dupré said that last year a company task force came up with suggestions on enhancing and managing the company's image, and he was subsequently hired, in part to conduct what he calls a 'research-based' communications and marketing plan.

"We want to convey, in a succinct way, what's distinctive about TagCorp. We're focusing on the excellent value we offer and the breadth of products we develop here."

**Answers:**

1. No
2. Yes
3. No
4. Yes
5. Yes

## Exercise B

161. A
162. B
163. B
164. D

## Exercise C

1. animal
2. employee
3. furniture
4. weather
5. material
6. room
7. shape
8. emotion
9. hobby
10. tool

# Day 23

## Reading Comprehension: Practice Questions and Follow-up Exercises

In this lesson, you will have the opportunity to practice Part VII of the TOEIC test. Before you do this, remind yourself of the tips you learned on Days 21 and 22:

- Allow enough time to read and reread the passages.
- Become familiar with the layout of texts used in the workplace.
- Read the sentence that introduces the text.
- Relate what you read to what you already know.
- Skim the entire passage quickly once to get an idea of what the passage is about.
- Read the questions before you read the text again.
- When you want to identify the main idea, read the title and the first sentence of each paragraph.

Now try this practice Part VII, working as if you were taking a real TOEIC test. Before you start, write the numbers 160–200 on a piece of paper to record your answers. First, read the directions and the example item, then work straight through the section. If you are not sure of the correct answer, choose the answer you think is closest. Do not leave any questions blank.

Remember that this part of the Reading section will take longer than the two previous reading parts. You may need to spend more than half of the 75 minutes on Part VII. Time yourself to see how long you spend on this practice Part VII.

*To the teacher:* Make sure the students spend no more than 45 minutes on practice Part VII. For homework, students could study the explanations for the questions they answered incorrectly, and class time could be spent discussing any general difficulties they had with these practice questions.

## PRACTICE QUESTIONS

## Part VII

*Directions: Questions 161–200 are based on a selection of reading materials, such as notices, letters, forms, newspaper and magazine articles, and advertisements. You are to choose the one best answer (A), (B), (C), or (D) to each question. Then, on your answer sheet, find the number of the question and mark your answer. Answer all questions following each reading selection on the basis of what is stated or implied in that selection.*

Read the following example.

The Museum of Technology is a "hands-on" museum, designed for people to experience science at work. Visitors are encouraged to use, test, and handle the objects on display. Special demonstra-

tions are scheduled for the first and second Wednesdays of each month at 13:30. Open Tuesday–Friday 12:00–16:30, Saturday 10:00–17:30, and Sunday 11:00–16:30.

When during the month can visitors see special demonstrations?

(A) Every weekend

(B) The first two Wednesdays

(C) One afternoon a week

(D) Every other Wednesday

*Sample Answer*

(A) ● (C) (D)

The reading selection says that the demonstrations are scheduled for the first and second Wednesdays of the month. Therefore, you should choose answer (B).

Now, begin work on the questions. The answers are printed at the end of this section.

**Questions 161–162 refer to the following page from a calendar.**

| Sunday | Monday | Tuesday | Wednesday | Thursday | Friday | Saturday |
|---|---|---|---|---|---|---|
| | | 1 | 2 | 3 | 4 | 5 |
| | | | Secretary's Day | | | 6 |
| 7 Company Picnic | 8 | 9 | 10 | 11 Annual Trade Show | 12 | 13 |
| 14 | 15 | 16 | 17 Founder's Day | 18 | 19 | 20 |
| 21 | 22 | 23 | 24 | 25 | 26 Board of Directors Meeting | 27 |
| 28 Independence Holiday All offices closed | 29 | 30 | | | | |

161. What event is scheduled for the fourth week of the month?

    (A) Secretary's Day

    (B) A company picnic

    (C) Founder's Day

    (D) A board meeting

162. How often is the trade show held?

    (A) Daily

    (B) Weekly

    (C) Monthly

    (D) Yearly

**Questions 163–164** refer to the following notice.

*You are cordially invited to view*

*CANADIAN LANDSCAPES*

*An exhibition of work by*

*Yoshiko Yamaguchi*

*Included will be works from her most*

*recent project in the Arctic Refuge*

**THE WHITMORE GALLERY**

8028 Lakeshore Boulevard

Opening Reception: 6:00 to 10:00 P.M.

Friday, April 6th

Show runs from 9:00 A.M. to 4:00 P.M.

Mon–Fri

12:00 to 5:00 P.M. Sat & Sun

Admission — Free

163. Where will the event be held?

    (A) In a garden

    (B) At a private home

    (C) At a gallery

    (D) In a movie theater

164. What time does the reception end?

    (A) 12:00

    (B) 4:00

    (C) 5:00

    (D) 10:00

**Questions 165–167** refer to the following information.

Friends of the Library

Supporting and Benefiting the Library

Be a Friend — Join Today! Friends of the Library get first selection at book sales, receive a newsletter about the library and the Friends program, and have the great satisfaction of benefiting the library. Be a part of it all — be a friend.

Friends Membership Schedule

    General ..................................... $10

    Family ...................................... $20

    Senior (65 and over) ............... $6

    Silver ...................................... $200

    Junior (17 and under) ............. $4

    Gold ...................................... $500

Here's what Friends do ...

- Work toward the development of a new branch library

- Raise funds to address financial needs that cannot be met by the library's regular budget

- Sponsor the summer reading program for children

- Supply "Begin with Books" packets to parents of newborns to encourage reading and library use

- Sponsor community programs

- Help establish a closer relationship between the library and the public it serves

Funds for the Friends' efforts are raised through book sales, membership dues, donations, and fundraisers. Annual membership expires April 30.

165. What is available to Friends of the Library?

    (A) A special newsletter

    (B) An updated list of newly acquired books

    (C) Reduced library fines

    (D) Extended hours for visiting the library

166. Who would be eligible for the least expensive membership rate?

(A) A married couple

(B) A 15-year-old child

(C) A 68-year-old woman

(D) A 35-year-old man

167. What is NOT an aspect of the Friends of the Library program?

(A) Programs for young readers

(B) Expansion of the library system

(C) Subsidy of library costs

(D) Classes for new parents

**Questions 168–169** refer to the following form.

At Lightning Clothing, we want to provide our customers with the best service possible. We value your feedback and welcome any comments you have. Please answer the questions below and mail this form to us in the enclosed postage-paid envelope. Thank you!

---

Name: *Michael O'Sullivan*
Address: *125 4 th Street*
Watertown, NY 11201
E-mail (for sales notices):

1. What motivated you to buy Lightning shoes?
   ❏ Friend ❏ Advertisement ❏ Catalog
   ❏ Store Display ❏ Web site ❏ Other

2. How many pairs of Lightning shoes have you owned prior to this purchase?
   ❏ 1 ❏ 2–3 ❏ 4–9 ❏ 10+

3. How satisfied were you with your shopping experience?
   ❏ Very ❏ Somewhat ❏ Not Satisfied

4. How old are you?
   ❏ Under 15 ❏ 16–22 ❏ 23–29 ❏ 29–60 ❏ 60+

5. Where did you purchase your Lightning shoes?
   ❏ Web site ❏ Mail-order catalog ❏ Store
   Comments:

---

168. What is the main purpose of this form?

(A) To collect customer information

(B) To allow customers to make special orders

(C) To offer customers a rebate

(D) To persuade customers to buy new products

169. Why did Mr. O'Sullivan buy Lightning shoes?

(A) A friend recommended them.

(B) A display in a shop attracted him.

(C) He received a discount coupon.

(D) He saw them in a mail-order catalog.

**Questions 170–172** refer to the following advertisement.

Have you ever wondered what your pet was thinking? Do you want to enhance your understanding of your dog or cat? Professor Shasta Ewing, a leading animal behaviorist, will be conducting an informative workshop entitled "Understanding Your Pet." This session will explore animal cognition and behavior commonly demonstrated by our pets. Professor Ewing has studied with the esteemed Drs. Nitz and Francis, authors of My Pet and Me. A demonstration of animal training will be given by Professor Edward West. All registered participants will receive a certificate of attendance. Audiocassettes will also be available for purchase.

| Location | Fee | Time |
| --- | --- | --- |
| **Halpern Hotel** | $25 | 11 a.m.–2:30 p.m. |

170. Who is going to lead this workshop?

(A) Professor Ewing

(B) Professor West

(C) Dr. Nitz

(D) Dr. Francis

171. What is the topic of the workshop?

(A) Photographing wildlife

(B) Animal behavior

(C) How to select a pet

(D) Grooming and caring for pets

172. What is provided with registration?

    (A) A recording of a previous workshop

    (B) An attendance certificate

    (C) A copy of My Pet and Me

    (D) A pet-training manual

**Questions 173–175** refer to the following notice.

### *Springdale Estate*

### Regulations for Weddings/Reception in Auerbach Hall or Gardens

1. The hall and/or approved areas in the gardens of Springdale Estate are available for weddings and receptions during normal operating hours, while the gardens are also open to the public. Hours: 8 A.M.–8 P.M.

2. The cost for a wedding or reception is £8.00 per person. If the reception includes catering, the cost will be an additional £20.00 per person.

3. All persons must depart the Gardens no later than the normal closing time. A late fee of £75 per hour will be charged until all persons have exited the property.

4. Rehearsal: If a rehearsal is planned prior to the wedding day, no more than 10 persons will be admitted free.

5. A security deposit of £100 must be made at least 30 days prior to the function. This deposit will be refunded provided the grounds are left free of damage and litter.

173. For whom are these instructions written?

    (A) People going to a business meeting

    (B) People planning to get married

    (C) People going to a late-night party

    (D) People planning to tour the gardens

174. What is the cost per person if no food is served?

    (A) £8.00

    (B) £20.00

    (C) £75.00

    (D) £100.00

175. For what reason would a security deposit not be refunded?

    (A) If the grounds were not left clean

    (B) If too many of people attended an event

    (C) If guests failed to leave before the closing time

    (D) If unauthorized areas of the estate were used

**Questions 176–177** refer to the following letter.

---

**Ardmore Express Box 6467 Miami, FL 33399**

Mr. Joseph Sung
2249 Oak St.
Champaign, IL 60602
Account Number: 2736-8273888-09

Dear Account Holder:

Thank you for contacting us with regard to the charge on your Ardmore Express Gold Card account. We have contacted Schroeder's Department Store on your behalf and are awaiting a reply.

If we find that the charge was made to your account in error, we will make a credit adjustment within one business day.

We appreciate your patience as it may take six to eight weeks to complete the research needed to resolve your claim. If we can be of any further assistance, please call (888) 555-9870 to speak with a customer service representative.

Sincerely,

*S. Nagle*

S. Nagle
Customer Service Supervisor

---

176. What is the topic of this letter?

    (A) A mistake in a credit card bill

    (B) A change to an account number

    (C) A complaint about customer service

    (D) A charge for a late payment

177. What is Mr. Sung asked to do?

(A) Contact the department store

(B) Wait six to eight weeks

(C) Adjust his account balance

(D) Pay his bill immediately

**Questions 178–180** refer to the following magazine article.

Lorraine Kulasingam has worked in the fashion industry as a stylist for ten years, choosing the clothing that models and movie stars wear for on-camera appearances. "I'm the one who decides how the actors look," she says. "I love it. Every day is different."

Although Lorraine routinely meets famous movie stars, there is a disadvantage to her job: she often works 18-hour days, and she has to accommodate everyone's schedule. "It's pretty tiring," she admits. "But I wouldn't change careers for anything."

178. What is indicated about Ms. Kulasingam's job?

(A) She has recently changed careers.

(B) She often works very long days.

(C) She gets tired of doing the same thing.

(D) She recently received a promotion.

179. What does Ms. Kulasingam do in her job?

(A) Hires the models who appear in advertisements

(B) Selects clothing for film stars and models

(C) Organizes filming of television programs

(D) Takes pictures for the fashion industry

180. What could be considered a benefit of her position?

(A) Meeting famous people

(B) Receiving free accommodation

(C) Being able to set her own work hours

(D) Being in a management-level position

**Questions 181–184** refer to the following schedule.

## Sanderson Training and Development, Inc.

| Course | Date | Time | Location |
|---|---|---|---|
| Evaluating Employees | Jan. 23 & 24 | 6 p.m.–9 p.m. | Richmond |
| Focusing on Quality | Feb. 6 | 9 a.m.–6 p.m. | Danville |
| Legal Issues for Supervisors | Feb. 21 & 22 | 4 p.m.–6 p.m. | Richmond |
| Motivating Employees | Jan. 18 | 9 a.m.–4 p.m | Richmond |
| Motivating Employees | Mar. 29 | 9 a.m.–4 p.m. | Corbin |
| Motivating Employees | May 5 | 9 a.m.–4 p.m. | Danville |
| Supervising Others | May 1, 8, & 15 | 9 a.m.–4 p.m. | Richmond |
| Issues Management | Feb. 24 | 9 a.m.–4 p.m. | Danville |
| Workplace Safety | Jan. 16 | 9 a.m.–4 p.m. | Richmond |
| Workplace Safety | Mar. 20 | 9 a.m.–4 p.m. | Danville |

Dates and times are subject to change. For up-to-date information, visit our Web site: www.satraining.ca.co.

Fees per course: $189, including lunch. Cancellations must be received in writing no later than seven days prior to the session in order to receive a refund. Companies will be billed for any of their employees not canceling in advance.

Registration begins December 1. Register by sending an e-mail to reg@satraining.ca.net, calling toll-free 1-888-555-1867, or visiting our office in Richmond.

181. For which employees are these training sessions primarily intended?

    (A) Receptionists

    (B) Supervisors

    (C) Maintenance staff

    (D) Office assistants

182. What is NOT a way to register for the sessions?

    (A) In person

    (B) By e-mail

    (C) By fax

    (D) By phone

183. Which course is offered only in the evening?

    (A) Issues Management

    (B) Customer Service

    (C) Workplace Safety

    (D) Evaluating Employees

184. According to the information, when are refunds provided?

    (A) When cancellations are received a week in advance

    (B) When the employee's supervisor cancels on the day of the session

    (C) When the instructor fails to attend the session

    (D) When the weather causes the session to be canceled

**Questions 185–187** refer to the following business profile.

**Business Profile:** Simon Technologies, Inc.

**Location:** Corporate headquarters in Chicago, manufacturing plants in Mexico City and Taipei.

**Business:** Design and manufacture switches used on equipment such as microwave ovens and gasoline pumps. Switches are custom-made for 80% of customers. Customers are in twelve countries and include major manufacturers of cellular phones.

**Employees:** 150 in Chicago, 500 worldwide.

**Sales:** Simon Technologies had $12.8 million in annual sales last year. Since then, sales have increased about 200% to over $38 million. Projected sales increase for the coming year: 25%.

**History:** Founded in 1979 as a division of H.A. Grady Co. Became independent in 1995.

**Future:** The industry leader in design and manufacturing, Simon Technologies focuses on being a world-class supplier of innovative products and on increasing annual growth by at least 10% each year.

185. What does Simon Technologies produce?

    (A) Switches

    (B) Microwave ovens

    (C) Gasoline pumps

    (D) Phones

186. In how many countries does Simon Technologies have facilities?

    (A) One

    (B) Two

    (C) Three

    (D) Twelve

187. What percent increase of sales is predicted for the next year?

    (A) 10%

    (B) 25%

    (C) 80%

    (D) 200%

**Questions 188–190** refer to the following memo.

From: Corinne von Schieveen, Human Resources
To: Hiroshi Nakamura
Date: October 9

This notice serves to confirm payment of your household goods move. A households goods move includes the relocation of your household goods from Toronto to one destination in the Atlanta area, and must be completed by the first anniversary of your employment. When you are ready to obtain an estimate of moving expenses, please pay a visit to the Human Resources department for assistance. We will put you in touch with our contracted carriers.

Once estimates are submitted to Human Resources for review and approval, we will issue a letter of acceptance to the carrier. If you should choose instead to hire a third party mover, we will provide direct payment to that mover at the conclusion of your move. Please feel free to contact me with any questions.

Corinne von Schieveen
Human Resources

188. Who wrote this message?

(A) A real estate agent

(B) A moving company employee

(C) A travel agent

(D) A personnel officer

189. What is the subject of the message?

(A) Payment of moving expenses

(B) Customer complaints

(C) Insurance claims

(D) Employee retirement plans

190. What is indicated in the letter?

(A) Actions must be completed within a year.

(B) Estimates have not been accepted.

(C) The value of Mr. Nakamura's home has increased.

(D) Payment must be sent immediately.

**Questions 191–192** refer to the following article.

Department stores in the capital region, suffering from a prolonged slump in sales, are changing tactics by marketing new products and making their displays more interesting.

Some stores are reducing the amount of floor space devoted to name brands in order to display more of their own house brands. Others are using existing floor space for their own specialty shops. Still others are targeting special segments of the population—businesspeople in their 20's for example.

Stores that are developing their own brands are able to offer quality clothing at 30 percent off name-brand prices. They also have increased flexibility in responding to shifting market trends.

191. What has caused department stores to alter marking strategies?

(A) Poor sales

(B) New tax regulations

(C) Lack of storage space

(D) Production costs

192. Which strategy is NOT being implemented?

(A) Purchasing additional floor space

(B) Developing in-store brands

(C) Marketing to specific groups of people

(D) Making displays more interesting

**Questions 193–195** refer to the following information.

When you receive your monthly gas bill from Broadgate Gas, you will find that the amount you pay is a total of several charges: Gas Purchased Charge, the Customer Charge, the Distribution Charge, and local taxes. The following information describes these charges.

The Gas Purchased Charge is the actual cost of the natural gas you used in the billing period, plus the cost of transporting it to the Broadgate Gas system. We do not earn a profit on the cost of the gas. If you choose to buy your natural gas from a non-regulated supplier through our Customer Choice Program, this part of your gas bill will indicate the choice.

The Customer Charge is a fixed monthly fee that includes our cost for the maintenance and repair of gas lines and other customer service functions.

The Distribution Charge is the cost of moving the natural gas through the Broadgate Gas system to your home. Prices fluctuate, depending on the amount of gas you use.

The local taxes are estimated and collected by Broadgate Gas and then remitted to the appropriate authority.

If you have any questions about your bill, call us at 807-555-9987. You may telephone us between the hours of 8:00 AM and 5:00 PM, Monday to Friday.

193. For whom is this information intended?

(A) Local tax officials

(B) Residential gas users

(C) Environmental activists

(D) Government energy officials

194. What do non-regulated suppliers provide?

(A) Information about taxes

(B) Natural gas

(C) Financial assistance

(D) Gas-line repair service

195. Which charge does NOT change from month to month?

(A) The local tax

(B) The Distribution Charge

(C) The Customer Charge

(D) The Gas Purchased Charge

**Questions 196–198** refer to the following information.

Employee Education Benefits Program

Foxdale will pay the course fees for full-time employees taking job-related courses up to a maximum of two courses per year. For part-time employees, Foxdale will pay fifty percent of the course fees for a single job-related course per year. Courses must be taken at an accredited university or technical college. Courses at uncertified schools, such as private business training schools, will not be accepted. All courses must be pre-approved by the supervisor; no reimbursement will be granted if prior approval has not been obtained. An employee is eligible for fee reimbursement starting six months from hiring date.

Procedures

1. Obtain a request form from the Human Resources department.

2. Submit request form to departmental supervisor a minimum of six weeks prior to start of course.

3. Upon approval, employee may enroll in course.

4. Fees must initially be paid by the employee. Foxdale will reimburse employees upon proof of successfully passing the course.

5. If an employee stops working for Foxdale during the time of the course, Foxdale will pay only that portion of the course that occurred while the individual was a Foxdale employee.

196. For how many courses per year can a part-time employee be reimbursed?

(A) 1

(B) 2

(C) 5

(D) 6

197. When will Foxdale pay for a course?

 (A) Immediately after a request form is submitted

 (B) Six weeks before the start of a course

 (C) At the beginning of a semester

 (D) After an employee has passed a course

198. Which requirement is mentioned in the information?

 (A) Courses must be taken at local business schools.

 (B) Courses must be related to the employee's job.

 (C) Courses must be on a list recommended by human resources.

 (D) Courses must be less than six months in duration.

**Questions 199–200** refer to the following order.

**Order Sheet**

**Computer Support Services**

**Background**: The 20 computer terminals in our office need a significant memory upgrade. After the Computer Support Services Department installed the new inventory programs on September 1, we began to have severe problems with memory capacity. At times we are unable to provide our customers with accurate and timely inventory information and have even had to send a messenger to the warehouse to check physically whether the needed chemical product was available in the quantity requested.

**Specific Request**: Installation of new memory chips into our 20 computer terminals, reconfiguration of programs, resetting of the computers, general troubleshooting.

**Date Requested for Service**: September 18

**Scheduling**: We expect that we will need one technician to spend one day to complete these operations.

Request made on September 10 by: Eleanor Thompson, Director, Inventory and Billing

Request approved on Sept. 12 by: Ronald Lopez, Manager, Computer Support Service

199. Why is Ms. Thompson's department having problems?

 (A) The computers do not have enough memory.

 (B) Supplies of chemical products have run out.

 (C) There are not enough workers on staff.

 (D) An inventory program has not been installed.

200. What will Mr. Lopez probably do?

 (A) Send a technician

 (B) File a complaint

 (C) Check warehouse inventory

 (D) Request staff hirings

| ANSWER KEY | |
|---|---|
| 161. D | 181. B |
| 162. D | 182. C |
| 163. C | 183. D |
| 164. D | 184. A |
| 165. A | 185. A |
| 166. B | 186. C |
| 167. D | 187. B |
| 168. A | 188. D |
| 169. A | 189. A |
| 170. A | 190. A |
| 171. B | 191. A |
| 172. B | 192. A |
| 173. B | 193. B |
| 174. A | 194. B |
| 175. A | 195. C |
| 176. A | 196. A |
| 177. B | 197. D |
| 178. B | 198. B |
| 179. B | 199. A |
| 180. A | 200. A |

## FOLLOW-UP EXERCISES

### EXERCISE A: THINKING ABOUT YOUR TIMING

How long did it take you to complete Practice Part VII? It took _____ minutes.

If it took you longer than 45 minutes, you may find yourself running out of time on the real TOEIC test. On Day 29, you will have another opportunity to try a Practice Part VII and compare your times.

### EXERCISE B: CHECKING YOUR ANSWERS

The correct answers are given at the end of today's lesson. Check your answers, then try again any that you got wrong.

### EXERCISE C: STUDYING THE EXPLANATIONS

Explanations of the answers for Practice Part VII are given below. Take time to study the explanations for any questions that you answered incorrectly—either on the first or the second attempt—and any others that you found difficult.

### PRACTICE QUESTION EXPLANATIONS

161. (D) Counting down from the top of the calendar, the fourth week is the one that begins on the 21st and ends on the 27th. The only event scheduled in that week is the Board of Directors Meeting, which is *a board meeting.* (A) Secretary's Day is in the first week of the month. (B) The company picnic is scheduled for the second week of the month. (C) Founder's Day is during the third week of the month.

162. (D) The word *annual* means "once per year." This lets us know that the trade show is held on a *yearly* basis. Neither (A) daily, (B) weekly, or (C) monthly means "once per year."

163. (C) The place where the event will be held is indicated by the name and address in the middle of the invitation. Because the name of this place is the *Whitmore Gallery*, we know that the event will be held *at a gallery*. (A) Although *landscapes* can be pictures of gardens, the event will not be *held* in a garden. (B) The address given is for an art gallery, not a private home. (D) There is no mention of a movie theater.

164. (D) Information about the reception is given in the section of the card that begins with the words *Opening Reception*. Because the hours for the reception are given as 6:00 to 10:00 P.M., we know that it ends at 10:00 P.M. (A) 12:00, (B) 4:00, and (C) 5:00 are mentioned as part of the opening hours for the exhibit in general, not for the reception.

165. (A) The notice states that Friends of the Library *receive a newsletter about the library and the friends program*. There is no mention of (B) new acquisitions, (C) library fines, or (D) extended visiting hours.

166. (B) The least expensive membership rate listed in the schedule is the Junior rate, which is $4 for individuals age 17 and under. A 15-year-old child would be eligible for this rate. (A) A married couple would pay $20 for the Family rate. (C) A 68-year-old woman would qualify for the Senior rate of $6. (D) A 35-year-old man would not fall under any of the special categories and so would have to pay the General membership rate of $10.

167. (D) The Friends of the Library supply special information packets to new parents, but do not offer classes to them. (A) The Friends run a *summer reading program* for children, or young readers. (B) The notice says that Friends *work toward the development of a new branch library*; in other words, they try to expand the library system. (C) The Friends *raise funds* to pay for things that the library other-

wise cannot afford; that is, the Friends *subsidize*, or pay part of, the library's costs.

168. (A) The paragraph at the top of the form states that Lightning Clothing values customer *feedback* and welcomes *comments*. The form itself asks for information about customer purchases. There is no mention of (B) *special orders* or (C) *a rebate* on the form. (D) The form asks questions about products that have already been purchased; it does not include advertising for new products.

169. (A) The first question on the form asks what *motivated*, or caused, the customer to buy Lightning Shoes. Mr. O'Sullivan has checked the box for "Friend," so a friend must have recommended Lightning Shoes to him. Neither the box for (B) *a shop display* nor (D) *a catalog* has been checked, so these are not reasons why Mr. O'Sullivan purchased the shoes. There is no mention of (C) *discount coupons* anywhere on the form.

170. (A) The advertisement states that Professor Shasta Ewing will be *conducting*, or leading, a workshop called "Understanding Your Pet." (B) Professor Edward West will be leading only a small part of the workshop, the demonstration of animal training. Though Professor Ewing has studied with (C) Dr. Nitz and (D) Dr. Francis, there is no indication that they will be participating in the workshop.

171. (B) The workshop will be led by an animal behaviorist. The advertisement says that the workshop will explore animal *cognition*, or thinking, as well as *behavior commonly demonstrated by our pets*. There is no mention of (A) photography, (C) pet selection, or (D) pet care and grooming.

172. (B) The advertisement states that all registered participants will receive a *certificate of attendance*. (A) Audiocassette recordings of this workshop may be purchased; these recordings are not provided with registration. (C) The book *My Pet and Me* is mentioned in the advertisement, but copies of this book will not be provided. (D) The advertisement mentions a demonstration of animal training, but it does not say that a training manual will be given away.

173. (B) The subheading at the top of the notice says that these are *regulations for weddings/receptions*; these instructions are therefore probably intended for people planning to get married. (A) There is no mention of anything related to a business meeting. (C) The hours of operation for Springdale Estate are 8 A.M. to 8 P.M., so the instructions cannot be for people going to a late-night party. (D) People who are only planning to tour the gardens would not need to know about catering costs and regulations concerning wedding rehearsals.

174. (A) The second paragraph states that there is a £8.00 charge per person for a wedding or reception. An additional fee is charged per person if the reception is *catered*, which is another way of saying that food is served. (B) £20.00 is the additional charge per person to have a reception catered. (C) There is a late fee of £75.00 per hour if guests do not leave the property on time; this charge is unrelated to the per person charges. (D) An advance deposit of £100 is required 30 days before an event, but this too is unrelated to the per person charges.

175. (A) The last paragraph of the notice says that the security deposit will be refunded if *the grounds are left free of damage and litter*, or trash. This is another way of saying that the grounds must be left clean after an event. (B) There is no mention of a limit on the number of people who may attend a reception. (C) A late fee of £75.00 will be charged if guests do not leave by the closing time; this is not related to the security deposit. (D) There is no mention of a penalty for use of unauthorized areas.

176. (A) The second paragraph of the letter says that, if a charge was made to Mr. Sung's credit card account *in error*, or by mistake, a credit adjustment will be made. Mr. Sung had apparently contacted the credit card company about a mistake in his bill, and this letter is the company's response to his complaint. (B) Mr. Sung's account number is printed at the top of the letter, but there is no indication that the number is being changed. (C) Though the third paragraph invites Mr. Sung to call a customer service representative, there is no

mention of a complaint about customer service. (D) There is no mention of a late payment charge.

177. (B) In the last paragraph of the letter, Mr. Sung is asked to have patience, or to wait, as the problem may not be resolved for another six to eight weeks. (A) The letter states that Ardmore Express has contacted the department store about the billing mistake. Mr. Sung does not need to contact the store. (C) Ardmore Express will adjust Mr. Sung's credit bill if an error has been made; Mr. Sung does not need to adjust his own account balance. (D) There is no mention of payment in the letter.

178. (B) The article says that Ms. Kulasingam *often works 18-hour days* and that she finds these hours *pretty tiring*. (A) Ms. Kulasingam has been working as a stylist for ten years, so she has not recently changed careers. (C) Ms. Kulasingam is quoted as saying that every day on her job is *different*; in other words, she does not do the same thing all the time. (D) There is no indication that Ms. Kulasingam has recently received a promotion.

179. (B) According to the article, Ms. Kulasingam's job involves *choosing the clothing that models and movie stars wear*. (A) Ms. Kulasingam chooses *clothes* for models appearing in advertisements; she does not select the models themselves. (C) The article mentions *actors* and *on-camera appearances*, but there is no indication that Ms. Kulasingam is responsible for filming television programs. (D) Ms. Kulasingam works with models prior to fashion photo shoots; she does not actually take photographs of the models.

180. (A) The article contrasts the disadvantage of Ms. Kulasingam's long working hours with one advantage of her job: the fact that she often meets famous movie stars. (B) The word *accommodate* in the article is used to mean *adapt*: Ms. Kulasingam has to adapt to everyone else's schedule. There is no mention of free *accommodation*, or lodging. (C) Again, since Ms. Kulasingam must accommodate models' and actors' schedules, she is not able to set her own hours. (D) There is no indication that Ms. Kulasingam has a management-level position.

181. (B) Many of the courses focus on activities that would be carried out by managers: *supervising*, *evaluating*, and *motivating* employees. *Supervisor* here has the same meaning as *manager*. (A) Receptionists and (D) office assistants are not usually responsible for supervising or evaluating other employees, so these courses are probably not intended for them. (C) The courses on workplace safety could possibly be for maintenance workers, but the question asks who the *primary* audience for the training sessions is. The majority of the courses clearly deal with supervisory or management issues.

182. (C) The schedule says that people may register for the sessions by (A) *visiting the office* in person, (B) sending an *e-mail* message, or (D) *calling* a toll-free telephone number. The only option *not* mentioned in the schedule is registration by fax, so (C) is the correct answer.

183. (D) The course titled "Evaluating Employees" runs from 6 to 9 P.M.; in other words, it is an evening class. (A) The "Issues Management" course is offered during the day, from 9 A.M. to 4 P.M. (C) The "Workplace Safety" course is also a daytime course, running from 9 A.M. to 4 P.M. (B) There is no "Customer Service" course being offered.

184. (A) The schedule states that refunds will be provided when cancellations are received *no later than seven days prior to the session*. (B) When an employee fails to cancel in advance, the company will be billed; in this case, *no* refund will be provided. There is no mention of either (C) an absent instructor or (D) a bad-weather policy.

185. (A) In the section of the profile titled "Business," a description of Simon Technologies is provided. The profile says that this company *designs and manufactures*, or in other words produces, *switches*. (B) Microwave ovens and (C) gasoline pumps are examples of the kinds of equipment that *use* switches made by Simon Technologies. (D) The profile states that manufacturers of cellular phones are among the *customers* of Simon Technologies.

186. (C) Under "Location," the passage states that Simon Technologies has facilities in three different countries. Its headquarters are in Chicago, USA, and it has manufacturing plants in Mexico City, Mexico and Taipei, Taiwan. (A) The company has one location for its headquarters, but it has three facilities total. (B) The company has factories in two countries, but the question asks about the total number of facilities, which would include the headquarters. (D) Simon Technologies has *customers* in twelve countries.

187. (B) In the section of the profile titled "Sales," a *projected sales increase* of 25% is mentioned for the next year. (A) Under "Future," the profile says that Simon Technologies focuses on *increasing annual growth* by 10% each year. This is a goal for the company to work toward for many years, not a prediction for next year's sales. (C) 80% is mentioned under "Business" as the percentage of switches that Simon Technologies custom-makes for customers. (D) 200% is the increase in sales from last year to this year.

188. (D) This message is from Corinne von Schieveen in Human Resources. A *personnel officer* is someone who works in Human Resources. (A) A real estate agent, (B) a moving company employee, and (C) a travel agent are all people who might be involved in helping an employee relocate, but this message is not written by any of these individuals.

189. (A) The first line of the message states that its purpose is to confirm payment of a *household goods move*. In other words, it is about the payment of expenses for moving from one place to another. Neither (B) customer complaints, (C) insurance claims, nor (D) retirement plans is mentioned in the message.

190. (A) The letter indicates that the employee's move must be completed *by the first anniversary of employment* or, in other words, within one year. (B) The letter gives instructions about *obtaining* estimates, but it does not indicate that estimates have been rejected. The letter does not say anything

about (C) the value of Mr. Nakamura's home, nor does it ask for (D) any kind of payment from Mr. Nakamura.

191. (A) The article says that department stores are changing strategies because of a *slump in sales*, or a period in which sales are low. This is another way of saying that sales have been poor. The article does not say anything about (B) tax regulations, (C) storage space, or (D) production costs.

192. (A) The article mentions several different strategies for increasing sales, but purchasing additional floor space is not among them. (B) The article says that some stores are *developing their own brands* so that they can sell them at lower prices. (C) It also says that some stores are *targeting special segments of the population*, or marketing to specific groups. (D) The first paragraph says that another strategy some stores are adopting is to *make displays more interesting*.

193. (B) Among the charges discussed is a *Distribution Charge*, which is defined as the cost of moving natural gas through the system and into the customer's home. From this, it can be inferred that the information is for residential gas users, or people who use gas in their homes. (A) The notice mentions local taxes, which are included in the monthly bill, but this information is not intended for tax officials. There is no mention of (C) environmental activists or (D) government energy officials.

194. (B) The second paragraph mentions that customers may *choose to buy natural gas* from a non-regulated supplier. Non-regulated suppliers do not provide (A) tax information or (C) financial assistance. (D) Gas-line repair service is provided by Broadgate Gas Company, not by a non-regulated supplier.

195. (C) The third paragraph states that the Customer Charge is *a fixed monthly fee*. In other words, this charge does not change from month to month. (A) The local tax, (B) the Distribution Charge, and (D) the Gas Purchased Charge would all change each month depending on how much gas is used.

196. (A) According to the passage, *part-time employees will be reimbursed for 50% of the course fees for a single job-related course per year*. (B) A *full-time* employee will be reimbursed for the course fees for two courses per year, but the question asks about *part-time* employees. There is no mention of any employee being reimbursed for (C) 5 or (D) 6 courses per year.

197. (D) Under "Procedures," the passage states that Foxdale will reimburse employees *upon proof of successfully passing the course*. In other words, Foxdale will only reimburse the course fees after the course has ended. There is no indication that employees will be reimbursed either (A) immediately after a request form is submitted or (C) at the beginning of a semester. (B) Employees must submit their request forms six weeks prior to the start of a course, but they do not receive any reimbursement at that point.

198. (B) The passage states that employees will be reimbursed for *job-related* courses, which must be approved by a supervisor. (A) According to the passage, courses may *not* be taken at private business training schools; only accredited universities and technical colleges are acceptable. (C) There is no mention of a list of schools recommended by human resources. (D) No limit on the length of a course is mentioned.

199. (A) The order sheet indicates that Ms. Thompson's department has been having *severe problems with memory capacity*. She asks that 20 computers in her department be *upgraded* with new *memory chips*, so the problem must be that the computers do not currently have enough memory. (B) Ms. Thompson indicates on the form that her staff has been unable use computers to keep track of the inventory of chemical products. She does not say that supplies themselves have run out. (C) There is no indication that there is a shortage of workers. (D) Ms. Thompson notes that the computers started having problems *after* the new inventory programs were installed.

200. (A) Mr. Lopez is the manager of the Computer Support Services Department. He will probably fulfill Ms. Thompson's request by sending a technician to perform the requested upgrade. There is no indication that Mr. Lopez will (B) file a complaint, (C) check inventory, or (D) request that staff be hired.

# Day 24

## Reading Section: Sample Questions from Parts V to VII, with Explanations of the Answers

In today's lesson, you will be able to try sample questions from all three parts of the Reading section of the TOEIC test and read detailed explanations for correct and incorrect answers. Use the TOEIC Sample Questions Answer Sheet on page 202 as you answer the questions.

For each question, select the correct answer and fill in the circles for the correct answers on your answer sheet. When you are finished with the questions, read the explanations carefully to find out why your answers are either correct or incorrect.

*To the teacher:* All three types of questions that appear in the Reading section are included here. You could present them using an overhead projector, showing the question first, then eliciting the correct answer and then an explanation of the choices from the students, and finally revealing the explanation given here. You could follow this procedure for just a few questions of each type and then ask the students to work individually.

## AUTHENTIC TOEIC READING QUESTIONS WITH EXPLANATIONS

### Part V Incomplete Sentences

25. Please note that customs regulations do not permit the shipment of - - - - - - - items.
    (A) perishable
    (B) compatible
    (C) sustainable
    (D) incredible

26. Brencorp has demonstrated a strong - - - - - - - to employee development through its many incentive programs.
    (A) committing
    (B) committed
    (C) committee
    (D) commitment

27. Prolonged - - - - - - - to moisture can adversely affect the proper functioning of this audio unit.

    (A) enclosure

    (B) exposure

    (C) exclusion

    (D) exertion

28. Despite an exceptionally small rice harvest, analysts predict that the Tarvo Republic will not need to rely on - - - - - - - staple foods this year.

    (A) import

    (B) imports

    (C) imported

    (D) importer

29. Warning! This strap must be fastened - - - - - - - around the crates in order to hold the load in place.

    (A) minutely

    (B) securely

    (C) portably

    (D) thickly

30. Construction engineers - - - - - - - that damage from last week's flood will exceed £50,000.

    (A) estimates

    (B) is estimating

    (C) have estimated

    (D) have been estimated

31. When changing jobs, it is important to consider - - - - - - - salary and benefits.

    (A) both

    (B) either

    (C) yet

    (D) or

32. The train station is - - - - - - - located near museums, monuments, and other tourist attractions in the city.

    (A) conditionally

    (B) conveniently

    (C) affordably

    (D) belatedly

33. Last year, requisition orders for children's clothes increased more than orders for all other types of - - - - - - - .

    (A) apparel

    (B) appearances

    (C) apparatus

    (D) appliances

34. Check - - - - - - - that information on the bill and the receipt match exactly before submitting your records.

    (A) care

    (B) careful

    (C) carefully

    (D) carefulness

## Part VI Error Recognition

35. The machinery <u>we sell</u> is <u>assembling in</u> this
               A         B

    country, but <u>most of the parts</u> come <u>from abroad</u>.
             C           D

36. The applicants <u>who</u> meet <u>the</u> requirements for the
            A      B

    position <u>they will</u> be contacted in order <u>to schedule</u>
            C               D

    an on-site interview.

37. <u>Because</u> rising incomes and falling mortgage rates,
    A

    sales <u>of residences</u> and <u>commercial buildings</u>
            B             C

    reached another <u>monthly high</u> last week.
                D

38. An important factor <u>should be</u> considered is
                  A

    Mr. Lopez's <u>ability</u> to keep the new restaurant
           B

    going <u>for several</u> months <u>with limited revenue.</u>
         C             D

39. This year, the judges had the difficult

    <u>yet enjoyable</u> task of selecting twelve <u>winning</u>
      A                          B

    photos <u>from</u> the many <u>who</u> were entered.
        C         D

40. <u>While</u> he worked as a <u>travel agency</u>, Mr. Nakamura
    A              B

    specialized <u>in arranging</u> tours of <u>the Middle East.</u>
           C            D

41. The accounting supervisor <u>was displeased</u> to learn
                  A

    that the <u>budget report</u> would not <u>be finished</u> <u>by time.</u>
           B             C    D

42. Electronics Superstore <u>has announced</u> that it will
              A

    <u>have closed</u> early <u>for</u> the upcoming
      B         C

    <u>holiday next week.</u>
      D

## Part VII Reading Comprehension

**Questions 43–44** refer to the following notice.

```
JWS TRAVEL SERVICES
8 NORTH MAIN STREET
BOSTON, MA 01731

MS. REBECCA JOHANNSON
52 ELM STREET
CAMBRIDGE, MA 02138

We are pleased to confirm your travel plans as follows:

WE  20 MAR   LV BOSTON           505P   EUROPEAN AIRWAYS  EA 832   WORLD TRAVELER
TH  21 MAR   AR LONDON–HEATH     455A

                                        SEAT 20-F
TH  21 MAR   LV LONDON–HEATH     720A   EUROPEAN AIRWAYS  EA 435   EURO TRAVELER
TH  21 MAR   AR STOCKHOLM        1057A

                                        SEAT 13-A

Thank you for your business.
```

43. For what kind of travel is this notice intended?
    (A) Airplane
    (B) Train
    (C) Luxury bus
    (D) Cruise ship

44. What is Ms. Johannson's final destination?
    (A) London
    (B) Stockholm
    (C) Cambridge
    (D) Boston

**Questions 45–47** refer to the following information.

---

**Information About Your New Furniture Upholstery**

*Upholstery Characteristics*

**Leather:** Leather hides can be treated in a number of different ways. This may include sanding or buffing, depending on the style of furniture. Leather hides may have characteristics referred to as "hallmarks of the trail." These characteristics include scarring from barbed wire, insect bite marks, or even branding marks that are used on ranches. Leather may also have shade variations. They can go from lighter colorations to darker colorations on the same piece of furniture. Leather may also have a natural aroma similar to that found on leather apparel when first unpacked. This aroma may dissipate after a short period of time.

**General Upholstery:** Striped or plaid fabrics that are designed to match may appear unmatched at delivery. In this case, try turning over or repositioning the cushions first. Many times, this alleviates the problem.

**Skirting:** The skirting located along the bottom of the sofa may be wrinkled or folded from the shipping process. These wrinkles will fall out with time. Wrinkles in fabric or skirting are quickly remedied with the use of steam.

---

45. For whom is this information intended?
    (A) Upholstery repairers
    (B) Manufacturers of leather furniture
    (C) Delivery personnel
    (D) Purchasers of new furniture

46. What is NOT mentioned as the source of a characteristic mark?
    (A) Barbed wire fences
    (B) Insect bites
    (C) Branding
    (D) Sanding

47. What should be done if fabric patterns do not match?
    (A) The furniture should be returned to the manufacturer.
    (B) The cushions should be rearranged.
    (C) Steam should be applied to the material.
    (D) The material should be unfolded carefully.

**Questions 48–50** refer to the following article.

**Annual School-to-Work Career Conference Survives a Storm**

The eighth annual School-to-Work Career Conference was held in Peterstown last Sunday, despite a major ice storm over the weekend that made travel in the area a considerable challenge.

More than 400 attendees came to the Jefferson Convention Center in downtown Peterstown. Students from local high schools, many of them accompanied by their families, received a variety of information about careers. Volunteers from the Peterstown Business Center helped students complete aptitude questionnaires and explore possible career paths. Presentations and workshops were given by local business leaders, and a large number of professionals were available to answer students' questions about careers.

The conference was sponsored by the Peterstown Business Association and the Peterstown school system. An association spokesperson commented that the willingness of people to come out in the poor weather was a good sign for the future of businesses in the area. He added that he hoped blue skies and a strong economy would be in the forecast for next year's conference.

48. For whom was the conference planned?

    (A) High school teachers

    (B) Community volunteers

    (C) High school students

    (D) New business owners

49. What was the purpose of the questionnaires?

    (A) To recruit volunteers

    (B) To provide family entertainment

    (C) To solicit funds

    (D) To help determine skills

50. What was an obstacle to the success of the conference?

    (A) The economy was weak.

    (B) The weather was unfavorable.

    (C) There were not enough volunteers.

    (D) Local business leaders were not available.

**Questions 51–54** refer to the following letter.

Bristol Motor Company
1 Gray Drive
Canberra ACT 0201

12 June

Vera Hsu, Director
Canberra Transit System
15 Central Street
Canberra ACT 0216

Dear Ms. Hsu:

I am writing to your office regarding the widening of the Centura Highway, due to begin this year. This important roadway passes the Bristol Motor Company. Many of our 2,000 employees use the Canberra public transportation system and access the bus station located opposite our facilities on Centura Highway.

Between the hours of 7:30 A.M. and 8:00 A.M., and 4:30 P.M. and 5:30 P.M., a considerable number of our employees cross Centura Highway as they go to and from work. To date we have not heard of any plan to provide a traffic signal, a walkway overpass, or the services of a traffic officer to ensure the safety of our employees. We believe that steps need to be taken to reduce the possibility of accidents both during the construction phase and beyond.

I would like to arrange a meeting with you as soon as possible to discuss the above options. We at Bristol Motor Company are willing to cooperate with your office to the fullest extent and would appreciate your immediate attention to this matter.

Sincerely,

Jeff Hall

Assistant Vice President
Bristol Motor Company

51. Which issue is discussed in the letter?

    (A) The modernization of a public transportation system

    (B) The expansion of a motor company

    (C) The promotion of safety awareness training

    (D) The widening of a major road

52. Which group of people is Mr. Hall concerned about?

    (A) Construction engineers

    (B) Bus and train operators

    (C) Motor company employees

    (D) City traffic officers

53. What is NOT mentioned as a possible solution?

    (A) Adding bus routes

    (B) Hiring a traffic officer

    (C) Building a walkway

    (D) Installing a traffic signal

54. How can Vera Hsu assist Bristol Motors?

    (A) By reducing bus fares

    (B) By decreasing work hours

    (C) By speeding up construction

    (D) By addressing traffic concerns

## TOEIC SAMPLE QUESTIONS ANSWER SHEET

25. Ⓐ Ⓑ Ⓒ Ⓓ
26. Ⓐ Ⓑ Ⓒ Ⓓ
27. Ⓐ Ⓑ Ⓒ Ⓓ
28. Ⓐ Ⓑ Ⓒ Ⓓ
29. Ⓐ Ⓑ Ⓒ Ⓓ
30. Ⓐ Ⓑ Ⓒ Ⓓ
31. Ⓐ Ⓑ Ⓒ Ⓓ
32. Ⓐ Ⓑ Ⓒ Ⓓ
33. Ⓐ Ⓑ Ⓒ Ⓓ
34. Ⓐ Ⓑ Ⓒ Ⓓ
35. Ⓐ Ⓑ Ⓒ Ⓓ
36. Ⓐ Ⓑ Ⓒ Ⓓ
37. Ⓐ Ⓑ Ⓒ Ⓓ
38. Ⓐ Ⓑ Ⓒ Ⓓ
39. Ⓐ Ⓑ Ⓒ Ⓓ
40. Ⓐ Ⓑ Ⓒ Ⓓ
41. Ⓐ Ⓑ Ⓒ Ⓓ
42. Ⓐ Ⓑ Ⓒ Ⓓ
43. Ⓐ Ⓑ Ⓒ Ⓓ
44. Ⓐ Ⓑ Ⓒ Ⓓ
45. Ⓐ Ⓑ Ⓒ Ⓓ
46. Ⓐ Ⓑ Ⓒ Ⓓ
47. Ⓐ Ⓑ Ⓒ Ⓓ
48. Ⓐ Ⓑ Ⓒ Ⓓ
49. Ⓐ Ⓑ Ⓒ Ⓓ
50. Ⓐ Ⓑ Ⓒ Ⓓ
51. Ⓐ Ⓑ Ⓒ Ⓓ
52. Ⓐ Ⓑ Ⓒ Ⓓ
53. Ⓐ Ⓑ Ⓒ Ⓓ
54. Ⓐ Ⓑ Ⓒ Ⓓ

## ANSWERS AND EXPLANATIONS

## Part V Incomplete Sentences

25. **(A)** *Perishable* **describes food that easily spoils or becomes rotten. Customs regulations would apply to such items.**

    (B) *Compatible* applies to people who get along or things that can be used well together.

    (C) *Sustainable* applies to something that can continue for a long period of time.

    (D) Incredible means *unbelievable*. It would not apply to items being shipped.

26. (A) Many verbs with an -ing ending can be used as nouns, but *committing* is almost never a noun.

    (B) *Committed* may be used as an adjective formed by adding -ed to the verb; however, it cannot be a noun.

    (C) *Committee* is a noun, the correct word form here. However, a committee cannot be demonstrated.

    **(D)** A *commitment* **is a promise and can be** *demonstrated*. **It is a noun modified by** *strong*.

27. (A) An *enclosure* is something that surrounds. Enclosure resembles the correct word but has a different spelling and meaning.

    **(B)** *Exposure* **to moisture would mean getting the audio unit wet. This could damage it.**

    (C) *Exclusion* is followed by *of*, not *to*. Excluding moisture would protect the unit, not harm it.

    (D) *Exertion*, meaning effort or exercise, is also followed by *of*. A nonliving thing cannot exert itself.

28. (A) *Import* can be a verb or a noun. An adjective is needed here.

    (B) *Imports* may only be used as a verb or a noun, and an adjective is needed here.

    **(C)** *Imported* **is an adjective describing or modifying staple foods. It is formed by adding -ed to the verb.**

    (D) An *importer* is a noun meaning a person or company that imports.

29. (A) *Minutely* applies to detail. It would not be used to describe how to tie a strap.

    **(B) The strap must be fastened** *securely* **so it will not come undone.**

    (C) Although the crates may be moved, the strap around them should remain in place.

    (D) While the strap may be thick, it cannot be fastened *thickly*.

30. (A) The present tense could be used here. However, *engineers* is plural, so the verb that follows should not have a final *s*.

    (B) Although the present progressive tense could also be used, *is estimating* is incorrect because it too is a singular verb.

    **(C) The present perfect tense is used to mean that the engineers have finished their estimates.** *Have estimated* **is the correct plural verb form.**

    (D) *Have been estimated* is a passive form. The engineers have *done* something, not had something done *to* them.

31. **(A) Someone changing jobs would consider** *all* **the important factors, including** *both* **salary and benefits.**

    (B) *Either* means a choice *between* two things, one *or* the other.

    (C) *Yet*, like *however*, implies a contrast. *Salary and benefits* are *important to consider*. No contrast is being made.

    (D) The conjunction *or* shows a comparison or choice *between* two things, not a decision including both of them.

32. (A)  The location of the train station does not depend upon a particular condition; therefore, *conditionally* is incorrect.

    **(B)  The train station is in a good, *convenient* location near tourist attractions.**

    (C)  While it may not cost much money to get from the train station to nearby attractions, the sentence is about location, not affordability.

    (D)  *Belatedly* means *too late*. While the station may have been built later than originally planned, the sentence is about location, not time.

33. **(A)  The sentence is about clothes. *Apparel* is a synonym for clothing.**

    (B)  *Appearances* is a less specific noun that does not relate to the subject of the sentence.

    (C)  *Apparatus* means a device or a machine. The sentence is about orders for clothing, not machinery.

    (D)  *Appliance*, similar to apparatus, means a device or machine. It is incorrect for the same reason as choice (C).

34. (A)  An adverb is needed to describe how the checking should be done. *Care* is a noun.

    (B)  *Careful* is an adjective, so it can only be used with a noun. Here, *check* is an imperative verb telling the reader to do something.

    **(C)  *Carefully* is an adverb that tells how to check the bill and receipt.**

    (D)  The thing to be checked is *information*, not carefulness. To check *carefulness* would not make sense.

## Part VI Error Recognition

35. (A)  The relative pronoun *that* is omitted. In this context, it is optional.

    **(B)  The passive voice should be used in this sentence. The machinery *is assembled* in this country.**

    (C)  This phrase is correctly used. The article *the* is sometimes mistakenly omitted.

    (D)  The phrase *from abroad* is correct.

36. (A)  *Who* refers to applicants. It begins the clause that tells which applicants will be contacted for an interview.

    (B)  The definite article *the* is needed before requirements to show that *specific* requirements must be met.

    **(C)  *They* is an extra word here since the sentence already has a subject, *the applicants*.**

    (D)  The phrase *in order* is followed by an infinitive verb, *to schedule*.

37. **(A)  *Of* follows *because* to introduce a noun such as *incomes*. *Because of* is a commonly used phrase.**

    (B)  In this case, the prepositional phrase *of residences* is correct and explains the kind of sales.

    (C)  The buildings are used for commercial, or business, purposes. They are *commercial* buildings.

    (D)  The sales again reached a high point for the month. They reached a new *monthly high*.

38. **(A)  *To be* or *that should be* are both possible here, but *should be* by itself is not grammatically correct. *Is* is the main verb of this sentence.**

    (B)  The phrase *ability to keep the new restaurant going* means that Mr. Lopez has the knowledge and skills to keep the new restaurant in business.

    (C)  *For several months* tells how long Mr. Lopez can continue to run the restaurant.

    (D)  *With limited revenue* means that the restaurant is not earning much money.

39. (A) *Yet* means *but* in this context. The task is difficult, but it is enjoyable.

    (B) Twelve photos won the contest. They are the *winning* photos. *Winning* is used here as an adjective.

    (C) Twelve photos were *selected from* many photographs that were entered.

    **(D) *Who* refers to people, not things. It cannot be used to refer to *photos*.**

40. (A) *While* expresses the idea of two things happening at the same time. Mr. Nakamura was working at the travel agency and arranging tours at the same time.

    **(B) Since Mr. Nakamura is a person, he must be an agent, not an *agency*. An agency is a company or office.**

    (C) The preposition *in* is followed by the gerund *arranging*. Mr. Nakamura specialized in arranging tours of the Middle East.

    (D) The article *the* precedes the names of geographical areas such as *the Middle East* or *the Southwest*.

41. (A) *Displeased* is an adjective here. The verb *was* is the correct verb tense to describe how the supervisor felt. He *was,* or felt, displeased.

    (B) *Budget* modifies report. The *report* about the budget will not be finished on time.

    (C) The complete verb is *would not be finished.* The passive voice is used because there is no mention of the person responsible for finishing the report.

    **(D) The correct phrase is *on time*, not *by time*.**

42. (A) The present perfect tense *has announced* is correct in this sentence. The verb is singular to agree with the singular noun *Superstore.*

    **(B) Either *will be closed* or *will close* may be used here, but *will have closed* is not the correct tense.**

    (C) The prepositional phrase *for the upcoming holiday* gives the reason the store will be closed.

    (D) No preposition is needed after *holiday. Next week* tells when the holiday will occur.

## Part VII Reading Comprehension

43. **(A) This notice must be for *airplane* travel, since the reservations are on European *Airways*.**

    (B) *Airways* is not used in reference to train travel.

    (C) The format of the travel plan or itinerary is typical of an airline ticket confirmation. *Airways* would not be used to refer to a bus company.

    (D) A cruise ship company would not be referred to as *airways,* and a passenger on a cruise ship would not usually receive a seat number.

44. (A) Ms. Johannson will *change planes* in London on her way from Boston to Stockholm.

    **(B) Ms. Johannson's final destination is Stockholm, where she arrives at 10:57 A.M. on Thursday, March 21.**

    (C) Ms. Johannson is currently living in Cambridge, since that is her address on the notice.

    (D) Boston is the location of the travel agency that sent the notice.

45. (A) The information is for people who do not know much about upholstery. *Upholstery repairers* would already know about the different kinds of upholstery and what to do in each case.

    (B) *Furniture manufacturers* would already know this information. A manufacturer would write this letter to provide information to customers.

    (C) *Delivery personnel* would need to know how to handle new furniture, but this notice is not intended for delivery personnel.

    **(D) The letter is meant to inform and reassure *purchasers of new furniture* so that they know what to expect.**

46. (A) *Barbed wire* used in fences may scar the hides or *skins* of animals.

    (B) *Insect bite* marks are also listed as typically found on leather hides.

    (C) *Branding marks* on the cattle are another "hallmark of the trail."

    **(D) *Sanding* is mentioned as a way of preparing leather hides, not as a source of marks**

47. (A) The passage does not mention *returning* the furniture for any reason.

    **(B) The passage suggests turning over or repositioning the cushions. This is the same as *rearranging* them.**

    (C) *Steam* is mentioned as a way to fix wrinkles in the skirting, not fabric that does not match.

    (D) The passage mentions that the fabric may be folded or wrinkled. However, the letter does not say to unfold anything.

48. (A) High school is mentioned, but *teachers* are not.

    (B) *Community volunteers* helped at the conference, but it was not planned for them.

    **(C) The article mentions *students* several times, and says that they came from *local high schools*.**

    (D) Local business owners helped to run the conference. The future of business is mentioned, but not *new* business owners.

49. (A) Volunteers had already been recruited. They helped the students with the questionnaires.

    (B) Many families attended the event, and they may have enjoyed themselves. However, the purpose of the questionnaire was not to entertain.

    (C) The words *business* and *economy* appear in the article, but nothing is written about soliciting, or *asking for,* funds.

    **(D) The students filled out questionnaires to help them find out their *aptitudes,* or *ability to acquire certain skills.***

50. (A) Although an association spokesperson said that he hoped for a strong economy next year, nothing is said about a weak economy for this year's conference.

    **(B) The first paragraph tells that a major ice storm made travel difficult on the day of the conference.**

    (C) Nothing is said about the number of volunteers who attended.

    (D) Local business leaders were at the conference to give workshops and presentations.

51. (A) Many company employees use the public transportation system, but that is not what is being modernized.

    (B) The Bristol Motor Company is not announcing plans to expand.

    (C) While safety is the major concern in the letter, safety awareness training is not listed as a solution.

    **(D) The widening of the Centura Highway presents a safety issue.**

52. (A) Construction engineers work on a highway expansion, but Mr. Hall does not mention them in his letter.

    (B) Bus and train operators are also not Mr. Hall's concern, nor does he mention them.

    **(C) Mr. Hall is worried about the safety of Bristol Motor Company employees who will have to cross the widened highway.**

    (D) A city traffic officer is mentioned as a possible solution to the safety problem, but not as a reason for concern.

53. **(A) Adding bus routes would not reduce danger to employees who must cross the highway to reach the buses. Mr. Hall does not suggest this as a solution.**

    (B) Having a traffic officer on duty where people cross is mentioned in Mr. Hall's letter.

    (C) Mr. Hall includes a walkway overpass in his suggestions.

    (D) Mr. Hall proposes providing a traffic signal as one way to prevent accidents.

54. (A) Bus *fares* are not mentioned in Mr. Hall's letter.

    (B) Mr. Hall lists the hours when many employees cross the highway. He does not ask Ms. Hsu to decrease work hours.

    (C) Construction is due to begin this year. Mr. Hall does not ask Ms. Hsu to speed up the schedule but rather to ensure safety during and after construction.

    **(D) Mr. Hall wants Ms. Hsu to meet with him to discuss ways to prevent accidents that might be caused by highway traffic.**

# Day 25

## Practice Test: Listening Comprehension Section

Today you will have the opportunity to work through a complete Listening Comprehension section of the TOEIC test. To use this practice section to your greatest advantage, treat it as if you were taking the Listening Comprehension section of a real TOEIC test.

- **Use the sample answer sheet provided.** On the following pages you will find a sample answer sheet similar to the one used on official TOEIC tests. Fill in your biographical information and answer the TOEIC Background Questionnaire before you begin the practice test. As you take the practice test for the Listening Comprehension section, take the time to fill in the circles on the answer sheet correctly, as you would during a real test.
- **Find a quiet place to take the practice test.** Answer the questions in a place where you will not be disturbed or have too many distractions for about an hour. Make sure that you have good audio equipment to listen to the recording. You will need a pencil and eraser.
- **Take the entire section at once.** Once you have started the recording, do not stop it. The recording will run for approximately 45 minutes.

# TOEIC®  Background Questionnaire

*Fill in the answers to the following questions in Section 11, "Questionnaire Responses," on side 2 of your answer sheet. Fill in only one answer for each question.*

## Section I _____

### A. Your educational and English language background

1. Please choose the highest level of education listed below that you have completed or that you are currently enrolled in.

   A. General secondary school
   B. Secondary school for university entrance qualification or equivalent
   C. Vocational school
   D. Business/trade school or technical school
   E. Post-secondary/undergraduate degree
   F. Graduate or professional degree

2. How much time have you spent studying English (in secondary and post-secondary school)?

   A. None (Skip to question 5.)
   B. Less than 1 year
   C. 1 year or more, but less than 2 years
   D. 2 years or more, but less than 5 years
   E. 5 years or more, but less than 10 years
   F. 10 years or more

3. How much time have you spent taking English courses (not including secondary or post-secondary school) that you paid for?

   A. None (Skip to question 5.)
   B. Less than 1 year
   C. 1 year or more, but less than 2 years
   D. 2 years or more, but less than 5 years
   E. 5 years or more

4. How often do/did these courses take place?

   A. Less than 2 hours per week
   B. 2 hours or more, but < 4 hours per week
   C. 4 hours or more, but < 10 hours per week
   D. 10 hours or more, but < 15 hours per week
   E. 15 hours or more per week

5. How much time altogether have you spent studying English in training sponsored by an employer?

   A. None (Skip to question 7.)
   B. Less than 1 year
   C. 1 year or more, but less than 2 years
   D. 2 years or more, but less than 5 years
   E. 5 years or more

6. How often does/did this instruction take place?

   A. Less than 2 hours per week
   B. 2 hours or more, but < 4 hours per week
   C. 4 hours or more, but < 10 hours per week
   D. 10 hours or more, but < 15 hours per week
   E. 15 hours or more per week

### B. Your experience using English in your personal life and work

7. Not including English classes, how often do you use (read, write, listen to, or speak) English now?

   A. Every day/almost every day
   B. 2 to 3 times a week
   C. Once a week
   D. Less than once a week

8. Have you ever lived in a country in which English is the main language spoken?

   A. No
   B. Yes, for less than 6 months
   C. Yes, for 6 months to 1 year
   D. Yes, for more than 1 year

### C. Your current status

9. Which of the following best describes what you do now?

   A. Employed full or part time
   B. Student (Skip to Section III.)
   C. Active duty in the armed forces (Skip to Section III.)
   D. Homemaker (Skip to Section III.)
   E. Unemployed (Skip to Section III.)
   F. Participating in a work-study or apprenticeship program (Skip to Section III.)

# TOEIC® Background Questionnaire – Side 2

**Section II** _____

### A. Your present employment situation

10. Which of the following categories best applies to your job? Choose one. (The positions shown in parentheses are examples only.)

   A. Management (legislator, official, department director)
   B. Scientific/Technical professional (engineer, research scientist)
   C. Marketing/Sales (market analyst, sales representative)
   D. Finance (financial auditor, accountant)
   E. Teaching/Training
   F. Professional specialist (business professional, economist, lawyer)
   G. Customer service (airline attendant, hotel staff, travel agent)
   H. Technician/Associate professional (junior engineer, medical technician, aircraft controller, safety inspector)
   I. Clerical (secretary, bookkeeper)
   J. Worker (trade person, machine operator, assembler, laborer)

11. What is your level in the company?

   A. Nonmanagerial/nonsupervisory
   B. Supervisory
   C. Managerial

12. About how many years have you been with your company?

   A. Less than 2 years
   B. 2 years or more, but less than 5 years
   C. 5 years or more, but less than 10 years
   D. 10 years or more

### B. Your current use of English on the job

13. About how much of your time at work do you spend using English?

   A. 0 to 10%
   B. 11 to 20%
   C. 21 to 50%
   D. 51 to 100%

**Questions 14–17.** How important is each of the following English skills to your work? (Choose one answer for each skill.)

14. Listening

   A. Important
   B. Somewhat important
   C. Not important

15. Reading

   A. Important
   B. Somewhat important
   C. Not important

16. Speaking

   A. Important
   B. Somewhat important
   C. Not important

17. Writing

   A. Important
   B. Somewhat important
   C. Not important

**Section III** _____

### A. Your experience taking the TOEIC test

18. Before today, how many times have you taken the TOEIC test?

   A. Never
   B. 1 time
   C. 2 times
   D. 3 times
   E. 4 or more times

19. When did you last take the TOEIC test?

   A. Less than 6 months ago
   B. 6 months ago or more, but less than 1 year ago
   C. 1 year ago or more, but less than 2 years ago
   D. 2 or more years ago

**LISTENING SECTION**

| 1 Ⓐ Ⓑ Ⓒ Ⓓ | 26 Ⓐ Ⓑ Ⓒ | 51 Ⓐ Ⓑ Ⓒ Ⓓ | 76 Ⓐ Ⓑ Ⓒ Ⓓ |
| 2 Ⓐ Ⓑ Ⓒ Ⓓ | 27 Ⓐ Ⓑ Ⓒ | 52 Ⓐ Ⓑ Ⓒ Ⓓ | 77 Ⓐ Ⓑ Ⓒ Ⓓ |
| 3 Ⓐ Ⓑ Ⓒ Ⓓ | 28 Ⓐ Ⓑ Ⓒ | 53 Ⓐ Ⓑ Ⓒ Ⓓ | 78 Ⓐ Ⓑ Ⓒ Ⓓ |
| 4 Ⓐ Ⓑ Ⓒ Ⓓ | 29 Ⓐ Ⓑ Ⓒ | 54 Ⓐ Ⓑ Ⓒ Ⓓ | 79 Ⓐ Ⓑ Ⓒ Ⓓ |
| 5 Ⓐ Ⓑ Ⓒ Ⓓ | 30 Ⓐ Ⓑ Ⓒ | 55 Ⓐ Ⓑ Ⓒ Ⓓ | 80 Ⓐ Ⓑ Ⓒ Ⓓ |
| 6 Ⓐ Ⓑ Ⓒ Ⓓ | 31 Ⓐ Ⓑ Ⓒ | 56 Ⓐ Ⓑ Ⓒ Ⓓ | 81 Ⓐ Ⓑ Ⓒ Ⓓ |
| 7 Ⓐ Ⓑ Ⓒ Ⓓ | 32 Ⓐ Ⓑ Ⓒ | 57 Ⓐ Ⓑ Ⓒ Ⓓ | 82 Ⓐ Ⓑ Ⓒ Ⓓ |
| 8 Ⓐ Ⓑ Ⓒ Ⓓ | 33 Ⓐ Ⓑ Ⓒ | 58 Ⓐ Ⓑ Ⓒ Ⓓ | 83 Ⓐ Ⓑ Ⓒ Ⓓ |
| 9 Ⓐ Ⓑ Ⓒ Ⓓ | 34 Ⓐ Ⓑ Ⓒ | 59 Ⓐ Ⓑ Ⓒ Ⓓ | 84 Ⓐ Ⓑ Ⓒ Ⓓ |
| 10 Ⓐ Ⓑ Ⓒ Ⓓ | 35 Ⓐ Ⓑ Ⓒ | 60 Ⓐ Ⓑ Ⓒ Ⓓ | 85 Ⓐ Ⓑ Ⓒ Ⓓ |
| 11 Ⓐ Ⓑ Ⓒ Ⓓ | 36 Ⓐ Ⓑ Ⓒ | 61 Ⓐ Ⓑ Ⓒ Ⓓ | 86 Ⓐ Ⓑ Ⓒ Ⓓ |
| 12 Ⓐ Ⓑ Ⓒ Ⓓ | 37 Ⓐ Ⓑ Ⓒ | 62 Ⓐ Ⓑ Ⓒ Ⓓ | 87 Ⓐ Ⓑ Ⓒ Ⓓ |
| 13 Ⓐ Ⓑ Ⓒ Ⓓ | 38 Ⓐ Ⓑ Ⓒ | 63 Ⓐ Ⓑ Ⓒ Ⓓ | 88 Ⓐ Ⓑ Ⓒ Ⓓ |
| 14 Ⓐ Ⓑ Ⓒ Ⓓ | 39 Ⓐ Ⓑ Ⓒ | 64 Ⓐ Ⓑ Ⓒ Ⓓ | 89 Ⓐ Ⓑ Ⓒ Ⓓ |
| 15 Ⓐ Ⓑ Ⓒ Ⓓ | 40 Ⓐ Ⓑ Ⓒ | 65 Ⓐ Ⓑ Ⓒ Ⓓ | 90 Ⓐ Ⓑ Ⓒ Ⓓ |
| 16 Ⓐ Ⓑ Ⓒ Ⓓ | 41 Ⓐ Ⓑ Ⓒ | 66 Ⓐ Ⓑ Ⓒ Ⓓ | 91 Ⓐ Ⓑ Ⓒ Ⓓ |
| 17 Ⓐ Ⓑ Ⓒ Ⓓ | 42 Ⓐ Ⓑ Ⓒ | 67 Ⓐ Ⓑ Ⓒ Ⓓ | 92 Ⓐ Ⓑ Ⓒ Ⓓ |
| 18 Ⓐ Ⓑ Ⓒ Ⓓ | 43 Ⓐ Ⓑ Ⓒ | 68 Ⓐ Ⓑ Ⓒ Ⓓ | 93 Ⓐ Ⓑ Ⓒ Ⓓ |
| 19 Ⓐ Ⓑ Ⓒ Ⓓ | 44 Ⓐ Ⓑ Ⓒ | 69 Ⓐ Ⓑ Ⓒ Ⓓ | 94 Ⓐ Ⓑ Ⓒ Ⓓ |
| 20 Ⓐ Ⓑ Ⓒ Ⓓ | 45 Ⓐ Ⓑ Ⓒ | 70 Ⓐ Ⓑ Ⓒ Ⓓ | 95 Ⓐ Ⓑ Ⓒ Ⓓ |
| 21 Ⓐ Ⓑ Ⓒ | 46 Ⓐ Ⓑ Ⓒ | 71 Ⓐ Ⓑ Ⓒ Ⓓ | 96 Ⓐ Ⓑ Ⓒ Ⓓ |
| 22 Ⓐ Ⓑ Ⓒ | 47 Ⓐ Ⓑ Ⓒ | 72 Ⓐ Ⓑ Ⓒ Ⓓ | 97 Ⓐ Ⓑ Ⓒ Ⓓ |
| 23 Ⓐ Ⓑ Ⓒ | 48 Ⓐ Ⓑ Ⓒ | 73 Ⓐ Ⓑ Ⓒ Ⓓ | 98 Ⓐ Ⓑ Ⓒ Ⓓ |
| 24 Ⓐ Ⓑ Ⓒ | 49 Ⓐ Ⓑ Ⓒ | 74 Ⓐ Ⓑ Ⓒ Ⓓ | 99 Ⓐ Ⓑ Ⓒ Ⓓ |
| 25 Ⓐ Ⓑ Ⓒ | 50 Ⓐ Ⓑ Ⓒ | 75 Ⓐ Ⓑ Ⓒ Ⓓ | 100 Ⓐ Ⓑ Ⓒ Ⓓ |

---

## PRACTICE TEST 1

## Listening Comprehension

In this section of the test, you will have the chance to show how well you understand spoken English. There are four parts to this section, with special directions for each part.

### Part I

*Directions: For each question, you will see a picture in your book and you will hear four short statements. The statements will be spoken just one time. They will not be printed in your book, so you must listen carefully to understand what the speaker says.*

*Sample Answer*

Ⓐ ● Ⓒ Ⓓ

When you hear the four statements, look at the picture in your book and choose the statement that best describes what you see in the picture. Then, on your answer sheet, find the number of the question and mark your answer.

Now, listen to the four statements. Statement (B), "They're having a meeting," best describes what you see in the picture. Therefore, you should choose answer (B).

1.

2.

3.

4.

5.

6.

7.

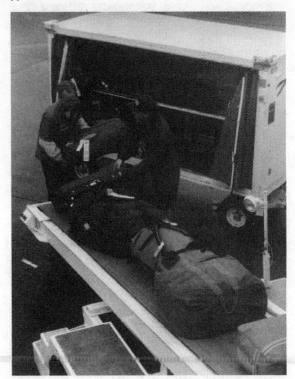

8.

9.

10.

11.

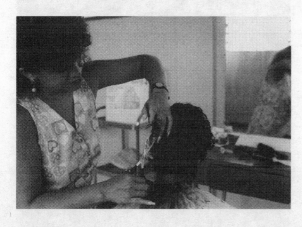

12.

13.

14.

15.

16.

17.

18.

19.

20.

**Part II**

*Directions: In this part of the test, you will hear a question or statement spoken in English, followed by three responses, also spoken in English. The question or statement and the responses will be spoken just one time.*

They will not be printed in your book, so you must listen carefully to understand what the speakers say. You are to choose the best response to each question or statement.

Now listen to a sample question.

You will hear:   ●

You will also hear:

The best response to the question "How are you?" is choice (A), "I am fine, thank you." Therefore, you should choose answer (A).

21. Mark your answer on your answer sheet.

22. Mark your answer on your answer sheet.

23. Mark your answer on your answer sheet.

24. Mark your answer on your answer sheet.

25. Mark your answer on your answer sheet.

26. Mark your answer on your answer sheet.

27. Mark your answer on your answer sheet.

28. Mark your answer on your answer sheet.

29. Mark your answer on your answer sheet.

30. Mark your answer on your answer sheet.

31. Mark your answer on your answer sheet.

32. Mark your answer on your answer sheet.

33. Mark your answer on your answer sheet.

34. Mark your answer on your answer sheet.

35. Mark your answer on your answer sheet.

36. Mark your answer on your answer sheet.

37. Mark your answer on your answer sheet.

38. Mark your answer on your answer sheet.

39. Mark your answer on your answer sheet.

40. Mark your answer on your answer sheet.

41. Mark your answer on your answer sheet.

42. Mark your answer on your answer sheet.

43. Mark your answer on your answer sheet.

44. Mark your answer on your answer sheet.

45. Mark your answer on your answer sheet.

46. Mark your answer on your answer sheet.

47. Mark your answer on your answer sheet.

48. Mark your answer on your answer sheet.

49. Mark your answer on your answer sheet.

50. Mark your answer on your answer sheet.

## Part III

*Directions: In this part of the test, you will hear thirty short conversations between two people. The conversations will not be printed in your book. You will hear the conversations only once, so you must listen carefully to understand what the speakers say.*

*In your book, you will read a question about each conversation. The question will be followed by four answers. You are to choose the best answer to each question and mark it on your answer sheet.*

51. Who called and left a message?

   (A) Mr. Murphy.

   (B) The operator.

   (C) Mr. Murphy's secretary.

   (D) The committee chairperson.

52. Where does this conversation take place?

   (A) In a coffee shop.

   (B) In an office.

   (C) In a post office.

   (D) In a supermarket.

53. Why is Mrs. Sompong leaving?

   (A) To join another company.

   (B) To start her own business.

   (C) To enter a race.

   (D) To have a break from working.

54. When does Claudia want to go to the play?

   (A) Monday.

   (B) Wednesday.

   (C) Thursday.

   (D) Saturday.

55. What is the woman's job?

   (A) Telephone operator.

   (B) Computer technician.

   (C) Sales representative.

   (D) Personnel supervisor.

56. When will the men see the movie?

   (A) At 1:00.

   (B) At 2:00.

   (C) At 4:00.

   (D) At 7:00.

57. What are the people doing with the furniture?

   (A) Rearranging it.

   (B) Designing it.

   (C) Buying it.

   (D) Assembling it.

58. How will they travel to the conference?

   (A) By plane.

   (B) By car.

   (C) By train.

   (D) By bus.

59. Why is the woman NOT able to buy Business News?

   (A) The magazines have all been sold already.

   (B) The truck was delayed because of the weather.

   (C) The store is closed on Mondays.

   (D) The delivery schedule has been changed.

60. Who is going to the convention?

   (A) Juan.

   (B) Ricardo.

   (C) Ms. Ortega.

   (D) Carla.

61. What are they likely to eat for lunch?
    (A) Soup.
    (B) Salad.
    (C) Sandwiches.
    (D) Hamburgers.

62. Where is the man's luggage?
    (A) In New York.
    (B) At the hotel.
    (C) In San Francisco.
    (D) On the bus.

63. How much vacation time is Susanna allowed this year?
    (A) One week.
    (B) Two weeks.
    (C) Three weeks.
    (D) Four weeks.

64. Where are the speakers?
    (A) In the cafeteria kitchen.
    (B) In the first-aid room.
    (C) In the mail room.
    (D) In the staff lounge.

65. Who are they talking about?
    (A) Yuri's daughter.
    (B) Yuri's son.
    (C) Yuri.
    (D) Yuri's wife.

66. When will Tom need to use Alan's office?
    (A) Thursday morning.
    (B) Friday morning.
    (C) Friday afternoon.
    (D) Monday afternoon.

67. What is Patricia looking for?
    (A) A file cabinet.
    (B) A report.
    (C) A memo.
    (D) A check.

68. Where does this conversation take place?
    (A) At the library.
    (B) At a restaurant.
    (C) At the office.
    (D) At a hotel.

69. Why is the man unable to speak to Ms. Krishnan?
    (A) She is on a sales trip overseas.
    (B) She no longer works for the company.
    (C) She has moved to another department.
    (D) She is too busy.

70. Where will the two men go next week?
    (A) To a hospital.
    (B) To a greenhouse.
    (C) To a building site.
    (D) To a factory.

71. Why is Ms. Mura pleased?
    (A) She won a contest.
    (B) She bought a new company.
    (C) She was just hired.
    (D) She finished her résumé.

72. What is the woman going to do?
    (A) Sell the camera.
    (B) Pay by check.
    (C) Fill out a form.
    (D) Write her name on the card.

73. Who will be sent to room 512?
    (A) A plumber.
    (B) An accountant.
    (C) An electrician.
    (D) A driver.

74. What is Ms. Lee waiting for?
    (A) A fax.
    (B) Her clients.
    (C) A document.
    (D) A phone call.

75. Why is Heidi leaving?

  (A) To go home.

  (B) To handle an urgent matter.

  (C) To make a telephone call.

  (D) To attend an office party.

76. What does the woman want to do?

  (A) Get a credit card.

  (B) Buy a sweater.

  (C) Return a present.

  (D) Pay a fine.

77. When will the presentation be made?

  (A) Monday.

  (B) Wednesday.

  (C) Over the weekend.

  (D) In seven weeks.

78. Why was the driver stopped?

  (A) He was driving too fast.

  (B) He turned the wrong way.

  (C) His car was not working properly.

  (D) He did not have a license.

79. When will the order be ready?

  (A) In a few minutes.

  (B) At 9:00 tonight.

  (C) Tomorrow.

  (D) The day after tomorrow.

80. Why did Olivia leave?

  (A) There was not enough work to do.

  (B) The division office asked her to.

  (C) She decided to retire.

  (D) Her contract was not approved.

## Part IV

*Directions: In this part of the test, you will hear several short talks. Each will be spoken just one time. They will not be printed in your book, so you must listen carefully to understand and remember what is said.*

*In your book, you will read two or more questions about each short talk. The questions will be followed by four answers. You are to choose the best answer to each question and mark it on your answer sheet.*

81. How long will the tour be?

  (A) 15 minutes.

  (B) 30 minutes.

  (C) 1 hour.

  (D) 3 hours.

82. What will the 3:00 talk be about?

  (A) Photography.

  (B) Sculpture.

  (C) Modern art.

  (D) Art collecting.

83. Who is speaking?

  (A) A hotel clerk.

  (B) A chef.

  (C) A waiter.

  (D) A farmer.

84. When is the speaker talking?

  (A) Early morning.

  (B) Late morning.

  (C) Mid-afternoon.

  (D) Evening.

85. Where would this announcement most likely be heard?

  (A) On a ship.

  (B) At a taxi stand.

  (C) On a train.

  (D) At an airport.

86. What must passengers have?

    (A) A seat assignment.

    (B) A credit card.

    (C) A local map.

    (D) A dinner reservation.

87. Who is the talk directed to?

    (A) Customer service representatives.

    (B) Potential franchise owners.

    (C) Shopping-center designers.

    (D) Bank officers.

88. What kind of business is Milton's?

    (A) A food retailer.

    (B) An employment service.

    (C) A recreational facility.

    (D) A travel agency.

89. What is Mr. Sandoval's position with the firm?

    (A) Sales manager.

    (B) Head of research and development.

    (C) Personnel manager.

    (D) Director of franchising.

90. What is Ms. Suzuki's profession?

    (A) Photographer.

    (B) Magazine editor.

    (C) Advertising director.

    (D) Newspaper publisher.

91. Where was Ms. Suzuki's most recent assignment?

    (A) Australia.

    (B) Japan.

    (C) Brazil.

    (D) The United States.

92. What is the purpose of the event?

    (A) To celebrate a new merger.

    (B) To honor workers.

    (C) To plan next year's strategies.

    (D) To announce profits.

93. How can you get tickets to the banquet?

    (A) Go to the hotel.

    (B) Call the president.

    (C) Contact the board of directors.

    (D) Telephone the personnel office.

94. What is the theme of the series?

    (A) Geology.

    (B) World history.

    (C) Travel.

    (D) Filmmaking.

95. How many films will be shown this week?

    (A) Two.

    (B) Five.

    (C) Seven.

    (D) Nine.

96. How long is tonight's film?

    (A) A half hour.

    (B) One hour.

    (C) An hour and a half.

    (D) Two hours.

97. What will happen after tonight's film?

    (A) The theater will be closed for renovations.

    (B) A short documentary film will be shown.

    (C) A prize will be awarded.

    (D) The filmmakers will be interviewed.

98. Who is speaking?

    (A) A political candidate.

    (B) A weather forecaster.

    (C) A radio-show host.

    (D) A newspaper reporter.

99. What is Ms. Valmont's job?

    (A) Computer programmer.

    (B) Government official.

    (C) Journalist.

    (D) Publisher.

100. What will be heard next?

    (A) Last week's election results.

    (B) A political commentary.

    (C) A candidate's speech.

    (D) Local news stories.

This is the end of the Listening Comprehension portion of the test.

■ Now, STOP the recording.

# Day 26

## Follow-up to the Listening Comprehension Section of the Practice Test

Start today's lesson by checking your answers to the practice test of the Listening Comprehension section that you worked on in Day 25. The answer key is printed below. For your reference, you should lightly mark the questions you answered incorrectly.

## ANSWER KEY FOR THE PRACTICE TEST: LISTENING COMPREHENSION SECTION

### Part I: Photographs

| | |
|---|---|
| 1. C | 11. D |
| 2. A | 12. A |
| 3. B | 13. B |
| 4. B | 14. D |
| 5. B | 15. D |
| 6. A | 16. A |
| 7. C | 17. B |
| 8. A | 18. C |
| 9. D | 19. D |
| 10. A | 20. C |

### Part II: Question–Response

| | |
|---|---|
| 21. C | 36. C |
| 22. B | 37. C |
| 23. B | 38. A |
| 24. C | 39. B |
| 25. B | 40. B |
| 26. A | 41. A |
| 27. B | 42. B |
| 28. B | 43. C |
| 29. A | 44. B |
| 30. C | 45. B |
| 31. B | 46. C |
| 32. A | 47. A |
| 33. C | 48. B |
| 34. B | 49. B |
| 35. B | 50. A |

## Part III: Short Conversations

| | | | |
|---|---|---|---|
| 51. C | 66. A |
| 52. B | 67. B |
| 53. A | 68. D |
| 54. B | 69. C |
| 55. A | 70. D |
| 56. D | 71. C |
| 57. A | 72. B |
| 58. C | 73. C |
| 59. D | 74. D |
| 60. A | 75. B |
| 61. B | 76. C |
| 62. A | 77. B |
| 63. C | 78. C |
| 64. A | 79. D |
| 65. A | 80. C |

## Part IV: Short Talks

| | |
|---|---|
| 81. B | 91. A |
| 82. B | 92. B |
| 83. C | 93. D |
| 84. D | 94. C |
| 85. C | 95. D |
| 86. A | 96. C |
| 87. B | 97. D |
| 88. A | 98. C |
| 89. D | 99. C |
| 90. A | 100. D |

Try again to answer any questions that you answered incorrectly on Day 25, finding the correct place on the recording for each one. It is often easy to see why you made an incorrect choice. Sometimes, however, you may still feel that you do not understand why the answer you chose was incorrect, and then it is useful to work with the question some more. Try doing the following:

1. If you had trouble understanding the recording, read the recording script while you look at the questions. The recording script for all the questions can be found at the end of this section. After each question, stop the recording and give yourself time to think about the choices carefully.

2. If you feel that you still do not understand why the answer you chose was incorrect, and why a different choice is the correct one, read the explanation of the answer for that question. On the following pages you will find explanations of the answers for all the questions in the practice Listening Comprehension section.

3. If you had difficulty with one particular question type, go back to the lessons in which you learned about that type of question, and review the tips.

## EXPLANATIONS OF THE ANSWERS FOR THE LISTENING COMPREHENSION SECTION ON DAY 25

## Listening Comprehension

### Part I Photographs

1.  (A) Since she is still working, the exchange, or *transaction*, has *not* been finished.

    (B) Neither woman is using a pen or pencil to write *by hand*.

    **(C) One of the women is typing; therefore, she is *using the keyboard*.**

    (D) The screen is part of the computer. It is *not* a television.

2.  **(A) People are seated at only a *few* of the tables.**

    (B) The water is in a river or lake *alongside* the restaurant but is not on its floor.

    (C) The tables are *round* in shape.

    (D) Since it has customers, the restaurant must *still be open* for business.

3.  (A) The photos have *already* been developed.

    **(B) The man is *both* talking on the phone and looking at photos.**

    (C) While he may be holding photos of scenery, he is *not* looking out the window.

    (D) He is *still* talking, with the phone at his ear.

4.  (A) No drivers can be seen in the cars, and the car lights are *not* on.

    **(B) There is a *ceiling* over the parking area.**

    (C) The picture shows *cars*, not cards.

    (D) The pictured cars are in a parking area, rather than in a *park*.

5.  (A) There is a bag on the sofa, but no one is touching it.

    **(B) The man and woman are sitting side by side, or *next to each other*, on the couch.**

    (C) They are *sitting* on the sofa, not moving it.

    (D) They are looking at *each other*, not at a display.

6.  **(A) The market is *busy* and full of people.**

    (B) The man is lifting vegetables, but he is not *in a garden*.

    (C) Since the vegetables, or *crops*, are for sale, they have *already* been harvested. *Yet to be done* indicates that a task remains.

    (D) The woman is *near*, but not *on*, a scale. The scale is for weighing vegetables.

7.  (A) They are placing the bags on a platform in front of them, but it is at *knee height* rather than *overhead*.

    (B) The suitcases had already been packed *before* they were moved.

    **(C) The men are transferring, or *moving*, luggage from one place to another.**

    (D) The picture does not show luggage being checked, or *inspected*.

8.  **(A) The man is looking at, or *examining*, the items for sale, or *merchandise*.**

    (B) The cases are actually quite full of items.

    (C) Since the man is looking at a watch, he is not rearranging the cases of merchandise.

    (D) Since the man is looking at a watch, he is not watching a movie.

9.  (A) The stairs are behind the woman, and the people are not climbing, but standing still.

    (B) Since they are turned to look at each other, they cannot also be looking in the *same direction*.

    (C) There is a railing in the picture, but neither person is touching it.

    **(D) The man and woman are standing opposite, or *facing*, each other.**

10. **(A) The train is _crowded_ with people.**

(B) The picture shows a _train_, not rain. The man is standing, but he is not trying to close the train door.

(C) The train is still in the station. It has not yet left.

(D) The man is still on the train, holding his briefcase. He has not left it anywhere.

11. (A) There is no indication that the woman's working hours have been decreased, or _cut_.

(B) The woman is not cutting out, or _clipping out_, an article.

(C) The picture shows _hair_, not _air_.

**(D) One woman is cutting the other woman's hair.**

12. **(A) Some of the people are riding the escalator up to a higher level.**

(B) The people are not climbing; therefore, the escalator is _in working order_.

(C) Since there is an escalator, there must be at least two levels.

(D) Because many people are visible, it is very unlikely that the _property_ is closed to the public.

13. (A) Since they have not yet eaten, they are not yet ready to pay their bill.

**(B) The waiter is writing while the man and woman have their menus open. Thus, he appears to be _taking their order_.**

(C) The woman is requesting, or _ordering, food_, not asking the men to leave.

(D) No dishes are on the table, so no dishes can be cleared away.

14. (A) The other person in the picture is not helping the woman.

(B) The store appears _full_ of items for sale. Thus, its _inventory_ is high.

(C) The man is kneeling in front of a shelf. He is not at a cash register ready to pay.

**(D) The woman has her arm out and appears to be _reaching for_ something on the top shelf.**

15. (A) There are files in the picture, but the man is _not_ putting anything away.

(B) The woman is opposite, or _across_ from, the man, but she is standing, not sitting.

(C) There are papers in the picture, but they do not look like _newspapers_.

**(D) The man is holding out a paper to give, or _hand_, to the woman.**

16. **(A) Three people are playing music together. They are a _trio_.**

(B) This performance is probably not a _musical_, or a play with songs, and it is _still taking place_.

(C) The instruments are being _used_, not put away in their cases.

(D) An _orchestra_ includes many musicians. These three people have _already_ entered the room and have begun to play.

17. (A) There is a wide body of water, perhaps a _river_, but no one is _in_ it.

**(B) The picture shows some people riding _bicycles_.**

(C) The trees in the photo have _many_ leaves.

(D) The water has not _overflowed_ onto the nearby land.

18. (A) There is paper and there may be flowers, but there is no _flowered wallpaper_.

(B) The women are seated, not walking, so they are most likely not _taking a tour_.

**(C) The three women appear to be working outdoors.**

(D) Papers are spread in front of them, but no food is being eaten.

19. (A) She is standing, not sitting.

(B) The people who are listening to her are sitting, not standing.

(C) The seats in the room are all taken, not empty.

**(D) The woman is making an informal speech, or _presentation_, to the people in the room.**

20. (A) The truck is parked on the side of the road. There is no traffic light in the picture.

(B) The man is *already* in the truck.

**(C) Large boxes are piled, or *stacked*, on the ground near the truck.**

(D) The picture shows men and boxes, but there are no men *carrying* boxes.

## Part II Question–Response

21. (A) answers a question about *where*.

(B) answers a question about *how long*.

**(C) The key question word is *when*, so a date is the correct answer.**

22. (A) repeats the word *arrive* from the question but does not respond to the main idea about the arrival time.

**(B) This is a request for information about time. Choice (B) shows that the woman is sorry not to have an answer; she didn't think of finding out the information.**

(C) does not respond to the main idea about the arrival time.

23. (A) mentions *where* someone lives.

**(B) The speaker asks *who* can deliver a memo. Only choice (B), *I can do it*, provides an appropriate response.**

(C) mentions *where* someone is from.

24. (A) is about where the reception takes place, not whether the man wants to go to it.

(B) A *reception* is a formal party; a *receipt* is a paper that shows payment.

**(C) The speaker gives a reason for not going to the reception.**

25. (A) The speaker asks *what*, not *who*.

**(B) The question asks for a name. Only choice (B) provides a name.**

(C) The question does not ask for a recommendation.

26. **(A) The key question word is *where*, so the answer should include a location.**

(B) answers *when*.

(C) answers *why*. Choice (C) mentions the view, but *Oceanview* is the name of a company, not a view from a window.

27. (A) uses the wrong subject and tense.

**(B) The speaker asks if a visit has been made. The answer should be in the past tense.**

In (C), a *plant* is referred to as a living thing, not as a factory.

28. (A) answers a *where* question. *It's* refers to an object, not a person.

**(B) The key question word is *who*, so the answer should include a person's name.**

(C) The new receptionist has *already* been hired.

29. **(A) The question asks *where* the conference will be held, so the answer should be a place.**

(B) *Here* and *hear* sound the same, but the woman is not asking about hearing.

(C) This answer merely confirms the first half of the question, since the first woman already knows that the conference will occur.

30. (A) gives a time but answers a *when* question.

(B) describes *what* the meeting was about, not *why* it began early.

**(C) The key words for this question are *why* and *early*. Only choice (C) gives a reason for *why* the meeting started early.**

31. (A) tells *what* is produced, but does not tell *how much*.

**(B) The key words *total* and *figures* indicate that the answer should include a number or an amount.**

(C) names a part of the factory but does not tell the amount produced.

32. **(A) Here, the question *how far* is about distance. Choice (A) measures distance by the time it takes to get to the park.**

    (B) This expression is a polite way of disagreeing.

    (C) The question is about a *park*, not about parking a car.

33. (A) The man asks whether the agenda is *prepared*, not *repaired*.

    (B) The agenda has been *prepared*, not *examined for likeness*, or *compared*, to another one.

    **(C) The speaker asks if a plan, or *agenda*, has been prepared. Choice (C) states that the agenda still needs to be reviewed, and is therefore *not yet* prepared.**

34. (A) The question does not ask for directions to the movie.

    **(B) The question is an informal invitation. Choice (B) is an informal way of agreeing.**

    (C) The question is not about how much more time the work will take.

35. (A) answers in the present tense. Moreover, in choice (A), *stock exchange* does not have the same meaning as *stock*, or inventory.

    **(B) Since the question is in the past tense, the answer should also be in the past tense.**

    (C) answers in the present tense.

36. (A) The question asks for the location of the *files*, not the *fire exit*.

    (B) *Merger* sounds like *emergency* but means the joining of two companies.

    **(C) The question is a request for help. Choice (C) is a polite reply.**

37. (A) The question asks about *sound equipment*, not *sounds*.

    (B) is about money spent on *room rental*, not equipment, although *rental* sounds like *departmental*.

    **(C) An important word in the question is *budget*; it asks where money, or *funding*, for the equipment came from.**

38. **(A) Only choice (A) answers the question of *where* the man will stay.**

    (B) tells *why* the man is going to Paris.

    (C) states *how long* he will be there.

39. (A) answers in the past tense, but the dinner has not yet taken place.

    **(B) The question is an invitation to dinner. Choice (B) is a polite refusal.**

    (C) does not answer a question about an invitation.

40. (A) In the question, *company* means a *business*, not a traveling companion.

    **(B) The word *deal* here means special discount, or reduced price. Choice (B) gives the percent of the discount.**

    In this choice, (C) to *deal* means to *give out the cards in a card game*.

41. **(A) The key question word is about *when* Mr. Mori will be free, so the answer should mention time.**

    (B) is a location that answers the question *where*.

    (C) is a location that answers the question *where*.

42. (A) refers to letters that have been mailed, not to supplies of stationery.

    **(B) The main idea of the question is *how* to obtain more supplies. Choice (B) explains the ordering procedure.**

    (C) *Letterhead* is official company paper, not a person who is department head.

43. (A) tells about the staff meeting itself.

    In this choice, (B) *present* means a gift, rather than *in attendance*.

    **(C) The question asks about Ms. Dubois's attendance at the meeting. Choice (C) indicates that she did not attend.**

44. (A) The word in the question is *assistant*, or *helper*, not *assistance*, or *help*.

    **(B) The man asks the woman to confirm whom she works for. Choice (B) politely corrects his mistake.**

    (C) This choice confuses two words that sound alike, *new* and *knew*. The man is not asking if the woman knows something but rather if she is the new assistant.

45. (A) The question does not ask about the actual sales, but about the sales *report*.

    **(B) The key question word is *when*. Choice (B) gives a time when the task can be done.**

    (C) tells how old the report is but not how to get one.

46. (A) tells *where* Mr. Danforth is, but does not explain his behavior.

    (B) starts with *no,* which can answer only a yes-no question, not an information question.

    **(C) Since the question asks *why*, the answer should explain the reason for the employee's mistake, and choice (C) does this.**

47. (A) An item that is on *sale* has had its price reduced, or *marked down*.

    (B) Although they sound similar, *marked down* is different from the *market* being closed down.

    (C) The question is about the price of the coat, not its color.

48. (A) The question is about lists of items, or *invoices*. It is not about voices.

    **(B) Only choice (B) answers the question *why*, by giving a reason for what Ms. Ortiz wants to do.**

    (C) Ms. Ortiz has not yet seen the invoices, so the answer should not be in the past tense. Also, *invoices* is plural, while *it* is singular.

49. (A) *Right* is a direction in the context of this question; it does not mean *correct* here.

    **(B) The question asks about *where* to put the cabinet, so the answer should be about its *location*.**

    (C) The question is about the file cabinet, not about the copies made by the copy machine.

50. **(A) The words *same* and *last* time suggest that an action is being repeated. Choice (A) explains that the situation has changed *since then*.**

    (B) The question is about a *business proposal*, not a marriage proposal.

    (C) The word used is *rejected*, meaning *not accepted*. An *injection* may be used in medicine to protect against sickness.

## Part III Short Conversations

51. (A) Mr. Murphy *himself* did not call.

    (B) The women do not mention a telephone *operator.*

    **(C) The second woman asks if Mr. Murphy's *secretary* called. The first woman answers yes.**

    (D) The women do not mention a committee *chairperson.*

52. (A) The man is looking for a place *to get* coffee, so he is probably not *already* in a coffee shop.

    **(B) Since the speakers mention the *employee lounge* and the *mailroom*, they are most likely in an *office* building.**

    (C) A *mailroom* is not the same as a post office.

    (D) The man is looking for a place *to get* coffee, so he is probably not *already* in a supermarket.

53. **(A) The speakers are talking about Mrs. Sompong's job situation, so the competitors must have made her a job offer to *join their company*.**

    (B) The speakers do not mention *starting* a business.

    (C) While competitors may *race* against each other, this conversation is not about racing.

    (D) The speakers also do not mention taking a vacation, or *break from working*.

54. (A) While there are performances of the play, or the play *runs*, from Monday to Thursday, Wednesday is the correct response.

    **(B) Claudia says that she wants to order tickets for *Wednesday*.**

    (C) While there are performances of the play, or the play *runs*, from Monday to Thursday, Wednesday is the correct response.

    (D) Saturday would be a weekend performance, and there are no performances available then.

55. **(A) The woman is a *telephone operator*, since she answers the phone and connects the caller to the department he requests.**

    (B) The company is called Standard *Computer* Services, but the woman is not a computer *technician*.

    (C) She offers to *transfer* the man's call to the sales department.

    (D) *Mr. Fong* works in the personnel department.

56. (A) There is no mention of a one o'clock show.

    (B) The movie is shown two *times*.

    (C) The *earlier* showing is at four o'clock.

    **(D) The men decide to go to the *later of* the two showings, which starts at seven o'clock.**

57. **(A) The speakers are talking about where to put the desk. They are probably *rearranging the furniture*.**

    (B) Since the furniture was already in place in the room, they cannot be designing it.

    (C) Since the furniture was already in place in the room, they cannot be buying it.

    (D) Since the furniture was already in place in the room, they cannot be putting it together or assembling it.

58. (A) The conference is *too close* for the complications of a plane trip.

    (B) They consider driving, but choose the train instead.

    **(C) The speakers decide to *take the train* so they can do work on the way.**

    (D) The man will pick up tickets at the *station*. Since they will take the train, he must mean the train — not bus — station.

59. (A) Since the *News* has not arrived, the copies *cannot* have been sold.

    (B) The truck is later than usual, but not due to the *weather*.

    (C) Monday is the *delivery* day, *not* when the store is *closed*.

    **(D) The *News* has not been delivered yet because the delivery truck has a new route. The man says it will come *soon*.**

60. **(A) Several names are mentioned. The woman calls the man, whom she asks to go to the convention, by the name *Juan*.**

    (B) Ricardo is the person who *cannot* go.

    (C) Ms. Ortega is *not* going, since she asks Juan to represent the firm.

    (D) Carla has made the travel arrangements.

61. (A) To *save money,* they will most likely order salad, not soup.

    **(B) *Salad* is the only choice actually mentioned. The woman has a *coupon* for the salad bar.**

    (C) To *save money,* they will most likely order salad, not sandwiches

    (D) To *save money,* they will most likely order salad, not hamburgers. A *health food* restaurant is not likely to serve hamburgers.

62. **(A) The airline sent the man's luggage to *New York* by mistake.**

    (B) The man himself is staying at a hotel.

    (C) The man himself is staying in San Francisco.

    (D) He can get to the shopping mall by bus.

63. (A) She asks if she can take her whole vacation *at once.* She does not say *one.*

    (B) Susanna has *worked for* the company for two *years.* She may take only *two* weeks' vacation at one time.

    **(C) Susanna is now allowed, or *entitled to, three* weeks of vacation.**

    (D) No mention is made of four weeks.

64. **(A) The men mention *kitchen staff, cans of corn,* and *menu,* which all relate to *food.* They are most likely in the cafeteria kitchen.**

    (B) First-aid room does not take into account the words that refer to food.

    (C) Mail room does not take into account the words that refer to food.

    (D) Staff lounge does not take into account the words that refer to food.

65. **(A) Yuri says that Anna, his *daughter,* got sick on their trip.**

    (B) Anna is his youngest *girl.*

    (C) Yuri is one of the speakers, but they are not talking *about* him.

    (D) Yuri's wife is referred to only indirectly when he mentions *our* daughter.

66. **(A) Several times are mentioned. *Thursday morning* is when Tom's office will be painted and he will need to use Alan's office.**

    (B) Alan will be *away* until Friday morning.

    (C) Friday *afternoon* is not mentioned.

    (D) Tom's project is *due* on Monday afternoon.

67. (A) She asks the other woman to *look* for it in the file cabinet.

    **(B) Patricia's question is about a marketing *report.***

    (C) The memo is on the desk, so it is not missing.

    (D) Patricia uses *check* as a verb meaning *look for,* not a noun meaning *a paper worth money.*

68. (A) *Booked* here is an adjective meaning *reserved,* not the noun *book* such as one would find in a library. A library is not a room where someone would stay *overnight.*

    (B) A restaurant is not a room where someone would stay *overnight.*

    (C) An office is not a room where someone would stay *overnight.*

    **(D) Since the conversation is about *finding a room* where the man can stay for the night, it most likely takes place in a hotel.**

69. (A) Although she now works in *overseas sales,* the woman does not say that she is on a sales *trip* overseas. Note that the order of the words in the two phrases is different.

    (B) Though Ms. Krishnan no longer works in this division, she *still* works for the company.

    **(C) Ms. Krishnan has been moved, or *transferred,* to the overseas sales department.**

    (D) The woman does not mention that Ms. Krishnan is too busy.

70. (A) *Operation* here means the way something works, not a procedure on a patient in a hospital.

    (B) A *greenhouse* is where *living* plants are grown.

    (C) The factory has *already* been built.

    **(D) *Plant* in this conversation means factory. The two men are planning a visit there.**

71. (A) Ms. Mura has good news about a *job*, not a contest.

    (B) Ms. Mura will be working with Mr. Shima's company, but she did not *buy* it.

    **(C) Mr. Shima has just *offered* the woman a *job*.**

    (D) Since Mr. Shima has *seen* her résumé and says it is very good, she must have finished it *already*.

72. (A) She is *buying*, not selling, the camera.

    **(B) The woman wants to *write a check* to pay for the camera.**

    (C) Filling out a form would not be a way to pay for something.

    (D) She may *show* a credit card in order to write a check. The card would already have her name on it.

73. (A) A *plumber* fixes a building's pipes.

    (B) An *accountant* helps with financial statements.

    **(C) The woman says that neither her hair dryer nor the lights in her room will work. This is an *electrical* problem, so an electrician will be sent to fix it.**

    (D) The woman is in a hurry, but she does *not* ask for a *driver* to take her somewhere.

74. (A) Ms. Lee will *send* a fax later in the day.

    (B) She is not waiting for clients, and in fact does *not* want to be interrupted.

    (C) She is *working on* the document for her client.

    **(D) Ms. Diaz mentions that Ms. Lee is *expecting* an international telephone call.**

75. (A) She is going back to help at the *office*, not home.

    **(B) The woman's office called to ask for Heidi's help. Since she must leave *right away*, it must be an important, or *urgent*, matter.**

    (C) She just *received* a phone call. She will make a call *later* but is not leaving to do so. (D) She is *already* at a party but may miss the rest of it.

76. (A) The man does not mention a credit *card*. He offers her a *credit*, which means to *apply the value of the sweater towards another item.*

    (B) She wants a suit *instead* of the sweater.

    **(C) The woman wants to *return* a sweater that she received as a *gift*, or present.**

    (D) She says it is *fine* if she gets a credit. She is not there to pay a fine.

77. (A) Next *Monday* is the day for making final changes.

    **(B) Several times are mentioned. However, *next Wednesday* is the day named for the presentation.**

    (C) The advertising staff has even had to *work* on the weekends.

    (D) They have been working hard for the *last* seven weeks.

78. (A) The man *asks* if he was speeding, but the officer tells him *no*.

    (B) There is something wrong with the turn *signal*, but he did not turn in the wrong direction.

    **(C) The turn signal on his car is *out of order*, or *not working*.**

    (D) He gives the officer his license when asked.

79. (A) Although he is in a hurry, the order will *not* be ready in a few minutes.

    (B) Nine o'clock tonight is not mentioned. The store *opens* at nine in the *morning*.

    (C) The store will be *closed* tomorrow, so he cannot get his order then.

    **(D) Several times are mentioned. The man must wait for the day *after* tomorrow to pick up his order.**

80. (A) A big contract was recently signed, so they expect an *increase* in work.

(B) There is no mention of her being *asked* to leave. In fact, the division office kept her position.

**(C) The people are talking about what happened to Olivia's position *when she retired*. That must be the reason why she left.**

(D) The *contract* mentioned is not Olivia's. It is for the whole company.

## Part IV Short Talks

81. (A) The man does not mention 15 minutes in his announcement.

**(B) The tour takes about half an hour (or 30 minutes).**

(C) The tour lasts *half* an hour, not an hour.

(D) The *sculpture* talk will start at three o'clock. Three hours is not mentioned.

82. (A) Although photography may be found in a museum, the man does not mention photography.

**(B) The tour guide invites people who like sculpture to the three o'clock talk, which will take place in the sculpture garden. The talk is likely about *sculpture*.**

(C) The tour that is starting *now* (not at three o'clock) is about modern art.

(D) Although art is collected in the museum, the tour guide's talk is not *about* collecting art.

83. (A) While most hotels have restaurants, a hotel *clerk* would not talk about serving *food*. (B) A chef *prepares* food in a restaurant but does not serve it.

**(C) Ivan mentions that he will be *serving* and taking the *order*, and he lists several menu items. He is most likely a *waiter* in a restaurant.**

(D) A farmer *grows* food but does not prepare *meals*.

84. (A) The correct answer cannot be early morning.

(B) The correct answer cannot be late morning.

(C) The correct answer cannot be mid-afternoon.

**(D) Ivan says that he is the server *tonight,* so it must be evening.**

85. (A) A ship would not have cars.

(B) A taxi would not have reserved seats or food service, or be likely to make such a long trip. Furthermore, announcements are not usually made at taxi stands.

**(C) The announcer mentions *limited express* and a rear car. This must be a train. Here, *car* means carriage.**

(D) While much of this announcement sounds like something heard on a plane, food service and telephones would be at passengers' *seats*, not in a rear car.

86. **(A) The announcer says that all seats are reserved, meaning assigned in advance.**

(B) No mention is made of credit cards.

(C) No mention is made of maps, either.

(D) Passengers need *seat* reservations, but they do not need a reservation for the *food* service.

87. (A) The listeners do not yet work for Milton's Pies.

**(B) A *franchise* is the right to sell a company's products. Dave Sandoval is telling his audience how to *become* franchise owners and *open* a franchise.**

(C) The talk is about the pie business. Milton's Pie Shops are *located* in shopping centers. (D) Listeners will be able to *borrow* money from banks to open new pie shops.

88. **(A) Pies are a *food*, so Milton's is a food retailer.**

    (B) Although the ideas in the talk refer to employment, there is no indication that Milton's is an employment service. The talk mentions eating, shopping, and different regions.

    (C) There is no indication that Milton's is a recreation facility.

    (D) There is no indication that Milton's is a travel agency.

89. (A) He does not claim to *be* a sales manager.

    (B) He does not claim to be head of research and development.

    (C) He does not claim to be a personnel manager.

    **(D) Dave Sandoval introduces himself as the *director of franchising*. He is trying to promote his company, increase *sales*, and *develop* business.**

90. **(A) Ms. Suzuki is introduced as a *photo*journalist and has worked as a staff *photographer*.**

    (B) She will join the magazine staff, but not as an *editor*, or *someone who revises the writing of others*. The talk mentions a *News Journal* and a *magazine*.

    (C) There is no indication that Ms. Suzuki is an advertising director.

    (D) There is no indication that Ms. Suzuki is a newspaper publisher.

91. **(A) The woman has just spent three years in *Australia*.**

    (B) She was *born* in Japan but has not worked there recently.

    (C) In six months she *will go* to work in Brazil.

    (D) The United States is not mentioned.

92. (A) There is no mention of a company *merger*, or the *combination of two organizations into one*.

    **(B) At a large formal dinner, or *banquet*, employee *awards* will be given to *honor* workers. In this situation, to honor employees means to present them with awards.**

    (C) *Year* is mentioned in connection with award winners, not strategies.

    (D) There is no mention of company profits.

93. (A) They must have tickets *before* they go to the hotel for the banquet.

    (B) The president will *attend* the banquet.

    (C) The board of directors will *attend* the banquet.

    **(D) To get tickets, people should call the *personnel office* right away.**

94. (A) Geology is the *study* of the earth. Although the movie is called *The Earth Is Round*, it is *not* about earth science.

    (B) The film tells the *story* of a journey around the world but is not about world history.

    **(C) The theme is travel. The key words *travel*, *journey*, and *voyage* are used.**

    (D) While the film*makers* will answer questions, the series is not about film*making*.

95. (A) A *couple* means two, but the couple mentioned here are the two *people* in the film. (B) Five *years* is the time it took the couple to make their journey.

    (C) Seven *days* is how long the series will last.

    **(D) *Nine* films will be shown during the series.**

96. (A) A half hour is a period of time that is not mentioned in the announcement.

    (B) One hour is a period of time that is not mentioned in the announcement.

    **(C) The film will take *ninety minutes*. That is the same as an hour and a half.**

    (D) Two hours is a period of time that is not mentioned in the announcement.

97. (A) No mention is made of closing the theater for repairs.

    (B) The featured film *is* a *documentary*, or one that *presents factual information*. Nothing will be shown *after* the film.

    (C) No mention is made of awarding a prize.

    **(D) The filmmakers will *answer questions*; in other words, they will be *interviewed*.**

98. (A) Ms. Valmont will speak *about* political candidates.

    (B) The weather forecast will come next, but the speaker is not a forecaster.

    **(C) The speaker, Vanessa Evans, has invited Ms. Valmont to be on her show.**

    (D) Ms. *Valmont* is a reporter, or *journalist*.

99. (A) There is no mention of computers in the passage.

    (B) Ms. Valmont writes about political parties, which are involved in government. However, she is not a *member* of government.

    **(C) Ms. Valmont is a newspaper journalist, or someone who writes about the news.**

    (D) She is an author who has *written* books, not a publisher who *issues* books.

100. (A) The interview will focus on last week's election results.

    (B) The commentary will come *after* the news.

    (C) Candidates will be talked *about*, but no candidate will *give* a speech on the program.

    **(D) Before the interview there will be local and regional news.**

## PRACTICE TEST SCRIPT FOR DAY 26

*These are the questions you heard during the Practice Test in Day 25.*

1.  (A) The transaction has been completed.

    (B) They're filling out the forms by hand.

    (C) The woman is using the keyboard.

    (D) They're watching a program on television.

2.  (A) Few of the tables are occupied.

    (B) There's water on the floor of the restaurant.

    (C) The shape of the tables is square.

    (D) The restaurant has gone out of business.

3.  (A) He's developing the photographs.

    (B) He's doing two things at once.

    (C) He's looking out the window at the scenery.

    (D) He's hanging up the telephone.

4.  (A) The drivers have turned on their car lights.

    (B) The parking area is covered.

    (C) The cards are sorted by number.

    (D) The park is closed to traffic.

5.  (A) They're picking up their bags.

    (B) They're sitting next to each other.

    (C) They're moving the sofa into the corner.

    (D) They're looking at a display in a museum.

6.  (A) The market is open for business.

    (B) The man is working in his vegetable garden.

    (C) The crops have yet to be harvested.

    (D) The woman is weighing herself.

7.  (A) They're placing the bags into the overhead compartment.

    (B) They're packing their suitcases.

    (C) They're moving the luggage.

    (D) They're going through customs inspection.

8.  (A) The man is examining the merchandise.

    (B) There are not many products for sale.

    (C) The display cases are being rearranged.

    (D) The man is watching a movie.

9.  (A) They're climbing the stairs together.

    (B) They're looking in the same direction.

    (C) They're holding onto the railing.

    (D) They're facing each other.

10. (A) There are a lot of people on the train.

    (B) The man is closing the door because of the rain.

    (C) The train has already departed from the station.

    (D) The man left his briefcase on the train.

11. (A) Her work hours have been cut.

    (B) She's finished clipping out the article.

    (C) There's not much air in this room.

    (D) She's giving the person a haircut.

12. (A) Some people are going up to the next level.

    (B) The escalator is out of order.

    (C) The building is only one story high.

    (D) The property is closed to the public.

13. (A) The customers are ready to pay their bill.

    (B) The waiter is taking their food order.

    (C) The woman is ordering the men to go away.

    (D) The waiter is taking away their dishes.

14. (A) The sales assistants are helping the customers.

    (B) The store inventory is low.

    (C) A man is paying for his purchases.

    (D) A woman is reaching for an item.

15. (A) He's putting her files away.

    (B) She's sitting across the desk from him.

    (C) They're reading the newspaper together.

    (D) He's handing her some papers.

16. (A) The musicians are playing as a trio.

    (B) The musical has just ended.

    (C) The instruments are in their cases.

    (D) The orchestra is entering the auditorium.

17. (A) Swimmers are getting out of the water.

    (B) People are cycling along the path.

    (C) The trees have lost all their leaves.

    (D) The river has flooded the surrounding area.

18. (A) They're putting up some flowered wallpaper.

    (B) They're taking a tour of the garden.

    (C) They're doing some work outside.

    (D) They're eating their lunch in the park.

19. (A) The speaker is seated in front of the class.

    (B) The men and women are standing along the wall.

    (C) There are many empty seats in the room.

    (D) She's making a presentation to the group.

20. (A) The truck is waiting at the traffic light.

    (B) The man is climbing into the truck.

    (C) Boxes are stacked outside the truck.

    (D) Men are carrying boxes across the street.

21. **(Man)**    When was Mr. Chen born?

    **(Woman)**    (A) In Hong Kong.

    　　　　　    (B) Since last June.

    　　　　　    (C) In 1958.

22. **(Woman 1)**   Did you ask them what time their flight would arrive?

    **(Woman 2)**   (A) Yes, they were happy to arrive.

    　　　　　　   (B) No, I didn't think of it.

    　　　　　　   (C) No, it was too dark to tell.

23. **(Man 1)**   Who can deliver this memo to Mr. Watanabe for me?

    **(Man 2)**   (A) Yes, Mr. Watanabe lives in Japan.

    　　　　　   (B) I can do it when I've finished typing this letter.

    　　　　　   (C) No, the delivery person is from Osaka.

24. **(Woman)**   Don't you want to go to the reception for Miss Gunther?

    **(Man)**   (A) No, in the hotel ballroom.

    　　　　   (B) I have the receipt.

    　　　　   (C) Sorry, but I'm not feeling well

25. **(Man 1)**   What's the name of the travel agency this company uses?

    **(Man 2)**   (A) Yes, that's his name.

    　　　　　   (B) I think it's called All Points Travel.

    　　　　　   (C) I recommend you use a carry-on bag.

26. **(Woman 1)**   Where did Maria leave the Oceanview contract?

    **(Woman 2)**   (A) She put it in Ms. García's mailbox.

    　　　　　　   (B) Just a minute ago, so you can still catch her.

    　　　　　　   (C) Because the mountain-view rooms were all booked.

27. **(Man)** Have you visited the main plant yet?

    **(Woman)** (A) Yes, they are.

        (B) Yes, I went there last week with the director.

        (C) Yes, the gardener is looking after them.

28. **(Woman)** Who is the new receptionist?

    **(Man)** (A) It's in the main office.

        (B) Her name is Olga Kaminsky.

        (C) Yes, we need a new receptionist.

29. **(Woman 1)** Will the conference be held here or at headquarters?

    **(Woman 2)** (A) It's scheduled for this building.

        (B) No, you will not be able to hear.

        (C) Yes, they will have the conference.

30. **(Man 1)** Why did the meeting begin so early?

    **(Man 2)** (A) Yes, at eight-thirty.

        (B) About the upcoming acquisition.

        (C) Everyone was in a hurry.

31. **(Woman)** What are your total production figures for this factory?

    **(Man)** (A) We produce pharmaceuticals.

        (B) Over 1000 units a week.

        (C) In the shipping department.

32. **(Man)** How far would you say Conrad Park is from here?

    **(Woman)** (A) It's about a ten-minute walk.

        (B) No, I wouldn't go so far as to say that.

        (C) Yes, parking there is very expensive.

33. **(Man)** Is the agenda prepared?

    **(Woman)** (A) No, it's still broken.

        (B) Yes, they compared very well.

        (C) Not yet, the vice president needs to review it.

34. **(Woman 1)** How about a movie when we finish up here?

    **(Woman 2)** (A) Just down the street at the Cinema Center.

        (B) That's a good idea.

        (C) About a half hour more, I think.

35. **(Man 1)** The product was in stock last week, wasn't it?

    **(Man 2)** (A) The stock exchange closes at five.

        (B) Yes, there was a large inventory on hand then.

        (C) No, they aren't.

36. **(Woman)** Can you locate the files on the merger, or should I ask Mr. Chang to do it?

    **(Man)** (A) The fire exit is located at the end of the hall.

        (B) Yes, I called security to handle the emergency.

        (C) I'll have them ready for you in a minute.

37. **(Man 1)** Didn't the sound equipment come out of your regular departmental budget?

    **(Man 2)** (A) We didn't hear any sounds.

        (B) Yes, the room is rented.

        (C) No, we got special funding.

38. **(Woman)** Where do you plan to stay while you're in Paris?

    **(Man)** (A) Our company has an arrangement with the Hotel Odeon.

    (B) I have a conference there next week.

    (C) I'll be in France for four days.

39. **(Man)** I was wondering if you'd like to join us for dinner this evening?

    **(Woman)** (A) Yes, it was a wonderful dinner.

    (B) Sorry, I have other plans.

    (C) I hope you weren't too lost.

40. **(Woman)** Does our company get any special deals on car rentals?

    **(Man)** (A) Yes, I'd like some company on the trip.

    (B) Twenty-five percent off the regular daily rate.

    (C) No, it's your turn to deal.

41. **(Woman 1)** Exactly when will Mr. Mori be free?

    **(Woman 2)** (A) In approximately two hours.

    (B) At the International Airport.

    (C) Near gate number 16.

42. **(Man 1)** How can I get more letterhead and envelopes?

    **(Man 2)** (A) Yes, the mail is picked up three times a day.

    (B) Contact Ms. McKay in the stockroom.

    (C) No, he isn't the head of the department.

43. **(Woman)** Ms. Dubois was present at this morning's staff meeting, wasn't she?

    **(Man)** (A) Once a week, on a Monday.

    (B) No, it wasn't a gift.

    (C) No, she wasn't there.

44. **(Man)** You're the new assistant to Mr. Lin, aren't you?

    **(Woman)** (A) No, I don't need assistance.

    (B) No, I work for Ms. Wong.

    (C) Yes, I knew about that.

45. **(Woman 1)** When can you get me a copy of the most recent sales report?

    **(Woman 2)** (A) Yes, they're selling well.

    (B) Right after lunch.

    (C) About four years old.

46. **(Man 1)** Why didn't Mr. Danforth bring the situation to the attention of his supervisor?

    **(Man 2)** (A) Yes, at his workstation.

    (B) No, he often doesn't pay attention.

    (C) He thought he could handle it himself.

47. **(Woman 1)** Is this coat already marked down?

    **(Woman 2)** (A) Yes, that's the sale price on the tag.

    (B) The market is closed this evening.

    (C) Yes, I have a red coat.

48. **(Woman)** Why does Ms. Ortiz want to see the invoices?

    **(Man)** (A) Yes, they have loud voices.

    (B) There's a problem with the shipment.

    (C) No, she didn't see it.

49. **(Man)** Should they move the file cabinet to the right or over by the copy machine?

    **(Woman)** (A) Yes, your thinking is correct.

    (B) I think it looks good where it is.

    (C) No, these copies didn't come out clearly.

50. **(Man 1)**   Isn't that the same proposal we rejected last time?

    **(Man 2)**   (A) Yes, but things have changed since then.

    (B) No, the wedding was called off.

    (C) No, it was a different injection.

51. **(Woman 1)**   I left a telephone message on your desk.

    **(Woman 2)**   Oh, did Mr. Murphy's secretary call again?

    **(Woman 1)**   Yes. She said the committee meeting is set for Tuesday.

52. **(Man)**   Is there anywhere I can get coffee or tea around here?

    **(Woman)**   Yes, I think there is. Go have a look in the employee lounge.

    **(Man)**   That's next to the mailroom, right? Want me to bring you anything?

53. **(Man)**   Did you hear about Mrs. Sompong's resignation?

    **(Woman)**   Yes. Our competitors made her an offer she couldn't resist.

    **(Man)**   I wonder if they'll appoint her as their new marketing manager?

54. **(Woman 1)**   I need to call the theater to order tickets for Wednesday.

    **(Woman 2)**   Why don't you see the play over the weekend, Claudia?

    **(Woman 1)**   It runs only Monday through Thursday.

55. **(Woman)**   Good morning, this is Standard Computer Services. Would you like to speak with someone in sales, service, or research?

    **(Man)**   Actually, I need to speak with Mr. Fong in personnel.

    **(Woman)**   Please hold while I transfer your call.

56. **(Man 1)**   When does the movie start?

    **(Man 2)**   There are two showings—one at four and one at seven.

    **(Man 1)**   Let's go to the later show.

57. **(Woman)**   Do you think the desk will fit under the window?

    **(Man)**   It might, but what about putting it next to the bookshelves? By the way, why are you changing things again?

    **(Woman)**   I just couldn't work comfortably in the old arrangement.

58. **(Man)**   What do you think is the best way for us to get to the conference?

    **(Woman)**   Well, it's too close to bother flying. We could drive there, but I think if we took the train we could get some work done on the way.

    **(Man)**   Yes, that's the best plan. I'll pick up tickets at the station on my way home from work.

59. **(Woman)**   Do you have this week's *Business News* yet?

    **(Man)**   No, the truck that used to deliver it on Monday has a different route. It should be here soon.

    **(Woman)**   I'll come back later this afternoon, I guess.

60. **(Woman)**   Juan, Ricardo will not be able to attend the meeting next week in Panama, so I'd like you to represent the firm. Would you be able to do it?

    **(Man)**   Yes, Ms. Ortega, I'd really like to go to that meeting. What about travel arrangements?

    **(Woman)**   That's all been taken care of. See Carla. You'll leave Sunday evening — and thanks.

61. **(Man)** I've heard nothing but praise for that new health food restaurant.

    **(Woman)** Same here. And I've got a coupon for the salad bar—buy one, get one free.

    **(Man)** I'm always looking to save some money. Let's check it out for lunch.

62. **(Man)** The airline sent my luggage to New York by mistake and it doesn't look like they'll be able to deliver it to me in time for this evening's dinner. Where can I go to buy a few things?

    **(Woman)** There's a shopping mall not far from here. You can get there by bus or cab from the hotel.

    **(Man)** Oh, that's right. I was there the last time I was in San Francisco.

63. **(Woman 1)** Because you've worked here now for two years, Susanna, you are entitled to three weeks' vacation.

    **(Woman 2)** Will I be allowed to take it all at once?

    **(Woman 1)** Most supervisors allow two weeks at a time

64. **(Man 1)** Let's get these boxes unloaded before the kitchen staff gets here.

    **(Man 2)** Okay. Should I put these cans of corn on the shelf?

    **(Man 1)** You can just leave them out on the counter. They're a part of today's menu.

65. **(Woman)** Hello, Yuri. I didn't think you would be back from your trip so soon.

    **(Man)** Well, we didn't expect to be back now, but Anna, our youngest girl, got sick while we were away.

    **(Woman)** I'm sorry to hear that. I hope she's feeling better now.

66. **(Man 1)** Alan, are you going to be in your office Thursday morning? If you're not, could I work there because my office is being painted then?

    **(Man 2)** You're in luck, Tom. I'll be out until Friday morning.

    **(Man 1)** That's great. I've got to get this project done by Monday afternoon.

67. **(Woman 1)** Did you leave that marketing report on my desk? I can't find it anywhere.

    **(Woman 2)** No, Patricia, the only thing I've put on your desk recently is a memo.

    **(Woman 1)** Could you please check in your file cabinet for it? I need it soon.

68. **(Woman)** I'm sorry, sir. We're completely booked tonight. There are no rooms available until tomorrow evening.

    **(Man)** I see. Is there someplace close by where I might be able to stay?

    **(Woman)** Let me call around and see if I can find a room for you.

69. **(Man)** Excuse me, could I speak to Ms. Krishnan, please?

    **(Woman)** Ms. Krishnan? I'm sorry, but she's no longer in this division. She was transferred last week to overseas sales.

    **(Man)** Perhaps you could give me her new number?

70. **(Man 1)** Would you like to visit our plant while you're in town next week?

    **(Man 2)** That would be great. I've always wanted to see your operation firsthand.

    **(Man 1)** OK. Let me know when you're available and I'll show you around.

71. **(Man)** Your résumé looks very impressive, Ms. Mura, and I would like to offer you a job with our company.

    **(Woman)** Thank you, Mr. Shima. I'm really looking forward to working with you.

    **(Man)** Good. You can sign the papers at the personnel office.

72. **(Man)** And how would you like to pay for the camera?

    **(Woman)** Could I write you a check?

    **(Man)** Certainly. I'll need some form of identification or a major credit card.

73. **(Woman)** Hello. I'm in room 512 [five-twelve]. I just plugged in my hair dryer and all the lights went out.

    **(Man)** I'm sorry. I'll send someone to take care of it right away.

    **(Woman)** Thanks. I have to go out at six o'clock, so I'm really in a hurry!

74. **(Woman 1)** Ms. Díaz, please make sure I'm not interrupted for the next hour. I'll be working on a document that I have to fax to a client today.

    **(Woman 2)** Will you take the international call that you're expecting, Ms. Lee?

    **(Woman 1)** Yes. That's the one exception I will make.

75. **(Woman)** I'm sorry to have to leave in the middle of things here, but that was the office calling. They need my help right away.

    **(Man)** Oh no, Heidi. You'll miss the rest of the party. Could you come back afterward?

    **(Woman)** Maybe. I'll phone before I leave to see if anyone's still here.

76. **(Woman)** I'd like to return this sweater, but I don't have the sales slip. It was a gift.

    **(Man)** In that case, we can only issue you a credit, not a refund.

    **(Woman)** That would be fine. I'll use it toward this suit.

77. **(Man)** The advertising department has been working really hard these last seven weeks.

    **(Woman)** I know, they've even been in the office on weekends. Do you think they'll be ready to make the presentation next Wednesday?

    **(Man)** That's the plan. They're making their final revisions on Monday.

78. **(Man 1)** Excuse me, sir. Could I see your driver's license and your insurance papers, please?

    **(Man 2)** Certainly, officer....Here you are. I wasn't speeding, was I?

    **(Man 1)** No sir, you weren't. The reason I pulled you over is because your left turn signal seems to be out of order.

79. **(Man)** Will my order be ready tomorrow? I must send it to a customer as soon as possible.

    **(Woman)** I'm afraid our store will be closed tomorrow for inventory. I'm sure we'll have it the following day.

    **(Man)** I see. I'll come and get it then. You open at nine, right?

80. **(Woman)** I thought the company wasn't going to hire anyone to take Olivia's place when she retired.

    **(Man)** The division office decided to keep her position open in case the workload increased in her department.

    **(Woman)** Oh, that's right. That big contract was signed just before she left.

**Questions 81 and 82** refer to the following announcement.

Good afternoon. I'm glad you could join me today for a tour of the museum's splendid modern art collection. The tour should last about a half an hour, during which time we will try to focus on some of the museum's best-known pieces. For those of you who enjoy sculpture, I'll be giving another talk at three o'clock in the sculpture garden.

**Questions 83 and 84** refer to the following speech.

Hello, my name is Ivan. I'll be serving you tonight. Let me tell you about some of our specials. We have grilled steak with sautéed vegetables. We also have a nice fresh salmon dish that comes with rice. Our soup of the day is clam chowder. I'll be back in a minute to take your order.

**Questions 85 and 86** refer to the following short talk.

This is the limited express bound for Munich. We will be making a brief stop in Frankfurt before reaching our final destination. We expect our traveling time today to be three hours and twenty minutes. All seats are reserved. Please check your ticket and make sure that you are sitting in the correct seat. Telephones and food service are available in the rear car. Thank you for your attention. We will be departing in a few minutes.

**Questions 87 through 89** refer to the following announcement.

Good evening. I'm Dave Sandoval, director of franchising for Milton's Pies. As you know, we're the fastest-growing franchisor in the southern region today. Last year we opened 300 shops, and now we hope to expand into the central region and put a Milton's Pie Shop in every mall and shopping center. No one should be too far from a great-tasting Milton pie. You're here tonight because you're interested in becoming a franchise owner, and we want to help you go into business! Most banks lend you the money you need to open a franchise because the Milton's name has customer appeal, and because our shops make money—for you, for us, and for the bank.

**Questions 90 and 91** refer to the following excerpt from a speech.

It is my pleasure to introduce to you the world-renowned photojournalist Michiko Suzuki. A native of Japan, Ms. Suzuki has been working in Australia for the past three years as a staff photographer for *The Sydney News Journal*. I'm very pleased that Ms. Suzuki has agreed to join our magazine for six months before she takes her next long-term assignment in Brazil. She'll be working closely with our staff, sharing some of the secrets of her innovative techniques.

**Questions 92 and 93** refer to the following announcement.

We are very pleased to announce that this year's annual employee awards banquet will be held in the grand ballroom of the elegant Adams Hotel. If you have not yet received your tickets, please call the personnel office immediately. We hope you'll join the president and board of directors in honoring this year's award winners.

**Questions 94 through 97** refer to the following announcement.

Good evening, ladies and gentlemen, and welcome to the Regent Theater. Tonight's film, *The Earth is Round,* documents the experiences of a young couple as they travel around the world on a journey spanning more than five years. This film begins our week-long series in which we'll show nine different films, each depicting a unique voyage. *The Earth is Round* runs for 90 minutes, and we invite you to join us at the end of the movie for a question-and-answer session with the filmmakers. Thank you, and we hope you enjoy the show.

**Questions 98 through 100** refer to the following talk.

This is Radio Talk Today. My name is Vanessa Evans and this afternoon we'll be talking with Sylvie Valmont about last week's election results. Ms. Valmont is a newspaper journalist and author of several books on politics and political parties. We'll be discussing her views on why some candidates fared well in the elections and why others didn't live up to expectations. She'll also tell us about the changing future of political parties in our country. But, before I bring on Ms. Valmont, here's the local and regional news and the weather forecast for the weekend.

# Day 27

## Practice Test: Reading Section, Parts V and VI

Incomplete Sentences and Error Recognition

Today you will have the opportunity to practice Part V, Incomplete Sentences, and Part VI, Error Recognition—questions 101–160 of the TOEIC test. These are the first two parts of the Reading section of the test, for which a total of 75 minutes is allowed. They are followed by Part VII, Reading Comprehension (questions 161–200), which you will practice on Day 29.

Work on Parts V and VI of the practice test as if you were taking the real TOEIC test so that you can learn how much time the questions will take and how it feels to work straight through questions 100–160 under conditions close to what you will experience during an actual test.

- **Use the sample answer sheet provided.** On the next page, you will find part of a sample answer sheet similar to the one used on official TOEIC tests. On Day 25, you completed the first sections of the sample answer sheet with your answers to the background questionnaire and details about yourself. As you answer questions 100–160, fill in the circles on the answer sheet under the heading "Reading Section."

- **Find a quiet place to take Parts V and VI of the practice test.** Answer the questions in a place where you will not be disturbed. You will need a pencil and an eraser.

- **Do not take a break between Parts V and VI.** It is important to pay attention to how long it takes you to work through these two parts. The time allowed for the entire Reading section (questions 101–200) is 75 minutes. As mentioned on Day 23, you will need to allow plenty of time for Part VII, questions 161–200, since it may take 40 or 45 minutes to complete this part. So try to do Parts V and VI in 30 to 35 minutes. If you find a question particularly difficult, fill in the answer that you think is closest and make a note next to the question so that you can come back to it later if you have time. Do not leave any questions blank.

*To the teacher:* Because of the one-hour-per-day format of this book, it is not possible for the students to take the entire practice Reading section on one day, so it has been split into two, with Part VII being taken on Day 29. If your class has 75 minutes available, you may prefer to ask them to take the entire section at once.

**READING SECTION**

| | | | |
|---|---|---|---|
| 101 Ⓐ Ⓑ Ⓒ Ⓓ | 126 Ⓐ Ⓑ Ⓒ Ⓓ | 151 Ⓐ Ⓑ Ⓒ Ⓓ | 176 Ⓐ Ⓑ Ⓒ Ⓓ |
| 102 Ⓐ Ⓑ Ⓒ Ⓓ | 127 Ⓐ Ⓑ Ⓒ Ⓓ | 152 Ⓐ Ⓑ Ⓒ Ⓓ | 177 Ⓐ Ⓑ Ⓒ Ⓓ |
| 103 Ⓐ Ⓑ Ⓒ Ⓓ | 128 Ⓐ Ⓑ Ⓒ Ⓓ | 153 Ⓐ Ⓑ Ⓒ Ⓓ | 178 Ⓐ Ⓑ Ⓒ Ⓓ |
| 104 Ⓐ Ⓑ Ⓒ Ⓓ | 129 Ⓐ Ⓑ Ⓒ Ⓓ | 154 Ⓐ Ⓑ Ⓒ Ⓓ | 179 Ⓐ Ⓑ Ⓒ Ⓓ |
| 105 Ⓐ Ⓑ Ⓒ Ⓓ | 130 Ⓐ Ⓑ Ⓒ Ⓓ | 155 Ⓐ Ⓑ Ⓒ Ⓓ | 180 Ⓐ Ⓑ Ⓒ Ⓓ |
| 106 Ⓐ Ⓑ Ⓒ Ⓓ | 131 Ⓐ Ⓑ Ⓒ Ⓓ | 156 Ⓐ Ⓑ Ⓒ Ⓓ | 181 Ⓐ Ⓑ Ⓒ Ⓓ |
| 107 Ⓐ Ⓑ Ⓒ Ⓓ | 132 Ⓐ Ⓑ Ⓒ Ⓓ | 157 Ⓐ Ⓑ Ⓒ Ⓓ | 182 Ⓐ Ⓑ Ⓒ Ⓓ |
| 108 Ⓐ Ⓑ Ⓒ Ⓓ | 133 Ⓐ Ⓑ Ⓒ Ⓓ | 158 Ⓐ Ⓑ Ⓒ Ⓓ | 183 Ⓐ Ⓑ Ⓒ Ⓓ |
| 109 Ⓐ Ⓑ Ⓒ Ⓓ | 134 Ⓐ Ⓑ Ⓒ Ⓓ | 159 Ⓐ Ⓑ Ⓒ Ⓓ | 184 Ⓐ Ⓑ Ⓒ Ⓓ |
| 110 Ⓐ Ⓑ Ⓒ Ⓓ | 135 Ⓐ Ⓑ Ⓒ Ⓓ | 160 Ⓐ Ⓑ Ⓒ Ⓓ | 185 Ⓐ Ⓑ Ⓒ Ⓓ |
| 111 Ⓐ Ⓑ Ⓒ Ⓓ | 136 Ⓐ Ⓑ Ⓒ Ⓓ | 161 Ⓐ Ⓑ Ⓒ Ⓓ | 186 Ⓐ Ⓑ Ⓒ Ⓓ |
| 112 Ⓐ Ⓑ Ⓒ Ⓓ | 137 Ⓐ Ⓑ Ⓒ Ⓓ | 162 Ⓐ Ⓑ Ⓒ Ⓓ | 187 Ⓐ Ⓑ Ⓒ Ⓓ |
| 113 Ⓐ Ⓑ Ⓒ Ⓓ | 138 Ⓐ Ⓑ Ⓒ Ⓓ | 163 Ⓐ Ⓑ Ⓒ Ⓓ | 188 Ⓐ Ⓑ Ⓒ Ⓓ |
| 114 Ⓐ Ⓑ Ⓒ Ⓓ | 139 Ⓐ Ⓑ Ⓒ Ⓓ | 164 Ⓐ Ⓑ Ⓒ Ⓓ | 189 Ⓐ Ⓑ Ⓒ Ⓓ |
| 115 Ⓐ Ⓑ Ⓒ Ⓓ | 140 Ⓐ Ⓑ Ⓒ Ⓓ | 165 Ⓐ Ⓑ Ⓒ Ⓓ | 190 Ⓐ Ⓑ Ⓒ Ⓓ |
| 116 Ⓐ Ⓑ Ⓒ Ⓓ | 141 Ⓐ Ⓑ Ⓒ Ⓓ | 166 Ⓐ Ⓑ Ⓒ Ⓓ | 191 Ⓐ Ⓑ Ⓒ Ⓓ |
| 117 Ⓐ Ⓑ Ⓒ Ⓓ | 142 Ⓐ Ⓑ Ⓒ Ⓓ | 167 Ⓐ Ⓑ Ⓒ Ⓓ | 192 Ⓐ Ⓑ Ⓒ Ⓓ |
| 118 Ⓐ Ⓑ Ⓒ Ⓓ | 143 Ⓐ Ⓑ Ⓒ Ⓓ | 168 Ⓐ Ⓑ Ⓒ Ⓓ | 193 Ⓐ Ⓑ Ⓒ Ⓓ |
| 119 Ⓐ Ⓑ Ⓒ Ⓓ | 144 Ⓐ Ⓑ Ⓒ Ⓓ | 169 Ⓐ Ⓑ Ⓒ Ⓓ | 194 Ⓐ Ⓑ Ⓒ Ⓓ |
| 120 Ⓐ Ⓑ Ⓒ Ⓓ | 145 Ⓐ Ⓑ Ⓒ Ⓓ | 170 Ⓐ Ⓑ Ⓒ Ⓓ | 195 Ⓐ Ⓑ Ⓒ Ⓓ |
| 121 Ⓐ Ⓑ Ⓒ Ⓓ | 146 Ⓐ Ⓑ Ⓒ Ⓓ | 171 Ⓐ Ⓑ Ⓒ Ⓓ | 196 Ⓐ Ⓑ Ⓒ Ⓓ |
| 122 Ⓐ Ⓑ Ⓒ Ⓓ | 147 Ⓐ Ⓑ Ⓒ Ⓓ | 172 Ⓐ Ⓑ Ⓒ Ⓓ | 197 Ⓐ Ⓑ Ⓒ Ⓓ |
| 123 Ⓐ Ⓑ Ⓒ Ⓓ | 148 Ⓐ Ⓑ Ⓒ Ⓓ | 173 Ⓐ Ⓑ Ⓒ Ⓓ | 198 Ⓐ Ⓑ Ⓒ Ⓓ |
| 124 Ⓐ Ⓑ Ⓒ Ⓓ | 149 Ⓐ Ⓑ Ⓒ Ⓓ | 174 Ⓐ Ⓑ Ⓒ Ⓓ | 199 Ⓐ Ⓑ Ⓒ Ⓓ |
| 125 Ⓐ Ⓑ Ⓒ Ⓓ | 150 Ⓐ Ⓑ Ⓒ Ⓓ | 175 Ⓐ Ⓑ Ⓒ Ⓓ | 200 Ⓐ Ⓑ Ⓒ Ⓓ |

## PRACTICE TEST: PARTS V AND VI

## Part V

*Directions: Questions 101–140 are incomplete sentences. Four words or phrases, marked (A), (B), (C), (D), are given beneath each sentence. You are to choose the one word or phrase that best completes the sentence.*

*Then, on your answer sheet, find the number of the question and mark your answer.*

You will read:

Because the equipment is very delicate, it must be handled with - - - - - - - .

(A) caring

(B) careful

(C) care

(D) carefully

Sample Answer

Ⓐ Ⓑ ● Ⓓ

The sentence should read, "Because the equipment is very delicate, it must be handled with care." Therefore, you should choose answer (C).

Now, begin work on the questions.

101. Answering telephone calls is the - - - - - - - of an operator.

(A) responsible

(B) responsibly

(C) responsive

(D) responsibility

102. A free watch will be provided with every purchase of $20.00 or more for a - - - - - - - period of time.

(A) limit

(B) limits

(C) limited

(D) limiting

103. The president of the corporation has - - - - - - - arrived in Copenhagen and will meet with the Minister of Trade on Monday morning.

(A) still

(B) yet

(C) already

(D) soon

104. Because we value your business, we have - - - - - - - for card members like you to receive one thousand dollars of complimentary life insurance.

(A) arrange

(B) arranged

(C) arranges

(D) arranging

105. Employees are - - - - - - - that due to the new government regulations, there is to be no smoking in the factory.

(A) reminded

(B) respected

(C) remembered

(D) reacted

106. Ms. Galera gave a long - - - - - - - in honor of the retiring vice president.

(A) speak

(B) speaker

(C) speaking

(D) speech

107. Any person who is - - - - - - - in volunteering his or her time for the campaign should send this office a letter of intent.

(A) interest

(B) interested

(C) interesting

(D) interestingly

108. Mr. Gonzales was very concerned - - - - - - - the upcoming board of directors meeting.

    (A) to

    (B) about

    (C) at

    (D) upon

109. The customers were told that no - - - - - - - could be made on weekend nights because the restaurant was too busy.

    (A) delays

    (B) cuisines

    (C) reservations

    (D) violations

110. The sales representative's presentation was difficult to understand - - - - - - - he spoke very quickly.

    (A) because

    (B) although

    (C) so that

    (D) than

111. It has been predicted that an - - - - - - - weak dollar will stimulate tourism in the United States.

    (A) increased

    (B) increasingly

    (C) increases

    (D) increase

112. The firm is not liable for damage resulting from circumstances - - - - - - - its control.

    (A) beyond

    (B) above

    (C) inside

    (D) around

113. Because of - - - - - - - weather conditions, California has an advantage in the production of fruits and vegetables.

    (A) favorite

    (B) favor

    (C) favorable

    (D) favorably

114. On international shipments, all duties and taxes are paid by the - - - - - - - .

    (A) recipient

    (B) receiving

    (C) receipt

    (D) receptive

115. Although the textbook gives a definitive answer, wise managers will look for - - - - - - - own creative solutions.

    (A) them

    (B) their

    (C) theirs

    (D) they

116. Initial - - - - - - - regarding the merger of the companies took place yesterday at the Plaza Conference Center.

    (A) negotiations

    (B) dedications

    (C) propositions

    (D) announcements

117. Please - - - - - - - photocopies of all relevant documents to this office ten days prior to your performance review date.

    (A) emerge

    (B) substantiate

    (C) adapt

    (D) submit

118. The auditor's results for the five-year period under study were - - - - - - - the accountant's.

    (A) same

    (B) same as

    (C) the same

    (D) the same as

119. ------- has the marketing environment been more complex and subject to change.

    (A) Totally

    (B) Negatively

    (C) Decidedly

    (D) Rarely

120. All full-time staff are eligible to participate in the revised health plan, which becomes effective the first ------- the month.

    (A) of

    (B) to

    (C) from

    (D) for

121. Contracts must be read ------- before they are signed.

    (A) thoroughness

    (B) more thorough

    (C) thorough

    (D) thoroughly

122. Passengers should allow for ------- travel time to the airport in rush hour traffic.

    (A) addition

    (B) additive

    (C) additionally

    (D) additional

123. This fiscal year, the engineering team has worked well together on all phases of project ------- .

    (A) development

    (B) developed

    (C) develops

    (D) developer

124. Mr. Dupont had no ------- how long it would take to drive downtown.

    (A) knowledge

    (B) thought

    (C) idea

    (D) willingness

125. Small-company stocks usually benefit ------- the so-called January effect that causes the price of these stocks to rise between November and January.

    (A) unless

    (B) from

    (C) to

    (D) since

126. It has been suggested that employees ------- to work in their current positions until the quarterly review is finished.

    (A) continuity

    (B) continue

    (C) continuing

    (D) continuous

127. It is admirable that Ms. Jin wishes to handle all transactions by ------- , but it might be better if several people shared the responsibility.

    (A) she

    (B) herself

    (C) her

    (D) hers

128. This new highway construction project will help the company ------- .

    (A) diversify

    (B) clarify

    (C) intensify

    (D) modify

129. Ms. Patel has handed in an ------- business plan to the director.

    (A) anxious

    (B) evident

    (C) eager

    (D) outstanding

130. Recent changes in heating oil costs have affected ------- production of furniture.

(A) local

(B) locality

(C) locally

(D) location

131. That is the position for ------- Mr. Kaslov has applied, but a final decision has not yet been made.

(A) which

(B) whom

(C) that

(D) what

132. Any unsatisfactory item must be returned within 30 days and ------- by the original receipt from this store.

(A) altered

(B) adjusted

(C) accepted

(D) accompanied

133. A list of telephone ------- that will be out of service while the new communications system is installed is available from the main office.

(A) extensions

(B) extending

(C) extended

(D) extends

134. Please ------- your flight number at least 24 hours in advance.

(A) confirm

(B) concur

(C) conduct

(D) concord

135. The first year's sales of the new calculator were so ------- that the firm decided to withdraw it from the market.

(A) discouragement

(B) discourage

(C) discouraging

(D) discouraged

136. From an investor's viewpoint, getting ------- advice is the key to making sound investment decisions.

(A) unjudged

(B) unbiased

(C) inanimate

(D) impatient

137. Staff members are reminded that professional ------- is a daily requirement of the company.

(A) attire

(B) ambivalence

(C) assembly

(D) approach

138. Ms. Lee did ------- good work on that project that she was quickly offered a promotion.

(A) too

(B) such

(C) so

(D) much

139. We have approached the proposal with a good deal of ------- since some of the ideas put forward are very unconventional.

(A) cautioned

(B) caution

(C) cautious

(D) cautiously

140. ------- higher ticket prices this year, attendance at area theaters remains above average.

(A) Even though

(B) Nevertheless

(C) In spite of

(D) Consequently

## Part VI

*Directions: Questions 141–160. Each sentence has four words or phrases underlined. The four underlined parts of the sentence are marked (A), (B), (C), (D). You are to identify the one underlined word or phrase that should be corrected or rewritten. Then, on your answer sheet, find the number of the question and mark your answer.*

**Example:**

All <u>employee</u> are required <u>to wear</u> their
    A                B

<u>identification</u> badges <u>while</u> at work.
  C             D

*Sample Answer*

● Ⓑ Ⓒ Ⓓ

The underlined word "employee" is not correct in this sentence. This sentence should read, "All employees are required to wear their identification badges while at work." Therefore, you should select choice (A).

Now, begin work on the questions.

141. The Pinebrook Inn <u>has</u> a courtesy bus
             A

<u>which runs</u> <u>every</u> thirty minutes both <u>to from</u>
   B      C               D

the downtown area.

142. We <u>appreciate it</u> your <u>interest in</u> our company
      A          B

and <u>look forward to</u> hearing <u>from</u> you soon.
     C           D

143. In the event <u>for</u> any changes need <u>to be made</u> in
       A                B

the <u>document</u>, please call our office <u>immediately</u>.
  C                 D

144. <u>Each</u> banking transaction <u>were handled</u> quickly
   A               B

and <u>efficiently</u> <u>by</u> well-trained tellers.
    C     D

145. We recommend that you follow the <u>formatted</u>
                      A

<u>shown</u> in this sample when <u>preparing</u> announce-
 B                 C

ments to be <u>displayed</u> on the bulletin board.
        D

146. Bennett International <u>has decided</u> to expand
                A

<u>its borrowing</u> to make up <u>with</u> a decline <u>in</u>
   B             C        D

investment returns.

147. Ms. Rivera <u>is going</u> to write <u>to manager</u> to
         A           B

complain <u>about</u> the poor service she received
      C

during <u>her stay</u> at the hotel.
      D

148. <u>One proposal</u> suggests <u>relocating</u> the central
   A           B

offices <u>at</u> the suburbs to obtain <u>needed space</u>.
    C               D

149. Consumers are usually willing to buy

<u>more</u> of an item <u>as</u> its price falls
 A         B

<u>because of</u> they want <u>to save</u> money.
  C           D

150. Substantial penalties <u>will be charging</u>
                A

whenever <u>a</u> customer withdraws <u>funds</u>
     B             C

from this account <u>prior to</u> the maturity date.
        D

151. We have <u>taken</u> special <u>caring</u> to see that the
           A          B

     merchandise <u>has been</u> packed <u>according</u> to
                C           D

     your instructions.

152. <u>For a list</u> of books <u>available</u> through the library
       A           B

     system, <u>consultation</u> the computer terminal <u>near</u>
             C                   D

     the reference desk.

153. Mr. Webber <u>was taken surprise</u> when he <u>was told</u>
               A               B

     the building he <u>was working</u> on had a severe
                 C

     <u>structural flaw.</u>
       D

154. <u>At</u> our company meeting the marketing
     A

     analyst <u>reported that</u> we have too <u>much</u>
           B              C

     sales representatives in Europe <u>these</u> days.
                        D

155. All passengers <u>must present</u> their boarding
              A

     passes <u>to</u> the <u>designate</u> agent <u>at</u> the airport gate.
         B     C        D

156. <u>Without</u> we receive a definite commitment <u>by</u> the
     A                          B

     end of the month, we will be forced <u>to reconsider</u> <u>our</u>
                             C     D

     original proposal.

157. The governor's panel of experts <u>reported that</u>
                           A

     supervisors should <u>continue</u> to review
                  B

     <u>safety standard</u> on <u>a regular</u> basis.
        C          D

158. For <u>each</u> workshop, you <u>must register</u> and pay
        A                  B

     <u>prior to</u> the date on which the conference <u>begin</u>.
       C                         D

159. Francesca Rosati <u>is perfect</u> candidate <u>for the</u>
               A            B

     position <u>because of her</u> experience in <u>administration</u>.
           C                 D

160. <u>Travel club</u> application forms <u>can find</u>
     A                  B

     <u>in front of</u> the main desk in the <u>hotel lobby</u>.
       C                     D

When you have finished working on the questions, do the following:

1. Note here how long it took you to answer questions 101–160: *It took _____ minutes.*

2. Check your answers with the answer key below. For your reference, mark on the key which questions you answered incorrectly. Did you find the Incomplete Sentence or Error Recognition questions more difficult? On Day 28, you will be able to study explanations for the answers. Pay particular attention to the question type that you found most difficult.

3. Now try again to answer any questions you answered incorrectly and check your answers once more.

# ANSWER KEY FOR THE PRACTICE TEST: PARTS V AND VI

## Part V: Incomplete Sentences

| | |
|---|---|
| 101. D | 121. D |
| 102. C | 122. D |
| 103. C | 123. A |
| 104. B | 124. C |
| 105. A | 125. B |
| 106. D | 126. B |
| 107. B | 127. B |
| 108. B | 128. A |
| 109. C | 129. D |
| 110. A | 130. A |
| 111. B | 131. A |
| 112. A | 132. D |
| 113. C | 133. A |
| 114. A | 134. A |
| 115. B | 135. C |
| 116. A | 136. B |
| 117. D | 137. A |
| 118. D | 138. B |
| 119. D | 139. B |
| 120. A | 140. C |

## Part VI: Error Recognition

| | |
|---|---|
| 141. D | 151. B |
| 142. A | 152. C |
| 143. A | 153. A |
| 144. B | 154. C |
| 145. A | 155. C |
| 146. C | 156. A |
| 147. B | 157. C |
| 148. C | 158. D |
| 149. C | 159. A |
| 150. A | 160. B |

# Day 28

## Follow-up to Parts V and VI of the Practice Test

On Day 27, you answered questions in Parts V and VI of the practice test and checked your answers. In today's lesson, you will be able to study the questions in detail.

## PART V: INCOMPLETE SENTENCES

Below, you will find explanations of the answers for questions 101–140. You will have plenty of time in this lesson to study all of the questions, not just the ones you answered incorrectly. To make the best use of the explanations, do the following:

First, read the question again. Try reading the sentence with each choice in turn, and think about how you would explain the correct answer to somebody else and how you would explain why each of the other choices is incorrect.

Next, read the explanation for that question. Did you give a similar explanation? The explanation for question 101 is given as an example:

### Example 1

101. **(D)** The definite article *the* shows you that a noun should be used here. *Responsibility* is a noun meaning *duty*. Choice (A), *Responsible*, is an adjective. Choice (B), *Responsibly*, is an adverb. Choice (C), *Responsive*, is an adjective.

*To the teacher:* Students can work in pairs on this. You could ask them to write down their explanations to make comparison with the printed explanations easier. Encourage the use of a dictionary to look up any words they do not know, particularly with the questions where they have to select the correct vocabulary item for the context. You could assign different questions to different pairs, rather than asking them all to work on all 40. Alternatively, you could ask each pair to work only on the questions they answered incorrectly.

## EXPLANATIONS FOR PRACTICE PART V

101. (A) *Responsible* is an adjective.

    (B) *Responsibly* is an adverb.

    (C) *Responsive* is an adjective.

    **(D) The definite article *the* shows you that a noun should be used here. *Responsibility* is a noun meaning *duty*.**

102. (A) The noun *limit* would not be used to modify the noun phrase *period of time*.

    (B) *Limits* is either a plural noun or a third-person singular verb. Neither of these would be used to modify *period of time*.

    **(C) *Limited* is used as an adjective to modify the noun phrase *period of time*. The expression *for a limited period of time* means *for a short time only*.**

    (D) The gerund *limiting* is sometimes used as an adjective, but it cannot be used in this expression.

103. (A) As an adverb, *still* is used for an action that started in the past but will continue for some time.

    (B) *Yet* is an adverb indicating that something has happened by or before now, but *yet* is most often used with *not* or in a question.

    **(C) In this sentence, the present perfect *has arrived* is used to indicate the immediate past. The adverb *already* shows that something has happened *by* or *before* now.**

    (D) *Soon* indicates an event in the near future, not in the immediate past.

104. (A) The verb *arrange* in its simple form cannot complete the present perfect tense.

    **(B) The past participle of the verb completes the present perfect tense *have arranged*.**

    (C) *Arranges* is a present tense form that cannot be used with *have* to form a verb tense.

    (D) While the present perfect continuous form *have been arranging* exists in English, *arranging* as a gerund would not be the object of the verb *have*.

105. (A) The past participle of a verb completes the present passive and explains something done to help employees remember the rule.

    (B) *Respected* is followed by *for* and the gerund of a verb: Employees are *respected* for working hard. *Respected* may also be followed by a noun phrase: The employees *respected* the rule.

    (C) *Remembered* would not be used in the passive voice in this sentence.

    (D) *Reacted* is an intransitive verb and cannot be used in the passive voice.

106. (A) A verb would not be used to complete the noun phrase.

    (B) *Speaker* is a noun, meaning a person who speaks, but *long* does not usually modify a person.

    (C) The gerund of a verb can be used as a noun, but it would not normally be used with the indefinite article *a*.

    **(D) Here, a noun is used to complete the noun phrase begun by *a long*.**

107. (A) *Interest* is a verb, not an adjective.

    **(B) An adjective should be used to describe *any person*. Someone who is *interested in* something is *curious about* it.**

    (C) *Interesting* is an adjective, but it is never followed by the preposition *in* when it is used to describe a person.

    (D) The adverb *interestingly* cannot be used in place of an adjective here.

108. (A) *Concerned* is not usually followed by the preposition *to*.

    **(B) The preposition *about* links *be concerned* and the *upcoming meeting*.**

    (C) *Concerned* is not usually followed by the preposition *at*.

    (D) *Concerned* can be followed by the preposition *upon*, but only when the preposition is followed by the gerund of a verb: I was *concerned upon hearing* the news.

109. (A) The verb used with *delays* is *cause*, not *make*.

(B) *Cuisines* are styles of food; verbs commonly occurring with *cuisines* are *serve* and *prepare*.

**(C) A noun describing something that can be made at a restaurant should be used here.**

(D) The verb *make* is not used with *violations*.

110. **(A) The connecting word *because* introduces the reason why the presentation was difficult to understand.**

(B) *Although* is not used to introduce the reason for something; rather, it is used to set up a contrast between two clauses.

(C) *So that* is used to introduce the purpose of an action.

(D) *Than* is used in a comparison, such as *more difficult than*.

111. (A) *Increased* is a verb, not an adverb.

**(B) The answer should be an adverb that modifies the adjective *weak*.**

(C) *Increases* is a plural noun or a third-person singular verb, not an adverb.

(D) *Increase* is a noun, not an adverb.

112. **(A) The preposition *beyond* would be used in the idiomatic expression *circumstances beyond its control*. The firm does not accept responsibility for the situation.**

(B) The preposition *above* is not used in this idiomatic expression.

(C) The preposition *inside* is not used in this idiomatic expression.

(D) The preposition *around* is not used in this idiomatic expression.

113. (A) *Favorite* is an adjective, but it is used to talk about a person's preferences.

(B) Neither the noun *favor* nor the verb *favor* can precede *weather conditions*.

**(C) An adjective that explains that the weather conditions are good should be used here.**

(D) An adverb cannot modify a noun.

114. **(A) A noun meaning a *person who receives something* should be used here.**

(B) This choice is a verb gerund.

(C) A *receipt* is a piece of paper showing *proof of payment*.

(D) This choice is an adjective.

115. (A) This choice is a pronoun and does not indicate possession.

**(B) The possessive adjective *their* shows that the creative solutions are the managers' own ideas.**

(C) *Theirs* is a possessive pronoun and can be used to refer to another noun: the textbook is *theirs*.

(D) This choice is a pronoun and does not indicate possession.

116. **(A) The answer should be a noun that indicates something that took place yesterday and is connected with the legal joining, or merger, of two companies. Mergers may involve a large amount of negotiation, or discussion with the aim of reaching an agreement.**

(B) *Dedications* are not usually associated with *mergers*.

(C) *Propositions* do not *take place*.

(D) *Announcements* are *made*. They do not *take place*.

117. (A) *Photocopies* is the object of the verb in the sentence. *Emerge* is an intransitive verb, so it cannot have an object.

    (B) *Substantiate* cannot be followed by the prepositional phrase *to this office.*

    (C) To *adapt* something means to change it; nothing in the sentence suggests that the requested documents should be changed before being submitted.

    **(D) The answer should be a verb that explains what employees should do with their photocopies. *Submit* means *hand in* or *send in*.**

118. (A) This choice includes parts of the required comparative phrase, but the entire phrase *the same as* is needed to complete the sentence.

    (B) This choice includes parts of the required comparative phrase, but the entire phrase *the same as* is needed to complete the sentence.

    (C) This choice includes parts of the required comparative phrase, but the entire phrase *the same as* is needed to complete the sentence.

    **(D) Two sets of results are being compared here. *The same* as is used to say that two things are equal.**

119. (A) *Totally* is an adverb, but it is not a frequency adverb.

    (B) *Negatively* is an adverb, but it is not a frequency adverb.

    (C) *Decidedly* is an adverb, but it is not a frequency adverb.

    **(D) Here, an adverb indicating infrequency should be used. It is placed at the beginning of the sentence for emphasis and causes inversion of the subject and verb.**

120. **(A) *The first* is a shortened version of *the first day*. The full expression here would be *the first day of the month*. The preposition of links day and month.**

    (B) *To* is often used in time expressions, but it means *until:* from the first *to* the fifth.

    (C) *From* is used in time expressions to mean *starting at: from* the end of the month.

    (D) *For* is used in time expressions to say how long something lasts.

121. (A) *Thoroughness* is incorrect unless preceded by the preposition *with.*

    (B) *More thorough* is an adjective, not an adverb.

    (C) *Thorough* is an adjective, not an adverb.

    **(D) The answer should be an adverb that tells how the contracts should be read. *Thoroughly* means *carefully*.**

122. (A) *Addition* is a noun. It would not be used to modify *travel time*.

    (B) *Additive* can be an adjective, but would not be used in this context.

    (C) *Additionally* is an adverb, and may not be used to modify a noun.

    **(D) An adjective that means *extra* should be used here.**

123. **(A) A noun is used here to complete the compound noun *project development*.**

    (B) *Developed* is a verb.

    (C) *Develops* is a verb.

    (D) *Developer* is a noun meaning a person who develops something.

124. (A) The noun *knowledge* should be followed by *of*.

    (B) *Had no thought* is not used to say *did not know*.

    **(C) The noun *idea* completes the phrase *had no idea*, meaning *did not know*.**

    (D) The noun *willingness* is not used to talk about what someone knows.

125. (A) The conjunction *unless* would introduce a conditional phrase. There is no conditional phrase here.

**(B) In this sentence, the verb *benefit* should be followed by the preposition *from* and a noun.**

(C) *To* is not used after the verb *benefit*.

(D) The preposition *since* might be used to introduce a reason or a starting time, but neither of these follows in this sentence.

126. (A) *Continuity* is a noun. A verb is needed after the subject *employees*.

**(B) The phrase *suggested that* should be followed by a complete sentence.**

(C) Used here, *continuing* would create an incomplete sentence.

(D) *Continuous* is an adjective; a verb is required to complete the sentence.

127. (A) This choice is a pronoun, but it is not a reflexive pronoun.

**(B) The reflexive pronoun *herself* is required, referring to Ms. Jin. It completes the phrase *by herself*, which means without help.**

(C) This choice is a pronoun, but it is not a reflexive pronoun.

(D) This choice is a pronoun, but it is not a reflexive pronoun.

128. **(A) The answer should be an intransitive verb that indicates what the company will do. *Diversify* means that the company will vary its work.**

(B) The verb *clarify* is usually transitive and requires objects. Its intransitive use in this sentence would not make sense.

(C) The verb *intensify* is usually transitive and requires objects. Its intransitive use in this sentence would not make sense.

(D) The verb *modify* is usually transitive and requires objects. Its intransitive use in this sentence would not make sense.

129. (A) A person can be *anxious* but a business plan cannot.

(B) The adjective *evident* would not normally be used to describe a business plan.

(C) A person can be *eager* but a business plan cannot.

**(D) An adjective should be used here to explain that the business plan is excellent, or *outstanding*.**

130. **(A) An adjective should be used here to modify *production*.**

(B) *Locality* is a noun.

(C) The adverb *locally* cannot modify *production*.

(D) *Location* is a noun that would not modify *production* in this sentence.

131. **(A) The relative pronoun *which* referring to *the position* would follow the preposition *for* in this sentence.**

(B) *Whom* is used to refer to a person.

(C) *That* could refer to *the position*, but would not follow *for* in this sentence.

(D) *What* is not a relative pronoun.

132. (A) An item can be *altered by* a person but not by a thing.

(B) An item can be *adjusted by* a person but not by a thing.

(C) *An item* could not be *accepted* by *a receipt*.

**(D) The answer should be a verb that can be followed by the preposition *by*. *Accompanied by* means the item must be returned *together with the receipt*.**

133. **(A) A noun that makes a compound noun with** *telephone* **should be used here.** *Telephone extensions* **are individual telephones that make up a telephone system.**

(B) This choice is a verb form. A verb cannot be used in this position in the sentence.

(C) This choice is a verb form. A verb cannot be used in this position in the sentence.

(D) This choice is a verb form. A verb cannot be used in this position in the sentence.

134. **(A) The answer should be a verb meaning *to check* or *verify*.**

(B) *Concur* means to *agree* about something.

(C) *Conduct* means to *lead* or *guide*. It would not be used to talk about a flight number. (D) *Concord* is a noun meaning *agreement*.

135. (A) Here the noun *discouragement* would not be used after *so*.

(B) *Discourage* is a verb, not an adjective.

**(C) An adjective that describes the first year's sales should be used.** *Discouraging* **sales would be poor sales.**

(D) *Discouraged* is the past participle of the verb *discourage*.

136. (A) *Unjudged* advice would not lead to sound investment decisions.

**(B) The answer should be an adjective.** *Unbiased* **is an adjective that means *impartial* or *fair*.**

(C) The adjective *inanimate*, which means *not living*, is not usually used to describe advice.

(D) A person can be *impatient*. Advice is not.

137. **(A) The noun *attire* means clothing. Professional clothing is often required by companies.**

(B) *Ambivalence* means uncertainty about something and would not be a requirement of a company.

(C) Although *assembly* can mean a professional *meeting*, the indefinite article *a* would need to precede the phrase in this context.

(D) If the noun *approach* were used, the indefinite article *a* would be needed.

138. (A) Sometimes *too* is used with an adjective, but it is not used with a *that* clause.

**(B) Here *such* emphasizes *good*. It is used together with a *that* clause (*that she was quickly offered a promotion*) to state the result of the good work.**

(C) A different word order is used with *so*: her work was *so* good that…

(D) *Much…that* is not used to show a result in the same way as *such…that*.

139. (A) *Cautioned* is the past participle of the verb.

**(B) A noun is used to complete the phrase *a good deal of*.**

(C) The adjective *cautious* would need to be followed by a noun.

(D) The adverb *cautiously* cannot complete this phrase.

140. (A) *Even though* is used to introduce a clause, not a phrase.

(B) *Nevertheless* can only be used to introduce the second idea in a series, not the first.

**(C) The prepositional phrase in spite of is used to introduce a contrast. Here, it connects the noun phrase higher ticket prices this year to the rest of the sentence.**

(D) Like *nevertheless* and *even though*, *consequently* is used to introduce a clause, not a phrase.

## PART VI: ERROR RECOGNITION

Below, you will find explanations of the correct answers for questions 141–160. Since the task for this question type is to identify the underlined word or phrase that is incorrect in the sentence, the explanation describes only why that word or phrase is incorrect. The other three underlined parts of the sentence are correct. You should have enough time to study all of the questions, not just the ones you answered incorrectly.

To make the best use of the explanations, do the following:

First, read each sentence again and think carefully about which underlined word or phrase is incorrect. Think about how you would explain to someone why it is incorrect.

Next, read the explanation of the correct answer for that question below.

Then, write out the corrected version of the test. It is useful to do this exercise, even though this is not something you are required to do in the test. It is better to have a correct sentence in your mind, rather than an incorrect one. There is a space after each explanation for you to write the corrected sentences.

**Explanations**

**141. (D)** The bus runs both *to* the downtown area and *from* the downtown area. *Downtown area* does not need to be used twice: The bus runs both *to and from* the downtown area.

Corrected sentence: _____

**142. (A)** The transitive verb *appreciate* takes one object. The object of *appreciate* is *your interest*; the word *it* is therefore redundant.

Corrected sentence: _____

**143. (A)** *That* is required here as part of the conjunctional phrase *in the event that*. This phrase means *in case* or *if*.

Corrected sentence: _____

**144. (B)** *Each* is always used with a singular verb, even though its meaning seems to be plural. The verb should be in the singular form of the passive, *was handled*.

Corrected sentence: _____

**145. (A)** The noun *format*, meaning *arrangement* or *style*, is needed here as the object of the verb *follow*. *Formatted* is the past tense or past participle of the verb *format*.

Corrected sentence: _____

**146. (C)** *Make up for* is a phrasal verb that means *compensate for*. The preposition *with* cannot be used in place of *for* in this phrasal verb.

Corrected sentence: _____

**147. (B)** The definite article *the* should precede the noun *manager*, since it refers to a specific individual (that is, the manager of the hotel where Ms. Rivera stayed).

Corrected sentence: _____

**148. (C)** The preposition *at* cannot be used with *the suburbs*. The offices will be moving, or *relocating*, *to* the suburbs.

Corrected sentence: _____

**149. (C)** *Because of* is a preposition and should be followed by a noun, as in the following sentence: I did not go out *because of* the rain. *They want to save money* is a clause, not a noun phrase. If this clause is used, the conjunction *because* is needed, rather than a preposition.

Corrected sentence: _____

**150. (A)** The first clause of this sentence requires a verb in the passive voice. The past participle of the verb *charge* should be used: Penalties *will be charged* or *are charged*.

Corrected sentence: _____

**151. (B)** The verb and noun combination *take care* means *make a special effort* to do something. The noun *caring* cannot be substituted for *care* in this expression.

Corrected sentence: _____

**152. (C)** In the second part of this sentence *the computer terminal* is the object of a verb. The verb form, *consult*, should replace the noun, *consultation*.

Corrected sentence: _____

**153. (A)** When something unexpected happens to someone, it is common to say that the person is *taken by surprise*. The preposition *by* cannot be left out of this expression.

Corrected sentence: _____

**154. (C)** *Too much* and *too many* are used before nouns to indicate a greater quantity than is necessary: I have *too much* work; there are *too many* chairs in the room. *Too many* must be used with a plural noun, such as *sales representatives*. *Too much* is used with uncountable, or mass nouns, such as *work*.

Corrected sentence: _____

**155. (C)** The past participle of the verb *designate* is needed before the noun *agent*. *Designated* acts as an adjective, and means that a particular agent has been given the job of checking travel documents.

Corrected sentence: _____

**156. (A)** *Without* should be followed by a noun or a gerund, a verb form acting as a noun. The sentence would be correct with the conjunction *unless* as the first word.

Corrected sentence: _____

**157. (C)** The compound noun *safety standard* is a countable noun. More than one safety standard is reviewed, so there should be an *–s* at the end of *standard* to indicate plurality.

Corrected sentence: _____

**158. (D)** A verb has to agree in number with its subject. *The conference* is the subject of the verb *begin*. Since the subject is singular, *begin* should be in the third person singular form: *begins*.

Corrected sentence: _____

**159. (A)** The noun *candidate* is a countable noun and is used in the singular here. It should be preceded by an article *(a or the)*.

Corrected sentence: _____

**160. (B)** The sentence requires a verb in the passive voice. The modal passive is formed here by *can* and the past participle *found*: applications *can be found* by guests at the hotel.

Corrected sentence: _____

# Day 29

## Practice Test: Reading Section, Part VII

Today you will have the opportunity to practice Part VII of the test, Reading Comprehension, which contains questions 161–200 of the TOEIC test.

Work on this section as if you were taking the real TOEIC test so that you can learn how much time the questions will take and how it feels to work straight through questions 161–200 under conditions similar to what you will experience during an actual test.

- **Use the sample answer sheet provided.** On the next page, you will find part of a sample answer sheet similar to the one used on official TOEIC tests. On Day 25, you completed the first sections of the sample answer sheet with your answers to the background questionnaire and details about yourself. As you answer questions 161–200, fill in the circles on the answer sheet under the heading "Reading Section."

- **Find a quiet place to take Part VII of the practice test.** Answer the questions in a place where you will not be disturbed. You will need a pencil and eraser.

- **Time yourself.** The time allowed for the entire Reading section (questions 101–200) is 75 minutes. Part VII may take 40 or 45 minutes. If you find a question particularly difficult, fill in the answer that you think is closest and make a note next to the question so that you can come back to it later if you have time. Do not leave any questions blank.

READING SECTION

| | | | |
|---|---|---|---|
| 101 Ⓐ Ⓑ Ⓒ Ⓓ | 126 Ⓐ Ⓑ Ⓒ Ⓓ | 151 Ⓐ Ⓑ Ⓒ Ⓓ | 176 Ⓐ Ⓑ Ⓒ Ⓓ |
| 102 Ⓐ Ⓑ Ⓒ Ⓓ | 127 Ⓐ Ⓑ Ⓒ Ⓓ | 152 Ⓐ Ⓑ Ⓒ Ⓓ | 177 Ⓐ Ⓑ Ⓒ Ⓓ |
| 103 Ⓐ Ⓑ Ⓒ Ⓓ | 128 Ⓐ Ⓑ Ⓒ Ⓓ | 153 Ⓐ Ⓑ Ⓒ Ⓓ | 178 Ⓐ Ⓑ Ⓒ Ⓓ |
| 104 Ⓐ Ⓑ Ⓒ Ⓓ | 129 Ⓐ Ⓑ Ⓒ Ⓓ | 154 Ⓐ Ⓑ Ⓒ Ⓓ | 179 Ⓐ Ⓑ Ⓒ Ⓓ |
| 105 Ⓐ Ⓑ Ⓒ Ⓓ | 130 Ⓐ Ⓑ Ⓒ Ⓓ | 155 Ⓐ Ⓑ Ⓒ Ⓓ | 180 Ⓐ Ⓑ Ⓒ Ⓓ |
| 106 Ⓐ Ⓑ Ⓒ Ⓓ | 131 Ⓐ Ⓑ Ⓒ Ⓓ | 156 Ⓐ Ⓑ Ⓒ Ⓓ | 181 Ⓐ Ⓑ Ⓒ Ⓓ |
| 107 Ⓐ Ⓑ Ⓒ Ⓓ | 132 Ⓐ Ⓑ Ⓒ Ⓓ | 157 Ⓐ Ⓑ Ⓒ Ⓓ | 182 Ⓐ Ⓑ Ⓒ Ⓓ |
| 108 Ⓐ Ⓑ Ⓒ Ⓓ | 133 Ⓐ Ⓑ Ⓒ Ⓓ | 158 Ⓐ Ⓑ Ⓒ Ⓓ | 183 Ⓐ Ⓑ Ⓒ Ⓓ |
| 109 Ⓐ Ⓑ Ⓒ Ⓓ | 134 Ⓐ Ⓑ Ⓒ Ⓓ | 159 Ⓐ Ⓑ Ⓒ Ⓓ | 184 Ⓐ Ⓑ Ⓒ Ⓓ |
| 110 Ⓐ Ⓑ Ⓒ Ⓓ | 135 Ⓐ Ⓑ Ⓒ Ⓓ | 160 Ⓐ Ⓑ Ⓒ Ⓓ | 185 Ⓐ Ⓑ Ⓒ Ⓓ |
| 111 Ⓐ Ⓑ Ⓒ Ⓓ | 136 Ⓐ Ⓑ Ⓒ Ⓓ | 161 Ⓐ Ⓑ Ⓒ Ⓓ | 186 Ⓐ Ⓑ Ⓒ Ⓓ |
| 112 Ⓐ Ⓑ Ⓒ Ⓓ | 137 Ⓐ Ⓑ Ⓒ Ⓓ | 162 Ⓐ Ⓑ Ⓒ Ⓓ | 187 Ⓐ Ⓑ Ⓒ Ⓓ |
| 113 Ⓐ Ⓑ Ⓒ Ⓓ | 138 Ⓐ Ⓑ Ⓒ Ⓓ | 163 Ⓐ Ⓑ Ⓒ Ⓓ | 188 Ⓐ Ⓑ Ⓒ Ⓓ |
| 114 Ⓐ Ⓑ Ⓒ Ⓓ | 139 Ⓐ Ⓑ Ⓒ Ⓓ | 164 Ⓐ Ⓑ Ⓒ Ⓓ | 189 Ⓐ Ⓑ Ⓒ Ⓓ |
| 115 Ⓐ Ⓑ Ⓒ Ⓓ | 140 Ⓐ Ⓑ Ⓒ Ⓓ | 165 Ⓐ Ⓑ Ⓒ Ⓓ | 190 Ⓐ Ⓑ Ⓒ Ⓓ |
| 116 Ⓐ Ⓑ Ⓒ Ⓓ | 141 Ⓐ Ⓑ Ⓒ Ⓓ | 166 Ⓐ Ⓑ Ⓒ Ⓓ | 191 Ⓐ Ⓑ Ⓒ Ⓓ |
| 117 Ⓐ Ⓑ Ⓒ Ⓓ | 142 Ⓐ Ⓑ Ⓒ Ⓓ | 167 Ⓐ Ⓑ Ⓒ Ⓓ | 192 Ⓐ Ⓑ Ⓒ Ⓓ |
| 118 Ⓐ Ⓑ Ⓒ Ⓓ | 143 Ⓐ Ⓑ Ⓒ Ⓓ | 168 Ⓐ Ⓑ Ⓒ Ⓓ | 193 Ⓐ Ⓑ Ⓒ Ⓓ |
| 119 Ⓐ Ⓑ Ⓒ Ⓓ | 144 Ⓐ Ⓑ Ⓒ Ⓓ | 169 Ⓐ Ⓑ Ⓒ Ⓓ | 194 Ⓐ Ⓑ Ⓒ Ⓓ |
| 120 Ⓐ Ⓑ Ⓒ Ⓓ | 145 Ⓐ Ⓑ Ⓒ Ⓓ | 170 Ⓐ Ⓑ Ⓒ Ⓓ | 195 Ⓐ Ⓑ Ⓒ Ⓓ |
| 121 Ⓐ Ⓑ Ⓒ Ⓓ | 146 Ⓐ Ⓑ Ⓒ Ⓓ | 171 Ⓐ Ⓑ Ⓒ Ⓓ | 196 Ⓐ Ⓑ Ⓒ Ⓓ |
| 122 Ⓐ Ⓑ Ⓒ Ⓓ | 147 Ⓐ Ⓑ Ⓒ Ⓓ | 172 Ⓐ Ⓑ Ⓒ Ⓓ | 197 Ⓐ Ⓑ Ⓒ Ⓓ |
| 123 Ⓐ Ⓑ Ⓒ Ⓓ | 148 Ⓐ Ⓑ Ⓒ Ⓓ | 173 Ⓐ Ⓑ Ⓒ Ⓓ | 198 Ⓐ Ⓑ Ⓒ Ⓓ |
| 124 Ⓐ Ⓑ Ⓒ Ⓓ | 149 Ⓐ Ⓑ Ⓒ Ⓓ | 174 Ⓐ Ⓑ Ⓒ Ⓓ | 199 Ⓐ Ⓑ Ⓒ Ⓓ |
| 125 Ⓐ Ⓑ Ⓒ Ⓓ | 150 Ⓐ Ⓑ Ⓒ Ⓓ | 175 Ⓐ Ⓑ Ⓒ Ⓓ | 200 Ⓐ Ⓑ Ⓒ Ⓓ |

## PART VII

*Directions: Questions 161–200 are based on a selection of reading materials, such as notices, letters, forms, newspaper and magazine articles, and advertisements. You are to choose the one best answer (A), (B), (C), or (D) to each question. Then, on your answer sheet, find the number of the question and mark your answer. Answer all questions following each reading selection on the basis of what is stated or implied in that selection.*

Read the following example.

The Museum of Technology is a "hands-on" museum, designed for people to experience science at work. Visitors are encouraged to use, test, and handle the objects on display. Special demonstrations are scheduled for the first and second Wednesdays of each month at 13:30. Open Tuesday–Friday 12:00–16:30, Saturday 10:00–17:30, and Sunday 11:00–16:30.

When during the month can visitors see special demonstrations?

(A) Every weekend

(B) The first two Wednesdays

(C) One afternoon a week

(D) Every other Wednesday

*Sample Answer*

Ⓐ ● Ⓒ Ⓓ

The reading selection says that the demonstrations are scheduled for the first and second Wednesdays of the month.

Therefore, you should select choice (B).

Now, begin work on the questions.

**Questions 161–162** refer to the following advertisement.

ESTATE AUCTION

An auction for the estate of Martina Jovanovic has been set for Saturday, July 19, at 12:00 noon. (Preview starts at 10:00 a.m.)

Location. The Jovanovic residence at 433 Walnut Drive

Some of the items to be auctioned:

\* 1997 Sports Car

\* Home Queen Appliances

\* Oriental Carpets

\* Stamp Collection

\* Hand-Carved Wooden Boxes, Dolls, and Utensils

\* China Teacups from Colonial America

\* Antique Furnishings

Parking three blocks south, in the Municipal Building lot, at 119 Walnut Drive

Questions? Please call Estate Planners Associates, 546-7000. The Jovanovics request that you do not phone their home.

161. What event is being advertised?

(A) A party for the Jovanovic family

(B) A fund-raising event at the Municipal Building

(C) A sale of the possessions of Martina Jovanovic

(D) A private viewing of museum pieces

162. Where will the event be held?

(A) At the Municipal Building

(B) At 433 Walnut Drive

(C) At the Estate Planners Associates' office

(D) In the city parking lot

**Questions 163–165** refer to the following form.

**Department of Public Health**
**Wellington, New Zealand**

**FOOD ESTABLISHMENTS CLOSED FOR HEALTH-CODE VIOLATIONS**

| Name of Business | Date Closed | Reasons Cited for Closing |
|---|---|---|
| Mandy's<br>910 12th St. | 1/16 | Inadequate ventilation<br>Improper food storage |
| Valley Restaurant<br>815 23rd Ave. | 1/16 | Plumbing fixtures in poor repair<br>No certified food supervisor |
| Market Grill<br>770 Golden Rd. | 1/16 | No certified food supervisor<br>Improper food temperature |
| Peppo Mart<br>(food sales section only)<br>104 Main St. | 1/17 | Operating without a health department permit<br>Inadequate refrigeration |
| Lawville's<br>872 N. Jackson St. | 1/18 | No hot water<br>Unclean food contact surfaces |

163. Why are these establishments closed?

(A) They are in violation of the building code.

(B) They have been cited for unsanitary conditions.

(C) They are undergoing renovations.

(D) They are open for only part of the year.

164. Which business will remain partially open?

(A) Peppo Mart

(B) Valley Restaurant

(C) Mandy's

(D) Lawville's

165. What should the Valley Restaurant do?

(A) Check its sinks and pipes

(B) Offer take-out service

(C) Change its menu

(D) Renew its permit

**Questions 166–168** refer to the following memorandum.

**MEMORANDUM**

TO: All Office Employees
FROM: Ruth Crawford
RE: New Phone System
DATE: May 22

As you know, we badly need to modernize our communications system. I have enclosed with this memo some descriptions of phone systems sent by sales representatives. Please read the materials carefully and send your recommendations to me.

The system should be able to handle at least one hold line and eight extension lines. My opinion is that a built-in answering machine is necessary. Conference calls and speed-dialing features are now standard in many systems and could prove useful.

At the present time our office uses twelve phones, and although we do not have a fixed limit for the unit price, it should be mid-range.

Recommendations should be in my office by the end of the week so an order can be placed through Supplies and Equipment by the first of the month.

Enclosures

166. What does the memo discuss?

(A) Holding a conference on telecommunications

(B) Repairing old telephone units

(C) Communicating by telephone less frequently

(D) Choosing a new telephone system

167. What should people do after reading the memo?

(A) Organize a conference to discuss the matter

(B) Order new phones right away

(C) Notify Ruth Crawford of a preference

(D) Contact Supplies and Equipment as soon as possible

168. What is a criterion for selecting equipment?

(A) Use of standard colors

(B) One hold line and at least eight extension lines

(C) Separate answering machine

(D) Low price per unit

**Questions 169–171** refer to the following news article.

This week Merrymaker Cruise Lines has filed a $700 million lawsuit against Wambaugh Marine Industries, a shipyard that filed for bankruptcy last November before completing a three-ship contract for Merrymaker. The suit contends that Merrymaker suffered $400 million in additional construction costs and lost passenger bookings and also seeks $300 million in punitive damages. In 1987, Merrymaker signed the $600 million contract with Wambaugh for three 2,600-passenger ships, but the bankruptcy halted all work at the shipyard. The suit also contends that the yard misrepresented its financial condition in order to get the Merrymaker contract.

169. What had Wambaugh agreed to do?

(A) Provide 2,600 passengers

(B) Build three ships

(C) File suit against Merrymaker

(D) Revise the Merrymaker contract

170. What was the value of the Wambaugh-Merrymaker agreement?

(A) $300 million

(B) $400 million

(C) $600 million

(D) $700 million

171. Why did work stop at the shipyard?

(A) Costs of materials were too high.

(B) Passenger bookings had decreased.

(C) The shipyard filed for bankruptcy.

(D) The ships were completed.

**Questions 172–173** refer to the following notice.

If you need to cancel or change your reservation for this tour, we will refund your deposit, in full, up to thirty days prior to departure. If you need to cancel your reservation after thirty days, no refund is possible, but you may sell your place or send a friend in your place. All group reservations are subject to a 90-day cancellation policy.

172. What percentage of the deposit will be refunded with a 30-day cancellation notice?

(A) 0

(B) 30

(C) 90

(D) 100

173. What is suggested as an alternative to cancellation?

(A) Joining a group tour

(B) Giving your place to a friend

(C) Traveling 30 days earlier

(D) Sending in a refund request

**Questions 174–176** refer to the following notice.

We would like to welcome you to the XYZ Machinery Company's International Symposium. As you are aware, XYZ employees from over twenty countries are in attendance at this year's conference. If you would like to meet your counterparts from other countries on a more personal level, be sure to sign up at the registration desk for special dinners, lunches, or breakfast meetings that are described below. Whether you are in Personnel, Sales, Management, or Research, you'll be able to discuss topics of common interest with colleagues of diverse backgrounds. Find out what your Indian, Japanese, or Moroccan counterpart can suggest for your department's current problems. Help your French, Colombian, or Russian colleague with a problem that you've tackled before. Take advantage of this rare opportunity to collaborate with your international partners. All meetings will be held in Lounge B.

| TIME | TOPIC |
|---|---|
| Monday Breakfast 7:00–9:00 | Legal Implications of Establishing Branch Offices in Asia |
| Tuesday Lunch 12:00–14:00 | Technologies in the Former Soviet Republics |
| Wednesday Dinner 19:00–21:00 | International Personnel Issues |
| Thursday Breakfast 7:00–9:00 | New Markets in Western Europe |

174. Who is the conference aimed at?

(A) International politicians

(B) People learning foreign languages

(C) International chefs

(D) Employees of a machinery company

175. What is the purpose of the notice?

(A) To give a list of participants

(B) To indicate room changes

(C) To announce special events

(D) To cancel several sessions

176. Which session would most likely deal with human resources?

(A) Monday breakfast

(B) Tuesday lunch

(C) Wednesday dinner

(D) Thursday breakfast

**Questions 177–180** refer to the following instructions.

Softwind's technical support staff provides free telephone assistance to registered Softwind users. In order to receive this free assistance, you must first register your product with Softwind. To do this, fill in the enclosed registration card, including the name of the retail outlet where you purchased this product. Softwind will then send you a personal identification number (PIN), which must be supplied to support staff whenever you request assistance. Registering your product will also enable us to send you timely information on updates and future releases. Before calling technical support, please try to find the answer to your question in the handbook that accompanies this product. In particular, we recommend that you check the section on frequently asked questions that begins in the back of your handbook.

177. Who were these instructions written for?

(A) Technical support staff

(B) Softwind engineers

(C) Retail sales personnel

(D) Softwind customers

178. What information is necessary in order to register this product?

(A) The name of the store that sold the product

(B) The user's personal identification number

(C) The dates of future releases

(D) The user's forwarding address

179. How can you receive a PIN?

(A) By requesting one from support staff

(B) By telephoning technical support

(C) By mailing in the registration card

(D) By signing up for one at a retail outlet

180. What should you do first if you have a problem with the product?

 (A) Read the manual

 (B) Change your PIN

 (C) Telephone technical support

 (D) Request updated instructions

**Questions 181–184** refer to the following letter.

**Smooth Skin**
3949 Marina Way West
Alta Vista, CA 92458

May 11

Mr. George Mackie
IFS Freight Forwarding
8471 S. Eastern Avenue
Chicago, IL 60647

Dear Mr. Mackie:

We have just received a complaint about a mishandled delivery from one of our trusted customers, Mr. C. Benson of Butterfly Beauty Care in Dubuque, Iowa.

Apparently, a member of your staff delivered two cartons of goods to the Butterfly Beauty Care facility despite the fact that the items they contained had been damaged in transit. Enclosed, you will find a copy of the transmittal form signed by Mr. Benson, on which he clearly indicated that he noticed the damage while your driver was still on the premises.

Mr. Benson reports that the driver refused to take the goods back, contrary to your company's stated policy. Furthermore, the driver indicated that our packing was responsible for the breakage. We can assure you that these boxes were packed with the usual care, and left our warehouse in perfect condition. We can only conclude that they were damaged during shipment.

We expect you to pick up the boxes immediately at absolutely no cost to Mr. Benson or Smooth Skin. We are far from satisfied with the actions of your employee, and in view of the fact that this is the third complaint we have received in six months, any further incidents of this nature will force us to reconsider the renewal of our contract with your firm.

Sincerely,

Peggy S. Rolf
Shipping Manager  Enclosure

181. What was sent to Mr. Mackie with this letter?

 (A) A check

 (B) Two cartons

 (C) A new contract

 (D) A shipping document

182. According to the letter, what did the delivery driver say?

 (A) Smooth Skin was responsible for the damage.

 (B) Butterfly Beauty should file a complaint.

 (C) The shipment was damaged in transit.

 (D) IFS should refund the customer's money.

183. Ms. Rolf refers to the IFS policy about

 (A) shipping charges.

 (B) returns.

 (C) weight limits.

 (D) travel expenses.

184. How does Ms. Rolf want the firm to respond to her letter?

 (A) By contacting her directly

 (B) By renewing the contract

 (C) By retrieving the goods

 (D) By paying for the damage

**Questions 185–186** refer to the following notice.

## FUEL ADJUSTMENT NOTICE

With the approval of the Price Control Commission, Velcorp Power announces that the fuel adjustment will be decreased to 1.8747 cents per kilowatt hour sold, effective with meter readings taken on or after November 1, and until further notice.

## VELCORP

185. Who issued this notice?

   (A) A law office

   (B) A gasoline station

   (C) The Price Control Commission

   (D) An electric company

186. What will happen on November 1?

   (A) The commission will have its monthly meeting.

   (B) Fuel will be sold by cubic meter.

   (C) Prices will change.

   (D) Meters will be read more often.

**Questions 187–188** refer to the following news article.

LONDON—One of the Mitchell Motor Company's main British plants remained closed today by an unofficial strike, even though the company's assembly-line workers have accepted a pay increase. About 550 maintenance technicians are on strike at the High-tower factory in northern England. In response, Mitchell has laid off 8,000 assembly-line workers there.

Mitchell's 32,000 assembly-line workers voted to accept a 6.2 percent pay increase this week. But the technicians argued that they were losing ground against unskilled workers and threatened to spread their strike to other plants. The strike has forced Framm to halt production of vans at its facility in southern England.

187. What have the assembly-line workers agreed to do?

   (A) Go on strike

   (B) Support the technicians' demands

   (C) Accept a pay increase

   (D) Move to another plant

188. What has been the result of the technicians' strike?

   (A) Assembly-line workers have been laid off.

   (B) 8,000 technicians have been fired.

   (C) Van models have been redesigned.

   (D) Their salaries have increased.

**Questions 189–190** refer to the following instructions.

## HOW TO INVEST MORE AT SMITH MUTUAL FUNDS

### By Mail

To add to your account, send a check or money order payable to Smith Funds along with the additional investment form that is attached to this statement. Please see minimum investment requirements for each fund in the appropriate prospectus.

### By Electronic Transfer

After an account has been established, you may purchase additional shares by electronic transfer. Please call Smith Funds for instructions.

### By Exchange

You can open a new account by exchanging from one Smith Funds account to an identically registered account. Please verify the investment guidelines for each Fund in the appropriate prospectus. The Fund may modify, suspend, or terminate the exchange privilege at its discretion.

189. What should clients do to invest by electronic transfer?

   (A) Mail a written request

   (B) Telephone for information

   (C) Send in another form

   (D) Terminate their exchange privilege

190. What can the Fund change at any time?

   (A) The investment guidelines

   (B) The account registration number

   (C) The minimum investment

   (D) The exchange privilege

**Questions 191–193** refer to the following letter.

Mr. S. Kayasit, President
Golden Crown Resorts
31/66 Raya Road
Patong Beach
Phuket 83150
Thailand

4-13-14 Shinohara Kitamachi
Chuo-ku, Osaka 541, Japan
March 22

Dear Mr. Kayasit:

Thank you very much for offering me the position of Properties Agent for your office in Phuket. I appreciate your discussing the details of the position with me and giving me time to consider your offer. I also enjoyed meeting Mr. Van Vliet, the current Properties Agent in Phuket.

You have a fine organization and there are many aspects of the position that are very appealing to me. However, I believe it is in our mutual best interest that I decline your kind offer. I have decided to accept a position as the Sales Director for a smaller company located in Kyoto. This has been a difficult decision for me, but I believe it is the appropriate one for my career and family at this time.

I want to thank you for the consideration and courtesy shown to me. It was a pleasure meeting you and Mr. Puapondh, the Head of Operations.

Sincerely,

*Ryusuke Hayashida*

Ryusuke Hayashida

191. Why was this letter written?

(A) To accept a new position
(B) To turn down a job offer
(C) To discuss employment opportunities
(D) To request further information from the personnel office

192. Who offered the opportunity for employment?

(A) The Company President
(B) The Head of Operations
(C) The Properties Agent
(D) The Sales Director

193. Who does NOT work for Golden Crown Resorts?

(A) Mr. Van Vliet
(B) Mr. Kayasit
(C) Mr. Hayashida
(D) Mr. Puapondh

**Questions 194–195** refer to the following notice.

All computer disks must be scanned immediately upon entry to this building. Standard Chemical Company policy prohibits the possession of any personal disks on site. Disks authorized for business must be declared, accompanied by a pass, and scanned for viruses. When entering the facility, failure to declare disks will result in confiscation. The term "disk" refers to any computer-data medium.

194. Where would this notice most likely be seen?

(A) In a health clinic
(B) At a computer terminal
(C) At the entrance of Standard Chemical
(D) In the company cafeteria

195. What will happen if a disk is not declared?

(A) It will be erased.
(B) It will be scratched.
(C) It will be duplicated.
(D) It will be taken away.

**Questions 196–197** refer to the following newspaper article.

**New Terminal For Digili**

DIGILI—Chaldea's Ministry of Planning and Investment has proposed building a new terminal at Digili International Airport. The *Economic Times* said the project would cost between US $180 million and $195 million, more than half of which would come from overseas. The plan calls for building a terminal that can process at least eight million passengers a year.

The ministry's proposal also calls for enlargement of the existing terminal to handle five million passengers a year. Late last year, the Aviation Science Institute unveiled an ambitious plan to renovate the country's four existing airports and build as many as six new airports.

196. Where is most of the funding for the project coming from?
    (A) *The Economic Times*
    (B) The Chaldean Ministry of Planning and Investment
    (C) International investors
    (D) The Digili Airport Authority

197. What is NOT included in the proposal?
    (A) Investing at least US $180 million
    (B) Increasing the size of an existing building
    (C) Constructing more than five new airports
    (D) Demolishing the old terminal at Digili

**Questions 198–200** refer to the following letter.

## Suarez Drilling Corporation
1217 Isabella Avenue, Buenos Aires, Argentina

Ms. Ursula Kahanian
Dienst and Klein Auditors
1001 Wellington Avenue
Toronto, Ontario
Canada

Dear Ms. Kahanian:

We will be pleased to welcome you to our headquarters for the year-end auditing procedures.

Paula Jenkins tells us that you will arrive in Buenos Aires on flight BA 209 on Monday, January 30, at 10:10 a.m. I have instructed my assistant, Carmen Sierra, to drive you directly to our main office and make sure that all the arrangements for your stay are satisfactory. We will put a computer terminal at your disposal in a private office. Should you have any special requirements, I would appreciate it if you would phone or fax us to let us know before your arrival.

We have booked a room at the Santa Catalina Hotel in the center of town, which serves breakfast and dinner. Alternatively, we can recommend many fine restaurants in the center of town. We have arranged for you to have prepaid lunches at our staff cafeteria. Ms. Sierra will take care of the transport arrangements for your return to the airport on Friday the third. I look forward to meeting you next month.

Sincerely,

*Rafael Ortiz*

Rafael Ortiz
Financial Director

198. Why is Ms. Kahanian going to Buenos Aires?
    (A) To visit a drilling site
    (B) To upgrade a computer system
    (C) To conduct an audit
    (D) To review various restaurants

199. Why might it be necessary for Ms. Kahanian to contact Mr. Ortiz prior to her arrival?
    (A) To arrange to use a computer
    (B) To tell him her flight number
    (C) To reserve hotel accommodations
    (D) To find out if she will have access to a copy machine

200. Where will Ms. Kahanian probably have her midday meals?
    (A) At the Suarez Drilling headquarters
    (B) At the Santa Catalina Hotel
    (C) In one of the town's restaurants
    (D) At a local coffee shop

**Stop! This is the end of the test.**

## FOLLOW-UP TO PART VII OF THE PRACTICE TEST

When you have finished working on the questions, do the following:

1. Note here how long it took you to answer questions 161–200: *It took _____ minutes.*

2. Check your answers with the answer key below. For your reference, mark on the key which questions you answered correctly.

3. On the pages following the answer key, you will find explanations of the answers for the practice test, Part VII. Study the explanations for the questions you answered incorrectly. If you have any more time, go on to study the explanations for the questions you answered correctly.

## ANSWER KEY FOR THE PRACTICE TEST: PART VII

| | |
|---|---|
| 161. C | 181. D |
| 162. B | 182. A |
| 163. B | 183. B |
| 164. A | 184. C |
| 165. A | 185. D |
| 166. D | 186. C |
| 167. C | 187. C |
| 168. B | 188. A |
| 169. B | 189. B |
| 170. C | 190. D |
| 171. C | 191. B |
| 172. D | 192. A |
| 173. B | 193. C |
| 174. D | 194. C |
| 175. C | 195. D |
| 176. C | 196. C |
| 177. D | 197. D |
| 178. A | 198. C |
| 179. C | 199. D |
| 180. A | 200. A |

## ANSWER EXPLANATIONS

### Part VII: Reading Comprehension

*To the teacher:* Students can work on the answer explanations in pairs, each pair looking only at those questions that they answered incorrectly. Alternately, each pair could be assigned a number of questions and asked to explain why a choice is correct or incorrect. Encourage students to use a dictionary and to give their own explanations before looking at the explanations on the following pages.

Below, you will find explanations of the answers for Questions 161–200. Before looking at the explanations, do the following:

Look carefully at each question you answered incorrectly. Read the question again. Make sure you understand what the question is asking for.

Next, try to decide why you answered the question incorrectly. Perhaps there were words you didn't understand in the text. Underline any words you are unsure of and look them up in a dictionary.

Write your own explanation for why you selected an incorrect answer and why another option is the correct choice. When you have finished, compare your answers with the explanations below. Number 161 is given as an example.

### Example 1

**161. What event is being advertised?**

**(C) A sale of the possessions of Martina Jovanovic**

Vocabulary – Estate Auction. An *estate* is a person's property or possessions and an *auction* is a type of sale.

## Explanations

161. (A) An *auction* is not a party.

(B) The advertisement does not indicate that this is a fundraising event.

**(C) An *auction* for the estate of Martina Jovanovic is being advertised. An *auction* is a kind of sale and an *estate* is the money or possessions people leave when they die.**

(D) Although there are several fine items, there is no indication that these are part of a museum collection.

162. (A) Cars can be parked at the Municipal Building lot, but the event will not be held there.

**(B) The *location* of the event, or the place where it will be held, is 433 Walnut Drive.**

(C) The event is organized by the Estate Planners Associates but it is not held at their offices.

(D) There is no mention of the city parking lot.

163. (A) It is not the *building code* that they are violating, it is the *health code*.

**(B) The establishments have been closed for *health code violations*, which means they have broken the health code by having unhealthy, or *unsanitary* conditions.**

(C) No mention is made of renovations.

(D) The passage does not state that the establishments can open for part of the year.

164. **(A) Only the *food sales section* of Peppo Mart has been closed, so Peppo Mart is *partially open*.**

(B) The passage does not indicate that any of these establishments has a section that is still open.

(C) The passage does not indicate that any of these establishments has a section that is still open.

(D) The passage does not indicate that any of these establishments has a section that is still open.

165. **(A) The form states that Valley Restaurant's *plumbing fixtures* (such as sinks and pipes) are *in poor repair*, meaning that they are broken, or nearly broken. Therefore, they should be checked.**

(B) Take-out service is not mentioned on the form.

(C) Menus are not mentioned.

(D) No mention is made of renewing permits.

166. (A) *Conference calls*, or calls involving more than two people, are mentioned, but the memo does not say anything about *a conference on telecommunications*.

(B) The company wants to choose a *new phone system*, not *repair* the old telephones.

(C) The memo does not say that employees are using the telephone too frequently.

**(D) The subject of the memorandum, or memo, is the new phone system. Employees are asked to choose a new phone system from some examples.**

167. (A) The memo does not state that employees need to organize a conference.

(B) The office employees receiving this memo cannot order the phone system themselves. It has to be ordered through Supplies and Equipment.

**(C) Employees are asked to read the descriptions of phone systems and send their recommendations, or *preferences*, to Ruth Crawford, who wrote the memo.**

(D) *Ruth Crawford* will contact Supplies and Equipment.

168. (A) Employees are not asked to consider color.

**(B) Office employees are asked to think about certain things when choosing the new equipment; these are *criteria*. One of the criteria is that the system should be able to handle *one hold line and at least eight extension lines*.**

(C) Ruth Crawford thinks the system should have a *built-in* answering machine. This is the opposite of *separate*.

(D) The memo states that the unit price should be *mid-range*.

169. (A) Wambaugh agreed to provide the ships, not the passengers.

   **(B) Wambaugh Marine Industries is a shipyard. Wambaugh had signed a contract for, or *agreed to build,* three passenger ships.**

   (C) Wambaugh has not filed a suit against Merrymaker.

   (D) There is no mention of revising the contract.

170. (A) Merrymaker is claiming $300 million in damages.

   (B) Merrymaker says it had to pay $400 million in additional construction costs.

   **(C) The value of the agreement, or *contract,* was $600 million.**

   (D) The lawsuit is for $700 million.

171. (A) Costs of materials did not cause work to stop.

   (B) Merrymaker lost passenger bookings *after* work on the ships stopped.

   **(C) The article states that it was Wambaugh's *bankruptcy* that *halted,* or *stopped,* work at the shipyard.**

   (D) Wambaugh became bankrupt *before* completing the contract for the ships.

172. (A) The refund is 0% if a person gives *less* than 30 days' notice.

   (B) 30 days is mentioned, but not 30%.

   (C) A 90-day cancellation policy is mentioned, but not 90%.

   **(D) The notice states that passengers who cancel 30 days *prior to departure,* meaning those who give 30 days' notice of cancellation, will get a refund of their *full* deposit, which is 100%.**

173. (A) Joining a group tour is not suggested.

   **(B) The notice states that you can *send a friend in your place,* or give your place to a friend. This is an *alternative* to cancellation.**

   (C) The notice does not suggest traveling earlier instead of canceling.

   (D) A refund request should be sent in *if people need to cancel,* not as an *alternative to cancellation.*

174. (A) The XYZ employees are from many different countries, but they are not politicians.

   (B) There is no mention of people learning foreign languages.

   (C) It is not a conference for chefs, or trained cooks.

   **(D) The notice welcomes employees of *XYZ Machinery Company* to the symposium, or conference. The conference is *aimed* at, or intended for, these employees.**

175. (A) The nationalities of some participants are given, but this is not a list.

   (B) There is no mention of room *changes.*

   **(C) The notice was written to give information about some special events: dinners, luncheons and breakfasts at which topics are discussed.**

   (D) Nothing has been cancelled.

176. (A) The discussion at Monday's breakfast is about legal matters.

   (B) The Tuesday lunchtime discussion is about *technologies,* not human resources.

   **(C) *Human resources* deals with a company's staff, or *personnel. Personnel issues* will be discussed at the Wednesday dinner.**

   (D) The Thursday breakfast discussion is about *markets,* not human resources.

177. (A) The instructions tell readers *about* the services of technical support staff.

   (B) *Softwind engineers* are not mentioned.

   (C) Retail sales personnel *sell* products. These instructions are for people who have already *bought* a product.

   **(D) The instructions are for people who have purchased a Softwind product, or in other words, *Softwind customers.***

178. **(A) Customers are asked to give the name of the *retail outlet* or *store* where they purchased the product.**

   (B) Customers will *receive* a personal identification number when they register.

   (C) *After* registering, customers will receive dates of future releases.

   (D) Forwarding addresses are not mentioned.

179. (A) The passage does not state that support staff give out PINs.

(B) This is the procedure for getting technical help *after* registering.

(C) **After Softwind has received the registration card, the customer will receive a PIN, or personal identification number.**

(D) No mention is made of signing anything at a retail outlet.

180. (A) **Customers are asked to look at the *handbook*, or *manual*, before calling technical support.**

(B) There is no mention of *changing* a PIN, or personal identification number.

(C) Customers are asked to do this *after* looking at the handbook; it is not the *first* thing they should do.

(D) No mention is made of updated instructions.

181. (A) There is no mention of a check.

(B) The letter is *about* two cartons of goods, but they were not sent with this letter.

(C) The letter mentions the contract between the two companies, but it was not sent with this letter.

(D) **A copy of the *transmittal form* is enclosed. This is a *shipping document* that the shipping company (IFS Freight Forwarding) gives to the person receiving the goods (Mr. Benson) when they are delivered.**

182. (A) **The driver *stated*, or *said*, that Smooth Skin's packing was responsible for the damage.**

(B) The driver did not suggest this to Mr. Benson of Butterfly Beauty.

(C) Peggy Rolf said this in the letter.

(D) The driver did not say anything about a refund.

183. (A) The policy about shipping charges is not mentioned.

(B) **Ms. Rolf's letter states that the delivery person acted contrary to the IFS policy of *taking damaged goods back*. In other words, the driver did not follow the policy about *returns*.**

(C) There is no mention of weight limits.

(D) *Travel expenses* would refer to the cost of *people* traveling, not of shipping goods.

184. (A) She does not ask IFS to contact her.

(B) Ms. Rolf may *reconsider* renewing the contract.

(C) **Ms. Rolf asks the firm to *take back*, or *retrieve*, the *boxes*, or *goods*. In other words, she may *not* renew the contract.**

(D) She does not ask IFS to pay for the damage.

185. (A) There is no mention of a law office.

(B) *Fuel* is mentioned, but not a *gasoline station*.

(C) Velcorp Power is acting with the *approval* of the Price Control Commission, but this notice is not issued by the Price Control Commission.

(D) **This is an announcement by Velcorp Power Company. A change in a price *per kilowatt-hour* is mentioned. This is a measure of electricity, so it can be assumed that this is an electric company.**

186. (A) A *meeting* is not mentioned.

(B) Cubic meters, as a measurement, are not mentioned.

(C) **According to the notice, the price will decrease, or *change*, from November 1.**

(D) Nothing is said about how often meters are read.

187. (A) It is the maintenance technicians who have gone on strike, not the assembly-line workers.

(B) The article does not state that the assembly-line workers support the technicians.

(C) **The assembly-line workers *voted to accept* a pay increase. This means that they *agreed to* accept one.**

(D) There is no mention of any workers moving to another plant.

188. **(A) The article states that Mitchell Motor Company has laid off assembly-line workers *in response to*, or *as a result of*, the technicians' strike.**

(B) It is assembly-line workers who have been fired, not technicians.

(C) There is no mention of changes to the designs of vans.

(D) The technicians have not received a pay increase.

189. (A) There is no mention of making a written request.

**(B) Investors are asked to *call for instructions* about investing by electronic transfer.**

(C) This is only necessary when investing by mail.

(D) *Terminating the exchange privilege* is not mentioned in connection with electronic transfer.

190. (A) *Verifying* the investment guidelines is mentioned, not changing them.

(B) There is no mention of changing the account registration number.

(C) Investors can *see* the minimum investment requirements, but there is no mention of changing them.

**(D) The Fund can change, or *modify*, the exchange privilege any time it feels it is necessary, or *at its discretion*.**

191. (A) Mr. Hayashida is accepting a job in Japan; this letter is written to a company in Thailand.

**(B) Mr. Hayashida is writing to *decline*, or *turn down*, the offer of a job.**

(C) A person would write to discuss employment opportunities *before* applying for a job.

(D) Though this is a personnel matter, Mr. Hayashida does not ask for any more information.

192. (A) The letter is written to the president of the company, thanking him for a job offer.

(B) Mr. Puapondh, the Head of Operations, is mentioned, but it was not Mr. Puapondh who made the job offer.

(C) The job Mr. Hayashida applied for was Properties Agent.

(D) Mr. Hayashida mentions that he will become Sales Director of a different company.

193. (A) Mr. Van Vliet is the Properties Agent of Golden Crown Resorts in Phuket.

(B) Mr. Kayasit is the president of Golden Crown Resorts.

**(C) Mr. Hayashida does not work for Golden Crown Resorts.**

(D) Mr. Puapondh is the Head of Operations of Golden Crown Resorts.

194. (A) Although disks will be scanned for computer *viruses*, there is no mention of a health clinic.

(B) This notice needs to be seen by people entering the building, so it would not be placed on a computer workstation *inside* the building.

**(C) The notice gives instructions on what must be done with computer disks *upon entry to this building*, meaning the *Standard Chemical Company* building.**

(D) It is unlikely that a notice about computer disks would be put in a cafeteria.

195. (A) No mention is made of erasing disks.

(B) No mention is made of scratching disks.

(C) No mention is made of duplicating disks.

**(D) If a disk is not *declared*, or officially made known, it can be *confiscated*, or taken away.**

196. (A) The Economic Times only *reported* where the funding would come from.

(B) The Chaldean Ministry of Planning and Investment has *proposed* the project.

**(C) According to the article, more than half of the money would come from *overseas*, meaning from international investors.**

(D) The Digili Airport Authority is not mentioned.

197. (A) The article mentions that between US $180 million and $195 million will be invested in the proposed project.

   (B) Part of the proposal involves *enlarging* the existing terminal, or in other words, increasing its size.

   (C) Building new airports was part of a plan put forward last year by an institute.

   **(D) The existing terminal will be *enlarged*, not destroyed, or *demolished*.**

198. (A) While she will conduct an audit for a drilling *company*, the letter does not indicate that Ms. Kahanian is going to Buenos Aires to visit a drilling *site*.

   (B) Mr. Ortiz writes that a *computer terminal* will be provided for Ms. Kahanian during her stay, but he does not mention that she will upgrade a computer system.

   **(C) The letter states that Ms. Kahanian is going to the Suarez Drilling Corporation headquarters in Buenos Aires for the *year-end auditing procedures*.**

   (D) Mr. Ortiz notes that the company can *recommend* restaurants to Ms. Kahanian; there is no indication that she will *review* the restaurants.

199. (A) Mr. Ortiz notes in the letter that the company will put a computer terminal at Ms. Kahanian's disposal, or in other words, make one available to her.

   (B) Mr. Ortiz mentions in the letter that he has already been informed of Ms. Kahanian's flight number.

   (C) Ms. Kahanian does not need to reserve a hotel room because the company has already *booked a room at the Santa Catalina Hotel*.

   **(D) Mr. Ortiz asks Ms. Kahanian to inform him of any *special requirements* by phone or fax *before* her arrival. A copy machine would be an example of a special requirement that Ms. Kahanian would need to mention.**

200. **(A) The letter states that arrangements have been made for Ms. Kahanian to have *pre-paid lunches*, or *midday meals*, at the Suarez Drilling Corporation's *staff cafeteria*.**

   (B) Ms. Kahanian can eat *breakfast* and *dinner* at the Santa Catalina Hotel, but no mention is made of midday meals at the hotel.

   (C) Mr. Ortiz mentions the town's restaurants as an alternative to *breakfast* and *dinner* at the hotel.

   (D) There is no mention of a local coffee shop in the letter.

# Day 30

# General Strategies for Taking the TOEIC Test

Now that you've become familiar with the TOEIC test and the types of questions found on it, you can focus on the actual day of the exam.

*To the teacher:* Students will expect to see a score from the practice test. The choice is to avoid the question of scoring and leave it up to the individual student or teacher to work out, or provide a very general chart.

Look at the answers to the questions below for some tips on how to prepare for the day of the exam.

1. How should I use what I've learned?

2. How can I maximize my test performance?

3. What should I keep in mind during the test?

4. What specific test-taking strategies should I use?

5. What can I do to improve my overall English proficiency?

## 1. How Should I Use What I've Learned?

For the past 29 days, you have been preparing to take the TOEIC test. You have had a chance to look at the different sections of the test in greater detail, and to complete various types of practice activities.

It is now time for you to assess what you have accomplished up to this point, and to spend more time improving your weaknesses.

Look at your scores from the different parts of the practice test.

• As a percentage correct, on which part did you receive the highest score?

Go back to the day that contains hints for the parts in which you received the highest score. Did the strategies that were provided there help you?

• As a percentage correct, on which part of the test did you receive the lowest score?

Go back to the day that contains hints for the part in which you received your lowest score. Reread the hints for that part of the TOEIC test. Have you been following the strategies?

Now, look at the practice test questions again. If you received your lowest score in one of the listening sections, listen to the tape again while reading the script.

Finally, look at the general tips below to help you on all parts of the TOEIC test.

## 2. How Can I Maximize my Test Performance?

Take good care of yourself before the test by following the advice below.

- **Eat.** It's important to eat a good meal before you go to the testing center. Don't eat so much that you feel sleepy, but make sure you eat enough to keep a steady level of energy.

- **Sleep.** Be sure to get plenty of rest the night before you take the TOEIC test. A good night's sleep before a test can be as good as, or better than, staying up all night studying.

- **Relax.** If you have worked through this book carefully and have completed all the practice exercises, you should feel confident when you sit down for the test. Be proud of what you can do on the test instead of worrying about what you cannot do.

## 3. What Should I Keep in Mind During the Test?

Remembering the following points will help you avoid making unnecessary mistakes.

- **Fill in all the required information.** Make sure you fill in your name and the name of the testing center on your answer sheet.

- **Be sure to read the instructions carefully.** You can practice by reading the instructions for each part of the test in this book. When you take the actual TOEIC test, you should read the instructions before each part of the test.

- **Mark only one answer to each question on your answer sheet.** If you mark more than one, both will be scored as incorrect.

- **Remember which materials you can and cannot bring into the testing center.**

  **Bring:** identification materials, extra pencils and erasers.

  **Do NOT bring:** dictionaries, papers, notes, rulers, calculators, listening devices, or study aids of **any** kind. They are **NOT** allowed in the testing room.

## 4. What Specific Test-taking Strategies Should I Use?

During the exam, keep the following test-taking strategies in mind.

- **Read the questions first.** Where possible, read the questions **before** you listen to the recorded voices in the Listening Comprehension Section. Looking at the questions first in the Reading Section will also help you find the information required.

- **Listen to or read the entire question before answering.** There may be more than one choice that seems to be correct. Don't rush into selecting one choice as your final answer.

- **Don't be upset by unknown words.** It's not always necessary to understand the meaning of every word. The question may be about only the main idea and may not be related to the word you don't know.

- **Summarize the main idea in your mind.** You may then find you already have the answer to the question!

- **If you are not sure, guess.** You will NOT be penalized for guessing when you take the TOEIC test, so you should guess rather than leaving the answer blank. Choose the answer that seems most likely. It is better to make a guess than to leave a blank space on the answer sheet.

- **Do not fall behind in the Listening Comprehension section.** Be careful not to spend too much time on each question. After a 5–8 second pause, you will hear the next question. Mark your answer as soon as you have made a decision. Don't try to go back to previous questions or you may miss the next question.

- **Always go back over your work in the Reading section if you have time.** Make sure to check your answers and fill in any spaces that you have left blank on the answer sheet.

## 5. What Can I Do to Improve my Overall English Proficiency?

As you know, the TOEIC test is not a test of specialized knowledge or vocabulary. It is a general proficiency test, and it measures how well you can function in English. A good way to prepare for the TOEIC test is to surround yourself as much as possible with spoken and written materials in English. Textbooks and grammar books can be very useful, but they do not always contain enough "real" English communication. The TOEIC test emphasizes authentic spoken and written language used in the global workplace. Here are some possible sources for appropriate English materials:

### CDs and Audiocassettes

Listen to English-language recordings of books, lectures, songs, and poetry. Listen several times until you can answer questions such as: *Who is speaking? What is the topic? What are the main ideas?* Try to write down what you hear.

### English Teachers/Native Speakers

Take every opportunity to talk with teachers or native speakers of English.

### Colleagues and Friends

While it is useful to talk English with native English-speakers, conversing with other non-native speakers can be just as helpful. Form an English-speaking discussion group with others interested in improving their English. Get together on a regular basis. For example, have lunch together and speak only English over lunch.

### Radio

Listen to broadcasts in English whenever possible. This is an excellent way to practice your listening skills. Don't be discouraged if you cannot understand every word. Start by trying to figure out what the topic is, who is speaking, and what issue is being discussed.

### Videotapes/Television

Watch an English-language video or television program. You can stop the tape and summarize the plot, or predict what is going to happen next. Or, you can take notes, and review the areas that were difficult for you to understand. It is also helpful to watch a video or TV show with a group of friends and discuss the program in English.

### Books

Find books in English that you can read **without** having to look up every word in a dictionary. Reading stories can increase your vocabulary and help you become familiar with different kinds of formal and informal English. Technical manuals or business texts can also be useful for building vocabulary.

### Brochures

You can visit or write to agencies and institutions such as tourist information offices in English-speaking countries, travel agencies, non-governmental organizations, universities, and large businesses. These places are good sources for brochures and other English-language materials.

### Magazines

Many airlines give away their in-flight magazines. These magazines often contain interesting articles related to the workplace. There are also many weekly news magazines that have short articles on a wide range of subjects. Fashion, food, and sports magazines are also good sources of authentic written English. Look at the pictures in the magazines and try to write brief descriptions of what is happening.

### Mail-Order Catalogs

Some companies doing business in English sell their products by mail order. Ask for catalogs or product information in English.

### Menus

Many restaurants have take-out menus. Ask for an English version.

### Newspapers

Read local newspapers written in English, or, if possible, international English-language newspapers. There are also special newspapers published for language learners. Summarize the news stories, or make up questions about the articles.

### World Wide Web and Internet

Visit ESL Web sites on the Internet. Many English-language newspapers and magazines also have online editions. Communicate in English with a friend, colleague or "e-pal" through e-mail.

### Songs and Music

Listen to popular music in English—you can practice singing along to acquire the stress patterns of spoken English, and you may learn many new words and expressions in the process.

### Journals/Notebooks

Keep a daily journal of your thoughts and activities in English. Set aside a few minutes for writing each day. This will give you a chance to practice new vocabulary and structures. Also, keep track of new words and expressions in a notebook. Write down the contexts in which you first heard or saw the new vocabulary. Then try to use the expression in other examples.

## WRITING PRACTICE

1. Here is an example of a letter requesting tourist information:

March 3, 20XX

6071 rue Valmont
Montréal, PQ H2C 4T6
Canada

Tourist Board of <u>Australia</u>
123 Water Street
Sydney, NSW   2001

To Whom It May Concern:

Please send me any printed information you may have on traveling in Australia. I plan to visit during the months of <u>June and July</u>, and I am particularly interested in <u>festivals</u>.

Thank you for your assistance.

Sincerely,

Jean-Luc Tremblay

Now go back and replace the underlined information with new information about yourself and your travel plans.

2. Here is a list of possible topics for your journal:

- A recent vacation
- My favorite childhood memory
- A movie I recently saw
- A description of my home or town
- What I do at school or work
- How to make a favorite food item
- Something I want to learn about
- Why I like (or don't like) a person
- What I would like to do for a living
- A news story that I have heard about
- Something I couldn't live without
- The most beautiful place I have ever been
- The most frightening experience I have ever had
- A list of things I've learned at school or work

# Master Script

The following is the master script for all of the recording you've heard on the CDs throughout the book.

*Lead-in to the first CD:*

**(N)**  Welcome to *30 Days to the TOEIC Test*, developed by The Chauncey Group International, a subsidiary of Educational Testing Service. Copyright 2002 by Educational Testing Service. All rights reserved.

This is the recording for the listening segments of *30 Days to the TOEIC Test*, a preparation guide that was written by the makers of the TOEIC test and published by Peterson's, part of The Thomson Corporation.

*Lead-in to the second CD:*

**(N)**  *30 Days to the TOEIC Test*, CD 2. Copyright 2002 by Educational Testing Service. All rights reserved. Published by Peterson's, part of The Thomson Corporation.

*Lead-in to the third CD (if necessary):*

**(N)**  *30 Days to the TOEIC Test*, CD 3. Copyright 2002 by Educational Testing Service. All rights reserved. Published by Peterson's, part of The Thomson Corporation.

## (N) DAY 1

## (N) SECTION 1: LISTENING COMPREHENSION

### (N) Part I: Photographs

1.  **(N)**  Look at the picture marked number 1 in your book.

    **(M1)** (A)  They're hiking in the mountains.

          (B)  They're working on a road.

          (C)  They're riding on their bicycles.

          (D)  They're driving in their vehicles. (5 seconds)

2.  **(N)** Look at the picture marked number 2 in your book.

    **(W1)** (A) The men are reading newspapers.

    (B) The men are copying blueprints.

    (C) The men are operating construction equipment.

    (D) The men are reviewing building plans. (5 seconds)

3.  **(N)** Look at the picture marked number 3 in your book.

    **(M2)** (A) She's picking up a test tube.

    (B) She's cleaning her glasses.

    (C) She's making something to drink.

    (D) She's removing her lab coat. (5 seconds)

4.  **(N)** Look at the picture marked number 4 in your book.

    **(W2)** (A) Customers are paying for their groceries.

    (B) Several kinds of fruit are on display.

    (C) The outdoor market is open for business.

    (D) The crop is ready to be harvested. (5 seconds)

## (N) Part II: Question-Response

5.  **(M1)** Where did Mrs. Romero go on her vacation?

    **(W1)** (A) I think she left on Monday.

    (B) She toured the south of France.

    (C) She'll probably go by plane. (5 seconds)

6.  **(M2)** Is production higher this month?

    **(W2)** (A) It's about the same as before.

    (B) No, they hired one last month.

    (C) It's on sale next week. (5 seconds)

7.  **(M1)** These books need to be returned to the library.

    **(M2)** (A) One of the librarians helped me.

    (B) I'll drop them off tonight.

    (C) I've already made a reservation. (5 seconds)

8.  **(W1)** When will they name a new treasurer?

    **(M1)** (A) In the safe deposit box.

    (B) I'm sorry, I don't know their names.

    (C) At the next committee meeting. (5 seconds)

9.  **(W2)** What's the train fare from here to New York?

    **(W1)** (A) It depends on when you travel.

    (B) About an hour and a half.

    (C) You're right; it isn't fair. (5 seconds)

## (N) Part III: Short Conversations

10. **(M1)** Have you finished writing that article yet?

    **(W1)** Almost. I'm doing a final edit right now.

    **(M1)** Good. Then it can go out in the morning edition. (8 seconds)

11. **(W1)** The waiting room's completely full again. Don't you think it's time to consider hiring more doctors?

    **(W2)** No, not yet. It's really a matter of space at this point. We need to make the admissions area bigger.

    **(W1)** Good idea. Let's look into that. (8 seconds)

12. **(M2)** Hello, I'd like to send a package to London overnight.

    **(M1)** I'm afraid today's shipments have already gone out. Our Tuesday shipment will get there by Wednesday at 9 A.M.

    **(M2)** Then I suppose a Tuesday shipment will have to do. (8 seconds)

13. **(M1)** What do you think accounts for the recent surge in your sales?

**(W1)** Well, for one thing, we've doubled our staff.

**(M1)** Oh really? I thought maybe you had changed your marketing campaign. (8 seconds)

14. **(W2)** I've been dying to try that new restaurant in town…uh…What's it called?

**(M2)** The Jade Garden? Me, too. I've heard they have great seafood. But I'm in a bit of a rush today. I've got a meeting at twelve-thirty.

**(W2)** Oh, OK. Then let's just run down to the cafeteria. (8 seconds)

## (N) Part IV: Short Talks

**(N)** **Questions 15 and 16** refer to the following excerpt from a talk.

**(W1)** There are four main exits from the plant, one for each wing. Two of these are emergency exits only. In the event of an emergency, an alarm will sound and all the doors will open automatically. You'll find floor plans posted in every hallway and at your workstations.

**(N)** Now read question 15 in your book and answer it. (8 seconds)

**(N)** Now read question 16 in your book and answer it. (8 seconds)

**(N)** **Questions 17 and 18** refer to the following telephone message.

**(M1)** Hello, Ms. Lee? This is Robert Grieg calling from the corporate office. Miratek is currently forming a committee to improve relations between the branches of our organization. Your name came up at a recent board meeting as a personnel manager who has connections in several geographic areas. If you would like to serve as a member of this committee, please let me know at your earliest convenience.

**(N)** Now read question 17 in your book and answer it. (8 seconds)

**(N)** Now read question 18 in your book and answer it. (8 seconds)

---

## (N) DAY 2

## (N) Example 1

**(M1)** The doctor and a nurse are talking with a patient.

## (N) Exercise A

**(M2)** 1.   The woman is carrying a tray of food. (5 seconds)

**(W1)** 2.   When will you be leaving Jakarta? (5 seconds)

**(M1)** 3.   I'd like to make an appointment with Doctor Simpson. (5 seconds)

**(W2)** 4.   He said he would meet us at Delano's restaurant. (5 seconds)

**(M2)** 5.   They're waiting to buy tickets from the box office. (5 seconds)

**(W1)** 6.   Ms. Tanaka is coming to the budget meeting, isn't she? (5 seconds)

**(M1)** 7.   I seem to have lost my umbrella somewhere. (5 seconds)

**(W2)** 8.   The two men are shaking hands. (5 seconds)

**(M2)** 9.   Have you met our new supervisor yet? (5 seconds)

**(W1)** 10.   Welcome to Flight three four six to Los Angeles. (5 seconds)

**(M1)** 11.   There's a table over there by the window. (5 seconds)

**(W2)** 12.   It's expected to rain this afternoon. (5 seconds)

## (N) Exercise D

1.  A. They're putting the violins away.
    B. The performance has begun.
    C. They're standing on a stage.
    D. The concert is taking place outdoors.
    E. The curtain is beginning to rise.
    F. They're drawing bows across the strings.
    G. They're giving a concert.

2.  A. There are buildings near a lake.
    B. The land in this area is very flat.
    C. Buildings are reflected in the water.
    D. There are houses on the hillside.
    E. The water is very calm.
    F. Factory chimneys rise above the village.
    G. People are boating on the river.

3.  A. The men are wiring an appliance.
    B. The men are all wearing hats.
    C. Wiring is being placed underground.
    D. A man is opening a window.
    E. The men are setting a table.
    F. The men are laying wheels on the ground.
    G. A man is pulling a cable.

## (N) Exercise E

**(M1)** 1.  He's putting the fish on the scales. (5 seconds)

**(W1)** 2.  Next to the bench, there's a bicycle. (5 seconds)

**(M2)** 3.  The concert's just finished. (5 seconds)

**(W2)** 4.  They're about to cut the tree down. (5 seconds)

**(M1)** 5.  She's sealing the envelope. (5 seconds)

**(W1)** 6.  The plane's going to land shortly. (5 seconds)

**(M2)** 7.  The restaurant isn't very crowded. (5 seconds)

**(W2)** 8.  It looks as if it's going to rain. (5 seconds)

---

## (N) DAY 3

## (N) Example

**(M1)** He's adjusting the dials on a television set.

## (N) Exercise D

### (N) Photograph 1

**(N)** Statement one: **(M2)** She's using a microphone.

**(N)** Statement two: **(M2)** She's using a pay phone. (5 seconds)

### (N) Photograph 2

**(N)** Statement one: **(W1)** She's writing in a book.

**(N)** Statement two: **(W1)** She's reading a book. (5 seconds)

### (N) Photograph 3

**(N)** Statement one: **(M1)** The passengers are getting off a bus.

**(N)** Statement two: **(M1)** The passengers are boarding the bus. (5 seconds)

### (N) Photograph 4

**(N)** Statement one: **(W2)** The man is folding up a newspaper.

**(N)** Statement two: **(W2)** The man is looking at a newspaper. (5 seconds)

### (N) Photograph 5

**(N)** Statement one: **(M2)** A woman is opening up the flip chart.

**(N)** Statement two: **(M2)** A woman is pointing to the flip chart. (5 seconds)

# (N) Day 4

## (N) Practice Questions

## (N) PART I

*Directions: For each question, you will see a picture in your test book and you will hear four short statements. The statements will be spoken just one time. They will not be printed in your test book, so you must listen carefully to understand what the speaker says.*

When you hear the four statements, look at the picture in your book and choose the statement that best describes what you see in the picture. Look at the sample below.

Now listen to the four statements.

**(M1)**     (A)    They're looking out the window.

          (B)    They're having a meeting.

          (C)    They're eating in a restaurant.

          (D)    They're moving the furniture.

Statement (B), "They're having a meeting," best describes what you see in the picture. Therefore, you should choose answer (B). The answers are printed at the end of this section.

1.    **(N)**    Look at the picture marked number 1 in your book.
      **(M1)** (A)    She's watering a plant.
           (B)    She's caring for a child.
           (C)    She's planting a tree.
           (D)    She's drinking some water. (5 seconds)

2.    **(N)**    Look at the picture marked number 2 in your book.
      **(W1)** (A)    She's looking for her glasses.
           (B)    She's picking up a pen.
           (C)    She's holding a piece of paper.
           (D)    She has a scarf around her neck. (5 seconds)

3.    **(N)**    Look at the picture marked number 3 in your book.
      **(M2)** (A)    They're riding horses.
           (B)    They're jumping the fence.
           (C)    They're feeding the animals.
           (D)    They're farming the land. (5 seconds)

4.    **(N)**    Look at the picture marked number 4 in your book.
      **(W2)** (A)    She's stepping onto the escalator.
           (B)    She's closing her handbag.
           (C)    She's lifting the handle.
           (D)    She's pushing the button. (5 seconds)

5.    **(N)**    Look at the picture marked number 5 in your book.
      **(M1)** (A)    The land around the building is flat.
           (B)    The stadium is now full.
           (C)    Planes have landed on the airfield.
           (D)    The warehouse is many stories high. (5 seconds)

6.    **(N)**    Look at the picture marked number 6 in your book.
      **(W1)** (A)    A man is withdrawing money.
           (B)    A man has hung a painting on a wall.
           (C)    A man is writing in a notebook.
           (D)    A man is on his hands and knees. (5 seconds)

7.    **(N)**    Look at the picture marked number 7 in your book.
      **(M2)** (A)    They're installing a sliding door.
           (B)    They're climbing down a ladder.
           (C)    They're working on the roof.
           (D)    They're loading the truck. (5 seconds)

8. **(N)** Look at the picture marked number 8 in your book.

   **(W2)** (A) The plates are being stacked.

   (B) The silver is being polished.

   (C) The shelves are being cleaned.

   (D) The floor is being mopped. (5 seconds)

9. **(N)** Look at the picture marked number 9 in your book.

   **(M1)** (A) He's writing a receipt for the customer.

   (B) He's oiling the motorcycle engine.

   (C) He's pumping up the car's tires.

   (D) He's putting fuel in the automobile. (5 seconds)

10. **(N)** Look at the picture marked number 10 in your book.

    **(W1)** (A) The equipment is all being used.

    (B) The workspace is being cleaned.

    (C) The tools are hanging on the wall.

    (D) The workshop has not been organized. (5 seconds)

11. **(N)** Look at the picture marked number 11 in your book.

    **(M2)** (A) Dogs are lying on the riverbank.

    (B) Birds are flying over the water.

    (C) Birds are landing in the trees.

    (D) People are swimming in the lake. (5 seconds)

12. **(N)** Look at the picture marked number 12 in your book.

    **(W2)** (A) The highway is busy with traffic.

    (B) Some people are crossing the street at the light.

    (C) All the buildings along the street are identical.

    (D) There are cars parked on both sides of the road. (5 seconds)

13. **(N)** Look at the picture marked number 13 in your book.

    **(M1)** (A) The waiter is removing the tablecloth.

    (B) The waiter is presenting the bill.

    (C) The woman is drinking coffee.

    (D) The customers are waiting to be served. (5 seconds)

14. **(N)** Look at the picture marked number 14 in your book.

    **(W1)** (A) He's playing some music.

    (B) He's laying some pipe.

    (C) He's talking to a friend.

    (D) He's marching in a band. (5 seconds)

15. **(N)** Look at the picture marked number 15 in your book.

    **(M2)** (A) The area is crowded with people.

    (B) People are collecting seaweed.

    (C) A person is walking along the water's edge.

    (D) A person is selling drinks by the ocean. (5 seconds)

16. **(N)** Look at the picture marked number 16 in your book.

    **(W2)** (A) People are working at the tables.

    (B) The librarians are opening the windows.

    (C) The library is closed for the day.

    (D) Students are leaving the building. (5 seconds)

17. **(N)** Look at the picture marked number 17 in your book.

    **(M1)** (A) The people are seated on a bench.

    (B) The woman is leaning on a railing.

    (C) The man is taking a picture of the view.

    (D) The people are looking for a parking place. (5 seconds)

18. **(N)** Look at the picture marked number 18 in your book.

    **(W1)** (A) Flowers are arranged in buckets.

         (B) Vegetables are planted in a garden.

         (C) The trees are in full bloom.

         (D) Sacks of flour are on the ground. (5 seconds)

19. **(N)** Look at the picture marked number 19 in your book.

    **(M2)** (A) The speaker is facing the audience.

         (B) They are changing the channel on the television.

         (C) They are closing the blinds.

         (D) The man is pointing toward the board. (5 seconds)

20. **(N)** Look at the picture marked number 20 in your book.

    **(W2)** (A) She's wearing gloves.

         (B) She's studying for a test.

         (C) She's tasting the food.

         (D) She's shaking hands. (5 seconds)

## (N) DAY 5

## (N) Exercise B

*Sample Question: Where is the nearest post office?*

1. Who's coming to the reception?
2. When are you taking your vacation?
3. Is it okay if I change the air filter?
4. Do you know why they built the new museum so far from the old one?
5. The play starts at 7:30, doesn't it?
6. You're not really taking a new job, are you?
7. Shouldn't we hire a new designer?
8. Would you like to join us for lunch?

## (N) Exercise C

**(M1)** 1. How about going for a walk during our lunch break? (5 seconds)

**(W1)** 2. Why don't you ask to switch offices? (5 seconds)

**(M2)** 3. How long will I have to wait for delivery? (5 seconds)

**(W2)** 4. How often do you go to the gym? (5 seconds)

**(M1)** 5. Could you hand me that file, please? (5 seconds)

**(W1)** 6. May I sit here? (5 seconds)

**(M2)** 7. Could you tell me how much this video player is, please? (5 seconds)

**(W2)** 8. Does anybody know whose umbrella this is? (5 seconds)

## (N) Exercise D

**(M1)** 1. How wide is the desk that's in your office? (5 seconds)

**(W1)** 2. When was the last time you visited the dentist? (5 seconds)

**(M2)** 3. Does Tom remember which travel agent he booked the tickets through? (5 seconds)

**(W2)** 4. Would you mind showing me how to use the copier? (5 seconds)

**(M1)** 5. You don't know whose coat this is, do you? (5 seconds)

**(W1)** 6. Why are you putting in so much overtime at work? (5 seconds)

**(M2)** 7. What about going to see a film over the weekend? (5 seconds)

**(W2)** 8. Why don't you apply for this job? (5 seconds)

## (N) Day 6

### (N) Exercise A

**(M1)** 1. Would you mind helping me with this suitcase? (5 seconds)

**(W1)** 2. He's not going to buy that car, is he? (5 seconds)

**(M2)** 3. She leaves on Friday, doesn't she? (5 seconds)

**(W2)** 4. Is this your first visit to the United Kingdom? (5 seconds)

**(M1)** 5. Would you like a ride to the theater this evening? (5 seconds)

**(W1)** 6. Should we stay late today, or finish this in the morning? (5 seconds)

**(M2)** 7. Did Mr. Richardson phone to confirm that appointment? (5 seconds)

**(W2)** 8. Would you prefer coffee, or tea? (5 seconds)

**(M1)** 9. We met at last year's conference, didn't we? (5 seconds)

**(W1)** 10. Do you think you will get that proposal done on time? (5 seconds)

### Example 1

Who's going to be in charge of processing paychecks now?

(A) Yes, I have a credit card.

(B) The assistant accountant.

(C) It's a complicated process.

### Example 2

Where is the employee cafeteria?

(A) He's out sick today.

(B) Yes, I'm really hungry.

(C) I'm not sure; I just started here.

### (N) Exercise D

*Sample Question: Where is the nearest post office?*

1. Who's coming to the reception?

2. When are you taking your vacation?

3. Is it okay if I change the air filter?

4. Do you know why they built the new museum so far from the old one?

5. The play starts at 7:30, doesn't it?

6. You're not really taking a new job, are you?

7. Shouldn't we hire a new designer?

8. Would you like to join us for lunch?

## (N) Day 7

### (N) Practice Questions

### (N) Part II

*Directions: In this part of the test, you will hear a question or statement spoken in English, followed by three responses, also spoken in English. The question or statement and the responses will be spoken just one time. They will not be printed in your test book, so you must listen carefully to understand what the speakers say. You are to choose the best response to each question or statement.*

Now listen to a sample question.

You will hear: **(W2)** Good morning, John. How are you?

You will also hear: **(M1)** (A) I am fine, thank you.

(B) I am in the living room.

(C) My name is John.

The best response to the question "How are you?" is choice (A), "I am fine, thank you." Therefore you should choose answer (A). The answers are printed at the end of this section.

21. **(W1)** Have they delivered our lunch yet?

    **(M1)** (A) I like chicken.

    (B) On Monday.

    (C) Yes, it's here. (5 seconds)

22. **(M2)** When did you begin your new job?

    **(W2)** (A) At nine o'clock every morning.

    (B) Three weeks ago.

    (C) A sales associate. (5 seconds)

23. **(M1)** What was that loud noise I just heard?

    **(W2)** (A) Yes, I think it was.

    (B) I don't know.

    (C) No, cameras are not allowed. (5 seconds)

24. **(W1)** When will my laundry be ready?

    **(M2)** (A) In about two hours.

    (B) Two dollars a shirt.

    (C) I've already cut it. (5 seconds)

25. **(W2)** Who will go with you on the business trip?

    **(M1)** (A) By train.

    (B) The Excalibur Hotel.

    (C) Ms. Preston. (5 seconds)

26. **(W1)** Has the director already left?

    **(M2)** (A) Yes, he had an appointment.

    (B) It's on the right, actually.

    (C) Yes, in three months. (5 seconds)

27. **(W2)** How long do you think the staff meeting will last?

    **(W1)** (A) An hour at the most.

    (B) In the conference room.

    (C) All the staff in our department. (5 seconds)

28. **(M1)** What time does the play begin?

    **(W2)** (A) This is the first time I've played.

    (B) I'll call the theater to find out.

    (C) I couldn't really hear the music. (5 seconds)

29. **(W1)** Don't you want to take your briefcase with you?

    **(W2)** (A) No, it's too heavy.

    (B) Because we're starting a new case.

    (C) No, she's in a hurry. (5 seconds)

30. **(M2)** Why is this train running late?

    **(M1)** (A) We met them two hours ago.

    (B) I think there are mechanical problems.

    (C) It's scheduled for Platform 7. (5 seconds)

31. **(M2)** You want me to retype this document, don't you?

    **(W1)** (A) That type would be best.

    (B) I would appreciate it.

    (C) I can't document that. (5 seconds)

32. **(W2)** Would you like to order a calendar for next year?

    **(M1)** (A) Yes, they can

    (B) Thanks, but I already have one.

    (C) Except for December. (5 seconds)

33. **(M2)** What do you think I should wear to the party?

    **(M1)** (A) A suit and tie.

    (B) A nice gift.

    (C) On Main Street. (5 seconds)

34. **(W1)** Shall we send you a reminder for your next dental appointment?

    **(W2)** (A) No, I can't remember.

    (B) Yes, that would be helpful.

    (C) No, I'd like a complete set. (5 seconds)

35. **(W1)** Where should I put these lab materials when I've finished using them?

    **(M2)** (A) I've had them since last week.

    (B) You can get them from any supervisor.

    (C) Take them to Dr. Reynold's office. (5 seconds)

36. **(M1)** Whose coffee cup is this on my desk?

    **(W2)** (A) It's not his desk.

    (B) I was wondering where I left it!

    (C) Cream and sugar, please. (5 seconds)

37. **(W1)** Why didn't you let us know you'd be late?

    **(M2)** (A) I couldn't find a phone.

    (B) I'll try again tomorrow.

    (C) You do have permission. (5 seconds)

38. **(M1)** Who's the new chef at Fontaine's bakery?

    **(M2)** (A) They now open at seven in the morning.

    (B) The bakery has been there for five years.

    (C) A man who worked at Central Pastry Shop. (5 seconds)

39. **(M1)** Why don't we go out this evening?

    **(W2)** (A) David and Caroline.

    (B) Sorry, I've already made plans.

    (C) I didn't enjoy that movie either. (5 seconds)

40. **(M2)** What is the fine for overdue books?

    **(W1)** (A) You can borrow videos, too.

    (B) Yes, it's an excellent book.

    (C) It's ten cents a day. (5 seconds)

41. **(M1)** You don't really want to start a new project this late in the day, do you?

    **(W2)** (A) In the beginning.

    (B) I still have time.

    (C) Yes, it really is. (5 seconds)

42. **(M2)** Should I wait here at the counter or follow you back to the warehouse?

    **(W2)** (A) I put the scale on the counter.

    (B) My house is not far from here.

    (C) Oh, come with me please. (5 seconds)

43. **(M1)** Your managing director resigned yesterday, didn't he?

    **(M2)** (A) Yes, it was quite a surprise.

    (B) The letter is ready for you to sign.

    (C) Yes, I can give you directions. (5 seconds)

44. **(W1)** How will you get to work tomorrow?

    **(M1)** (A) I'll get my car back from the mechanic tonight.

    (B) I go home early on Fridays.

    (C) I applied for several jobs. (5 seconds)

45. **(M2)** Is Ms. Liu from the payroll department here today, or is she still on vacation?

    **(M1)** (A) She works in payroll.

    (B) She'll be back on Monday.

    (C) I haven't been on vacation. (5 seconds)

46. **(W2)** Where should we meet so we can all go to the game together?

    **(W1)** (A) The team is very good this year.

    (B) Let's meet at the stadium entrance.

    (C) It should be over by ten o'clock. (5 seconds)

47. **(M2)** How can we be sure that the order will arrive on time?

   **(M1)** (A) Express service is very reliable.

   (B) At about five in the afternoon.

   (C) To buy some. (5 seconds)

48. **(W2)** Didn't anyone train the new employee to use the copier?

   **(M1)** (A) John takes the bus to work.

   (B) The copier's in the staff room.

   (C) Mike showed him how everything works. (5 seconds)

49. **(W1)** What do you think, plain or patterned carpet in the waiting room?

   **(W2)** (A) Not much longer, I hope.

   (B) There's no room on the plane.

   (C) Either one is fine with me. (5 seconds)

50. **(M2)** Wilma gets reimbursed for the cost of driving her car to the meeting, doesn't she?

   **(W2)** (A) I'll have a look in my purse.

   (B) Yes, but she has to submit a claim form.

   (C) No, we've already met, several times. (5 seconds)

## (N) DAY 8

## (N) Example 1

**(W1)** Have you heard? Mr. Olmos is going to Africa.

**(M1)** Is that right? I guess he'll be gone for some time.

**(W1)** Not too long, really. Just for fourteen days.

## (N) Example 2

**(W2)** Is that today's paper? I want to see if our advertisement is in it.

**(M2)** No, this is yesterday's. Today's hasn't come in yet.

**(W2)** Oh, I'll call downstairs and see if they have a copy.

## (N) Exercise A

1. **(W1)** Where are the pictures from the Atlanta Conference?

   **(M2)** I put them upstairs in your office. Didn't you want them there?

   **(W1)** Well, I left them here in the break room for people to look at. (8 seconds)

2. **(M1)** Have you shipped the electrical equipment to the European trade show?

   **(W2)** We have to make some modifications to it, but that won't be difficult. I'm sure we can do it.

   **(M1)** We've got to do it quickly. We don't have that much time. (8 seconds)

3. **(W1)** I thought you had an economics class on Tuesday nights.

   **(M1)** No, it was switched to Wednesdays, and the finance class was canceled, so now I'm free on Tuesdays and Thursdays.

   **(W1)** Well, since you're free, why don't we meet at the library later? (8 seconds)

## (N) Example 3

**(M2)** Thanks for your help with our trip to New Orleans. The hotel was beautiful, and we had a great time.

**(W2)** My pleasure. I guess you're planning another trip?

**(M2)** Yes, and I'll be needing plane tickets, a rental car, and of course, a hotel recommendation.

## (N) Exercise B

1. **(W1)** I didn't expect to see so many people here this early. The show doesn't start for another hour, and half the seats are already full.

   **(M2)** Well, the lead actor is very popular these days. He's been in a number of successful plays.

   **(W1)** Not only that, but the set design is supposed to be quite unique. (8 seconds)

2. **(W2)** Your story on last night's game was very good, but I've suggested some changes.

   **(M1)** I hope it won't take much time. I've got to get to the stadium for an interview this afternoon.

   **(W2)** You just need to make it a bit shorter. We want to add another photo. (8 seconds)

3. **(M2)** And this is the latest model. You'll save money because it doesn't use much hot water or electricity.

   **(W2)** I don't know. The restaurant can get very busy. How fast is it?

   **(M2)** Faster than the machine you're using now. You'll find it cleans pots and pans better, too. (8 seconds)

4. **(W1)** I understand you had to shut down the third assembly line this morning. What happened?

   **(M1)** A power supply problem. The electrician had to replace a cable. It was off for about an hour.

   **(W1)** Have him check the cables in lines one and two and let me know if there are any more problems. I'll be in my office. (8 seconds)

5. **(M1)** We should have just ordered from the catalog. This will take all afternoon.

   **(W2)** This store is cheaper, and they deliver. Besides, I don't want to see a picture; I want to see what we're getting.

   **(M1)** Well, we need filing cabinets, desks, and chairs. Let's look at the cabinets first. (8 seconds)

## (N) DAY 9

## (N) Example 1

**(M1)** Sally, can you give me a hand with this marketing project this afternoon?

**(W1)** Well, I need to finish this product proposal today, then I'm going to catch a train at 5:15.

**(M1)** OK. Could we start on it first thing tomorrow morning, then?

## (N) Exercise A

1. **(M1)** We've tried different colors and different fabrics, but we haven't been able to satisfy the client.

   **(W2)** This client isn't interested in new colors and fabrics. You'll have to try changing the style. I don't want to lose this account.

   **(M1)** I'll go back to production and get started again. (8 seconds)

2. **(M2)** Did you hear that Mr. Brewer is retiring next month?

   **(W2)** I know. Is he an area manager or a partner?

   **(M2)** He's a partner. He started forty years ago as a driver and worked as a salesman, too. (8 seconds)

3. **(W1)** I hear you took some French clients to the baseball game last night. How was it?

   **(M1)** They said that they still prefer soccer and rugby to baseball.

   **(W1)** Maybe you should try basketball next time. It's more exciting. (8 seconds)

## (N) Example 2

**(M2)** I'm very tired. At least it's Friday and I can sleep late tomorrow.

**(W1)** I won't be sleeping late. I'll be up at five since the plane for Hawaii leaves at seven.

**(M2)** That's right. Tomorrow, you're starting your vacation. Have a good time!

## (N) Exercise C

**(M1)** I'm calling to let you know that your credit card payment is several weeks overdue.

**(W2)** Hmm…I thought I paid that last month. Perhaps it was delivered to the wrong address.

**(M1)** Well…please check your records to see if you've already paid.

## (N) Exercise D

1.  **(M2)** Could you take me to the station after my meeting?

    **(W1)** Sorry, I'm not going downtown. I have a doctor's appointment near here.

    **(M2)** That's OK. I'll get a taxi.  (8 seconds)

2.  **(W1)** We're planning to go to the new Italian restaurant this afternoon. Would you like to join us?

    **(M1)** I'd love to, but I've already made plans for lunch. Maybe we can go some time next week.

    **(W1)** OK. If it's good, I'm sure everyone will want to go back again.  (8 seconds)

3.  **(M1)** I heard this morning that Wednesday's reception for the visiting professors has been postponed.

    **(W2)** Really? I was looking forward to meeting Dr. Greene and the others.

    **(M1)** They've rescheduled it for the beginning of next month.  (8 seconds)

---

## (N) DAY 10

## (N) Practice Questions

## (N) Part III

*Directions: In this part of the test, you will hear 30 short conversations between two people. The conversations will not be printed in your test book. You will hear the conversations only once, so you must listen carefully to understand what the speakers say.*

In your book, you will read a question about each conversation. The question will be followed by four answers. You are to choose the best answer to each question. The answers are printed at the end of this section.

51.  **(M1)** Don't stack more than four boxes on top of one another, Bill.

     **(M2)** Should I move them down to that area over there?

     **(M1)** Yes, that's near where the truck will drop off the rest of the crates.  (8 seconds)

52.  **(W2)** I'd like to return this blouse. I have the receipt here.

     **(M1)** What's the reason for the return?

     **(W2)** It doesn't fit very well.  (8 seconds)

53.  **(M2)** So, Jennifer, how are you enjoying your new job?

     **(W2)** Well, so far it's not very interesting, actually.

     **(M2)** Hmm. Maybe things will get better after the first few months.  (8 seconds)

54.  **(W1)** This printer doesn't seem to be working.

     **(M1)** Uh …check the cord. It may have been unplugged.

     **(W1)** You're right. Maybe someone used it with a laptop computer.  (8 seconds)

55. **(W2)** May I bring this bag with me onto the flight?

    **(M2)** I'm afraid that's too large ma'am. You'll have to check it in.

    **(W2)** OK, as long as it's handled carefully. (8 seconds)

56. **(W1)** Have you read Joan Smith's new novel?

    **(W2)** No, but I didn't really like her last story about the journalist.

    **(W1)** I love her books. She writes so well. (8 seconds)

57. **(M1)** What are you doing in your Business Writing class today?

    **(W2)** I'm giving a test. What about you?

    **(M1)** We're still reviewing. My students are having trouble with business letters. (8 seconds)

58. **(M2)** Why weren't you at the training session?

    **(W1)** I thought it was canceled.

    **(M2)** No, yesterday's session was canceled, but not today's. (8 seconds)

59. **(M1)** I'd like to make a reservation for the night of September fourth.

    **(W1)** Yes, of course. Would you like our business traveler rate, which includes breakfast in the room?

    **(M1)** Yes. I'd also like to be on either the first or second floor. (8 seconds)

60. **(W2)** This soup is much too salty. I think I'll send it back.

    **(M2)** I'm surprised. The food here is usually very good.

    **(W2)** I know. I've brought clients here many times. (8 seconds)

61. **(M1)** That's funny. I'm sure there used to be a pharmacy on this corner.

    **(M2)** Well, now it's a barbershop.

    **(M1)** Let's go in. Maybe the barber will know where the pharmacy moved. (8 seconds)

62. **(M2)** How late can we submit this bid?

    **(W1)** Well, the notice of tender gives a May tenth deadline.

    **(M2)** Wow! We'd better get moving on this then! (8 seconds)

63. **(M1)** Two tickets for the 12:30 tour, please.

    **(W2)** Here you go. We're running about thirty minutes behind schedule, so you'll be leaving at one.

    **(M1)** That's fine. We have to go exchange some more money anyway. (8 seconds)

64. **(M2)** We need to send a buyer to New York to look at the new lines of summer clothes.

    **(M1)** Winter isn't even over yet! How can they plan so far in advance?

    **(M2)** Designers are always at least two seasons ahead. (8 seconds)

65. **(M1)** Ms. Lee, why are you interested in transferring to another department? You've worked in Customer Service for almost six years.

    **(W1)** Well, my current manager, Mr. Parker, suggested I apply.

    **(M1)** I see. Well, I'll send your résumé to Ms. Foley. (8 seconds)

66. **(M2)** Where would you like to put these plants, Ms. Kim? By the window?

    **(W2)** No, they don't need that much light. How about over here by the water cooler?

    **(M2)** OK. I'll push them back so they're away from the door. (8 seconds)

67. **(M1)** Can I help you, sir?

    **(M2)** Yes, I'd like to know if this table is marked down.

    **(M1)** Yes, that one has been reduced for our clearance sale. (8 seconds)

68. **(W1)** How often do you come to Argentina?

    **(W2)** Well, usually twice for business and at least once for leisure each year.

    **(W1)** Really. So you're here quite often? (8 seconds)

69. **(M2)** Susan, I hear that you finally decided to buy that house you were looking at!

    **(W1)** Yes, I did, Roberto. I hope it's the right decision.

    **(M2)** My friends Douglas and Beth bought a house in that same area last year. They're very pleased so far. (8 seconds)

70. **(W2)** What's that café across the street like?

    **(M1)** They have a great menu, but it's kind of small and a bit overpriced.

    **(W2)** That's okay, as long as it has something different from all the other places around here. (8 seconds)

71. **(M1)** If we replace the workstations, we'll need to re cable the whole floor.

    **(W1)** How can we be sure of that? Let's check with the installers first.

    **(M1)** OK. I'll find the phone number. (8 seconds)

72. **(M2)** Mr. Garcia, did the new tenant sign his lease yet?

    **(M1)** No, he's busy unpacking some boxes that just came off the moving van.

    **(M2)** Please get his signature on it by the end of the day. (8 seconds)

73. **(W2)** I'm giving a presentation to the board of directors today.

    **(M1)** Make sure to give a clear statement of our marketing strategy.

    **(W2)** I think they'll be more interested in how the money's being spent—at least initially. (8 seconds)

74. **(M1)** It's been good talking with you, Sam. I guess I'd better let you get back to work.

    **(M2)** Yes. I need to finish this design so I can submit it by Friday. The company wants to have it ready for next month's magazine.

    **(M1)** Yes. Once that's done, you'll be able to relax a little bit! (8 seconds)

75. **(W1)** I'd like to buy some aspirin, please.

    **(M2)** We have bottles with 50, 100, or 150 tablets. Which would you like?

    **(W1)** The smallest one, please. (8 seconds)

76. **(M2)** Excuse me, the sun is shining right on my seat and it's a bit warm. Would you mind if I opened the window?

    **(W2)** Yes, actually. I have a cold and I'd rather keep it closed.

    **(M2)** Oh, I'm sorry. Never mind. (8 seconds)

77. **(M1)** I'm thinking of having the lobby redecorated this year.

    **(W1)** Are you going to hire an interior decorator this time?

    **(M1)** Not until I talk to someone in Accounting! (8 seconds)

78. **(W2)** Can we use the conference room for an Administration Department meeting tomorrow morning?

    **(W1)** No, it's already been reserved. It _is_ free in the afternoon, though.

    **(W2)** OK. We'll reschedule for tomorrow at 2 P.M. Can you make the reservation, please? (8 seconds)

79. **(W1)** I just received an e-mail from Mr. Smith at the factory. He needs product specifications immediately. Are you still planning to see him today?

    **(M2)** Yes, I'll be leaving in about a half hour.

    **(W1)** Great. I'll get the information ready and you can give it to him when you see him. (8 seconds)

80.  **(W2)** Do you think we should hire some temporary workers to finish this data entry?

**(W1)** Yes, then the two of us can concentrate on writing the reports.

**(W2)** All right, I'll call Brenda in Personnel and see what she can do.  (8 seconds)

---

# (N) DAY 11

## (N) Example 1

**(W2)** Good afternoon and welcome aboard Global Air Flight 875 from Copenhagen to Bangkok, with intermediate stops in Dubai and Calcutta. We are preparing to depart in a few minutes. At this time, your seat back should be returned to its full upright position and your seat belt should be fastened. Our anticipated flying time to Dubai is six hours and twenty-five minutes. We hope you enjoy the flight.

## (N) Exercise A

**(N)** **Questions 1 and 2** refer to the following report.

**(M1)** And for all of you getting ready for your drive home, I'm happy to report that there are no major traffic delays in the metropolitan area. There are, however, a few minor problems. On Route 9 near River Road, expect delays due to paving. Also, because of the rebuilding of the Lincoln Bridge, only one lane will be open. Stay tuned for an update in twenty minutes.

## (N) Exercise B

**(W1)** It's your life. Live each moment to the fullest! Imagine living in a spacious, modern apartment in a country-club setting where activities and facilities can keep you constantly busy. Close to the city, yet rural enough to grow a garden and have a pet. We offer luxurious one-bedroom apartments for $1,500 [fifteen hundred dollars] a month. Your rent includes membership in our private health and fitness club. Find out how beautiful life can be. Call or write for a free brochure or video, or make an appointment for a tour. Don't delay, call today. Only a limited number of one-bedroom apartments remain.

## (N) Example 2

**(M2)** The baseball game scheduled for 7:00 [seven o'clock] tonight has been postponed due to rain.

**(M2)** The baseball game scheduled for 7:00 [seven o'clock] tonight has been postponed due to rain. The game will be played on Saturday at 4:00 [four] P.M. instead.

## (N) Exercise C

**(M1)** 1.  Many people believe that making your own candles is difficult. We're here today to show you that it's not so hard. Just watch this quick and simple technique.

**(N)** Now answer the question that is printed in your book.  (8 seconds)

**(W1)** 2.  The Crosstown Bridge project was originally scheduled for completion by the end of this August. However, work has been slowed down by the recent storms, delaying the proposed completion date until early October.

**(N)** Now answer the question that is printed in your book.  (8 seconds)

**(W2)** 3.  History books have long reported that the town of Compton was founded 300 years ago. But surprising new evidence shows that it was probably really founded closer to 500 years ago.

**(N)** Now answer the question that is printed in your book.  (8 seconds)

## (N) Exercise D

**(N)** **Questions 1 and 2** refer to the following report.

**(M2)** The Eastern Gas Company has been given permission to increase the charges for natural gas service. The revised rate for natural gas service will not be effective until March first of next year. The overall increase will amount to 20 cents per cubic meter. Details of this change are available at the gas company billing office.

---

# (N) DAY 12

## (N) Example

**(N)** Questions 1 and 2 refer to the following announcement.

**(M1)** I'd like to take this opportunity to welcome you all to our seventh annual electronics sales convention. This year we are proud to announce...

## (N) Exercise A

**(N)** Talk Number 1

**(N)** Questions 1 through 3 refer to the following radio advertisement.

**(M2)** Are you tired of spending hours waxing your car? Now you can get the shine without the work! Introducing new Super Wax. Cheaper than most waxes...

**(N)** Now answer the questions that are printed in your book. (8 seconds)

**(N)** Talk Number 2

**(N)** Questions 4 through 7 refer to the following tour information.

**(W1)** Welcome to Franklin Dairy. Tours of the cheese factory are given every hour beginning at two o'clock. If you'd like to join a tour, please go to the ticket window…

**(N)** Now answer the questions that are printed in your book. (8 seconds)

**(N)** Talk Number 3

**(N)** Questions 8 through 11 refer to the following news report.

**(W2)** In local news, the new park was dedicated this morning in a ceremony attended by the mayor. The park, called Gordon Park because it is located on Gordon Avenue, has a playground, tennis courts…

**(N)** Now answer the questions that are printed in your book.

## (N) Exercise B

**(M1)** Welcome to Hoffberg Fine Instrument Company. I'm Paul York and I'll be conducting the tour today. Our facility here, one of the five operated by Hoffberg, is where the company's famous violins are manufactured. To start, we'll tour the production area, where we'll observe skilled craftsmen completing the assembly process. Then we'll visit the audiovisual room, where we'll see a short film on the history of Hoffberg Fine Instruments. Before we begin, are there any questions?

## (N) Exercise C

**(W1)** Happy Travel is pleased to announce three new vacation packages. The first is a grape-picking holiday in Southern Italy. We offer reasonably priced room and board and a discounted round-trip airline ticket. Make friends and enjoy the beautiful scenery. Our second package is a fun-for-all beach-resort vacation. Shopping, snorkeling, and bike rentals are all available, and there are supervised activities for the young. Thrill seekers will want to try our luxury scuba diving package off the coast of Greece. Our top-class diving instructors will make sure you have an underwater experience that's out of this world! Call now for details on all three packages.

## (N) Exercise D

(N) **Questions 1 through 4** refer to the following short talk.

(M2) Our next topic today is the schedule change for the construction of the new office building on Center Street. We're starting construction in November of this year—not in March of next year, as we had originally planned. As a result of this change, we'll need all preliminary drawings, site plans, and renderings ready for the client in two weeks. I realize this new schedule may present a challenge to many of you, so we will adjust your workload to accommodate the extra work.

## (N) DAY 13

## (N) Practice Questions

## (N) Part IV

*Directions: In this part of the test, you will hear several short talks. Each will be spoken just one time. They will not be printed in your test book, so you must listen carefully to understand and remember what is said.*

In your book, you will read two or more questions about each short talk. The questions will be followed by four answers. You are to choose the best answer to each question. The answers are printed at the end of this section.

(N) **Questions 81 and 82** refer to the following message.

(SP) Ms. Giovanni, this is Janet from Dr. Rossi's office calling to remind you of your annual physical exam tomorrow at 10:30. Please be on time. The appointment should take about an hour.

(N) Now read question 81 in your book and answer it. (8 seconds)

(N) Now read question 82 in your book and answer it. (8 seconds)

(N) **Questions 83 and 84** refer to the following announcement.

(SP) Attention, all employees. The power outage in plant number two has been resolved. However, our main computers are still down. We will be closing the production line early today so that technical services can correct the problem. Plan to leave by 2:30 P.M. unless told otherwise by your supervisor. Please make sure all manufacturing equipment is turned off before you leave. Thank you.

(N) Now read question 83 in your book and answer it. (8 seconds)

(N) Now read question 84 in your book and answer it. (8 seconds)

(N) **Questions 85 through 87** refer to the following short talk.

(SP) Good morning everyone. As you know, we have been holding interviews for a new editor to join our team. Ms. Patricia Wright has been chosen for the position. She will begin her orientation program this week and will be on staff by the end of the month. Ms. Wright has a good deal of experience in our field, both here and abroad. She worked for a major publication in Hong Kong for over two years before returning to this country.

(N) Now read question 85 in your book and answer it. (8 seconds)

(N) Now read question 86 in your book and answer it. (8 seconds)

(N) Now read question 87 in your book and answer it. (8 seconds)

(N) **Questions 88 and 89** refer to the following announcement.

(SP) This is to announce the new departure time for Flight 109 to Jakarta. Severe thunderstorms delayed the connecting flight from Tokyo. The plane is on the ground and is being serviced. Departure time is now scheduled for 8:30. Meal vouchers will be available for passengers scheduled on this flight. Passengers are asked to please be back to the gate by 8:00 for boarding.

(N) Now read question 88 in your book and answer it. (8 seconds)

(N) Now read question 89 in your book and answer it. (8 seconds)

(N) **Questions 90 and 91** refer to the following conference announcement.

(SP) Ladies and gentlemen, some of you have been asking for additional conference programs. Unfortunately, we can't give anyone an extra program until we're sure that we have enough for the conference guests who haven't arrived yet. If you've lost yours and need to check your meeting schedules, you can use the copies that we have at the information desk. Those of you who still need an extra program can check with us this afternoon. By then, we will have additional copies.

(N) Now read question 90 in your book and answer it. (8 seconds)

(N) Now read question 91 in your book and answer it. (8 seconds)

(N) **Questions 92 and 93** refer to the following short talk.

(SP) This dishwasher might look intimidating, but it's really quite easy to use. Start by taking an empty dish rack and load the dishes so that none of them are touching each other. Place the rack at the opening of the machine and hit the power switch so that the rack automatically feeds through the machine. Check the dishes when they come out on the other side and if they aren't completely clean, run the rack through the machine again. When they're done, take the dishes out and stack them on the dish cart.

(N) Now read question 92 in your book and answer it. (8 seconds)

(N) Now read question 93 in your book and answer it. (8 seconds)

(N) **Questions 94 and 95** refer to the following announcement.

(SP) Though we have no official dress code for traveling while on business, employees should remember that their physical appearance affects customers' impressions of our company. Beginning this Thursday, I will offer the first in a series of three workshops on business dress and conduct for travel in foreign countries. I hope the sessions will be informative and thought provoking.

(N) Now read question 94 in your book and answer it. (8 seconds)

(N) Now read question 95 in your book and answer it. (8 seconds)

(N) **Questions 96 through 98** refer to the following talk.

(SP) As you can see, the house is in excellent condition. It's worth far more than the asking price. The present owners carried out some renovation work recently and put in a whole new bathroom and kitchen. They were careful to retain the charming character of the house, as I'm sure you'll appreciate. When you go upstairs, you'll see how cozy the bedroom is. The house is a bit small, but you could easily build an extension over the old garage. The property is in a very desirable location—just minutes away from the train station, a supermarket, and some restaurants.

(N) Now read question 96 in your book and answer it. (8 seconds)

(N) Now read question 97 in your book and answer it. (8 seconds)

(N) Now read question 98 in your book and answer it. (8 seconds)

**(N)** **Questions 99 and 100** refer to the following talk.

**(M1)** I've called this meeting because, since the beginning of the year, our store has been losing over 1500 [fifteen hundred] euros a month due to theft. Last month, this figure rose to nearly 2000 [two thousand] euros. We believe that a group of shoplifters has been operating in the building for the last few weeks and that this may account for the losses that occurred in September. We've been in touch with our security consultants, who will be investigating the matter and drawing up a report on their findings.

**(N)** Now read question 99 in your book and answer it. (8 seconds)

**(N)** Now read question 100 in your book and answer it. (8 seconds)

---

## (N) Day 14

---

## (N) Authentic TOEIC Listening Comprehension Questions with Explanations

## (N) PART I: Photographs

**(N)** **Number 1**

**(M1)** (A) The people are waiting outside a hotel.

(B) All the people have left the room.

(C) Several people are gathered near a table.

(D) Two women are drinking coffee. (5 seconds)

**(N)** **Number 2**

**(W1)** (A) She's talking on the telephone.

(B) She's reading a newspaper.

(C) She's copying a document.

(D) She's standing in a telephone booth. (5 seconds)

**(N)** **Number 3**

**(M2)** (A) The drivers are leaning against the trucks.

(B) The trucks are lined up along the road.

(C) The engines are being repaired.

(D) The workers are unloading the trucks. (5 seconds)

**(N)** **Number 4**

**(W2)** (A) He's filling in a form.

(B) He's using a keyboard.

(C) He's signing a contract.

(D) He's writing on a board. (5 seconds)

**(N)** **Number 5**

**(M1)** (A) A crane is moving material to the top of a building.

(B) The frame of a building is exposed.

(C) The construction of a building is completed.

(D) People are attending a groundbreaking ceremony. (5 seconds)

## (N) PART II: Question-Response

**(N)** **Number 6**

**(M2)** Would you mind changing seats with me?

**(W1)** (A) No, I don't mind at all.

(B) Sorry, I don't have change.

(C) There are no more seats available. (5 seconds)

**(N)** **Number 7**

**(W2)** Why don't you let me leave the tip?

**(W1)** (A) Because I need you here.

(B) It's not too far.

(C) I've already taken care of it. (5 seconds)

**(N)  Number 8**

**(M1)**  Haven't you worked here longer than Mrs. Kim?

**(M2)**  (A)  No, it's very close to the office.

(B)  No, we were hired at the same time.

(C)  No, she won't have to wait much longer. (5 seconds)

**(N)  Number 9**

**(W2)**  The leadership training with Mr. Garcia begins at ten o'clock, doesn't it?

**(M1)**  (A)  No, it leaves at eleven.

(B)  It's not raining now.

(C)  I thought it was at nine. (5 seconds)

**(N)  Number 10**

**(M2)**  Should I turn off these lights?

**(M1)**  (A)  Just keep driving straight along this road.

(B)  No, only the ones in your office.

(C)  Yes, it's too heavy for me. (5 seconds)

**(N)  Number 11**

**(W1)**  Do you like this hot weather, or do you prefer the cold?

**(W2)**  (A)  I have trouble with the heat.

(B)  It's just an allergy.

(C)  Yes, I'm feeling much better, thanks. (5 seconds)

# (N) PART III:  Short Conversations

**(N) Number 12**

**(W1)**  Here's the schedule. Do you have everything you need?

**(M1)**  I can't find my folder with the guidelines in it.

**(W1)**  You just had it in your hand a minute ago! (8 seconds)

**(N) Number 13**

**(M1)**  Before I leave, is there anything else I need to know, doctor?

**(W1)**  Well, you should start your medication this evening and take it for two weeks. I'll need to see you here again after that.

**(M1)**  OK. I'll make an appointment on my way out. (8 seconds)

**(N) Number 14**

**(M1)**  Excuse me, I think I dropped my watch in the fitting room when I was trying on a suit here this morning. Has anyone found it?

**(W1)**  I don't see it here, but if you leave your name and phone number, I'll call you if it turns up.

**(M1)**  Thanks. I'll give you my office number and my home number. (8 seconds)

**(N) Number 15**

**(W1)**  They've started the road repairs on Main Street.

**(M1)**  I know. For the next three months, it'll take over an hour to get downtown.

**(W1)**  Yes, but after that we'll be able to get there much faster. (8 seconds)

**(N) Number 16**

**(M1)**  Good evening, front desk. May I help you?

**(W1)**  Yes, I have a 7:45 flight tomorrow morning, so I'll need a wake-up call. How long does it take to get to the airport?

**(M1)**  If you get a cab from here by 6:30, it should only take 15 minutes. Should I call you at 5:45? (8 seconds)

**(N)** Number 17

**(M1)** It's so hard to find an apartment in this city. They're either too small or too expensive.

**(W1)** Have you looked over by the university? Rents are low around there, and some of the apartments are really nice.

**(M1)** I tried that area, but there's nothing available until summer. (8 seconds)

## (N) PART IV: Short Talks

**(N)** Questions 18 and 19 refer to the following announcement.

**(M1)** Attention, health-club members. Back by popular demand, our expert instructor, Elena Pappas, will again offer her International Folk Dancing sessions beginning January 15. Enjoy the fun of moving to music, gain the benefits of physical conditioning, and meet new people while you learn the basics of folk dances from around the world. Enrollment is limited to sixteen. See Maria Sandor at the front desk for details.

**(N)** Questions 20 through 22 refer to the following announcement.

**(W2)** The anniversary committee is finalizing plans for the celebration of our twenty-fifth anniversary on Saturday, June second. In the event of rain, the celebration will be held on June ninth. The official ceremonies are scheduled to begin at five o'clock in Oak Park and will include speeches by visiting dignitaries and the dedication of two cherry trees as a salute to past presidents of the association. Special events for children are also being planned. Anyone who would like to assist the anniversary committee should contact Tom Suzuki before April twenty-ninth.

**(N)** Questions 23 and 24 refer to the following report.

**(M2)** Union workers at Gemini Industries are in their fifth day of a strike in protest of the growing use of temporary workers. More and more workers are seeing their full-time jobs replaced by non-salaried, short-term positions without benefits or job security. Gemini President Raymond Singh insists that the company reduce payroll costs to remain competitive.

## (N) DAY 25

### (N) Practice Test : Listening Comprehension

**(N)** In this section of the test, you will have the chance to show how well you understand spoken English. There are four parts to this section, with special directions for each part.

Part I

**(N) Directions: For each question, you will see a picture in your test book and you will hear four short statements. The statements will be spoken just one time. They will not be printed in your test book, so you must listen carefully to understand what the speaker says.**

When you hear the four statements, look at the picture in your book and choose the statement that best describes what you see in the picture. Then, on your answer sheet, find the number of the question and mark your answer. Look at the sample below. Now listen to the four statements.

**(M1)** (A) They're looking out the window.

(B) They're having a meeting.

(C) They're eating in a restaurant.

(D) They're moving the furniture.

**(N)** Statement (B), "They're having a meeting," best describes what you see in the picture.

Therefore, you should choose answer (B).

**(N)** Now let us begin Part I with question number one.

1.  **(N)** Look at the picture marked number 1 in your book.

    **(M1)** (A) The transaction has been completed.

    (B) They're filling out the forms by hand.

    (C) The woman is using the keyboard.

    (D) They're watching a program on television. (5 seconds)

2.  **(N)** Look at the picture marked number 2 in your book.

    **(W1)** (A) Few of the tables are occupied.

    (B) There's water on the floor of the restaurant.

    (C) The shape of the tables is square.

    (D) The restaurant has gone out of business. (5 seconds)

3.  **(N)** Look at the picture marked number 3 in your book.

    **(M2)** (A) He's developing the photographs.

    (B) He's doing two things at once.

    (C) He's looking out the window at the scenery.

    (D) He's hanging up the telephone. (5 seconds)

4.  **(N)** Look at the picture marked number 4 in your book.

    **(W2)** (A) The drivers have turned on their car lights.

    (B) The parking area is covered.

    (C) The cards are sorted by number.

    (D) The park is closed to traffic. (5 seconds)

5.  **(N)** Look at the picture marked number 5 in your book.

    **(M1)** (A) They're picking up their bags.

    (B) They're sitting next to each other.

    (C) They're moving the sofa into the corner.

    (D) They're looking at a display in a museum. (5 seconds)

6.  **(N)** Look at the picture marked number 6 in your book.

    **(W1)** (A) The market is open for business.

    (B) The man is working in his vegetable garden.

    (C) The crops have yet to be harvested.

    (D) The woman is weighing herself. (5 seconds)

7.  **(N)** Look at the picture marked number 7 in your book.

    **(M2)** (A) They're placing the bags into the overhead compartment.

    (B) They're packing their suitcases.

    (C) They're moving the luggage.

    (D) They're going through customs inspection. (5 seconds)

8.  **(N)** Look at the picture marked number 8 in your book.

    **(W2)** (A) The man is examining the merchandise.

    (B) There are not many products for sale.

    (C) The display cases are being rearranged.

    (D) The man is watching a movie. (5 seconds)

9.  **(N)** Look at the picture marked number 9 in your book.

    **(M1)** (A) They're climbing the stairs together.

    (B) They're looking in the same direction.

    (C) They're holding onto the railing.

    (D) They're facing each other. (5 seconds)

10. **(N)** Look at the picture marked number 10 in your book.

  **(W1)** (A) There are a lot of people on the train.

  (B) The man is closing the door because of the rain.

  (C) The train has already departed from the station.

  (D) The man left his briefcase on the train. (5 seconds)

11. **(N)** Look at the picture marked number 11 in your book.

  **(M2)** (A) Her work hours have been cut.

  (B) She's finished clipping out the article.

  (C) There's not much air in this room.

  (D) She's giving the person a haircut. (5 seconds)

12. **(N)** Look at the picture marked number 12 in your book.

  **(W2)** (A) Some people are going up to the next level.

  (B) The escalator is out of order.

  (C) The building is only one story high.

  (D) The property is closed to the public. (5 seconds)

13. **(N)** Look at the picture marked number 13 in your book.

  **(M1)** (A) The customers are ready to pay their bill.

  (B) The waiter is taking their food order.

  (C) The woman is ordering the men to go away.

  (D) The waiter is taking away their dishes. (5 seconds)

14. **(N)** Look at the picture marked number 14 in your book.

  **(W1)** (A) The sales assistants are helping the customers.

  (B) The store inventory is low.

  (C) A man is paying for his purchases.

  (D) A woman is reaching for an item. (5 seconds)

15. **(N)** Look at the picture marked number 15 in your book.

  **(M2)** (A) He's putting her files away.

  (B) She's sitting across the desk from him.

  (C) They're reading the newspaper together.

  (D) He's handing her some papers. (5 seconds)

16. **(N)** Look at the picture marked number 16 in your book.

  **(W2)** (A) The musicians are playing as a trio.

  (B) The musical has just ended.

  (C) The instruments are in their cases.

  (D) The orchestra is entering the auditorium. (5 seconds)

17. **(N)** Look at the picture marked number 17 in your book.

  **(M1)** (A) Swimmers are getting out of the water.

  (B) People are cycling along the path.

  (C) The trees have lost all their leaves.

  (D) The river has flooded the surrounding area. (5 seconds)

18. **(N)** Look at the picture marked number 18 in your book.

  **(W1)** (A) They're putting up some flowered wallpaper.

  (B) They're taking a tour of the garden.

  (C) They're doing some work outside.

  (D) They're eating their lunch in the park. (5 seconds)

19.  **(N)**  Look at the picture marked number 19 in your book.

    **(M2)**  (A)  The speaker is seated in front of the class.

        (B)  The men and women are standing along the wall.

        (C)  There are many empty seats in the room.

        (D)  She's making a presentation to the group.  (5 seconds)

20.  **(N)**  Look at the picture marked number 20 in your book.

    **(W2)**  (A)  The truck is waiting at the traffic light.

        (B)  The man is climbing into the truck.

        (C)  Boxes are stacked outside the truck.

        (D)  Men are carrying boxes across the street.  (5 seconds)

## Part II

*(N) Directions: In this part of the test, you will hear a question or statement spoken in English, followed by three responses, also spoken in English. The question or statement and the responses will be spoken just one time. They will not be printed in your test book, so you must listen carefully to understand what the speakers say. You are to choose the best response to each question or statement.*

Now listen to a sample question.

You will hear:  **(W2)**  Good morning, John. How are you?

You will also hear:  **(M1)**  (A) I am fine, thank you.

        (B) I am in the living room.

        (C) My name is John.

The best response to the question "How are you?" is choice (A), "I am fine, thank you." Therefore, you should choose answer (A).

Now let us begin Part II with question number 21.

21.  **(M1)**  When was Mr. Chen born?

    **(W1)**  (A)  In Hong Kong.

        (B)  Since last June.

        (C)  In 1958.  (5 seconds)

22.  **(W2)**  Did you ask them what time their flight would arrive?

    **(W1)**  (A)  Yes, they were happy to arrive.

        (B)  No, I didn't think of it.

        (C)  No, it was too dark to tell.  (5 seconds)

23.  **(M2)**  Who can deliver this memo to Mr. Watanabe for me?

    **(M1)**  (A)  Yes, Mr. Watanabe lives in Japan.

        (B)  I can do it when I've finished typing this letter.

        (C)  No, the delivery person is from Osaka.  (5 seconds)

24.  **(W2)**  Don't you want to go to the reception for Miss Gunther?

    **(M2)**  (A)  No, in the hotel ballroom.

        (B)  I have the receipt.

        (C)  Sorry, but I'm not feeling well.  (5 seconds)

25.  **(M1)**  What's the name of the travel agency this company uses?

    **(M2)**  (A)  Yes, that's his name.

        (B)  I think it's called All Points Travel.

        (C)  I recommend you use a carry-on bag.  (5 seconds)

26. **(W1)** Where did Maria leave the Oceanview contract?

 **(W2)** (A) She put it in Ms. García's mailbox.

 (B) Just a minute ago, so you can still catch her.

 (C) Because the mountain-view rooms were all booked. (5 seconds)

27. **(M2)** Have you visited the main plant yet?

 **(W1)** (A) Yes, they are.

 (B) Yes, I went there last week with the director.

 (C) Yes, the gardener is looking after them. (5 seconds)

28. **(W2)** Who is the new receptionist?

 **(M1)** (A) It's in the main office.

 (B) Her name is Olga Kaminsky.

 (C) Yes, we need a new receptionist. (5 seconds)

29. **(W1)** Will the conference be held here or at headquarters?

 **(W2)** (A) It's scheduled for this building.

 (B) No, you will not be able to hear.

 (C) Yes, they will have the conference. (5 seconds)

30. **(M1)** Why did the meeting begin so early?

 **(M2)** (A) Yes, at eight-thirty.

 (B) About the upcoming acquisition.

 (C) Everyone was in a hurry. (5 seconds)

31. **(W2)** What are your total production figures for this factory?

 **(M1)** (A) We produce pharmaceuticals.

 (B) Over 1,000 units a week.

 (C) In the shipping department. (5 seconds)

32. **(M2)** How far would you say Conrad Park is from here?

 **(W1)** (A) It's about a ten-minute walk.

 (B) No, I wouldn't go so far as to say that.

 (C) Yes, parking there is very expensive. (5 seconds)

33. **(M1)** Is the agenda prepared?

 **(W2)** (A) No, it's still broken.

 (B) Yes, they compared very well.

 (C) Not yet, the vice-president needs to review it. (5 seconds)

34. **(W1)** How about a movie when we finish up here?

 **(W2)** (A) Just down the street at the Cinema Center.

 (B) That's a good idea.

 (C) About a half hour more, I think. (5 seconds)

35. **(M2)** The product was in stock last week, wasn't it?

 **(M1)** (A) The stock exchange closes at five.

 (B) Yes, there was a large inventory on hand then.

 (C) No, they aren't. (5 seconds)

36. **(W2)** Can you locate the files on the merger, or should I ask Mr. Chang to do it?

 **(M2)** (A) The fire exit is located at the end of the hall.

 (B) Yes, I called security to handle the emergency.

 (C) I'll have them ready for you in a minute. (5 seconds)

37. **(M1)** Didn't the sound equipment come out of your regular departmental budget?

 **(M2)** (A) We didn't hear any sounds.

 (B) Yes, the room is rented.

 (C) No, we got special funding. (5 seconds)

38. **(W1)** Where do you plan to stay while you're in Paris?

 **(M2)** (A) Our company has an arrangement with the Hotel Odeon.

 (B) I have a conference there next week.

 (C) I'll be in France for four days. (5 seconds)

39. **(M2)** I was wondering if you'd like to join us for dinner this evening?

 **(W1)** (A) Yes, it was a wonderful dinner.

 (B) Sorry, I have other plans.

 (C) I hope you weren't too lost. (5 seconds)

40. **(W2)** Does our company get any special deals on car rentals?

 **(M1)** (A) Yes, I'd like some company on the trip.

 (B) Twenty-five percent off the regular daily rate.

 (C) No, it's your turn to deal. (5 seconds)

41. **(W1)** Exactly when will Mr. Mori be free?

 **(W2)** (A) In approximately two hours.

 (B) At the International Airport.

 (C) Near gate number 16. (5 seconds)

42. **(M1)** How can I get more letterhead and envelopes?

 **(M2)** (A) Yes, the mail is picked up three times a day.

 (B) Contact Ms. McKay in the stockroom.

 (C) No, he isn't the head of the department. (5 seconds)

43. **(W1)** Ms. Dubois was present at this morning's staff meeting, wasn't she?

 **(M1)** (A) Once a week, on a Monday.

 (B) No, it wasn't a gift.

 (C) No, she wasn't there. (5 seconds)

44. **(M2)** You're the new assistant to Mr. Lin, aren't you?

 **(W2)** (A) No, I don't need assistance.

 (B) No, I work for Ms. Wong.

 (C) Yes, I knew about that. (5 seconds)

45. **(W1)** When can you get me a copy of the most recent sales report?

 **(W2)** (A) Yes, they're selling well.

 (B) Right after lunch.

 (C) About four years old. (5 seconds)

46. **(M2)** Why didn't Mr. Danforth bring the situation to the attention of his supervisor?

 **(M1)** (A) Yes, at his workstation.

 (B) No, he often doesn't pay attention.

 (C) He thought he could handle it himself. (5 seconds)

47. **(W2)** Is this coat already marked down?

 **(W1)** (A) Yes, that's the sale price on the tag.

 (B) The market is closed this evening.

 (C) Yes, I have a red coat. (5 seconds)

48. **(W2)** Why does Ms. Ortiz want to see the invoices?

 **(M2)** (A) Yes, they have loud voices.

 (B) There's a problem with the shipment.

 (C) No, she didn't see it. (5 seconds)

49. **(M1)** Should they move the file cabinet to the right or over by the copy machine?

 **(W1)** (A) Yes, your thinking is correct.

 (B) I think it looks good where it is.

 (C) No, these copies didn't come out clearly. (5 seconds)

50. **(M1)** Isn't that the same proposal we rejected last time?

 **(M2)** (A) Yes, but things have changed since then.

 (B) No, the wedding was called off.

 (C) No, it was a different injection. (5 seconds)

# PART III

(N) *Directions: In this part of the test, you will hear thirty short conversations between two people. The conversations will not be printed in your test book. You will hear the conversations only once, so you must listen carefully to understand what the speakers say.*

In your book, you will read a question about each conversation. The question will be followed by four answers. You are to choose the best answer to each question and mark it on your answer sheet.

Now let us begin Part III with question number 51.

51.  **(W1)** I left a telephone message on your desk.

   **(W2)** Oh, did Mr. Murphy's secretary call again?

   **(W1)** Yes. She said the committee meeting is set for Tuesday.  (8 seconds)

52.  **(M2)** Is there anywhere I can get coffee or tea around here?

   **(W1)** Yes, I think there is. Go have a look in the employee lounge.

   **(M2)** That's next to the mailroom, right? Want me to bring you anything?  (8 seconds)

53.  **(M1)** Did you hear about Mrs. Sompong's resignation?

   **(W2)** Yes. Our competitors made her an offer she couldn't resist.

   **(M1)** I wonder if they'll appoint her as their new marketing manager?  (8 seconds)

54.  **(W1)** I need to call the theater to order tickets for Wednesday.

   **(W2)** Why don't you see the play over the weekend, Claudia?

   **(W1)** It runs only Monday through Thursday. (8 seconds)

55.  **(W2)** Good morning, this is Standard Computer Services. Would you like to speak with someone in sales, service, or research?

   **(M2)** Actually, I need to speak with Mr. Fong in personnel.

   **(W2)** Please hold while I transfer your call.  (8 seconds)

56.  **(M2)** When does the movie start?

   **(M1)** There are two showings—one at four and one at seven.

   **(M2)** Let's go to the later show.  (8 seconds)

57.  **(W2)** Do you think the desk will fit under the window?

   **(M2)** It might, but what about putting it next to the bookshelves? By the way, why are you changing things again?

   **(W2)** I just couldn't work comfortably in the old arrangement.  (8 seconds)

58.  **(M1)** What do you think is the best way for us to get to the conference?

   **(W2)** Well, it's too close to bother flying. We could drive there, but I think if we took the train, we could get some work done on the way.

   **(M1)** Yes, that's the best plan. I'll pick up tickets at the station on my way home from work.  (8 seconds)

59.  **(W2)** Do you have this week's *Business News* yet?

   **(M1)** No, the truck that used to deliver it on Monday has a different route. It should be here soon.

   **(W2)** I'll come back later this afternoon, I guess. (8 seconds)

60. **(W1)** Juan, Ricardo will not be able to attend the meeting next week in Panama, so I'd like you to represent the firm. Would you be able to do it?

**(M2)** Yes, Ms. Ortega, I'd really like to go to that meeting. What about travel arrangements?

**(W1)** That's all been taken care of. See Carla. You'll leave Sunday evening—and thanks. (8 seconds)

61. **(M1)** I've heard nothing but praise for that new health food restaurant.

**(W2)** Same here. And I've got a coupon for the salad bar—buy one, get one free.

**(M1)** I'm always looking to save some money. Let's check it out for lunch. (8 seconds)

62. **(M2)** The airline sent my luggage to New York by mistake and it doesn't look like they'll be able to deliver it to me in time for this evening's dinner. Where can I go to buy a few things?

**(W1)** There's a shopping mall not far from here. You can get there by bus or cab from the hotel.

**(M2)** Oh, that's right. I was there the last time I was in San Francisco. (8 seconds)

63. **(W2)** Because you've worked here now for two years, Susanna, you are entitled to three weeks' vacation.

**(W1)** Will I be allowed to take it all at once?

**(W2)** Most supervisors allow two weeks at a time. (8 seconds)

64. **(M1)** Let's get these boxes unloaded before the kitchen staff gets here.

**(M2)** Okay. Should I put these cans of corn on the shelf?

**(M1)** You can just leave them out on the counter. They're a part of today's menu. (8 seconds)

65. **(W1)** Hello, Yuri. I didn't think you would be back from your trip so soon.

**(M2)** Well, we didn't expect to be back now, but Anna, our youngest girl, got sick while we were away.

**(W1)** I'm sorry to hear that. I hope she's feeling better now. (8 seconds)

66. **(M2)** Alan, are you going to be in your office Thursday morning? If you're not, could I work there because my office is being painted then?

**(M1)** You're in luck, Tom. I'll be out until Friday morning.

**(M2)** That's great. I've got to get this project done by Monday afternoon. (8 seconds)

67. **(W2)** Did you leave that marketing report on my desk? I can't find it anywhere.

**(W1)** No, Patricia, the only thing I've put on your desk recently is a memo.

**(W2)** Could you please check in your file cabinet for it? I need it soon. (8 seconds)

68. **(W1)** I'm sorry, sir. We're completely booked tonight. There are no rooms available until tomorrow evening.

**(M2)** I see. Is there someplace close by where I might be able to stay?

**(W1)** Let me call around and see if I can find a room for you. (8 seconds)

69. **(M1)** Excuse me, could I speak to Ms. Krishnan, please?

**(W1)** Ms. Krishnan? I'm sorry, but she's no longer in this division. She was transferred last week to overseas sales.

**(M1)** Perhaps you could give me her new number? (8 seconds)

70. **(M2)** Would you like to visit our plant while you're in town next week?

    **(M1)** That would be great. I've always wanted to see your operation firsthand.

    **(M2)** OK. Let me know when you're available and I'll show you around. (8 seconds)

71. **(M1)** Your résumé looks very impressive, Ms. Mura, and I would like to offer you a job with our company.

    **(W1)** Thank you, Mr. Shima. I'm really looking forward to working with you.

    **(M1)** Good. You can sign the papers at the personnel office. (8 seconds)

72. **(M2)** And how would you like to pay for the camera?

    **(W2)** Could I write you a check?

    **(M2)** Certainly. I'll need some form of identification or a major credit card. (8 seconds)

73. **(W1)** Hello. I'm in room 512 [five-twelve]. I just plugged in my hair dryer and all the lights went out.

    **(M1)** I'm sorry. I'll send someone to take care of it right away.

    **(W1)** Thanks. I have to go out at six o'clock, so I'm really in a hurry! (8 seconds)

74. **(W2)** Ms. Díaz, please make sure I'm not interrupted for the next hour. I'll be working on a document that I have to fax to a client today.

    **(W1)** Will you take the international call that you're expecting, Ms. Lee?

    **(W2)** Yes. That's the one exception I will make. (8 seconds)

75. **(W1)** I'm sorry to have to leave in the middle of things here, but that was the office calling. They need my help right away.

    **(M1)** Oh no, Heidi. You'll miss the rest of the party. Could you come back afterward?

    **(W1)** Maybe. I'll phone before I leave to see if anyone's still here. (8 seconds)

76. **(W2)** I'd like to return this sweater, but I don't have the sales slip. It was a gift.

    **(M1)** In that case, we can only issue you a credit, not a refund.

    **(W2)** That would be fine. I'll use it toward this suit. (8 seconds)

77. **(M2)** The advertising department has been working really hard these last seven weeks.

    **(W1)** I know. They've even been in the office on weekends. Do you think they'll be ready to make the presentation next Wednesday?

    **(M2)** That's the plan. They're making their final revisions on Monday. (8 seconds)

78. **(M1)** Excuse me, sir. Could I see your driver's license and your insurance papers, please?

    **(M2)** Certainly, officer....Here you are. I wasn't speeding, was I?

    **(M1)** No sir, you weren't. The reason I pulled you over is because your left turn signal seems to be out of order. (8 seconds)

79. **(M1)** Will my order be ready tomorrow? I must send it to a customer as soon as possible.

    **(W2)** I'm afraid our store will be closed tomorrow for inventory. I'm sure we'll have it the following day.

    **(M1)** I see. I'll come and get it then. You open at nine, right? (8 seconds)

80. **(W1)** I thought the company wasn't going to hire anyone to take Olivia's place when she retired.

    **(M1)** The division office decided to keep her position open in case the workload increased in her department.

    **(W1)** Oh, that's right. That big contract was signed just before she left. (8 seconds)

# Part IV

(N) *Directions: In this part of the test, you will hear several short talks. Each will be spoken just one time. They will not be printed in your test book, so you must listen carefully to understand and remember what is said.*

In your book, you will read two or more questions about each short talk. The questions will be followed by four answers. You are to choose the best answer to each question and mark it on your answer sheet.

(N) **Questions 81 and 82** refer to the following announcement.

(M1) Good afternoon. I'm glad you could join me today for a tour of the museum's splendid modern art collection. The tour should last about a half an hour, during which time we will try to focus on some of the museum's best-known pieces. For those of you who enjoy sculpture, I'll be giving another talk at three o'clock in the sculpture garden.

(N) Now read question 81 in your book and answer it.  (8 seconds)

(N) Now read question 82 in your book and answer it.  (8 seconds)

(N) **Questions 83 and 84** refer to the following speech.

(M2) Hello, my name is Ivan. I'll be serving you tonight. Let me tell you about some of our specials. We have grilled steak with sautéed vegetables. We also have a nice fresh salmon dish that comes with rice. Our soup of the day is clam chowder. I'll be back in a minute to take your order.

(N) Now read question 83 in your book and answer it.  (8 seconds)

(N) Now read question 84 in your book and answer it.  (8 seconds)

(N) **Questions 85 and 86** refer to the following short talk.

(W1) This is the limited express bound for Munich. We will be making a brief stop in Frankfurt before reaching our final destination. We expect our traveling time today to be three hours and twenty minutes. All seats are reserved. Please check your ticket and make sure that you are sitting in the correct seat. Telephones and food service are available in the rear car. Thank you for your attention. We will be departing in a few minutes.

(N) Now read question 85 in your book and answer it.  (8 seconds)

(N) Now read question 86 in your book and answer it.  (8 seconds)

(N) **Questions 87 through 89** refer to the following announcement.

(M1) Good evening. I'm Dave Sandoval, director of franchising for Milton's Pies. As you know, we're the fastest-growing franchisor in the southern region today. Last year, we opened 300 shops, and now we hope to expand into the central region and put a Milton's Pie Shop in every mall and shopping center. No one should be too far from a great-tasting Milton's pie. You're here tonight because you're interested in becoming a franchise owner, and we want to help you go into business! Most banks lend you the money you need to open a franchise because the Milton's name has customer appeal, and because our shops make money—for you, for us, and for the bank.

(N) Now read question 87 in your book and answer it.  (8 seconds)

(N) Now read question 88 in your book and answer it.  (8 seconds)

(N) Now read question 89 in your book and answer it.  (8 seconds)

(N) **Questions 90 and 91** refer to the following excerpt from a speech.

**(W2)** It is my pleasure to introduce to you the world-renowned photojournalist Michiko Suzuki. A native of Japan, Ms. Suzuki has been working in Australia for the past three years as a staff photographer for *The Sydney News Journal*. I'm very pleased that Ms. Suzuki has agreed to join our magazine for six months before she takes her next long-term assignment in Brazil. She'll be working closely with our staff, sharing some of the secrets of her innovative techniques.

**(N)** Now read question 90 in your book and answer it. (8 seconds)

**(N)** Now read question 91 in your book and answer it. (8 seconds)

**(N)** **Questions 92 and 93** refer to the following announcement.

**(M2)** We are very pleased to announce that this year's annual employee awards banquet will be held in the grand ballroom of the elegant Adams Hotel. If you have not yet received your tickets, please call the personnel office immediately. We hope you'll join the president and board of directors in honoring this year's award winners.

**(N)** Now read question 92 in your book and answer it. (8 seconds)

**(N)** Now read question 93 in your book and answer it. (8 seconds)

**(N)** **Questions 94 and 97** refer to the following announcement.

**(W1)** Good evening, ladies and gentlemen, and welcome to the Regent Theater. Tonight's film, *The Earth is Round*, documents the experiences of a young couple as they travel around the world on a journey spanning more than five years. This film begins our week-long series in which we'll show nine different films, each depicting a unique voyage. *The Earth is Round* runs for 90 minutes, and we invite you to join us at the end of the movie for a question-and-answer session with the filmmakers. Thank you, and we hope you enjoy the show.

**(N)** Now read question 94 in your book and answer it. (8 seconds)

**(N)** Now read question 95 in your book and answer it. (8 seconds)

**(N)** Now read question 96 in your book and answer it. (8 seconds)

**(N)** Now read question 97 in your book and answer it. (8 seconds)

**(N)** **Questions 98 through 100** refer to the following talk.

**(W2)** This is Radio Talk Today. My name is Vanessa Evans and this afternoon we'll be talking with Sylvie Valmont about last week's election results. Ms. Valmont is a newspaper journalist and author of several books on politics and political parties. We'll be discussing her views on why some candidates fared well in the elections and why others didn't live up to expectations. She'll also tell us about the changing future of political parties in our country. But, before I bring on Ms. Valmont, here's the local and regional news and the weather forecast for the weekend.

**(N)** Now read question 98 in your book and answer it. (8 seconds)

**(N)** Now read question 99 in your book and answer it. (8 seconds)

**(N)** Now read question 100 in your book and answer it. (8 seconds)

**(N)** This is the end of the Listening Comprehension portion of the test.

<u>End of Recording.</u>